The Last
Pool of
Darkness

The Last Pool of Darkness

THE CONNEMARA TRILOGY: PART TWO

Tim Robinson

MILKWEED EDITIONS

Published 2023 by Milkweed Editions
Printed in the United States of America
Cover design and illustration by Mary Austin Speaker
Author photo by Brian Farrell
23 24 25 26 27   5 4 3 2 1
First US Edition

Library of Congress Cataloging-in-Publication Data

Names: Robinson, Tim, 1935-2020, author.
Title: The last pool of darkness / Tim Robinson.
Description: First US Edition. | Minneapolis : Milkweed Editions, 2021. | Series: Connemara ; vol. 2. | "Original edition first published by Penguin Books Ltd, London © 2008 Text by Tim Robinson | Summary: "The second volume of the Connemara trilogy from cartographer Tim Robinson"-- Provided by publisher.
Identifiers: LCCN 2021011587 (print) | LCCN 2021011588 (ebook) | ISBN 9781571313744 (paperback) | ISBN 9781571319852 (ebook)
Subjects: LCSH: Connemara (Ireland)--Description and travel. | Connemara (Ireland)--History. | Connemara (Ireland)--Folklore. | Robinson, Tim, 1935-2020--Travel--Ireland--Connemara. | Landscapes--Ireland--Connemara.
Classification: LCC DA990.C7 R615 2021 (print) | LCC DA990.C7 (ebook) | DDC 941.7/4--dc23
LC record available at https://lccn.loc.gov/2021011587
LC ebook record available at https://lccn.loc.gov/2021011588

Milkweed Editions is committed to ecological stewardship. We strive to align our book production practices with this principle, and to reduce the impact of our operations in the environment. We are a member of the Green Press Initiative, a nonprofit coalition of publishers, manufacturers, and authors working to protect the world's endangered forests and conserve natural resources. *The Last Pool of Darkness* was printed on acid-free 100% postconsumer-waste paper by Sheridan Saline, Inc.

CONTENTS

The Last
Pool of
Darkness

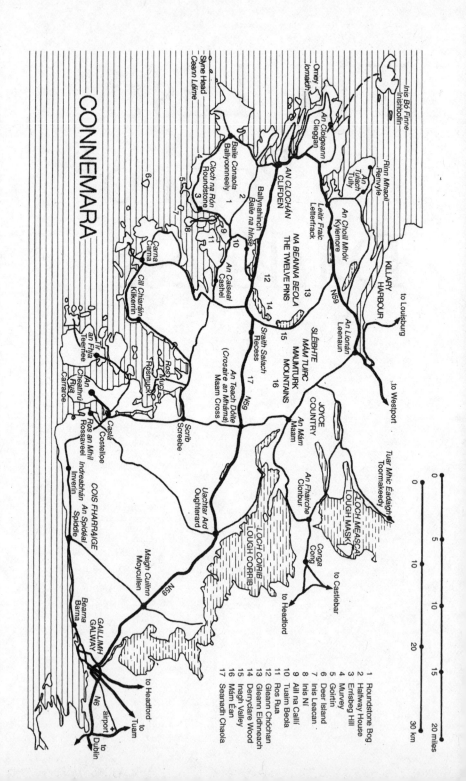

CONNEMARA

Inis Bó Finne
Inishbofin

Flinn Mhaoil
Renvyle

An Tulách
Tully

Omey
Iomaidh

An Cloigeann
Cleggan

An Choill Mhóir
Kylemore

Leitir Fraic
Letterfrack

Slyne Head
Ceann Léime

Baile Conaola
Ballyconneely

Cloch na Rón
Roundstone

Ballynahinch
Baile na hinse

AN CLOCHÁN
CLIFDEN

NA BEANNA BEOLA
THE TWELVE PINS

KILLARY
HARBOUR

to Louisburg

An Caiseal
Cashel

Carna
Carna

Cill Chiaráin
Kilkerrin

Sraith Salach
Recess

SLÉIBHTE
MÁM TUIRC
MAUMTURK
MOUNTAINS

An Lionán
Leenaun

to Westport

Tuar Mhic Éadaigh
Toormakeedy

LOCH MEASCA
LOUGH MASK

An Teach Dóite
(Crosaire an Mháma)
Maam Cross

JOYCE
COUNTRY

An Máim
Maam

An Fhairche
Clonbur

Conga
Cong

Ros
Muc
Rosmuck

Scríb
Screebe

N59

Uachtar Ard
Oughterard

LOCH COIRIB
LOUGH CORRIB

to Castlebar

Tír
an Fhia
Teernee

An
Cheathrú
Rua
Carraroe

Ros an Mhíl
Rossaveel

Casla
Costelloe

Indreabhán
An Spidéal
Inverin
Spiddle

COIS FHARRAIGE

Maigh Cuilinn
Moycullen

to Headford

to Headford

Bearna
Barna

GAILLIMH
GALWAY

N6

to Dublin

N59

to Tuam

airport

to Tuam

0   5   10   10   20   30 km
0   5   10   15   20 miles

1 Roundstone Bog
2 Halfway House
3 Errisbeg Hill
4 Murvey
5 Goirtín
6 Deer Island
7 Inis Leacan
8 Inis Ní
9 Aill na Caillí
10 Tuaim Beola
11 Ros Rua
12 Gleann Chóchan
13 Gleann Eidhneach
14 Derryclare Wood
15 Inagh Valley
16 Mám Éan
17 Seanadh Chaola

Introduction

When first he finds me, I am red-faced and soaked to the skin—by tears and by rain. Salty rivers have traced their path on my winter skin. I have, only a single day before, stepped into a dark pool of the vastest, darkest grief I have ever known. I try on a green tweed jacket in a secondhand shop, and there he is, in my inside pocket. Outside, snow has begun to fall on the auld Edinburgh streets. I have just left Ireland to live in Scotland, and I am heartsore. But here I am, in another Celtic land, holding—now, in my hands—a gift from another individual who has known what it means to be affected by geography. Who knows what it means to lean back into a place until you are at one with the rocks and the lichen, the river and the wren song, the blue flower and the grey skies. Rather—until you realise that you *are* these things too. That you hold, deep within you, all the darkness of this world, and all the light too.

The gift of which I speak was a tattered map of the Burren, one of the exquisite objects by which the—English by birth, Irish by belonging—writer and cartographer Tim Robinson is best known. I place much value on very particular parts of the lives people choose to live: the landscapes they feel drawn to, the creatures with which their lives become entwined, how they give voice to this eternal but ever-shifting song of what it means to be human on this achingly beautiful earth—often forgetting that others might appreciate the smaller, everyday details that constitute a life too.

So, I should tell you first that Robinson was a mathematician, an artist, a cartographer, a writer, a partner. I shall tell you that he was so taken by the landscape of Ireland that he, with his wife and creative collaborator Máiréad, rooted himself on that island so firmly that he became part of the soil itself. I could tell you that he embedded himself so fully in the West of Ireland that upon visiting some parts of the Burren, it is almost as if his voice is calling to you, above the stone and the silence. You see, some lives do not allow themselves to dwell in any one place too long—least of all in those corners that house the run of the mill, the everyday, the ordinary. Some lives are much more about vast open bogland than they are about lists of accomplishments (of which one might, when speaking of him, list many).

Tim Robinson is less like the stone of which he writes so exceptionally in this, the second of his beloved Connemara trilogy, and more like the water that has moved over it, ebbing and flowing, moving—always moving.

Within these pages we find history, geography, sociology, religion, folklore, art—all the things that make up a life lived: Robinson's own (in a line, as the crow flies) shared with those who walked that westerly part of that westerly island both before and alongside him.

Any book about the landscape of Ireland, Tim Robinson knew well, would have—at its heart—the *people* of Ireland, and this book is, too, about those humans, both well-known and not. The philosopher Ludwig Wittgenstein, the artist Dorothy Cross, and the poet W. B. Yeats share space with a wee boy paying rent in the winter of the endless rains of 1878 (when conditions almost reached the horrific level they had been in An Gorta Mor, the Great Famine), a group of whistling schoolgirls, and a pair of architects employed to encourage healing within a community deeply traumatised by abuse of children—a thing held in the land as well as the heart.

"What is to be done, to reclaim this tear-drenched land?" he asks, and I feel this question is the one at the heart of this incredible book—a work of excavation, examination, reparation, and more.

Why would this writer, this artist who has sculpted a life hung upon geography, cast his clever eye upon issues of the heart and soul, turn his careful hand to recording issues of the past and all it holds beneath the surface, within the soil? For here we find much more than a telling of rock and sand, of sea and land. Well, what, he seems to ask us, even now, is geography but *a measure of the earth*? And how might we even begin to measure this glistening, aching, ever-shifting earth without listening to the stories it holds within its strata—human and more than, folkloric and historical—from here and there, from then, from now, and from all that is yet to come?

Robinson writes Ireland in a way I have never encountered before, giving her his whole being, holding all her complexities in the palm of his hand, this "land without shortcuts."

Tim Robinson finds me, for the second time, at another moment of vast change. It is the start of April 2020, the first spring of the global pandemic, one of four seasons that my second book—*Cacophony of Bone*—seeks to record.

My journal entry for the fourth day of that fourth month reads:

Discovered Tim Robinson has died.

A writer who has always compelled me to consider how best to be in a place.

'I am too restless to sink into the moment for more than a moment at a time. Horizons beckon, and what's beyond them.'

Must write to R.

The "R" is Robert Macfarlane, who described the Connemara trilogy as "one of the most remarkable nonfiction projects undertaken in English."

Macfarlane is not alone in his admiration for Robinson; many of us have been deeply inspired by his work, spurred on in our own writing of the earth by his compassionate, unflinching words and images alike.

In response to Folding Landscapes—Robinson and Máiréad's publishing house—being granted a Ford Ireland Conservation Award by the mayor of Madrid in 1987, Robinson wrote it was an "ethical attitude of informed love" that had guided his path.

Hold these words inside you for a moment.

Let them echo on your insides before you read this book.

Then, as you read it, ask yourself what exactly it is that he loved so dearly, what it is that he is asking you to love too.

. . .

Tim Robinson finds me for the third time in this my first spring living in the West of Ireland—on Traught Beach, at the edge of the ancient Burren, across the bay from Roundstone, where he and his wife's ashes were scattered into the sea in this the place they made home.

The day is Good Friday.

The weather is fine.

The sea is turquoise blue, the sky a darker blue that you only really see in the West of Ireland.

I have come here to write this introduction to this special book, by an equally special man. I've come here today because this is how I learn, through the doing, and I have learned so much from Tim Robinson. I wonder what I will remember of today. How does anyone experience place? Will I remember the gently lapping water, the grey of the sand, the mustard yellow and clementine orange shells—so tiny, so egglike? Will I remember how it feels to just *be here*?

As we hurtle even further toward climate emergency, housing emergency, toward human emergency, it is so important—it is vital—to consider what place means.

That's something that Tim Robinson taught me: that place encompasses everything and everyone around me.

We share this earth with our kith and kin, both human and non, and I wonder what it means—and what it will continue to mean—to think about place in terms that are different from how we have been taught to until now.

Just now the clouds are turning grey and I must take my young son by the hand, away from the sand and the shoreline.

I hope that you will love these words that Tim Robinson shares with us as much as I have.

On this Good Friday—free from any weight: religious, political, or other—I would ask you only one thing: *Imagine a life spent loving what is already good.*

KERRI NÍ DOCHARTAIGH
West of Ireland, 2023

Preface

THE DARK NIGHT OF THE INTELLECT

In 1948 Ludwig Wittgenstein fled the seductions of Cambridge, where he was the unchallenged star of the Philosophy Department, to a friend's holiday cottage in Rosroe, a fishing hamlet on a rugged peninsula separating the mouth of Killary Harbour from the bay of Little Killary. 'I can only think clearly in the dark,' he said, 'and in Connemara I have found one of the last pools of darkness in Europe.' His thought, a mental ascesis that matched his frugal and solitary existence there, was directed to an end, or rather to its own end. As he had written, 'The real discovery is the one that makes me capable of stopping doing philosophy when I want to. The one that gives philosophy peace, so that it is no longer tormented by questions which bring itself into question. 'The particular question preoccupying him at this time concerned the difference between seeing something, and seeing it as something. For instance, his farming neighbours see this strange figure in their landscape, and see him as a madman. There he stands, stock-still for minutes on end, staring at something he has drawn with his stick in the mud of the roadside. If I see this diagram (a roundish shape with a dot in the middle, and two long appendages on one side) first as a duck's head and bill, and then as a rabbit's head and ears, not a particle of the mud has moved. What then has changed—a mysterious mental picture I can show to no one else? The temptation, he writes, is to say 'I see it like this,' pointing at the same thing for 'it' and 'this.' Hence arises a philosophical pseudo-problem. But by analysing how we use language in such cases, we can 'get rid of the idea of the private object.' His neighbours, though, know a duck-rabbit when they see one, and forbid him to cross their land lest he frighten the sheep. Wittgenstein also lifts his eyes to the forbidden hills in search of examples of change-of-aspect: The concept of 'seeing' makes a tangled impression. Well, it is tangled . . . I look at the landscape, my gaze ranges over it, I see all sorts of distinct and indistinct movements; this impresses itself sharply on me, that is quite hazy. After all, how completely ragged what we see can appear! And now look at all that can be meant by 'description of what can be seen.'

'Wie gänzlich zerrissen uns doch erscheinen kann, was wir sehen!'—what rippings and tearings in that *'zerrissen'*! And this landscape has indeed been torn. Great thicknesses of stone from ages whose names—Silurian, Ordovician—speak of ancient uncouth states of the earth have been broken through and thrust one over the other. Little Killary was gouged out of the fault-weakened rock by a glacier in the Ice Age. At the head of the bay the fault is visible as a deep notch in the hillside, forming a steep and narrow pass. People from the now-deserted village on the mountainside beyond used to bring their dead through this pass to an ancient ruined chapel, holy well and graveyard in a mossy wood by the shore. The way is steep and rough, and in winter more like a stream-bed than a path. On the one hand rises an angry-looking broken-down cliff; the slopes on the other are boggy and slippery. The chapel and holy well are dedicated to a St Roc, unknown to history, who legend says struggled with the Devil here. When the fiend tried to drag him off to Hell on a chain the saint resisted so violently that the chain cut deep into the hillside, creating the pass and funerary way. Thus geology reveals itself as mythology; both are systems of 'description of what can be seen' in terms of what lies too deep to be seen. What were the temptations that chained the saint to the Devil? 'Are you thinking about logic or your sins?' Bertrand Russell once asked, when the young Wittgenstein, then his pupil, had been striding up and down Russell's room in silence for hours. 'Both!' was the reply. Half a lifetime later in Ireland, logic was no longer the problem—a tectonic shift separates the two phases of Wittgenstein's thought—but his self-lacerating effort to exorcize the delusions called up by everyday forms of speech was driven by

the same passionate and intransigent ethic. In some future legendary reconstitution of the past it will be Wittgenstein's wrestling with the demons of philosophy that tears the landscape of Connemara.

TIM ROBINSON
Roundstone, 2008

A Suspect Terrane

Skirragohiffern, or Sciorradh go hIfreann, a slide down to Hell, is the name of a ravine-torn hillside on the Mayo side of Killary Harbour, directly opposite the little Connemara village of Leenaun, and it is by no means the steepest of the slopes along that northern shore of the fiord, which becomes almost a precipice further west where the narrow waterway squeezes between the huge bulk of the Mweelrea Mountains and the hills of north Connemara to find the Atlantic. Pillars of eternity, at first glance, these majestic features of the landscape, as viewed from the mountain that dominates Leenaun; but to the eyes of geology they are provisional arrangements or over-hasty conclusions soon to be undone by tremendous reconsiderations, while according to fireside tales they are the Devil's work. Ordnance Survey maps name that summit behind Leenaun as Devilsmother, and some ten miles to the west of it is the pass of Salrock, cleaving the rocky height separating the bay of Little Killary from Killary Harbour, which came into existence through the aforementioned struggles of the Devil with St Roc, as recorded by the travel-writing couple Mr. and Mrs. Hall in the early 1840s:

> The sanctity of the Saint having grievously annoyed the Tempter, he threw a chain over him while asleep; unable to bear the sight of his glance or the mark of the cross, he leapt to the opposite side of the mount, but still held fast the Saint by the chain—the friction produced by the struggle forming this pass, and the victorious Saint having in the morning the felicity of seeing a way for travellers by a much shorter route than any that had previously existed.

Another version of the tale, inserted in a romantic and Oirishizing novella, *Noreen Dhass* (Pretty Noreen), published anonymously in

1902, has St Patrick himself chaining the 'Divil' to a rock in the mouth of the Killary, and the fiend tearing open the pass as he drags the chain after him as far as 'another big mountain in the County Mayo, below Asleagh, that they call "The Divil's Mother".'

But where exactly is this mountain? The boundary between County Galway and County Mayo runs up the middle of Killary Harbour and then inland from its head, and the old six-inch OS maps place Devilsmother about two miles east of Leenaun and just south of the boundary, therefore in Galway and indeed in Connemara, since Connemara is widely understood to include the Joyce Country. But when I was mapping the area in the 1980s I found that that mountain was called Binn Gharbh, rough peak, and that its map name was unfamiliar to the people of Leenaun and the Maam Valley—or, if they knew of it, they seemed anxious to stress that Devilsmother was 'over in Mayo,' in agreement with the speaker in *Noreen Dhass* and as if they were happy to disown it. But I finally got the truth from the late Bina McLoughlin, styled the Queen of Connemara.

I first met Bina when I was nosing around the bottom end of the Leenaun graveyard and she detached herself from a funeral that was going on above me to scramble down the terraced rows of tombs and check out what I, a stranger, was at. (If the afterlife is lived in the western ocean, as Irish mythology suggests, the dead of Leenaun have a fine start to it, for their graveyard falls westwards from the road to the waters of Killary Harbour, which seem to flow riverlike into the sunset. But of course, as Christians expecting resurrection from the east, they set their backs to this view of eternity.) Bina, I learned later on, had been given her title long ago (by another almost folkloric local figure, Dan the Street Singer) for her renditions of Francis Fahy's mellifluous ballad about a boat:

Oh! She's neat, oh she's sweet, she's a beauty in ev'ry line!
The 'Queen of Connemara' is that bounding bark of mine . . .

Bina herself, on the other hand, was ample and earth-rooted; however, she was always majestically adorned with numerous ropes of massive beads, and for her appearances at the great occasions of

Connemara—Clifden Pony Show, Maam Cross Fair, the pattern at Mám Éan—she would sport some extravagant ornament on her brow like a tiara; I remember one in the form of a large bow studded with fat pearls.

At that graveyard meeting she gifted me with some amazing placelore concerning various boulders on her farm, a few miles to the south in the Maam Valley, under which were buried sundry personages including Fionn Mac Cumhaill's mother; St Oliver Plunkett too, she told me, had had many adventures in the locality. So, a few years later when Michael Viney and David Cabot were making a TV film about my mapping career, it seemed a good idea to stage a conversation with the archetypal Connemara woman on her farm. Thus after I had appeared prancing on precipices in the Aran Islands and dragging myself through bramble bushes in the Burren, I came hopping over a Connemara field wall to greet the flamboyantly rubicund Bina, who was surrounded by her fat, woolly, individually named and loved sheep and wore what looked like a Mycenaean gold mask of an alligator among the profusion of jewels on her bosom. And what she had to tell amazed me, on camera. I asked her about the peaks and valleys forming the eastern backdrop to the scene, and she named them: Binn Gharbh, which I already knew; north of it, Gleann na nÉan, the glen of the birds; and north of that again and hardly visible, Magairlí an Deamhain, which she blushingly confirmed meant 'the Devil's balls.'

Back at home, I looked more closely at my blurry photocopies of pre-Ordnance Survey maps, and found that some sixteenth-and seventeenth-century maps have 'Magharladone' rather indeterminately located south of the Killary; one of them indeed labels the whole massif of the Twelve Pins as 'Magher ladone als the devyils Balocks xii great hylles or mountains'—an even more impressive symbol of the Devil's potency. Those old maps are vague and approximate as to details, but William Larkin's 1819 map of County Galway is more precise, and it has 'Muggerleendoon' in the right position, just north of the Galway–Mayo border. Later on I returned to Leenaun to view the heights from all angles in hope of determining the exact application of the name, and found that Magairlí an Deamhain (for which 'Devilsmother' is obviously a nineteenth-century euphemism) is a ridge extending northwards across the county border from Binn Gharbh and terminating in two swellings high over the Leenaun–Westport road that an inflamed imagination could indeed see as a pair of giant testicles. I confess I took an unholy pleasure (for the Devil has us all enchained) in informing the Ordnance Survey that they had had the wrong name on the wrong mountain for the last 150 years; and now that the name 'Magairlí an Deamhain' has appeared on their recent Discovery Series map of the area (though still attached to the wrong mountain!) I am egotistically peeved that the first modern and correct application of it was not on my own map of Connemara, which had been published by the time of my second audience with the Queen of Connemara.

Killary Harbour (the anglicized name derives from the Irish Caolaire Rua, the latter word meaning 'reddish' and the former combining *caol*, thin, and *sáile*, salt, into a term for a narrow sea inlet) is so long (nearly ten miles) and narrow (less than half a mile over most of its course) that Leenaun, with its white houses scattered along the curves of the coast road, and the steep mountain slopes immediately behind them, has the air of a middle-European lakeside village rather than an Atlantic seaport. Líonán Cinn Mhara is the original Irish, meaning the reef or shallow at the head of the sea, and the sandbank from which it is named is the product of small rivers that pour into it the swarf from the valleys they have been rasping out of the surrounding hillsides ever since the last Ice Age. The Killary itself is a true fiord, a sea-invaded glacial valley, even if it lacks the towering walls of the Norwegian fiords. It was excavated by a glacier creeping seawards from a vast ice-dome that would have overtopped all the mountains of Mayo and Connemara. Some tributary glaciers coming off Leenaun Hill, south of the village, and especially Mweelrea, a few miles to the north-west, have left corries like empty eye-sockets on the rocky hillsides where they originated. All the most striking features of the scenery, then, have been thrown together during or since the Ice Age that ended about ten thousand years ago. But the main glacier was exploiting a pre-existent set of faults that had weakened a zone now marked by the Erriff river valley (the route followed by the Leenaun–Westport road) and the Killary itself. To help me make head or tail of the profound convulsions and serial reconsolidations of the region, long pre-dating these Ice Age remodellings, I got in touch with a young man who had just finished his Ph.D. on the region and had the latest theories and radiometric rock-datings at his fingertips.

Kieran Ryan met me with his car in Leenaun for a tour of the region. To understand the Killary it was necessary, he said, to look at what the geologists call the South Mayo Trough—and here was a preliminary hint of the magnitude of the changes we would be considering, for this so-called 'trough' is largely occupied by Connacht's highest mountain, Mweelrea (2,688 feet), and its colossal sprawling entourage of hills. So we drove round the head of the Killary and along its Mayo shore towards Bundorragha (Bun Dorcha, dark bottom place), a mountain-shadowed hamlet in the mouth of a steep-sided valley coming down from the north. Just before we reached the turning into the valley I remarked on three jagged teeth outlined against the sky on the profile of the mountain ahead of us; Kieran told me these were the outcroppings of strata of volcanic rocks, marking three periods of eruptions separated by age-long compilations of the outwash of huge river systems. And in fact the day was to be dominated by vulcanism, much of Kieran's work having been directed towards dating these and other such strata. From Bundorragha we drove up the oppressively grand mountain glen past Delphi (too often a rain-soaked and Gothic-gloomy obverse of the classic site of sunstruck oracles it was named after) and the gloomy waters of Doo Lough, black lake, and out into the gentler country beyond. Then we pulled into a little roadside quarry to look at a (to my eyes) nondescript greyish rock exposure, in which Kieran pointed out two bands of a slightly paler grey. These narrow strata, he told me, were composed of tuffs: concretions of volcanic ash that had rained out of the sky and sunk to the bottom of a sea. Presumably these layers were more or less horizontal when they were laid down; now they were rearing up northwards at almost forty-five degrees, while those we had glimpsed near Bundorragha were steeply inclined in the opposite direction. In fact to comprehend the topography one had to subtract the whole Mweelrea massif, which did not exist at the time of these volcanic events.

That time was almost half a billion years ago, in the geological period known as the Ordovician. (Nineteenth-century geologists had a confusing antiquarian custom of naming such periods not after the areas in which their characteristic rocks were first described or are most prevalent, but after the Celtic tribes that inhabited those areas many millions of years later, in this case the Ordovices of North Wales.) This was long before the Atlantic had begun to open up, and the disposition of the continental masses around the globe then was quite different from what it is at the moment and from what it will be at similarly remote periods of the future, for the various plates making up the Earth's surface crust, on which the continents and ocean beds are carried, are ever shifting to and fro, stirred by slow convection currents in the white-hot rock of the mantle on which the crust rests. There was at that time an ocean comparable to the present-day Atlantic, the Iapetus; it separated Laurentia, which is more or less today's North America and Greenland, from Baltica and Gondwana, which comprised South America, Africa and most of the rest. Ireland was not yet a whole; what is now the north-western portion of it was a sector of the Laurentian shores of Iapetus, while the south-eastern portion on the other side of Iapetus formed part of Eastern Avalonia, a minor continental fragment close to Baltica. But the Iapetus Ocean was slowly but steadily closing, which meant that the edges of the oceanic plate underlying it, composed of dense rocks, were being forced under the edges of the lighter converging continental plates. As the oceanic material was driven deep into the hot interior of the globe it began to melt, and some of it made its way to the surface again through volcanic vents; thus each of the approaching continental margins was fringed by an arc of volcanic islands. The South Mayo Trough was a small marginal basin of Iapetus, between the Laurentian continent and its offshore chain of volcanos. But this was no Hawaiian paradise; Kieran's account of it was a vision of Hell. In the various tuff bands he showed me that day, some of them insignificant-looking streaks a couple of inches across and others boldly upstanding reefs a dozen or more yards in thickness, he had been able to identify minute shards of glass formed by the cooling of lava flung high into the atmosphere by violent explosions, bombardments of boulders that had sunk into seabeds of ash, and the traces of *nuées ardentes*, dense clouds of red-hot dust that come racing down the slopes of volcanos. The intervening strata of sandstone bore signs of having been consolidated out of huge thicknesses of sediments that had slumped and avalanched down submarine slopes, in events that must have caused vast tsunamis. And Laurentia itself, as yet unprotected by the vegetable world that would hardly begin to invest the land for another fifty million years, was a naked wasteland, subject to ferociously erosive weathers that could grind down mountains as fast as the folding and refolding of the rocks, in the oncoming collision of continents, could heave them up.

Some of the volcanic tuffs of south Mayo, I learned, had the chemistry of lava that had forced its way up through light continental-plate rocks; this implied that in places the coastal margin of Laurentia had overrun its preceding island arc, which was thrust down into the mantle. Connemara, it appears, originated as such a place, a broad promontory pierced through by volcanos, far from its present position next to south Mayo. Its ancient Dalradian rocks, its quartzites and schists, are much older than the deposits of the South Mayo Trough; they originated near to the similarly Dalradian rocks of Donegal and Scotland. This promontory of the Laurentian coast was sheered off by a major fault parallel to the coast (like the present-day San Andreas fault in California) along which the opposing micro-continent of Eastern Avalonia was approaching. Forced eastward along the Laurentian margin, Connemara was eventually grafted onto another peninsula that had been built up by the erosion products and volcanic outpourings of Laurentia's coastal mountains. Such chips off continental masses, which have been shifted, rotated and emplaced in geologically discordant surroundings, are called 'suspect terranes,' I learned. Connemara's rocks, folded, faulted and piled high by the age-long impact, were then worn down by rivers and deposited as alluvial fans in the South Mayo Trough. These deposits have gone through many a remoulding since then, and have now become the thousands of feet of sandstone strata of the Mweelrea Mountains; they are interrupted by welded-tuff bands that Kieran has found to be some 470 million years old, the work of Connemaran volcanos that have been totally deleted from the earth's surface by erosion.

I had been hoping to hear that the great trench of Killary Harbour marked the site of the suture between Connemara and the south Mayo rocks, in which case the widely accepted definition of Connemara as the land south of the Killary could have claimed a most ancient and natural validation. But reality is always more complex than our concepts of it. To follow the construction of Connemara further, or at least to view the mighty ruins left by ice's deconstruction of it, we had now to visit the southern shores of the Killary. So we returned to Leenaun—and for me it was as if we were simultaneously fleeing the mountainy gloom and grandeur of today's Delphi Valley and the Ordovician hell of the South Mayo Trough, our little time capsule of a car ploughing through shallow seas hissing under downpours of volcanic ash. Then we drove down the south side of the fiord towards Rosroe, the small peninsula separating Little Killary from the mouth of the Killary itself. The rocks of the hillsides we passed over on the way were largely mudstones and sandstones, which all looked much of a muchness to me but for the geologist bore the signs of having been deposited in varying situations, the earliest layers on dry land, then some on a continental shelf, then more in deep ocean, and the most recent in shallow inshore waters. It seems that in the final stages of its life the ever-narrower Iapetus Ocean overflowed the Laurentian margin for a while, and erosion of the coastal mountain ranges dumped these sediments into it. This was in the Silurian period (so named from the Silurian Celts of the Welsh borders), 440 to 410 million years ago. And somewhere under that pile, which grew to a thickness of a couple of miles, is the join between Connemara and the Mweelrea rocks of the South Mayo Trough.

By the end of the Silurian period Iapetus had ceased to exist and the two halves of what was to become Ireland had been fused together; the suture, according to a recent study, runs up Galway Bay (crossing the southern tip of Gorumna Island in south

Connemara) and thence to Clogher Head in County Louth. Local effects of this cataclysmic unification include the dramatic-looking fault at Salrock, where the older Ordovician rocks of Rosroe have been uplifted and forced southwards over the younger Silurian rocks. A more profound remodelling of the land derives from the bundle of faults running from north of Doo Lough across the Killary to Leenaun and down the Maam Valley to Lough Corrib and Galway city, the land on the east of these faults being displaced southwards by four miles or so relative to that on the west. The ravines of Sciorradh go hIfreann and the broad Maam Valley itself are the much later work of glaciers and rivers attacking the rock-beds sapped by these faults.

All the tremendous landforms I have described had been eaten away by erosion by the middle of the Carboniferous period some 300 million years ago and reduced to a plain, which then was gently and slowly uplifted into a plateau as a result of another remapping of the globe, the drifting apart of the continents that had converged and united in Ordovician times. The continent formed out of Laurentia and Baltica, in which Ireland was embedded, was ripped in two again by this opening of the new-born Atlantic in the Jurassic period, the time of the dinosaurs—a process that continues today and that one day may well be reversed, with America and Europe marching to yet another provisional Armageddon, one or the other preceded by a rank of volcanos. Finally (to compress unimaginable tracts of time into a few words) the plateaux of the West of Ireland and Scotland were uplifted by the spreading mantle currents that were bearing America and Europe apart; and then, a mere million years ago, the Ice Ages came to the Connemara–Mayo plateau and dissected it by glaciation into a number of massifs—the Twelve Pins of Connemara and the Mweelrea, Sheefry, Partry, Maamtrasna and Maumturk ranges.

What appals and exhilarates me in the contemplation of these shiftings of matter—which of course are trivial in scope of space and time when compared to the bursting forth of the universe from next to nothing, the condensation of the galaxies, the stellar explosion that spewed out the dust of which the Earth is made, and all the rest of the cosmic creation-story—is that none of it mattered.

Only after the evolution of life and then, billions of years later, that of consciousness, of mentality, was there any thing or person that could care whether the dice fell this way or that. Values arise from purposes, purposes from desires, desires from the ability to imagine what is not, an aptitude that is virtually ours alone, at least in this neck of the universal wood. Reaching the end of our day's travels across abyssal time and clashing continents, Kieran and I strolled up a side road to inspect what we saw as the sandstones of the Rosroe formation, which, he told me, is a small terrane that originated far away as fans of material washed down from the eroding Laurentian margin to form a peninsula was sheered off by a fault, carried westwards and wedged in between the Connemara terrane and the Mweelrea formation. Immersed strata-deep in our cogitations we passed a brusquely phrased notice forbidding unauthorized entry onto the premises of the salmon farm that seems to have commandeered the western end of the Rosroe peninsula. Soon an angry bellow from a distant figure reminded us that other people, for defiantly non-geological reasons such as profit and privacy, value the most out-of-the-way bits and pieces of the geographical outcome of the ages' convulsions, and so we abandoned our trespassing. I shall have much to write about the intensity of feelings, the conflicts of interest and the small daily struggles of saints against the father of evil that humanize such phenomena as the Salrock fault, the Rosroe formation and the rest of the stark and stony features, from Killary Harbour to Slyne Head in the extreme south-west, that make up Connemara's Atlantic face.

Faults

The townland of Foher: population in 1841, 165; ten years later, 28. Of the various meanings of the Irish word *fothair* listed in Dinneen's dictionary, the most apt to the situation of this townland are 'a grass-grown surface sloping over and down a cliff' and 'a ravine or deep glen.' A half-mile strip of 'improved land' lies along the southern shore of Killary Harbour, a sequence of ragged, closely grazed fields, each slanting down to the seaweedy rocks from the wall that separates them from the heathery mountainside above. It is terminated to the west by a precipitous shoulder of the mountain thrust out to the water's edge; the slot-like fault-valley of Salrock hacks its way through this obstruction. An old track coming along the shore from the east forks on reaching the pasturage; one branch climbs obliquely across the fields and squeezes through the narrow pass, the other keeps low and then clambers across the bare rocky ribs and grassy hollows of the mountain shoulder. This latter way originated as a famine-relief work, a penny-pinching tinkering with a famished topography; the hollows have been roughly levelled here and there with low drystone revetments, but one has to pick one's way across the intervening outcrops with care, especially when they are slippery with rain, mindful of the deep water steeply below.

No one lives in Foher east of the pass nowadays; in fact the population of the townland is reduced to a couple of households west of the pass, at the head of Little Killary. There are two derelict cottages in the pasturage area, one by each track, that look as if they date from the Congested Districts Board days of a century or so ago; the lower one is hulled in an immense rhododendron bush, and the upper one has a patch of daffodils before it—two mementos of somebody's efforts to soften their bleak surroundings. The field walls and drainage channels run straight and parallel downslope from the mountain wall to the coast, a tidy arrangement attributable to General Alexander Thomson, the owner in the Famine years of what was known as the Cushkillary estate (Cois Chaolaire Rua, meaning Killary-side). In 1848, writing to the Board of Works about proposed improvements to his lands, the General stated that eighty-two acres in Foher had been cleared of stones, chained and fenced:

> It has all been under partial cultivation and thickly inhabited but the distress of the county has caused such mortality and emigration that there are only a few tenants remaining on the property. I am contemplating making the whole into a sheep walk.

And if one looks carefully about this rationalized desolation there are traces of older, irregular walls and hut foundations. A discreet memorial to this vanished community is a holy well, a glint of spring water in a little hole surrounded by a few stones, by the wayside about fifty yards west of the upper cottage. It is dedicated to St Joseph, I am told—and of course St Joseph knew what it was to be forced to lead one's family into unknown lands.

The last journey of those who died in Foher or in the scattered farmsteads further up and on either shore of the Killary was by the pass through the mountain shoulder to the ancient graveyard of Salrock, in the woods at the head of Little Killary. The way is dramatic, even now that the ESB has inexcusably routed its poles and wires through the pass. I followed it recently on a winter's day when squalls were chasing packs of white wave crests down the green-black waters of the fiord and a bitter east wind was whetting itself like a knife in the V-shaped gorge. The cliff on the right seemed to rear up like a breaker to a black crest against the sky, and the scree fallen from it interrupted the path in places. Among the heaps of jagged boulders I could easily have missed the shattered remains of some curious stone platforms the Killary folk used to rest the coffins on at the highest point of the way. It was the custom for each mourner to throw a pebble into one of the cupboard-like recesses in these platforms. The pebbles are still there, in some numbers, fossil-beds of grief.

As one descends from that point the path moderates its asperity and becomes almost grassy, the cliff puts on a ragged cloak of gorse and grey-green cotoneaster, while a vista is revealed of the Little Killary's wooded southern shore and its distant opening to the ocean. At the head of the bay, to the left of the foot of the pass, the modest grey tower of a small Protestant church rises among old ash trees and sycamores, the graveyard of Salrock lies hidden in the woods beyond it, and Salruck House (as the Thomson family always spelled it), still in the possession of the General's descendants, can just be glimpsed among the ancient trees of its gardens. What a cut-off world this is, and how beautiful, in its rugged, unkempt way! Just one adventurous side road twists and climbs over the steep hills that rim it round to the south, passing the gates of Salruck House, running around the head of the bay and down the north side of it, and eventually coming to a stop on the shore of the greater Killary, at the village and harbour of Rosroe. Nothing, it seems at first glance, has changed since Mr. and Mrs. Hall came by, shortly before the Famine:

> There are few human habitations in this wild neighbour-hood; and but one gentleman's house within a circuit of many miles. Just at the entrance to a little bay, completely shut out from the world, surrounded by stupendous mountains through which a road has been formed by almost incredible labour, resides, with his family, General Thomson—a veteran officer, native of Scotland, who after having passed through the whole of the continental war, and taken part in almost every battle fought in the Peninsula, has retired from active and most honourable service to pass the remainder of his days in this primitive district. It would be difficult to imagine a greater contrast between his past life and his present; and it would not be easy to picture a healthier or a happier household. Under his superintending care, a little paradise has grown up among the barren rocks. All his arrangements seem to have been conducted with generous and considerate zeal for the welfare of the tenants, who are gathering about him. He is reclaiming land, encouraging

fishing, having regard to education; and is, in short, the benefactor of a rising colony.

And then, walking on to the end of the road, one discovers that Rosroe for decades has been blighted by neglect . . . but I will face that in due course.

'Salrock' is 'Sal Roc' in Irish, the first word being probably from *sabhall*, a barn, as in the names of several ancient churches including Saul near Downpatrick, where St Patrick was given a barn to use as his place of worship. St Roc—he whose struggles with the Devil produced the nearby cleft—is said to have been Patrick's nephew and the Abbot of Inishbofin in Lough Derg. Nothing visible remains of the saint's church; old maps indicate that the last traces of its ruins disappeared in the latter half of the nineteenth century. As recently as the middle of the last century it was still the practice here to distribute clay pipes for the mourners to smoke after a funeral, and to leave them on the gravestones; a photograph in the National Library shows them scattered in dozens on the flat slabs. The graveyard is hummocky with old burials, knotty with tree roots, dark with pendant leafage. One can dimly make out parts of what was a circular wall that once surrounded a holy well, as described by the lady-novelist duo Somerville and Ross, who spoke to a local woman here in 1893:

A circle of stones like a rudimentary wall stood round some specially sacred spot . . . inside the stones the ground was bare and hard, like an earthen floor, and in the centre was a small round hole, with the gleam of water in it. 'That's the Holy Well of Salrock,' said the woman. 'There'll be upwards of 30 sitting round it some nights prayin' till morning. It's reckoned a great cure for sore eyes.'

This shadowed space of sanctified neglect is of course the Catholic burial ground; for the Protestants, the gentry, there is a separate enclosure by its gate, and here the atmosphere is quite different. In pride of place is the tomb of the Thomsons, a massive slab of limestone supported on six cannonball-like granite globes and surrounded by black iron railings with lions' feet. Here lie: Hugh Thomson of Barcalden, Argyleshire, died 1838; his son Alexander Thomson, CB, late Lt General in the army and Colonel of Her Majesty's 74th Highlanders, died 1856; his grandson James Douglas Thomson of the Light Infantry, killed near Lucknow in the East Indies, 1857; the General's wife Mary Eliza, died 1867 in Surrey; her son Captain Colin Hugh Thomson of the 74th Highlanders, died at Salrock, 1905; and the latter's daughters Laura, died aged three, and Olive Thomson, died 1913. The prestige of death in battle extends to generations both before and after the cross-section of the genealogy noted on this tomb. General Alexander Thomson acquired the 8,000-acre Cushkillary estate by an earlier marriage to the widow of a Brigadier General Charles Miller, whose ancestors had come to Ireland with Cromwell and who died in the Peninsular War. And, more recently, Violet, another of Colin Thomson's daughters, married a Walter Browne Barber, the Brownes of Nottingham being another military family, and lost her two sons, Captain Colin Browne Barber MC and Major Robert Heberden Barber, in the Second World War. I have been told that a cousin of theirs deserted from the army and so survived, and when a local man dared to remark to the grieving mother, 'Isn't it a pity your sons didn't do the same, and then they'd be alive today,' she replied magnificently, 'I would have shot them myself!'

The little grey-plastered Protestant church, chilly and damp within, is perched above the road and almost hidden in trees; a rope has been strung along the churchyard wall to help its fading congregation up the steep flight of steps to the porch. It used to have a spire, according to a drawing made in its heyday, but that is long gone, leaving it with a low, square tower with modest battlements. Until recently one service a year was celebrated here, on the third Sunday in August, in memory of General Thomson, who had it built in the 1840s. To gain entrance at other times, I remember, one had to count out so many paces from the door and look for the key under a certain stone; but now the church is disused and even the stone is gone. The incumbent, until his death at the age of one hundred in 1997, was Canon Willoughby; his wife Ruth, who did not long outlive him, was the chatelaine of Salruck House and the daughter of Violet Barber. The Canon was very old and silvery and vague when I knew him, with an extraordinarily refined face of almost transparent delicacy and spirituality. Ruth too was elegant and gracious; I had called in at Salruck House in the course of my map-making (cartography for me being mainly an excuse to enter anywhere and question anyone), and once we had bridged an ideological gap—I had raised my eyebrows over her inability to tell me the Irish name of a little creek at the bottom of her garden, and permitted myself some remark about the Anglo-Irish relationship to the land of Ireland, whereupon she quite rightly told me not to be patronizing—we became friends. At her invitation M and I once spent a rather chilly and hermetic Christmas in a couple of small storerooms or tack rooms she had refurbished as a guest suite in the outhouses across the yard behind the main house. We had permission to ramble in the house, where we sometimes came across the Canon chuckling quietly to himself over some little incident of his youth, as we sidled between massive Victorian sofas and sideboards, inspecting bookshelves and documents and portraits. Ruth's great-grandfather the General seemed to rule over the house from his place above the drawing-room fireplace, stipulating 'No change!' By opposites the house made me think of the classical rhetoricians' art of memory: they would memorize a long speech by associating each part of it with some object situated in a certain position in a certain room of an imagined building, which they would then visit according to a mental itinerary. Here, though, a real building was so stuffed with memorabilia, which themselves must have been overflowing with memories for those who lived among them, that the visitor's powers of memory were defeated. Even the notes I diligently began to make from the archives Ruth piled on a table for me to finger through soon degenerated into an eye-wearied scribble in which accounts of complicated property matters and family relationships peter out or become illegible at crucial points.

But what of the local memories of Salruck House, seen from outside? How did Mrs. Willoughby, representing the only landed family of Connemara to remain in situ since pre-Famine times, and carrying the legacy of her forebears' reputations, relate to the descendants of their tenants? She once told me that she was afraid to complain about one local family's rascalities for fear they would burn the place down. That same family was very ready to tell me that General Thomson had evicted people from Foher 'to make fields of it.' Mrs. Willoughby was indignant about a recently published history of Connemara that named the General as an evicting landlord and failed to mention the soup kitchen he set up during the Famine. I have tried to follow out some of the social fault-lines of mutual incomprehension that persist from those stressful times, with the aid of a few of the General's letters that have been published; written witness from the other side is of course not to be had.

In 1846, when the Famine had declared itself, Thomson joined with the other local gentry on the Ballynakill Relief Committee in appealing to the government for funds and for public works, and promised £200 to give employment on the building of a pier at Rosroe. At the same time he was arranging for improvements to Salruck House, including the installation of a fashionable Wyatt window (a window of three lights under a segmental arch) in the dining room. The committee also called for donations to purchase meal and establish food depots; the General contributed an extra £60 towards the Rosroe depot. In the depths of the following winter, impatient at the government's delays, he went to Westport to purchase four tons of flour and a ton of meal, and shipped it on-board his own hooker. But during the voyage home:

> About 10 o'clock at night they were boarded with a boat and a number of men, and on challenging the people—the men on the Hooker three in number were beaten, pelted with stones, and forced under the hatch in the forecastle till they plundered the Hooker of everything on board.

He appealed to the government to make good the loss so that he 'may be enabled to keep the store as usual for the supply of a population of upwards of 1,000 souls,' but it seems there was no response to this. In January 1847 representatives of the

Quaker relief effort reached the area and arranged for the establishment of soup kitchens at Cleggan and Salrock. The British Relief Association was funding the provision of food for children through the school system; the older children prepared the soup in big boilers, the girls made shirts, and in the school at Salrock, which was under the direction of the Thomsons, the boys were employed in making nets. The Quakers also promoted the establishment and equipment of fishing stations, and advanced the General £52 towards one at Rosroe.

Little sowing was done in that fever-ridden and bitterly cold year of Black Forty-Seven, and by May Thomson was in despair:

> We are in a most wretched state of destitution and I fear we shall be worse . . . Many of my tenants have thrown up their holdings not being able to sow them but they are keeping still possession of their houses and what to do with them I know not—I am giving employment to such of them as are not on the public works as yet, putting down my own crops, but what way I can manage after my crops are down I know not for tho' in my debt for rent I am obliged to pay them weekly in cash which will not last always —unless I take money for the general improvement and reclamation of the whole Estate—but if I did that I could not profitably employ all my tenants and squatters who are now more numerous than the original tenants that I set the land to—as for paying rent there is not a thought about it, and this outdoors Relief Bill with all the rates to be levied to carry it out will make the proprietors as bad as the poorest man on their estates for they will not be able to pay it.

In fact the General had already decided to borrow £2,500 under the provisions of the Landed Property Improvement Act, use £600 to assist some of the poorest of his tenants on their way to America, and follow the advice he had given to his neighbour Henry Blake of Renvyle: 'to get quit as soon as he could of half if not two thirds of his present pauper tenancy' and relet the land in reasonably sized farms to men of capital. Such policies for dealing with the Too Many, the people whose names appear in no rent rolls or leases, would appear to the landlords as sensible and even generous; among the mountainous prejudices and class ravines of that era's grossly malformed society the line between pitiless eviction and charitably assisted emigration is hard to make out, as is the line between the Christian act of feeding hungry children and the bribing of their parents to abjure the faith they had grown up in. Ever since coming into possession of the Cushkillary estate in the 1830s the Thomsons had conceived it as their duty to extricate the souls of their tenants from the toils of Romish priestcraft. The 'spiritual awakening of the country' had been undertaken by the Connemara Christian Committee, set up in 1836 by the Revd Anthony Thomas, Rector of Ballynakill, and two curates including the Revd Brabazon Ellis; their plan was to acquire an area of bogland, drain and divide it into small farms and establish a colony of convertites on it. Thomson was keen to have the colony on his own land—one can imagine the attractions of a decent Protestant social geography to a landlord newly come into possession of the squalid tangle of handkerchief-sized plots and teeming hovels in Foher—but the project lapsed when no clergyman could be found to undertake it.

'Souperism,' the purchase of souls with food, was the charge that naturally and unavoidably arose with the advent of the Irish Church Mission Society. This aggressively proselytizing organization, energized by the belief that God had ordered up the Famine to make the Irish amend their papist ways, had been welcomed into Connemara in 1846 by most of the Protestant clergy, including the Revd Anthony Thomas of Ballynakill; one of the most contentious of their missions was at Moyrus near Carna, on old church land leased for them by Thomson from the Bishop of Tuam. The ICMS rapidly established mission schools throughout the region, including one at Salrock. A drawing made in 1850 by an English supporter of the society, Fanny Bellingham, who later married Hyacinth D'Arcy, the Rector of Clifden, depicts 'Feeding time at Salruck' as a charming *fête champêtre* with plump and pretty children lining up to have their soup cans filled, tenderly watched over by the spire of the Thomsons' recently built little church. But the soup was contaminated by sectarianism and its bitter aftertaste still lingers in the mouth of Connemara.

All that was a century and a half ago; since then there have been great changes. The Protestant missionary movement faded out even during the General's lifetime and the convertites-of-convenience no doubt quietly reverted to their old faith. In the time of his son Colin some of the estate was sold privately, and under his grandson Alexander most of the remainder was bought out by the Congested Districts Board to be divided among the tenantry. Independence came, and then the Civil War; the head of the local IRA called on Colin's widow, Mary, late one night to assure her that the house would not be harmed, as she had always been good to the people. But the district remained obstinately impoverished. When Wittgenstein visited in 1934 he was shocked by the cottages in the locality: 'I thought I had struck rock bottom in Poland—but this is even more primitive.' Rosroe was in General Thomson's time solely a fishing village; according to Richard Griffith's *Valuation*, in 1855 the 296 acres of the townland all belonged to the General and his twelve tenants had no land; indeed only two of them had even a small garden. Today Rosroe still fishes, in a small way, but the seaward view from its little quay is dominated by ugly sheds, gaunt walkways and a rusty hulk associated with a salmon farm. The former thatched coastguard cottage (which served as the food depot during the Famine) has been replaced by a dingy utilitarian pebble-dashed building, until recently a youth hostel but currently closed. There are a few neat cottages, but the atmosphere is blighted by tin-roofed sheds of concrete blocks with dogs tied to them, a storm-damaged mobile home and clutters of useless-looking plastic fishing gear; in short the place is an insult to its setting in Connemara's most magnificent gateway to the ocean. Is there some connection between this slovenliness, this indifference or hostility to order and regulation, and a memory of landlordism, a resentment brewed up in the soup kitchen and still undigested?

But here, as a writer and as a resident of Connemara, I face a difficulty. Just as, at a certain minute scale of things, the laws of classical physics have to give way to the much more difficult and paradoxical considerations of quantum theory, so at some low level of population the generalities of social history dissipate into the life-stories of individuals, with all their unknowable and contradictory motivations. The people of this little locality are so few that I may already have trespassed on their private spaces. As reparation, I will conclude with the testimony of one of those individuals to the fact that life in Rosroe has been one of self-respecting toil and closely calculated returns.

Among those small tenants listed in the *Valuation* I see the name of Michael Mortimer. The Mortimers figure as 'a cargo of rogues' in *Noreen Dhass*, and today it is the Mortimer face—toughened by salt spray and with a slow-burning and indeed roguish twinkle in the eye—that visitors are likely to carry away in their memories and their cameras. So, let Festy Mortimer, who died a few years ago and whose reminiscences were written down by Paul Gannon in the 1990s, speak for the passing generations of Rosroe villagers. Festy was a boatbuilder as well as a fisherman; there used to be currachs lying belly-up outside his roadside shed, and the bite of fresh tar in the air. He made his first currach in 1938; the white deal for the framework was delivered from Westport, the nine yards of canvas at tenpence a yard came from Stanley's in Clifden and another nine yards of reject calico from a Westport factory, while a gallon of tar cost him 1s 6d. He sold this currach for £3, with which he bought enough materials to make two more. So the making of each currach—signed with the cross in seawater, he says (which tells me that seawater was holy water in those days), and launched 'in the name of the Father and of the Son and of the Holy Ghost, three men that never failed'—capitalized the labour of making more currachs; by the 1950s he was charging £60 a currach and in the 1990s, around £900.

The main fishery in the Killary was for salmon, and in Festy's young days it was worked by draught-net, with two to row and one to throw out the net, and a fourth man on shore holding the end of it to prevent the salmon from escaping as the net was drawn in around them. In a good year they might catch 400 or 500 salmon, but the fishery was very unpredictable. The older men would spend all the day on station no matter how badly the fishing went, while the youngsters would get fed up and head for home; Festy learned the value of patience from the old hands, and always felt more comfortable on water than on land. From 1968 drift-net fishing was permitted in the Killary and many fishermen invested in bigger boats, but Festy stuck to the old ways. Herring and mackerel were fished too, and fetched around two shillings a 'long hundred,' that is, 126, the extra fish being to compensate the buyer for any spoiled in transit. Festy used to make his own lobster pots of sally rods, and often had ten or eleven dozen lobsters ready for the dealer, who had storage tanks at Glassillaun, on the south side of the Little Killary; lobsters sold for eleven shillings a dozen, but the dealer often claimed that some of them had died on their way to Dublin, and the price was not forthcoming, which caused suspicion and ill-feeling. By the 1940s Festy was getting three shillings a hundredweight for winkles, but the dealer's lorry did not always turn up to collect them, so that they died and the back-breaking labour of gathering them among the seaweed and stones of the shore went to waste. Later on a Frenchman, Mauger, set up his lobster and shellfish tanks at Aughrus near Cleggan and the fishermen were assured of fairer deals.

But of late the salmon and other fisheries have fallen away to nothing, and in Festy's eyes the rafts and lines of buoys of the new mussel farms were so much 'clutter and rubbish." I was able to rear a family of ten from fishing and making currachs in days gone by,' he ends; 'but if I was starting out all over again today, as a young man, I know there is no way fishing and currach-making alone would sustain me and that is what saddens me most after all these years.'

And maybe that is the meaning of the wasteland that lurks in the corners of such villages as Rosroe: the disappointment of Connemara; its failure, 'after all these years'—after the unimaginable climb out of the common grave of the Famine, the division of the land between the dwellers on it, the economic dreariness and then the material ebullience of the new Ireland—to renew its old ways of life, its language and skills, so that the young need not leave for the cities and the attempts to employ them here would not disfigure the countryside. As it is, land and sea look bleakly on Rosroe and grumble together over its present state, and even the splendid Atlantic sunsets the little port opens on to throw money at the problem in vain.

Looking around Rosroe in sadness, wondering what curse has lighted on it, I have in mind the times when the cottage by the quayside, later replaced by the youth hostel, housed mental effort so intense and sustained that one could imagine the thrum of cerebration reverberating there still. Quay House originated as a coastguard station and then became a holiday home; its occupiers have included the painter Paul Henry and the poet Richard Murphy, both of whom I will write about later on, in connection with other parts of Connemara. During his stay here Richard Murphy happened to notice a wad of paper tucked under a tile in the roof of an outhouse to stop it rattling; it was a letter, and it began 'Dear Wittgenstein.' The philosopher, it turned out, had spent two periods in Quay House, a fortnight or so in the rainy September of 1934 and nearly four months in the summer of 1948. The house belonged to the brother of one of his pupils, Maurice O'Connor Drury, whose family, of Irish origins but long settled in England, had ties with the area; I note 'Pamela Drury, died at Salruck Cottage, 1918 aged 76' among the words on tombstones in the Protestant burial ground of Salrock. Con Drury, as he was called, was of a religious temperament, but perhaps his most trying struggles of faith centred on his teacher, by whom his life history was repeatedly directed. It is largely owing to the witness of Con Drury (as conveyed in his *Conversations with Wittgenstein*) and one or two others of Wittgenstein's devoted and brilliant young acolytes that the depth of the remorselessly analytical thinker's engagement with religion is understood today.

Ludwig Wittgenstein was born into an extremely wealthy and cultured Viennese family in 1889, and went to Manchester to study engineering; a problem in the design of propellers led him to mathematics, and his absolutist mind soon focused on the philosophical foundations of the subject. Through the writings of Bertrand Russell he became aware of the pioneering work done on this topic by Gottlob Frege, a professor at the University of Jena and father figure of modern logic. Frege redirected him to Russell, and so Wittgenstein enrolled for study in the University of Cambridge. Ever since I went to Cambridge myself as a hero-worshipping young student of mathematics, the successional relations between Frege and Russell, and then between Russell and Wittgenstein, have been my paradigm of disinterested intellectuality; perhaps I have been naive in this, and the truth is rather more ambivalent and contradictory, but still I want at least to point out, from this ragged corner of Connemara, a distant glimpse of the noble escarpment that links those three peaks of mental endeavour.

Frege set out to show that the truths of arithmetic could be derived purely from the laws of logic, and that in particular the natural numbers (1, 2, 3, etc.) could be defined in terms of classes, a 'class' being merely a collection or set of objects considered as a totality—surely, one might think, the most basic and trouble-free of logical concepts. Having published the first volume of what he intended to be the definitive work on the foundations of arithmetic in 1893, he was about to publish the second when he received a letter from a young Fellow of Trinity College, Cambridge, Bertrand Russell, pointing out a flaw in his argument. It is roughly this: it seems intuitively obvious that one class may be a member of another; e.g. the class of cats, a very large class, is a member of the class of large classes. If so, then it should be possible for a class to be a member of itself, as, for instance, the class of large classes is itself a large class. So, what about the class of classes that are members of themselves—and, even trickier, the class of classes that are not members of themselves? Is this last class a member of itself? If so, it is a member of the class of classes that are not members of themselves and therefore is not a member of itself; if, on the other hand, it is not a member of itself, it is a member of that class, i.e. of itself. If it is, it isn't, and if it isn't, it is—a paradox, like the old classical chestnut of the Cretan who says all Cretans always lie. The concept of a class is not so rock-solid as it might seem, and a mathematics founded on it might be expected to collapse at some unexpected juncture. Frege responded to this disastrous communication with candour and magnanimity:

> Your discovery of the contradiction has surprised me beyond words and, I should like to say, left me thunderstruck, because it has rocked the ground on which I meant to build arithmetic . . . It is all the more serious as the collapse of my law V seems to undermine not only the foundations of my arithmetic but the only possible foundation of arithmetic as such . . . Your discovery is at any rate a very remarkable one, and it may lead to a great advance in logic, undesirable as it may seem at first sight.

He also added an appendix to the second volume of his long-laboured-over *Grundgesetze der Arithmetik*:

> Hardly anything more unfortunate can befall a scientific writer than to have one of the foundations of his edifice shaken after the work is finished. This was the position I was placed in by a letter of Mr. Bertrand Russell, just when the printing of this volume was nearing its completion . . . What is in question is not just my particular way of establishing arithmetic, but whether arithmetic can possibly be given a logical foundation at all . . .

Young Bertie Russell was not trying merely to be clever at the expense of his elders, and he well understood what was at stake, both scientifically and humanly: 'As I think about acts of integrity and grace, I realise that there is nothing in my experience to compare with Frege's dedication to truth. His entire life's work was on the verge of completion . . . and upon finding that his fundamental assumption was in error, he responded with intellectual pleasure clearly submerging any feelings of personal disappointment.' Russell was equally passionate about the search for certainty, and much of his life effort for decades thereafter, in collaboration with Alfred Whitehead, was expended on his *Principia Mathematica*, a vast and labyrinthine work deducing the theorems of mathematics from the properties of sets or classes, plus some complicated rules of class-membership designed to ward off the paradox that had undermined Frege's work. Nowadays set theory is founded on axioms that preclude a set from belonging to itself, but Russell's paradox retains its fascination, as do its linguistic kin the conundrums about sentences that refer to themselves, and sundry thinkers have investigated the fascinating consequences of breaking the taboo—two whose work I have puzzled my head over are the heterodox mathematician George Spencer-Brown and the French theorist of the event, Alain Badiou, while a self-respecting text like this of mine can hardly avoid the paradoxes of self-reference.

Then arose Wittgenstein—'the most perfect example of genius as traditionally conceived,' according to Russell, 'passionate, profound, intense, and dominating.' He studied under Russell, graduated, went off to fight in the Austrian army in the First World War, and to Russell's amazement emerged in 1918 from an Italian prison camp bearing the manuscript of a treatise: 'It appeared that he had written a book in the trenches—he was the kind of man who would never have noticed such small matters as bursting shells when he was thinking about logic.' This work claimed not only to have solved all the problems of philosophy, but also to have shown how little is achieved in doing so. In passing it remarked that 'the theory of classes is completely superfluous in mathematics'; a sufficiently precise symbolism, according to Wittgenstein, could 'show,' could make immediately and indubitably apparent, what all Russell's elaborate theory failed to say. Russell was temporarily flattened, as he wrote to his lover Lady Ottoline Morrell: 'I saw that he was right, and I saw that I could not hope ever again to do fundamental work in philosophy. My impulse was shattered, like a wave dashed to pieces against a breakwater. I became filled with utter despair.' (But he soon got over this mood, he tells us, in a footnote to his autobiography.) Later on came Kurt Gödel's astounding proof that not only mathematics, but even mere arithmetic, the theory of numbers, cannot be founded on the laws of logic, that indeed there can be no complete set of axioms for it of whatsoever nature; mathematics is essentially and eternally unfounded and adrift on unfathomable seas. This unexpected closure of the question of the 'logical foundations of mathematics' announced the end of the topic's dominance in philosophy.

Wittgenstein's thesis was published in German in 1921 and the following year in English. Despite the various stinging remarks in it about his own work, Russell contributed a generously welcoming introduction:

> . . . As one with a long experience of the difficulties of logic and of the deceptiveness of theories which seem irrefutable, I find myself unable to be sure of the rightness of a theory, merely on the ground that I cannot see any point on which it is wrong. But to have constructed a theory of logic which is not at any point obviously wrong is to have achieved a work of extraordinary difficulty and importance. This merit, in my opinion, belongs to Mr. Wittgenstein's book, and makes it one which no serious philosopher can afford to neglect.

Nothing could be more different in style from Lord Russell's aristocratically poised and supple prose-flow than the terse propositions, numbered according to a precise decimal system and hammered into place like so many nails, of Wittgenstein's *Tractatus Logico-Philosophicus*, as the English version of his treatise was titled. It begins:

1. The world is all that is the case.
1.1 The world is the totality of facts, not of things.

And it ends (in the ringing words of the first English version):

7. Whereof we cannot speak, thereof we must remain silent.

In between it offers—no, it enforces—a vision of reality as compounded from objects 'that fit into one another like the links of a chain,' and a corresponding vision of language in which these relationships of objects can be expressed with crystalline clarity. Propositions depict facts as a painting depicts a landscape by virtue of having a structure in common with it; the elements of a proposition and their logical relationships are in a one-to-one correspondence with the objects and relationships constituting a fact. The dauntingly abstract symbolism and aphoristic intensity of Wittgenstein's text persuades one that it makes all things crystal clear, if only one were intelligent enough to follow it. But, as Wittgenstein was to write later on, 'If a lion could talk we would not understand him.'

An expressed aim of the *Tractatus* is to draw a boundary in language, inside which lies all that can be said (and for Wittgenstein that meant all that could be said clearly), and outside which lies all that cannot be said without uttering nonsense. Since he devotes seventy-two pages of his text to the former region, which comprises the propositions of science, mathematics and logic, and just the last three pages to the latter, including religion, ethics and aesthetics, it is no wonder that his work appealed to the severest of rationalists, and it was energetically wielded by the Viennese school of logical positivists in their attempt to scourge meaningless metaphysics out of philosophical discourse. However, it has now become clear, thanks largely to the witness of some of his young disciples, including Drury, that to Wittgenstein what mattered was exactly that which cannot be said. To delineate a coastline is to delimit the land and simultaneously to indicate the illimitable ocean beating upon it; to show the limits of what can be said is to acknowledge the immensity of what Wittgenstein calls *das Mystische*, the transcendental and ineffable. The function of that terrible two-handed engine, the 'whereof / thereof' that smites one at the exit door from the *Tractatus*, is to sever our heads, freeing the soul from the trammels of reason to bathe in the immediacy of beauty and goodness.

And having thus finished, and finished with, philosophy, Wittgenstein disappeared from public view, divested himself of all his money in favour of his relatives, and found work first as an elementary school teacher in a remote Austrian village and then as a gardener's assistant in a monastery. After a few years of this Tolstoy-inspired self-abnegation he returned to lecturing in Cambridge, where he formed a close attachment to his pupil Con

Drury. Having graduated with a first-class degree Drury enrolled in a theological college in Cambridge, intending to become an Anglican clergyman. Wittgenstein strongly disapproved: 'I would be afraid that one day that collar would choke you. 'This was not irreligion on Wittgenstein's part but rather the opposite; once when Drury remarked that he would be happy working as a priest among people who shared his beliefs, his severe mentor retorted that he had better make sure that his religion was a matter between himself and God alone. On visiting Drury in the college and noticing a crucifix over his bed, Wittgenstein looked at him sternly and said, 'Drury, don't allow yourself to become too familiar with holy things.' And so it was to be; such observations made Drury feel that his life hitherto had been 'superficial and aesthetic,' he abandoned the road to priesthood and followed Wittgenstein's advice to leave Cambridge and work among 'ordinary people.' After a spell in Newcastle helping unemployed shipyard workers build a social centre he considered becoming a nurse in a mental hospital, but Wittgenstein had other ideas: 'Now there is to be no more argument about this: it has all been settled already, you are to start work as a medical student at once. I have arranged with two wealthy friends of mine to help you financially, and I shall be able to help you myself.' And so it was to be, again.

In 1934 Wittgenstein and his closest friend and student Francis Skinner came to stay with Drury at Rosroe. Dinner the first evening was of the best Connemara could provide: roast chicken followed by suet pudding and treacle. Wittgenstein ate in silence, and then announced, 'Now let it be quite clear that while we are here we are not going to live in this style. We will have a plate of porridge for breakfast, vegetables from the garden for lunch, and a boiled egg in the evening.' And so it was, once again. For Drury, Wittgenstein's moral attitudes had the standing of commandments, revelations that struck him with awe. One day the party rowed across Killary Harbour to walk the great beaches on the opposite shore, and observed a local family, the Mortimers, making hay in one of the precipitous little fields nearby, as Drury tells:

WITTGENSTEIN: 'We are going back. These people are working and it is not right that we should be holidaying in front of them.'

I thought of the many times I had been to these sands and such an obvious thought had never occurred to me.

But Wittgenstein's exacting moral sense was never on holiday; he had a determinate ethical stance for every situation, real or potential. During the Second World War Drury served in military hospitals and as a medical officer of a landing craft on the Normandy beaches—a conflict he went into bearing this advice from Wittgenstein: 'If it ever happens that you get mixed up in hand-to-hand fighting, you must just stand aside and let yourself be massacred.'

After the war, unable to settle down after such experiences, Drury went through a time of turmoil and uncertainty in which, 'dreading the powerful influence he had over me, and wanting to make my own decisions,' he did not see Wittgenstein for over a year. Eventually he became a psychiatrist at St Patrick's Hospital in Dublin, and went on to a serviceable and honourable career there. Wittgenstein, who had been appointed Professor of Philosophy at Cambridge in 1939 ('Having got the professorship is all very flattering and all that but it might have been very much better for me to have got a job opening and closing crossing gates'), resigned the chair in 1947 and, in search of a quiet milieu in which to think, came to stay in Dublin at Ross's Hotel (now the Ashling), not far from St Patrick's Hospital. He visited the hospital with Drury, and was deeply concerned by the heavy demands made on him by his duties there. He also told Drury off for his manners in a philosophical discussion with a patient: 'When you are playing ping-pong you mustn't use a tennis racquet.'

In the following year, after a period of depression and an unproductive stay in a Wicklow farmhouse, Wittgenstein went down to Rosroe to 'think in the dark,' in silence and solitude. And his mode of thought was utterly new, for in that high philosophical escarpment I have indicated on the horizon of this chapter, Mount Wittgenstein has two peaks, and it is the second of these that came to dominate anglophone philosophy for a generation or two after his death, leading Russell to note with philosophical detachment that 'Wittgenstein's philosophy replaced mine at both Cambridge and Oxford.' This work eventually resulted in his posthumously published *Philosophical Investigations*, which is astonishingly different from the pillared and light-flooded hall of certainties we are hurried through in the *Tractatus*, being rather a Dantesque dark wood in which one gropes and stumbles and backtracks, and occasionally senses the nearness of a forest ride or a clearing. Wittgenstein himself wrote that the nature of his new investigations 'compels us to travel over a wide field of thought criss-cross in every direction' and he described his book as 'a number of sketches of landscapes made in the course of these long and involved journeyings.' The work also involved severe self-criticism: looking back at the *Tractatus* he noted, 'I have been forced to recognise grave mistakes in what I wrote.' Many of his most basic assumptions were now subjected to a shattering re-examination and thrown aside. In particular the idea that propositions describe facts as pictures show their subjects is abandoned; there are many modes of description and many sorts of proposition other than descriptions, and the meaning of a proposition is not a corresponding reality but the role the proposition plays in a particular linguistic situation, to be elucidated by the most subtle and painstaking observation of its behaviour in the stream of life.

The day-to-day of Wittgenstein's life at Rosroe was not entirely conducive to these lonely explorations. He was grieving for the loss of Francis Skinner, who had died of polio; 'Let grief into your heart. Don't lock the door on it. Standing outside the door, in the mind, it is frightening, but in the *heart* it is not,' he advised himself. Also, his neighbours the Mortimers (unaware, of course, of the exquisite consideration Wittgenstein had shown towards them years before), were unwelcoming, and indeed regarded him as mad, especially when he complained about the barking of their dogs, and forbade him access to their land, so that he had to make a long detour to walk the hills. Housework, to Wittgenstein's demanding standards, was a chore. A Tommy Mulkerrins, who acted as caretaker for the Drurys and brought him turf and milk each day, drenched the cottage in DDT to rid it of the woodlice Wittgenstein was so disturbed by, and saved up his own family's wet tea leaves to scatter on the floor to lay the dust, according to the philosopher's instructions. Tommy also told him the names of the seabirds in the fiord ('though perhaps they weren't always the right names I told him,' he confessed later on). After a few months Wittgenstein was minded to move in with the Mulkerrinses, but Tommy, thinking of his narrow cottage and multitudinous family, politely declined the honour. And when Wittgenstein finally left Rosroe Tommy would have inherited the task of feeding the garden birds Wittgenstein had taught to come to his hands, had not the village cats taken advantage of their tameness to eat them all.

In August Wittgenstein moved to Dublin and settled into Ross's Hotel again. Drury went to meet him there almost daily, for walks in the Zoological Gardens and for discussions, of which Drury noted down many invaluable particulars. Wittgenstein was writing copiously at that period and often continued to do so for some time after Drury's arrival; on one occasion he said, 'Just wait a minute until I finish this,' and went on writing for two hours before breaking off, apparently quite unaware that it was now long past lunchtime. Drury was often stressed by his own work, and came close to resigning after losing his temper with an alcoholic woman who threw a glass of medicine over him, but Wittgenstein steadied him, saying that 'one keeps stumbling and falling . . . and the only thing to do is to pick oneself up and try to go on again.' And on another occasion, when Drury was feeling that there was something 'all wrong' with him in that he had not lived a religious life, Wittgenstein took the question in hand with his customary incisiveness and with the utmost seriousness:

WITTGENSTEIN: 'It has troubled me that, in some way I never intended, your getting to know me has made you less religious than you would have been had you never met me.'
DRURY: 'That thought has troubled me too.'
WITTGENSTEIN: 'I believe it is right to try experiments in religion. To find out, by trying, what helps and what doesn't.
. . . Now why don't you see if starting the day by going to

Mass each morning doesn't help you to begin the day in a good frame of mind? I don't mean for a moment that you should become a Roman Catholic. I think that would be all wrong for you. It seems to me that your religion will always take the form of desiring something you haven't yet found.'

The following year Wittgenstein was diagnosed with anaemia. Then during a visit to the United States he became seriously ill with cancer, and returned to Cambridge, where, as previously arranged, he moved into the house of a medical colleague of Drury's to await death. Drury, who had married the matron of St Patrick's, was summoned soon after his return from their honeymoon, in April 1951, and found Wittgenstein unconscious and dying; 'Tell them I've had a wonderful life!' had been his last words. His forgathered friends could not decide whether to have the Office for the Dying said, until Drury remembered that Wittgenstein had once hoped that his Catholic friends would pray for him, and advised that whatever was customary should be done. And so it was. At the very last it was Drury who directed his soul-friend's departing life.

'Death is not an event in life . . . Eternal life belongs to those who live in the moment,' Wittgenstein had written in the *Tractatus*. He had visited the peaks of intellect, and must have lived strange and disturbing moments of eternal happiness. But, to quote the *Tractatus* again, 'The world of the happy man is different to that of the unhappy man,' and as for Drury, who rose to be Senior Consultant Psychiatrist at St Patrick's and worked there until his death in 1976, what I read of him does not suggest the happy man. I think his scrupulous self-doubt may have deflated that pressure of presence in the moment necessary to burst it open to eternity. Also, Wittgenstein, that Saturn of the philosophical solar system (I was going to write 'Jupiter,' but Wittgenstein's manner was never jovial), exerted a terrible perturbation on the orbits of lesser bodies that came too near him. But Drury's own modest record of his relationship with greatness does suggest a selfless, devoted and disinterested man, a good man. The memory of Con Drury's decency, as much as that of Wittgenstein's genius, stands me in good stead as I sigh over the dereliction of contemporary Rosroe.

The Mermaid

Cryptozoologists occasionally show some interest in the Connemara coast west of Killary Harbour because of old tales of strange sea-beings sighted there. The best-authenticated records are from Fuaigh na mBan, the cove of the women, in Letterbeg, just south of the tip of the Renvyle peninsula; despite the place-name it seems that the creatures observed there were male. In 1936 the *Connaught Tribune* reported that two local fishermen saw a floating object in the cove that they took to be some item of windfall, rowed up close to it and got a fright when it turned and revealed the features of a man, growled at them in annoyance and dived beneath their currach. They backed off hastily, and one of them tried to hit the thing with his oar, but the other told him not to, believing it to be supernatural. The apparition pursued them for over 200 yards before disappearing into the depths. It was also remembered at the time that thirty years earlier Mr. Laurence Henry, son of Mitchell Henry of nearby Kylemore Castle, had seen something similar while passing the cove in his steam launch, and would have shot it had his crew not mutinied and refused to put the boat about.

There is, surely, nothing in these merman stories except perhaps exotic sea-mammals storm-blown in from Iceland or further afield, or, more likely, the usual factors of drink, prank, exaggeration and lies. But north Connemara does have its mermaid. Her name is Dorothy Cross and she lives in Mullaghglass, about five miles west of Little Killary. Dorothy is an artist and perhaps the leading member of the extraordinary cohort of Irish women artists that have emerged over the last two decades. Most of her creations no longer exist, having been made for specific sites and periods of time; hence the title of one of the monographs on her: *Gone*. So, like most people, I have to rely on hearsay, photographs and retrospective reconstructions to visualize them.

As an elemental artist Dorothy has had almost nothing to do with fire, some dealings with earth and air, and an overwhelming devotion to water. For the purposes of this book she is attendant upon the zone of ebb and flow, the oceanic unutterable, the contested, fluctuating boundary of that whereof we cannot speak but cannot remain silent. (I borrow the word 'attendant' from the title of her obscenest piece, which was located in a disused underground gent's lavatory, with signs directing 'Irish' one way and 'English' another, but both ethnicities nevertheless finding themselves conducted into the same space, faced with adjacent urinals mounted in maps of England and Ireland and drained by mutually yearning penises; an untenanted cubicle with a dimly illuminated sign, ATTENDANT, presides over this dismal, guilt-stained confusion of the politico-historical waters.)

This affinity with water is almost innate. Dorothy was a child prodigy of the swimming pool, swam two hours of lengths before breakfast and missed qualification for the Olympics by a tenth of a second. This apprenticeship has shaped her: her limbs are long and restless; when she wears her big shaggy black cardigan her stretchings and anglings give her the wingspread of a cormorant. It was the presence of a diving school at Glassillaun, the great beach just west of Little Killary, that brought her to Connemara. She swims most days in a cove and sea-cave below her house; she sometimes takes a can of sardines down into the depths of Killary Harbour to feed conger eels, black monsters as long as herself that come wavering out of holes and like to rub themselves through her hands. She says she is getting pudgy now, but when I give her a hug on greeting or parting she feels as streamlined as the stuffed gannet that plunges to its death in a construction of hers I once saw in the Irish Museum of Modern Art.

Dorothy's art tends to be written about in terms drawn from advanced theory, especially of the Lacanian sort; she herself reads little of this stuff, her personal mode being gestural, exclamatory, spontaneous. I had seen her once or twice at artistic functions over the years, not knowing who she was but noting her spare, decisive build and distinguished profile, and saying to myself, 'There is a person I would like to talk to.' And one day in September 2007 there she was, perched on the steps of the Station Theatre in Clifden as I was hanging around for my lift home after some event of the Arts Week. She cried out, 'I must introduce myself to this man,' which she did, adding, 'Artangel is in love with you!' This was gratifying. Artangel is a London-based fund-raising organization that finances radical artistic projects; it had expressed an interest in my West-of-Ireland activities, and M and I had visited its HQ, with no immediate scheme in mind, and had left with unspecific hopes of a future collaboration. Since then I had been hatching an idea concerning a certain cluster of ruined cottages by a little jetty on a peninsula in the west of Connemara, which had been progressively deserted in the century between the Famine and the 1950s. The village, almost lost in the wood of sycamores, rowans and old apple trees that had grown up through it, had a quiet and reflective atmosphere despite its negative history; the web of field walls was overgrown and tumbled, but the stones were all there and with care one could have reconstituted each little potato patch, rocky path and narrow 'street,' as the space before a vernacular dwelling is called. Its convivial and unhierarchical layout suggested the true meaning of the traditional term for a next-door neighbour: *comharsa bhéal dorais*, literally, 'neighbour of the door-opening.' Now, if Artangel could be persuaded to buy the place and supply a few million pounds' worth of gold leaf, one could gild the entire village, down to each bramble thorn and cow hoofprint, with nostalgia, at a cost vastly greater than all the wealth the little community had generated during the centuries of its existence. And now, here was Dorothy Cross, whose best-known work has been her mysteriously evocative *Ghost Ship*, a disused lightship she covered in luminous paint and moored off Dublin, where it glowed fadingly each night for a while. Who better to make my land-based dream a reality, or to throw it in the wastebin and come up with a better idea to put to Artangel? When I told her about the village she was eager to see it, but winter weather and the usual lava-flow of events intervened each time we made a date for the visit. In the meantime she came to see us in Roundstone, and in the spring I visited her in Mullaghglass.

Mullaghglass, An Mullach Glas, the green top, so named from a verdant glacial hill in it, is one of the townlands that slant down from Connemara's northern mountain range to the coast just west of the mouth of Killary Harbour. A narrow road and its accompanying straggle of bungalows meanders through it; Dorothy's is above the road and revels in a superb vista of ocean rimmed by mountains and islands: the grand bulk of Mweelree beyond Killary Harbour to the left, then faraway Clare Island and Achill, and in the middle distance Caher Island and Inishturk; Inishbofin is hidden by the Renvyle peninsula to the right. Her studio, next to the house, is a simple and elegant rectangular plank-clad building, rising slightly from rear to front and consisting virtually of a single huge room looking out through a good twenty or thirty square yards of glass onto the same vast arena of sky and sea as the house, but here rather attenuated by the young trees and shrubs of the garden. Here and there in the drive and on the lawn sloping down from the house are stacks of driftwood, a beachcomber's booty, some of it half assembled into loose structures that might someday become works of art. Indoors are innumerable clusters of objects, the pickings of Dorothy's world-wide travels; I noted a bizarre entity which on inspection resolved itself into a conventional little brass figure of a mermaid on a rock, her body sprouting a clutch of Amerindian barbed fish-spears, and one of her arms prolonged by the horn of some South-African deer species. There are stills from Dorothy's video works too, such as *Storm in aTeacup*, in which a famous scene from Robert Flaherty's film *Man of Aran* showing a three-man currach braving fearsome waves is apparently being enacted on the surface of the tea in a fancy old-fashioned cup sedate on its saucer on a tabletop. That idea is as bold and simple and disturbing as a nursery tale; much more complex in structure and implications is her *Chiasm* (which, I gather, is a term used by the phenomenologist Merleau-Ponty for a psychic structure of two separate but interwoven elements). In this work, video imagery of waves surging up and down in the great rectangular tidal pool below the cliffs of Aran called the Wormhole is projected onto the floors of two adjacent handball alleys; in each alley is an opera singer, one male and one female, who sing the most passionate of musical phrases culled from the great romantic operas, but who are inexorably separated by the wall between them. In *Chiasm*, or the mental image I have of it, for I never saw the event itself, the creative power of unassuageable human desire resonates with the self-destructive longing of the sea for its shores. Other troubling images I glanced at in the conventional setting of Dorothy's bright and well-regulated domesticity seemed to cross dangerous boundaries; I remember a most elegant photograph of a hand holding a dogfish gently by the head so that its body lies along the forearm in apparent erotic fusion.

Soon Dorothy's black Labrador, Louis, was demanding his daily walk, so we let him into the back of her car, where he turned himself into a whirlpool of noisy delight, and we drove down to the great beach at the foot of the next townland to the east, Lettergesh (a name of ancient provenance—*leitir*, a rough, wet hillside, and *ceis*, a causeway or bog track of wattles). The beach was at its widest just then, at the lowest ebb of a spring tide; Louis circled wildly, printing loops and spirals into the soggy sand. We took off our shoes and waded across a small river that winds an ever-changing course in the sands of its estuary, and clambered over dunes and crags and spilling prehistoric shell-middens to a further stretch of beach. Dorothy once found a horror near here, she told me: a sheep that had thrust its head into a discarded lobster pot, got caught by its horns and starved to death. She kept an eye on the corpse until it had largely rotted away, and salvaged the encaged skull. This item of found Surrealism, which she called *Wrong Death*, prompted her to accept an invitation to lecture at the Salvador Dali museum in Florida. Another of her gruesome finds on one of these beaches was the body of a Cuvier's whale; I had already seen photographs of it being carried home for her, draped across the bucket of a digger and dangling down to the ground on either side; its remains have not yet mutated into anything rich and rare. Then, as the tide was beginning to flow, we called in the dog and returned to the river, which was backing up a little but was still fordable, and so to Dorothy's for tea.

As well as her house and studio above the road Dorothy owns a stripe of land that slopes from the road to the low-cliffed shoreline.

We took our tea and cake halfway down it to a grassy tree-shaded enclosure dotted with primroses, celandines and bluebells, where there are the ruins of a cottage, a few old garden huts, and a small barrel-roofed barn of corrugated sheeting that houses a rather spartan bedroom she sleeps in now and then. The dappled shade was full of strange objects, all the raw material of potential works: the whale's vertebrae laid out to lose the last of their smell on long planks resting on trestles; its skull, on a small Victorian table; an old hip-bath that belonged to Dorothy's father and that she intends to plumb in someday where it stands; clusters of brightly coloured plastic buoys, a clutch of skittles among nettles in a corner of the ruin; a blue gardening glove on a stick, raised as if in greeting or drowning. I photographed everything, knowing my memory was overloaded; but even with the photographs I cannot now identify half the shapes wallowing in the grass or piled against trees in this museum, not of bygones, but of things to be.

A few days later we met again for the expedition to the deserted village. A mile of rough track leads from the coast road across the bog from which the villagers used to cut their turf for export to the offshore islands. The only inhabitant of this wide tract of land now is a hermit whose cottage is reached from a certain point of the track by half a mile of stepping stones set in the bog; I told Dorothy of how, one glorious Easter Sunday morning, I was coming down the track with some friends when we heard a distant vigorous baritone making the great spaces ring: 'Rejoice in the Lord always, and again I say, Rejoice!'—and the hermit appeared far off, strode across the stepping stones, processed singularly and solemnly up the track to us and shook hands with each of us in turn, never pausing in his psalmody the while. A little way beyond the beginning of the stepping stones another track diverges from the main one and winds into the distance; it used to be known as the Scholars' Road, for this was the way the village children took to school. Just beyond that junction the land begins to fall to the sea, and the village, or rather the wood that enshrouds it, appears. As we picked our way from dwelling to dwelling through the undergrowth, and Dorothy videoed and noted everything with rapt concentration, I told her what I had gathered of the village lore from its last inhabitant: that the cottage nearest to the crooked little jetties of the harbour was the storytelling house, and all the boatmen would call in there on returning from fishing or shipping turf to the islands; how the lads used to test their strength by trying to lift a certain round granite boulder lying on the shore outside it; and how, when a high tide threatened to invade this cottage, as it did now and again, the woman of the house would take up her tongs and lift the glowing turfs off the hearth and place them in the big pot that hung on its chain over the fire, until the sea had gone out again, and otherwise would make no more of this wet caller than of any rain-or spray-soaked human guest.

Finally I led Dorothy around a little point of the coastline to see a more recent curiosity: a boat, a lumpy homemade thing of concrete, perhaps fifty feet long, high on the shore and never to sail again, indeed almost built into the land by a stone-built ramp by which one could board it. A big teddybear, tipped forward onto its nose and toes, was propped against the deckhouse. We peered down into the body of the boat; it was dark and smelled of mould, and looked as if it had been squatted in by generations of junk-hoarders. A billowy-petticoated doll lay abandoned in silky disarray. I picked up a book, its cover washed blank, its pages sealed into a block. My eyes rebelled against the details; it seemed that all the soiled stuff of humanity was composting away down below decks. But Dorothy was fascinated; she eeled her way down ladder-like steps and disappeared into a nether compartment; I returned to the sunshine. Her voice came, detailing her finds. Clearly this meant more to her than had the village. When she emerged at last I said, 'Should we ask Artangel to buy it?' Dorothy has an odd way of sharpening up her lips and looking at you with one glinting eye like a seagull, which is childish and comic and at the same time anciently wise, when she rejects an idea: 'Too ugly!' she said. But her unbridled imagination has led her into dark places before now; I am thinking of her installation of metal cutouts representing the thirty species of shark known to have made unprovoked attacks on humans, which hung in chains and rusted away in a sluiceway channelling the effluent from a toxic dump down a cliff into the Niagara River. She is an adept of the deathly and the impure; she will say the unspeakable. But she would not take on board this cargo of grime disfiguring one of Connemara's precious shores. There was something to think about in this discrimination.

That night I dreamed I was walking along an old stone jetty like the one by the village; pure limpid water covered it to a depth of a few inches and flowed caressingly over my feet. Suddenly I was at the end of the jetty, or at a gap in it, and was struggling in deep water. I woke with a start, the phrase 'in deep water' in my head. Or perhaps it was, 'out of my depth.'

Moaning About the Chimneys

In 1917 W. B. Yeats brought his bride George down to Renvyle, the northernmost of Connemara's Atlantic peninsulas, to visit the country home of his friend Oliver St John Gogarty. George was a handsome and intelligent young woman, but she may have been aware that in Yeats's mind her middle name was Not-Maud-Gonne. However, if Yeats's inextinguishable old flame and implacable muse had held him (at a distance) with the terrible beauty of physical force, George had a countervailing attraction: a ready access to and familiarity with the spirit world. From her girlhood she had been a medium, and here, in the old house with its crooked corridors, creaky panelling and ten tall gale-strummed chimneys, she had the perfect theatre for the display of her talents. There was even a ghost to hand, a representative of the Blake family who had had the house before Gogarty acquired it, which expressed its resentment of newcomers by poltergeistical tricks. The door of an upstairs room, the only one with bars on its windows, could not be opened one evening; someone climbed up by ladder to saw through the bars, and reported that a heavy linen chest had been moved a few inches to hold the door shut. Even the sceptical and worldly-wise Gogarty had once been frightened by unaccountable footsteps in dark passages, and so it was to be expected that his poetical and mystical guests would see things invisible to his 'unenchanted eyes,' as Gogarty put it.

One evening, George having announced that she had seen a face looking out at her from the glass in her room, the Yeatses and two other guests held a séance downstairs, while a rival party, more pranksters than occultists, locked an emissary into the haunted room until he screamed and fainted and had to be rescued by Gogarty, having witnessed the apparition of a boy of twelve or so, dressed in brown velvet with ruffles at his wrists, who indicated in horrid mime how he had gone mad and hanged himself. The ghost also communicated with the Yeats party, through automatic writing, and Yeats, exercising his authority over the spirit world, a characteristic he prided himself on, had served it with a five-point antisocial behaviour order:

1. You must desist from frightening the children in their early sleep.
2. You must cease to moan about the chimneys.
3. You must walk the house no more.
4. You must not move furniture or horrify those who sleep near by.
5. You must name yourself to me.

Mrs. Yeats, the hardened seer, went up to the haunted room by herself to receive the ghost's response. 'What courage she had!' thought Gogarty. 'But we attribute courage to those whose professions to us are unfamiliar: to the soldier, sailor, aviator, none of whom claims credit for it for himself. So, too, the psychic researchers are unfamiliar with fear in their vocation.' Rejoining them after her vigil, George extinguished her candle and gave her husband a curt nod: 'Yes, it is just as you said.' After a whispered consultation with her, Yeats explained that she had seen a red-haired boy take shape in the middle of the room. 'He had the solemn pallor of a tragedy beyond the endurance of a child. He resents the presence of strangers in the home of his ancestors. He is Athelstone Blake. He is to be placated with incense and flowers.' A gathering of flowers from various bowls was put together, with a collection of scent bottles, and handed to Mrs. Yeats, and, so far as Gogarty's reminiscences tell us, the ghost gave no further trouble. Gogarty was left wondering how on earth (or elsewhere) Yeats could have guessed that it was the custom of the Blakes to name their sons after the Heptarchy, the kings of Saxon England, and to have found out the name of this particular child, a thing Gogarty himself had never been able to learn.

What has survived of the history of Renvÿle House is discontinuous, episodic. A haunted house is really one that itself haunts the corridors of its past, evoking crises that hang like cracked and bulging old history paintings and faded portraits in certain alcoves and staircases, and usually leaving long intermediate passages unilluminated by record or memory. I shall take a leaf out of George's book of spells—one of the functions of form or theme in literature being to maintain the writer's interest in the subject matter (not the reader's interest, which is no business of the writer's at all)— and summon up from critical moments of their lives the remarkable men and women who have paced those corridors. I have rearticulated their bones with the aid of unreliable memoirs and sporadic documentation, but if in some cases they turn out to be misarticulated, say with a leg where an arm should be, then I would point out that 'Athelstone Blake' does not correspond so perfectly to his historical precursor as Gogarty pretends to believe, as will appear.

James Hardiman, the Galway historian, tells us that in May 1653, just over a year after the surrender of the town to the Cromwellian army, a party of soldiers was sent into Connemara to capture Colonel Edmund O'Flaherty, who had taken part in the rebellion of 1641 and therefore stood accused of treason and murder. Colonel Edmund was not to be found in or near his tower house of Renvyle, and the soldiers were turning back after a long search when they noticed ravens hovering and croaking above a small dark wood. Led by these birds (sent by Providence to avenge the Protestants O'Flaherty had killed in a raid on a castle in Clare, according to Hardiman's local source for these details), they found a cavity in a rock in the centre of the wood, and pulled out of it a miserable-looking man and a poorly dressed and emaciated woman: the Colonel himself, and his wife Margaret, daughter of Sir Christopher Garvey of Kent and Lehinch in Mayo. 'And truly who had seen them would have said they had been rayther ghosts than men, for pitiful looked they, pyned away for want of food, and altogether ghastly with fear,' it was reported. The Colonel was tried in Galway, found guilty and hanged; what became of poor Margaret I have not learned.

The lost territories of the Renvyle O'Flahertys had been granted to Richard Nugent, Earl of Westmeath; one of the leaders of the Royalists, he was lucky to escape with his life after the

Cromwellian victory, but lost his rich estates and was given most of the land from Renvyle and Cleggan eastwards to Lettergesh and Pollacappul in boggy compensation. He went into the service of the Spanish king, and so probably never saw his new holdings. On the restoration of the monarchy in 1660 he regained his estates, and later sold most of the Connemara lands to one Henry Blake, a member of one of the thirteen Catholic and mercantile families, Anglo-Norman in origin, known as the Tribes of Galway. Henry had been sent off to Montserrat as a remittance man, did well in the West Indies trade, and returned with money in his pocket with which he bought not only the 2,068 acres of north-west Connemara but land at Lehinch in County Mayo too. For generations the Blakes were absentees, renting most of the Renvyle lands to one of Colonel Edmund's three sons, another Edmund, who had gone to England, become an army captain and now returned to farm the family's former property. For some generations thereafter the O'Flahertys stayed on as middlemen, renting land and subletting to lesser tenants, and living like virtual landlords, if not indeed as Gaelic chieftains of the old order. This Captain Edmund too had a son called Edmund, who died in poverty in 1749 on his own little estate, attractively named Cluain Idir Dhá Abhainn, the meadow between two rivers, a mile or so east of the old Ballynakill church; he was the legendary Éamonn Láidir who used to fight with Nimble Dick Martin, and I will not disturb his gigantic bones here, for they were on display in a niche of the church wall for many years. It was probably his son Anthony who built himself a house where Renvyle House now stands, cementing its stones with lime made from the great prehistoric deposits of oyster shells in the nearby sand dunes.

There the O'Flahertys of Renvyle enjoyed an Indian summer in what was a relatively prosperous time for Connemara as a whole. When continental sources of alkali for glass-making and linen-processing were cut off during the Napoleonic Wars, kelp was in great demand, and the sea heaped its riches on every Connemara shore; the farmers of Meath needed all the calves Connemara's thin pastures could breed, to fatten on their richer grasslands; industrializing Ulster consumed the oatmeal from Connemara's little plots of oats; potatoes grown on seaweed-enriched soil were bounteous. The herring fisheries centred on nearby Inishbofin attracted hundreds of boats from up and down the western coast. Smuggling flourished; the ramifying bays and multitudinous offshore islands made it easy to evade the few Revenue cutters patrolling the coast, and Anthony was the chief patron and financial backer of the famous smuggler of Ballynakill, George O'Malley. The law was far away; Clifden had yet to come into being, and what roads existed were mere bridle-paths. When the blithe young Chevalier de La Tocnaye came rambling through Connemara in 1796, staying one night with Humanity Dick Martin at Ballynahinch and the next with Anthony O'Flaherty, he found that it occasioned no surprise if he entered into a cabin and called for brandy or claret, although the good woman of the house might have to say, 'There is nothing at present in the house, but my husband is at sea, and if you come back in a month you can have all you want.' All this commerce and productivity was of course extremely precarious—agricultural and kelp prices were to fall at the end of the continental wars, the herring shoals had a treacherous way of disappearing beyond ocean horizons, the potato crop was subject to failure through drought or drenching, and ultimately through the blight—but for the time being all was well. The population soared and holdings were subdivided, but there was still enough to go round, and plenty of time for singing songs and dancing and telling stories. Then, in 1811, when Anthony had reached the golden age of eighty-six, out of the blue came the first crisis in the history of the house: the arrival of the true landlord.

The Lehinch Blakes' estates had descended from generation to generation, and on Henry's great-great-grandson dying without issue had passed to a relative, Valentine Blake of Mullaghmore in east Galway; the family had long conformed to the established Church and to the mentality of the anglicized landlord class by this period. It was Valentine's son, another Henry, who in 1811 descended on the O'Flahertys, most unlooked-for and uncalled-for.

What had prompted this visit, beyond perhaps a growing aware-ness of the possibility of making something out of

Connemara at last, was the news that a ship had been wrecked on a beach (probably Glassillaun) on his property, and that it was necessary for him to assert his manorial right to it, which had been usurped by the middleman. On a stormy day in the depths of winter he and a friend, accompanied by an armed party to see them through the Joyce Country, set off from Mullaghmore on the sixty-mile journey. They entered the Joyce Country by the isthmus between Loughs Corrib and Mask, and the following day went on into the Maam Valley, where they had to cross the fords of the Béal na mBreac river, 'or rather to ride for several miles in the bed of a mountain torrent, which formed the track by which we were gradually led to the pass of Mam Turk.' This brought them down into the Inagh Valley and the 'mountain road' from Galway to Ballynakill and Renvyle. Towards the end of that day's travel they saw the wreck on the white sands ahead of them, pressed on and made themselves known to the leader of 'a party of as wild looking fellows as can be imagined' who were running in and out of a hovel dug into the sand, in which the salvaged timbers were being stored. This 'person of superior rank' turned out to be the son-in-law of Anthony O'Flaherty, and he immediately invited them to what he called 'the big house.' Blake was delighted to have the opportunity of seeing the establishment of 'a middleman, possessed of an income of 1500*l* per annum, arising from his good management of profit rents, surrounded by a numerous and untutored tenantry, utterly unconscious of any other claims on the land' and moreover one 'claiming to be a lineal descendant from the old Kings of the West, O'Flaherties of centuries long since gone by.' Blake proceeds to give us an unrivalled insight into the domestic life of such a person:

'The big house,' then, was a thatched cabin about sixty feet long by twenty wide, and to all appearance only one storey high. It ostensibly contained an eating parlour and sitting-room, out of which opened two small bedrooms. We had oral evidence in the night, that there was other accommodation in the thatch, but those who had the benefit of it were placed beyond our ken. Conceive then our surprise at being gradually introduced to at least two dozen individuals, all parlour boarders. There was mine host, a venerable old man of eighty-six, his young and blooming wife, a daughter with her husband, three or four gay young ladies from Galway, two young gentlemen, two priests, and several others, evidently clansmen and relations. As they filed in, we sat by, wondering whence they came, but when the adjournment to the dining-room took place, it was evident, from the profusion with which the hospitable table was spread, that there would be no deficiency in their entertainment. Among a variety of curious articles on the table, we particularly noticed a fine dish of sea-kale . . . A room full of company, the fumes of a large dinner, and the warmth of a bright turf fire, rendered the heat almost insupportable, and during the feast, amid the clatter of knives and forks, and the mingled voices of our party, we were indulged *ad libitum* with the dulcet notes of the bag-pipe, which continued its incessant drone until the ladies retired from the table. I need not expatiate on the wines and spirits, though both had probably been imported duty free many years before, and were certainly good enough to tempt the whole party to pay a sufficient devotion to the jolly god . . .

Blake, however, was on his guard, and when 'the expected attack' came and the son-in-law, after many compliments to the Blake family and self-congratulations on his own industry, asked for a renewal of the lease, was ready to reply 'in general but decisive terms' that while he would be unwilling to remove an old tenant or his family, he was resolved not to have a middleman between himself and 'the immediate cultivators of the soil.' This brought an abrupt end to the conversation, and the party soon adjourned to join the ladies.

The next day, before he left for home, Blake formally laid claim to the wreck, but in the end neither he nor the O'Flahertys made much on it as the owner and the Admiralty stepped in and asserted their prior rights. However, he had been delighted with the beauty of the region, and planned to settle there, a determination to which the general improvement in conditions during those years would have helped persuade him. There was a feeling abroad that a profit could be wrung out of Connemara. John D'Arcy was beginning to consider building the seaport that would become 'Newtown Clifden' on his estate, the Martins were looking into marble quarries and copper mines, and Blake himself, during this first visit, got wind of a slate bed on his land at Lettergesh, and returned to inspect it in the following year. Although the Blakes took themselves off to London for a few years, and it would be over a decade before he moved his family to Renvyle, the end of the O'Flaherty regime was clearly at hand, as another episode soon proved. Blake was informed that a large trunk of bog-timber had been found on the estate, and he instructed a steward to claim it on his behalf; a mob gathered, the steward was sent about his business, and the log was shouldered and carried off in triumph, preceded by the O'Flaherty piper. 'I could not thus suffer my authority to be set at naught,' writes Blake, 'and after some communication between our mutual men of business, the timber was restored . . . This may be regarded as the dawn of law in this part of Connemara.' It certainly marked the displacement of one law by another. Anthony O'Flaherty soon afterwards retired to an estate of his own (presumably Cluain Idir Dhá Abhainn), because, according to Blake, it had been demonstrated publicly that 'he was not king *de jure.*'

By the time the Blake family moved to Renvyle and took over the big house, which they had had refurbished and (probably) reroofed with slates from the Lettergesh quarry, the condition of the West of Ireland had deteriorated sharply. Projects initiated in the years of hope were still advancing, but the hopes of D'Arcy at Clifden and Nimmo at the new harbour and fishing village of Roundstone had already been undermined by the halving of agricultural prices on the conclusion of the Napoleonic Wars, the decline of the kelp trade now that industry had another source of alkalis in the saltwort marshes of Spain, and finally the potato crop failure of 1816 and the general food shortages of 1821 and 1822. A clutch of bank failures followed on the bankruptcy of big graziers, and the overnight disappearances of small rent-defaulting tenants together with their stock left many landlords with depopulated and disused lands. Nevertheless by January 1823 Henry, his English wife Martha, *née* Attersol, the first four of their children and Martha's sister Anne Attersol were *in situ*, and the last-named was able to write to their distant London friends:

> Henceforward you are to consider us as cut off from the ordinary routine of society, leading somewhat of a patriarchal life; or rather living in the style of the old feudal Barons. Enjoying, in proud solitude, the grandeur of our rocks and mountains, surrounded by warm-hearted faithful dependants, and with no rival chieftain within a distance of fifteen miles.

Thus begins the first of a series of letters that were later published by John Murray, his eye on the Romantic cult of Scotland, under the title *Letters from the Irish Highlands*. Henry himself contributes the retrospective account of his earlier visit I have quoted above, and several astute analyses of the political economy and the woes of the times, while the ladies provide humane and sympathetic insights into the lifestyles of their tenants and dependants, as well as wry observations on their own establishment. The letters were published anonymously; all are intelligent and enlightened in their attitudes, within the unquestioned parameters of landlordism, but those signed with an 'A,' and presumably written by Anne Attersol, are particularly vigorous in the defence of the Irish against the commonplace charges of idleness brought against them by her London correspondents:

> Instead of bewailing the faults of the Irish as incurable, or bewildering ourselves in a vain search after hidden causes, the effects of which are as plain as the sun at noon-day, we may be comforted with the assurance, that they possess the seeds of all the opposite virtues, which only lie dormant, until, by proper management, they may be called forth into life and activity. If they are now dirty and indolent, it is still certain they have been endowed by Providence with the capacity of becoming both cleanly and industrious: if profuse

and improvident, it is not from any moral inability of being careful and economical.

And it is the clear duty of the landlord class to provide the 'proper management' that will enable those hidden virtues to come into play. The judicious distribution of charity and the charitable imposition of justice occupy much of their thought and time. Both evangelical Protestant bigotry and superstitious Romish practices—the filthy bottles of holy water, the priest's exactions and negligences—are to be reprehended, but controversy is to be avoided:

> At present, the most hopeful plan, and the best preparation for that purer system of Christianity, which must be the great object of all our wishes and of our prayers, appears to be, the gradual enlightenment of their minds by education and employment; and the proving to them, by a steady course of charity and forbearance, that the only end we have in view is their own well-being.

Nevertheless there had already been a sectarian row over a Catholic chapel that Anthony O'Flaherty had built 'within a hundred yards of the house'; since O'Flaherty had not obtained a grant of the site, the chapel now was Henry Blake's property, and 'it was natural that he should wish to be relieved from the inconvenience of a Catholic place of worship so close to his own door.' While the house was still being refurbished in preparation for the family's settling there, Blake decided to convert the chapel into a school, and offered to assist liberally in the building of a new chapel on a site donated by him (that now occupied by the church in the village of Tully Cross, two miles to the east), but delays ensued and eventually he had the altar rails and altar of the old chapel removed and a lock put on its door. The priest, however, continued to say Mass in it, borrowing the key now and then, and finally putting his own lock on the door. Blake called in constables and carpenters, the lock was removed, and after an 'explanation' with the Catholic archbishop the priest was transferred out of the parish. That is the Blakes' version, but an uncharacteristic inaccuracy in it perhaps hints at an uneasy conscience in the matter, for the chapel was in fact a quarter of a mile from the house (its ruins can still be made out, by the road leading to the main gates). We shall never get to the bottom of the story, but local tradition is that Blake allowed his cattle to get into the chapel and so desecrated it. The new chapel at Tully Cross was, it seems, not built until about 1837, at least seventeen years after this incident. The school flourished for four years, according to the Blakes, but then it closed because the people, however much they appreciated the advantages of an education for their children, feared the priest's curse more.

The living conditions of many of their tenants are described with appalled humanity by the Blakes, and there is no doubt that they exerted themselves to alleviate suffering where they could; but circumstances—the succession of bad harvests, the desertion of the herring shoals, the collapse of agricultural prices—were against them. Their family increased mightily and patriarchally: seven sons, whose first names—Edgar, Harold, Ethelbert, Egbert, Ethelred, Ethelstane and Herbert—romantically harked back to the Heptarchy, the 'seven kingdoms' of Anglo-Saxon times, and all with Henry as their second names, were followed by two daughters, Emelia and Eleanor. (The Yeatses were a little out with their naming of the ghost as 'Athelstone': Ethelred was the son who died young and, says local legend, mad, aged fourteen or so, while Ethelstane's widow was living in Tullymore cottage, not far away, for years after her husband's death, if not indeed at the time of the Yeatses' visit.)

Maria Edgeworth, in the course of her Connemara tour of 1833, came on to Renvyle after her stay at Ballynahinch, mentioned in my first volume; unfortunately (for us readers of her brilliant letters) the Blakes were away from home, but they sent word that she was to consider their house as her own and instructed their agent to make her and her party comfortable. Edgeworth describes the excellent sitting room and the Turkish-carpeted and oak-panelled library 'looking as if it had been lived in constantly and happily,' in contrast to the house's bleak and cold situation 'within a stone's throw or wave's dash of the vast Atlantic—a magnificent, awful, shivering November view.' Just as she had done with Ballynahinch,

Edgeworth viewed Renvyle as literature; Henry Blake, who she tells us had suffered various reverses, she identified with a certain character in one of her own short stories:

> He brought over an English broad-wheel wagon, and it was landed on the sea shore and could never be got further. He brought over a herd of English cattle—Southdown sheep used to warmth and tender care and good living, and having made no sort of provision for them, and it being desperate cold in the latter end of October and the beginning of November, they and their ewes all died. And Mr. Blake, though a very ingenious, philanthropic and active man, has been, I am afraid, too Pierce Marvelish and, in short, is ruined and wants to sell Renvyle and quit.

Finally the potato-blight crisis of 1845–9 brought Blake to despair. In the year remembered as Black '47 he wrote to Labouchère, the Chief Secretary for Ireland:

> Having resided in this country for nearly thirty years, having preserved the peace of it for the same time, I am now after having spent £30,000 in attempting to improve my estate, in building and in farming, in broken health and with the prospect of utter ruin before my eyes.

His neighbour Alexander Thomson had a copy of this letter, and he wrote to a John Galway describing Blake's predicament and his own brisk proposals for dealing with it:

> Poor Blake of Renvyle he is very desponding and I fear will hurt his health and that of his family by his gloomy forebodings and calculations; he had nearly dismissed all his servants and calls himself a ruined man that will not be able after all he has expended for the last 30 years on improvements etc. etc. to support his family but will actually be reduced to destitution—I strive to rouse him sometimes and a few days ago I proposed to him to borrow money to improve the Estate

which would pay him well. His answer was how could he do it—where would he get tenants to pay the instalments—I said my view on that subject was very simple to get quit soon as he could of half if not two thirds of his present pauper tenancy—to fence and divide his property to reasonable sized farms and then let them to farmers of sound capital that would employ the remaining poor on his Estate so as to do away with those half labourers half farmers that he has no control over either as labourers or farmers—till he got things into that state to farm his Estate himself . . . but all would not do, there were insurmountable difficulties in his way tho' this year he acknowledged he had plenty of stock but they would all be taken away from him by the Poor Rate—he never leaves the house and looks miserably ill.

Henry Blake's last years must have been sad; he lived through whatever tragedy it was that led to young Ethelred's death, and saw two more of his fine heptarchy of sons die in their twenties. Mrs. Blake died in 1853, and Henry followed her in 1856.

The estate survived, however, and was inherited by Edgar, Henry's eldest son, although by then the eastern portion, almost two-thirds of the whole, had been leased to a Canon Wilberforce. As Edgar himself died in 1872, it was his widow Caroline who was left to run the estate in the dangerous years of the Land War, and by her manner of doing so became a heroine of the Unionist cause. The endless rains of the winter of 1878–9 brought conditions in the West to a nadir almost as deep as that of the Great Famine; the Land League, founded in Mayo as a relief organization, a physical force to protect tenants from eviction, and a political movement with the slogan 'The land for the people,' soon spread to Connemara, bringing its practices of boycotting landlords and driving cattle onto their land, and withholding rent. The Catholic clergy in Clifden were supportive: landlordism, they declared, was 'as vile and detestable system as ever cursed any district under the sun,' and they undertook 'to agitate until the order of death by eviction and extermination shall be drawn from within the right which landlords enjoy.' Caroline Blake bore the brunt of this—including such petty horrors as the slicing off of her donkey's ears—and came through. But the rentless years left her with heavy debts and a dilapidated house. Sympathizers set up a 'Blake Fund' to help her, to which the Prime Minister A. J. Balfour contributed, and this enabled her in 1883 to open the house as a hotel.

A few years later Charles Stewart Parnell, who had become president of the Land League in the hope of steering it as a political engine, was accused by *The Times* of complicity in agrarian outrages and murders, and a special commission was set up to investigate the allegations. Caroline Blake and her young son Henry travelled to London to give evidence before it. The commissioners were anxious to hear from her whether or not there had been coercion of tenants who were otherwise able and willing to pay their rent:

> *Towards the end of 1879 was there any difficulty with some of the tenants as to the payment of rent?*—There was some difficulty when the agitation began; none before. I was on the very best of terms with the tenants. The family had lived some 200 years in that part of the county [i.e. Connemara. In fact the family had been there some fifty or sixty years] . . . Afterwards they refused to pay unless with a reduction, and they came round the house in a number and said they would be killed if they paid, and asked would I support their children if they were murdered; they had the rent, but dared not pay. I went out to them and said I would give no reduction demanded in that way, but I would consider every case on its merits, and give time or reduction according to what I thought right.
>
> *After that did they come to you?*—Some of them came secretly, and one old man came with a little boy, and the little boy had the money in his sleeve. It was taken out of the sleeve—£5 or £6 —and he paid his rent, and got a receipt pinned inside the jacket of the little boy, for fear he might be searched.

The question of cattle-driving and the killing of stock was also raised; Caroline deposed that in December 1879 over a hundred sheep belonging to tenants who paid rent were thrown into the sea, and a bullock was pushed in:

> About this time police protection was given me. The people used to drive their cattle onto my land to trespass in great numbers, and one could get no one to drive them off. Even the most friendly would not do so unless you were with them to give them the support of your presence, and I had myself to go and help to drive the cattle off. I have driven 50 sheep, 16 head of cattle, and nine horses off one grass farm where they were trespassing . . . When I had to go out sometimes at night at 11 o'clock to drive them off I thought I ought to have protection.

A few of Mrs. Blake's tenants appeared before the commissioners too, and provided some light relief:

> *Do you know what boycotting means?*—I do not, Sir.
> *Don't know what 'boycotten' means?*—Oh, 'bycotten,' I know him. (Laughter.) I have not much good English to speak.
> *You put the accent on the second syllable?*—Witness looked puzzled, and at last said, 'I go about my own business.' (Loud laughter.)

In the end the commission exonerated Parnell and the other leaders of the Land League of the particular charges against them, but found that they had incited their followers to intimidation, which had led to criminal outrages. The verbatim account of all this in *The Times* made Caroline Blake a national celebrity. Somerville and Ross, both of them of land-owning families and deeply sympathetic to her predicament, happened by in the course of their jaunt by governess cart through Connemara in 1893, and saw her plain:

> We looked as hard at Mrs. Blake as politeness would permit, while the broad columns of the *Times* seemed to rise

before our mind's eye, with the story sprinkled down it through examination and cross-examination of what she had gone through in the first years of the agitation. It required an effort to imagine her, with her refined, intellectual face and delicate physique, taking a stick in her hand and going out day after day to drive off her land the trespassing cattle, sheep, and horses that were as regularly driven onto it again as soon as her back was turned. We did not say these things to Mrs. Blake, but we thought about them a good deal while we sat and talked to her, and noted the worn look of her face and the anxious furrows above her benevolent brows.

By that time the Congested Districts Board, set up in response to the Land League agitation to undertake the decent burial of landlordism, was in negotiations with Caroline and her son Henry Edgar Valentine Blake (who was now a surgeon with a house in Howth, Dublin) that led eventually to the purchase of 522 acres of the estate for a sum of £3,750, and its division among the tenants. The reign of the Blakes was drawing to an end. Henry died in 1911, and Caroline soon afterwards. In the uncertain years of the Great War tourism fell away, and the family found themselves in growing financial difficulties. In 1917 the house itself and another 200 acres were put up for sale and were acquired—as if to mark the end of an era all the more pointedly—by a Dublin littérateur in search of peace rather than of profit.

My house . . . stands on a lake, but it stands also on the sea. Water-lilies meet the golden seaweed. It is as if, in the fairy land of Connemara at the extreme end of Europe, the incongruities flow together at last, and the sweet and the bitter blended . . . Behind me a wing of the long sea-grey house stretches for forty yards. In the evening the lake will send the westering sun dancing on the dining-room panels, the oak of which sun and age have reddened until it looks like the mahogany of a later day. The sun is shining up at me from the lake and down at me from the sky. We have not long to live in the sun; and here even the sunlight is not assured. Therefore let us enjoy it while we may.

Oliver St John Gogarty was the quintessential Dublin man-about-town. A surgeon by trade, at different stages of his life a champion cyclist, an aviator, a whisky salesman, a senator, a wit contaminated by the thoughtless anti-Semitism of his time, a versifier whose masterpieces of well-crafted if puerile innuendo flew from mouth to mouth, he was most celebrated as an unquench-able talker. As an undergraduate at Trinity College, Dublin, he shared quarters in a Martello tower with James Joyce, and figures in *Ulysses* as 'stately, plump Buck Mulligan'; Yeats selected what many thought to be an inordinate number of his poems for inclu-sion in *The Oxford Book of Modern Verse*; and the daring plunge into the Liffey by which he escaped assassination by anti-Treaty gunmen during the Civil War was celebrated in a ballad that ends with an accurate portrait in a phrase:

Cried Oliver St John Gogarty, 'A Senator am I!
The rebels I've tricked, the river I've swum, and sorra the
    word's a lie.'
As they clad and fed the hero bold, said the sergeant with
    a wink: 'Faith, thin, Oliver St John Gogarty, ye've too
    much bounce to sink.'

Gogarty first visited Connemara, and fell in love with its scenery, in 1906 on his honeymoon with his bride, Martha Duane of Garraunbawn House. In ancient times the O'Duanes were a subject clan of the O'Flahertys and had come with them into Connemara in the fourteenth century, settling mainly in Ballynakill; in the nineteenth century and more recently the Duanes of Garraunbawn were wealthy middlemen with tenants here and there in west Connemara. The O'Flaherty connection probably counted for something with Gogarty in his decision to buy the former O'Flaherty house at Renvyle. Since Gogarty knew everybody and was amply hospitable, many famous names found their way down to Renvyle, among them the film-director Robert

Flaherty, the painter Augustus John, the high-society Ladies Leslie and Lavery, Gogarty's old TCD master in the art of talk, John Mahaffy, Lord Beaverbrook and, as mentioned, W. B. Yeats and his wife George. Yeats's play *The Hawk's Well* was performed there by players of the Abbey Theatre in 1930, with masks and costumes by Edward Dulac. Dermot Freyer, the son of Sir Peter Freyer the surgeon, of Sellerna House near Cleggan, was a life-long friend; another local friend was the wealthy landowner and sportsman Talbot Clifton, squire of Lytham, whose holiday home was Kylemore House.

As Ireland sank into civil war, it was the misadventures of Talbot Clifton that warned Gogarty that even remote Renvyle would not be spared. Clifton's superb Lanchester car was 'commandeered' by the local lads of the IRA; Talbot, on realizing that his precious vehicle was running to and fro between Clifden and Leenaun, took his rifle and ambushed it as it passed his house at midnight. He wounded one of the passengers, and worse might have transpired had not Mrs. Clifton hurried out with the plea, 'You can get many Lanchesters; but you cannot bring back human life!'; she extracted a promise from the IRA men that if they were allowed to keep the car they would not molest her house or alarm her children. This was agreed, but Talbot was warned to leave the country that night, which he did. Mrs. Clifton soon followed him, after coming over by pony-car to leave her diamonds with Gogarty for safe keeping. Gogarty too decided to get out with his car before the blowing-up of bridges made it impossible to do so, and delivered the jewels to Dublin. But Gogarty, despite his well-known patriotism, was a target for the anti-Treaty Republicans once he accepted his appointment as a senator by the Free State government. There followed his abduction and celebrated escape, and then came yet another crisis in the history of Renvyle House: in January and February of 1923 the homes of thirty-seven senators, including Gogarty's, were burned down by the IRA. His grief over the destruction of his beloved Renvyle (which was no doubt the work of local men whom he would have known) was tinged by a patrician *ressentiment*:

Why should they burn my house? Because I am not an Irishman? Because I do not flatter fools? If the only Irishman who is to be allowed to live in Ireland must be a bog-trotter, then I am not an Irishman. But I object to the bog-trotter being the ideal exemplar of all Irishmen. I refuse to conform to that type.

So Renvyle House, with its irreplaceable oak panelling, is burned down. They say it took a week to burn. Blue china fused like solder . . . Memories, nothing left now but memories . . . Books, pictures, all consumed: for what? Nothing left but a charred oak beam quenched in the well beneath the house. And ten tall square towers, chimneys, stand bare on Europe's extreme verge.

A staunch Sinn Féiner and the close friend of Arthur Griffith and Michael Collins, Gogarty came to loathe Éamon de Valera—a 'half-breed' who looked like 'something uncoiled from the Book of Kells' and 'did more damage to our country than England did in seven hundred years.' But the fratricidal blood-letting for which Gogarty blamed de Valera wore itself out at last. By 1930 the house had been rebuilt, and Gogarty decided to open it as a hotel. And since the ground it stands on is of the essence of a house, the new Renvyle House was related closely enough to its predecessor to inherit its ghosts.

But if ghosts there were in the new hotel, they were mere courtiers and jesters at the court of the Gogartian life-force, which a bedazzled visitor, the Italian literary scholar Mario Rossi, describes for us:

This region is animated by the presence of a man who recalls the great Italians of the quattrocento. For me, at least, to know Gogarty was to realise the enthusiasm of the man who lives with full consciousness for that admirable phenomenon which is called life . . . Surgeon, conversationalist, politician, airman, poet, he has sufficient humanity for all that he does, and he is equally at ease whether he laughs at his neighbour or scans a poem, like a natural force which adapts itself at once to a thousand manifestations. He sums up Ireland. Renvyle House is the kingdom of Gogarty, the most westerly hotel in Europe, beaten by all the Atlantic winds, crowded with guests, a peculiar combination of the great Atlantic hotel and the hospitable home . . .

When the onset of the Second World War ended this Renaissance fantasy, and having failed, at the age of sixty, to get into the RAF as a doctor, Gogarty took himself off to America, leaving his wife to manage the hotel. He flourished there as a writer for magazines, a lecturer, a society lion, the exemplary Irishman, an untiring word-trotter; also he played the novel role of salesman, promoting Irish Mist, his son-in-law's brand of whiskey, with great enthusiasm. But he found the world becoming less attentive to him, and he aged and turned bitter; once when he was silenced in mid-anecdote by a jukebox he exploded, 'Oh dear God in heaven, that I should find myself thousands of miles from home, at the mercy of every retarded son-of-a-bitch who has a nickel to drop in that bloody illuminated coal-scuttle!'

The hotel ultimately failed to prosper and was sold off in 1953. In the following year Gogarty died, after a heart attack, in a New York hospital. His body was flown to Shannon, and he was buried in the old cemetery by the ruined chapel of Ballynakill. Most of his colleagues from the great days of the Irish literary revival had pre-deceased him, as had his comrades of the fight for independence, but the former President W. T. Cosgrave attended, as did the great scholar Monsignor Pádraig de Brún, President of the University in Galway and translator of Dante into Irish, who whispered one of Gogarty's ribald verses into the ear of Ulick O'Connor, Gogarty's future biographer, as the priest intoned his Latin and sprinkled holy water from a whiskey bottle.

Renvyle House, expanded and modernized, is still a hotel, in the hands of the Coyle family (D. D. Coyle was one of three Galway businessmen who bought it from the Gogarty family in 1953), and by all accounts it is a fine one, an unpretentious country house comfortable with its distinguished past. I had intended to finish this chapter with an account of a stay there, but it does not feel quite right to footnote or postscript myself into its history, and in any case luxurious hotels are not my favourite haunts; I feel my own presence becoming dim, querulous and ghostlike in such surroundings. So I shall drift away through its walls and briefly describe the reaches of the peninsula tapering off into the Atlantic beyond it. Like all the western promontories of Connemara it is a stark and sometimes forbidding terrain, a ragged, virtually treeless lowland of glacially moulded rock outcrops and boggy little fields, with a spattering of cottages and bungalows under an untidy scribble of electricity and telephone wires. Its beauties lie not in this middle scale of habitation but in the immensities of boisterous air and shifting tides into which it seems to push forward with hunched shoulders and upturned collar, and in its endlessly fascinating details of stone and plant and human individuality. Also, it turns out to be as ghost-ridden as Renvyle House itself.

Immediately outside the hotel is Loch Roisín Dubh, named from the townland we are in here, Roisín Dubh, meaning 'small black headland'; it is held apart from the ocean by a stout shingle bank, from which storms have been known to pick up stones to hurl through the hotel's windows. The wave-smoothed, bulbous and particoloured brown and grey pebbles of the shingle bank are composed of conglomerate, that is, of rock made up of a previous generation of assorted pebbles cemented together by mud hardened into stone; this shingle has been brought here by glaciers or stormy seas from the extensive exposures of such rock a few miles to the north-east. A nineteenth-century geologically minded visitor wrote eloquently about these conglomerates and the pebbles of which they are composed, revenants from a lost world of the Silurian period:

> Your correspondent asks were those rocks 'furnished from the detritus of land formerly covered by the waters of the Atlantic.' To this I may answer that they were formed in a sea that existed long before our present Atlantic, and concerning whose boundaries and extent it would now be in

vain to speculate. Many a time have the land and the water interchanged their positions—miles in thickness of strata have been deposited in successive seas; and whole organisms have died out, and others have appeared since the pebbles that form those conglomerates were rolled on a primaeval shore.

In the 'lake of the small black headland' a botanic rarity was discovered in 1932, an unobtrusive, straggly, aquatic weedy thing, *Hydrilla verticillata*, previously unknown in Ireland; indeed its discoverer, a W. H. Pearsall, was probably until then the only visitor to Renvyle who could have recognized it, for by an extraordinary coincidence his father had reported it twenty-one years previously from Esthwaite Water in the Lake District. The Esthwaite waterweed, as it is called, has never been observed to flower in Britain or Ireland, and although it still persists at Renvyle its hold on existence seems to be tenuous and its appearances and disappearances mysterious. It is long gone from Esthwaite Water (so that its name is orphaned), but has been found in a lake of the Scottish lowlands, while the Galway ecologist Cilian Roden recently discovered masses of it while snorkelling in Ballynakill Lake; to see it elsewhere in Europe one would have to travel as far as eastern Poland or Lithuania. Máire Scannell, then of the National Botanic Gardens in Dublin, took a specimen of it for propagation in an aquarium some years ago, and she told me of her enchantment in seeing it exude and clothe itself in tiny silvery bubbles, which kept it afloat and serenely vertical. Cilian Roden made his find while in search of another rarity, *Najas flexilis*, similarly obscure, but with small green flowers, and difficult to find as it keeps to deep water. It is, as one flora puts it, 'extremely local in quiet bays in lakes in the Lake District, Scotland and W. Ireland,' and among these quiet watery retreats is this lake by the hotel, which thus inherits a special responsibility for it. The slender naiad is its name, which brings a spectral glimmer of classical antiquity to the waters of Renvyle.

The ruins of the age of the O'Flahertys lie about a mile west of the hotel. The square, four-storey tower house, on a slight rise over the road, lacks its roof and parapets and the larger part of its northern and eastern walls, and exhibits hungry-looking vaults and the spinal cord of its spiral staircase to the passer-by. This dissection is said to have been the work of Grace O'Malley, who put a shot into the place from one of her ships during some cooling of her generally good relations with her O'Flaherty relatives. I remember that the first time I saw the castle there were stacks of lobster pots in it. That was in the wintry April of 1979 when I was still living in the Aran Islands and had come across the water to cycle around Connemara and reconnoitre the possibilities of making a map of it. I had a small traditional turf-basket of woven sally rods on the handlebars of my old bike, the work of Joeen na gCloch of Árainn, and as I coasted down the road to the castle a little man who was bundling up sea rods hailed this *cléibhín*, this signal from the old days before life had left him behind, with such joyful recognition that I was delighted to stop and chat with him. Sea rods are the long thick stems of deep-water seaweed, cast up by winter storms on the shore and gathered for sale to an alginates factory in Cill Chiaráin; the price he was getting for them was £40 a ton, which did not amount to a decent day's wages for the trouble of gathering and drying them. He remembered when there used to be a hundred tons of sea rods piled by the roadside here. He used to hate the tourists photographing him in his old clothes and with dirty hands doing this work. For some reason we had a lot of laughter together over this, his laughter a wintery wheeze caught on the seaweed banks. At the time I wondered why I had struggled against wind and rain to this last desolate desultory promontory to talk to this man about the most marginal of economic activities; a quarter of a century later I can only hope that the completion of this book will answer that question.

As with all the O'Flaherty castles of Connemara, legends of tyranny are associated with Renvyle. Two cliff-sided coves of the shoreline near it are named Fó Chaití and Fó Mhairéid from two of the castle's serving women who are said to have witnessed a man being murdered by hanging; one can imagine Caití and Mairéad timidly peeping out of the now vanished windows of the castle at the deed being enacted in the bawn below. They fled with their dreadful knowledge, and when pursued flung themselves into the sea rather than be captured. Another scrap of folklore reflects the local belief that the castle was built by the Joyces and then taken over by the O'Flahertys. The story is preserved in rather incoherent form by Caroline Blake, who wrote it up under the title 'The Interrupted Wedding' for a magazine, *Today's Woman*, in 1895. So far as I can follow her, one day when the castle was nearly finished the Joyces, to celebrate the marriage of the young heir to the chieftainship, held a feast in their old dwelling, a building on piles in a swamp near 'the white sands,' a beach about three miles away to the east. When the meat had been eaten someone took up the bare shoulder blade, held it to the light and prophesied, 'There is one of the company who has tasted of the meat but will never taste of the broth.' The young bridegroom tried to dispel the alarm this caused his timid bride by lifting a bowl of broth and saying jovially, 'It is not me!'—at which moment the O'Flahertys of Bunowen burst in to slaughter them, and in an instant his brains were dashed into the bowl. And 'even to this day they tell you that at the dead hour of the night when spirits walk along the sea-beaten coast an O'Flaherty does not like to tread lest the ghosts of the wedding feast, bearing grudge through the long lapse of years, should rise to revenge.'

A few hundred yards up a boreen inland of the castle in an ancient and overgrown graveyard is a small medieval parish church, roofless and missing its western wall. It is dedicated to the Seven Daughters, of whom Roderick O'Flaherty, writing in 1684, says, 'some call them by tradition the daughters of a British King, others of a King of Leinster. 'Their holy well is just over a hundred yards to the north of the church, and hard to find in the long tussocky grass. One comes across wells of the Seven Daughters at several places in Connemara—on Cleggan Head and by the hill of Bunowen in the west, in Leitir Deiscirt and Maínis in the south, and in Muintir Eoghain Thoir near Mám—and there are traces of another Cill na Seacht nIníon or Church of the Seven Daughters in Inis Oírr in the Aran Islands. O'Flaherty's nineteenth-century editor James Hardiman adds a footnote that there used to be a cursing stone by the Renvyle well, until the parish priest took it away and buried it, 'at which the people were much dissatisfied.'

Beyond this nucleus of medieval Renvyle lies the last cluster of houses before America. I mentioned above the details of human habitation; here is one. When, a few years after that first visit, I came to map this area in detail, I stayed with a friend in the most westerly of these houses. He was a tough-sounding young Dubliner who had been driven down here by his demons, had recovered himself, and was teaching in Letterfrack National School, of which he later became Principal. Before his recent retirement he always used to introduce himself modestly as 'a country schoolmaster'; in fact he is a widely esteemed educationalist. Decades before it was usual he brought a holistic vision of learning and an environmentalist agenda to his curriculum. In the vacations his school becomes the centre for two annual events he directs, 'Bog Week' and 'Sea Week,' during which a sort of composite pied piper of archaeologists, biologists, poets and musicians leads the participants out into the land-and seascapes of Connemara and Inishbofin in celebration of nature and tradition. Leo Hallissey—let such men be praised while they are still with us, rather than placated as revisiting ghosts by history, that age-old study in coming too late.

The tip of the peninsula is the townland of Curragh, from *corradh*, the Irish for a moor or marsh. The marsh itself was drained by the Blakes at some time after the Famine and is now a grassy sea-plain of glacial drift, in which the long slate-roofed buildings of their home farm lie derelict. There used to be a large lake in the southern portion of this townland, in which, Caroline Blake's story seems to imply, the O'Flahertys dwelled in a house on piles before they took over the castle; this suggests that it would be worth the archaeologists' while to search for traces of a crannog or lake dwelling here. The sea has bitten into the soft drumlins that form two extreme points of the land, carving out cliffs of clay in which variously coloured boulders stick out like fruit in a cake, and at the south-west point of the townland a curious knoll rears up steeply on the brink of a hundred-foot cliff: Cathair an Dúin, the fort of the promontory, also known as Cnoc na Síóg, the fairy hill. It is in fact a promontory fort, perhaps of the Iron Age or Bronze Age—certainly pre-dating the O'Flahertys' coming, though they might have occupied it before

Connemara's belated age of castle-building in the fifteenth century. An oval area about a hundred paces long is defended (if its function was indeed military rather than domestic and/or ritual) by the cliff on one side and on the other by a nine-yard-high earthen bank, a wide ditch and a lesser bank. In the enclosure are the remains of one of the Local Defence Force lookout posts that once ringed the coast, left over from the 'Emergency' of 1939–45. (The next such post to the south is also in a prehistoric fort, on Doon Hill at Bunowen.) The folklore of the fairy king of this fort will fit better into a later chapter of my story; here I'll merely note that the stony beach below it is a place of bad luck to the fishermen, where they say full-rigged sailing ships have been seen at all uncanny hours of day or night.

Finally, the last, north-western point, off which is a low-lying islet, Oileán na Maoile, the island of the *maol*, a word that covers bare or flat-topped things including rocks and hillocks. The name 'Renvyle' has been explained in several ways, but I think the most economical derivation is from this *maol*: Rinn na Mhaoile or Rinn Mhaoile, the point of the flat islet. And that brings to mind the haunting folk song 'Amhrán Rinn Mhaoile,' 'the Song of Renvyle,' concerning a matter that pre-dates and outdates Blakes, O'Flahertys and even the builders of the cliff-top fort. A girl longs to own a cow and sheep and be married to her village love, but another young woman is coming between them every second day. This verse from it lends a particular resonance to the placename:

'S tá mé 'mo shuí ó d'eirigh an ghealach aréir,
A' cur na tine seo síos dho mo mhian is dhá fadú liom fhéin;
Ó a Mhuire 's a Chríost, nach cloíte le n-aithris mo scéal:
Na coiligh a' glaoch 's Rinn Mhaoile 'na codladh ach mé
    fhéin.

(And I'm sitting up since the moon rose last night, setting this fire for my love and keeping it burning alone. O Mary and Christ, isn't my story sad to tell: the cocks crowing and all Renvyle asleep but myself.)

Placenames are pedlars' packs full of assorted items; only the placename itself holds them together. Time is the pedlar, but if I were he, in this instance I would have the name of Renvyle include this night-waking spirit in preference to the Yeatsian hocus-pocus of a boy dressed in brown velvet with ruffles at his wrists.

The Sublime and the Religious

Touristic pioneers of the mid nineteenth century, all following the same itinerary through Connemara—from Galway to Oughterard, Ballynahinch, Clifden, Leenaun, and so on to Westport—carried with them a set of concepts: the Picturesque, the Beautiful and the Sublime. Like a camera, or more accurately like a camera's viewfinder, this mental gadgetry enabled them to find the view: to identify what was worth looking at, to select and frame it, to record it as a verbal construction portable by memory with a view to publication. The Sublime came into play invariably as they passed through the Parish of Ballynakill, and more especially the pass of Kylemore, which cuts through the mountains eastwards from the village of Letterfrack, with the frowning gabbro of Dúchruach (the name means black stack) on the left, and the glinting quartzite of Diamond Hill on the right. Henry Inglis, travelling in 1835, was one of the earliest, and was much quoted by his successors:

> I do not hesitate for a moment to say, that the scenery in pas-
> sing from Clifden to the Killeries and Leenane is the finest
> in Ireland. In bold-ness of character, nothing at Killarney
> comes at all near to it . . . in the part of Ireland of which I am
> now speaking there are undoubted approaches to the sub-
> lime, with all of the picturesque besides that depends upon
> form.

A guidebook of 1854 expands on this, and introduces us to the Coill Mhór, big wood, from which Kylemore gets its name:

> The road, cut out of the base of the mountain, is carried along
> the margin of the lake for nearly three miles. Grey crags ris-
> ing to a stupendous height above the road, and seemingly
> about to topple over into the lake, impart a kind of wild

grandeur to this secluded spot . . . On our left, the old birch wood, interspersed with gnarled oak and green holly, takes root amid the interstices of the rocks, adorning the front of the broken ledges, and garlanding immense crags piled one above the other in rude and apparently detached masses . . . and waving as if in triumph its tiny branches from the bold projection of the impending cliffs. This natural wood, with the placid lake beneath, renders the scenery of Kylemore a combination of the sublime and the beautiful.

A dissenter was the spoilsport Thackeray, suffering the journey in 1842:

After leaving Clifden, the friendly look of the country seemed to vanish; and though picturesque enough, was a thought too wild and dismal for eyes accustomed to admire a hop-garden in Kent, or a view of rich meadows in Surrey, with a clump of trees and a comfortable village spire. 'Inglis,' the Guide-book says, 'compares the scenes to the Norwegian Fiords. 'Well, the Norwegian Fiords must, in this case, be very dismal sights! And I own that the wildness of Hampstead Heath (with the imposing walls of 'Jack Straw's Castle' rising stern in the midst of the green wilderness) is more to my taste than the general views of yesterday.

A long time later I came through the pass on my rusty black Raleigh bike; it was my first visit to north Connemara and I scarcely knew where I was, as my diary reminds me. I had set off up the Inagh Valley from Recess on a wet-looking April morning:

It got worse; the mountains & even the lakes invisible in driving mist and rain, and a gale hammering through the valley that brought me to a halt again and again. At the Kylemore Hotel I went in to have a drink & reconnoitre but it was so empty & dreary & it was still so early in the day, I felt I'd rather go on struggling. Then the scenery changed dramatically as I entered the valley of the Coill Mhór—the woods climb dizzy slopes & there's an opulent brown river & old stone bridges. When I saw a church tower off in the woods to the right I backtracked & took a private-looking but open way towards it, looking for Kylemore Abbey and not knowing what to expect. The neat plot of nuns' graves outside the shut church told me it was a convent. I pressed on, & passed a girl who looked to me as if she'd been sent there to have her baby in decent obscurity, gloomily stumping along. The castellated abbey appeared and disappeared almost unseen; a group of schoolgirls broke off from a religiose chant to whistle at me as I cycled deeper into the woods. Half a mile further on the path ran up to huge wooden gates, locked from without; I could glimpse freedom beyond them. I turned back with trepidation; another winding and dwindling forest track eventually delivered me onto the high road, where I ate my sandwich on the parapet of a bridge above the tumbling river.

This watery valley—a rain-trap for clouds fresh off the Atlantic—is occupied by two long lakes, which are really one lake, as they lie head to tail and are separated only by a neck of land fifty or so yards wide. The eastern one is Kylemore Lake, and the craggy hillside soaring up from its northern shore is Léim na hEilte, the doe's leap; Fionn Mac Cumhaill's dog Bran jumped from the heights into this lake in pursuit of the doe, says ancient tradition. The western lake is Loch Pholl an Chapaill, the lake of the pool or hole of the horse—but why so called, ancient tradition itself has forgotten. Kylemore Castle, which only became an abbey and a girls' school when the exiled Benedictine Dames of Ypres acquired it after the First World War, stands on a terrace close above the northern shore of this second lake, magnificently backgrounded by forested steeps. It was built as a Manchester capitalist's plaything in the late 1860s; before that time there was a fishing lodge on the site, built by a Revd Robert Wilberforce, son of the great parliamentarian and humanitarian William Wilberforce.

What crises of conscience were suffered here in this mountain-shadowed vale of tears we shall never know. Robert was a Catholic convertite, settled here with the express intention of combating the influence of the Evangelical Protestant missioners, but he had been an archdeacon and a leading theologian of the established Church, at a time when the Anglican clergy were being woken from their traditional concerns of lepidopterology and preferment by the Evangelicals on the one hand and the High-Church Oxford Movement on the other. In fact in 1842 when John Henry Newman, a leader of the Oxford Movement, was racked by a 'frightful suspicion' that the Roman Church was in fact the one true Church, Robert Wilberforce was the first friend he confided in. Robert's response was a cry of anguish:

> I don't think that I was ever so shocked by any communication, which was ever made to me, as by your letter of this morning. It has quite unnerved me . . . I am ready to grieve, that I ever directed my thoughts to theology, if it is indeed so uncertain, as your doubts seem to indicate.

His mental turmoil was intensified by family strife, as two of his brothers were also following the wake of Newman through the Oxford Movement into Roman Catholicism, thus losing the faith of their eminent father (we shall meet one of them, Henry, in Inishbofin, of all places), while another had risen in the Church of England hierarchy to become an intransigent and controversial Bishop of Oxford. Soon Robert too was being dragged along by the force of Newman's example, but kept his doubts a secret from his pious wife up to her death in 1853. Planning to renounce his living, retire as a layman and devote himself to his books, he bought the eastern two-thirds of the Blake estate, amounting to some 9,000 acres of valley-bottom meadows and upland blanket bog. Perhaps Kylemore seemed to offer him a decent obscurity, a pool of darkness in less painful contrast with his inner darkness than the glare of publicity he was fleeing. The British establishment was shaken by the prospect of losing him. 'He stands at the head of our living divines,' said Gladstone. 'His withdrawal from the Church of England could be compared to nothing but that of Newman and Manning, and I am not sure that the blow would not be as great as either.' The parting of the ways took place in 1854, when he was received into the Catholic Church in Paris. Withdrawing to his Kylemore estate, Robert set about improving the lot of his tenants, for instance by establishing thirty cottages, each on its stripe of land, in the townland of Mullaghglass, near Tully Cross. But only three years were allotted to him for these good works, and they were not happy ones. Although he found the Catholic liturgy attractive he confessed that 'one does not accustom oneself in a hurry to the worship of the saints.' And he evidently felt he was entering into the valley of the shadow of death: 'We shall soon be old men,' he wrote to his brother the Bishop. 'Then there awaits us the Churchyard and what lies beyond it.' However, Henry Manning, who had converted a few years before him and was like Newman to become a cardinal of the Catholic Church, was pressing him to accept ordination, and in 1856 on the Pope's nomination he entered the Accademia Ecclesiastica in Rome. But while still in minor orders he was stricken with gastric fever, and died in Albano in 1857.

Apart from Robert Wilberforce's retreat by the lake shore, the only buildings those early tourists found worthy of mention in the vicinity were a gentleman-farmer's residence and its large outhouses, set back from the road a little way west of Loch Pholl an Chapaill. Here a Mr. Thomas Eastwood had taken up a holding of valley bottom and mountainside from the landlord of Letterfrack, Francis Graham, in 1847, and with his brother had undertaken improvements that were commended by several passers-by:

Two gentlemen, brothers, of the name of Eastwood, have purchased a large tract of land, and are cultivating it in a most spirited manner; they are young, and evidently have no small share of youth's energy. The chief scene of their farming operations lies in a sort of 'flat,' surrounded by mountains; through the farm a salmon river passes; which they have bridged over, and the road across it led us up to a comfortable house of considerable size; this, with the adjoining large farm buildings, they have built, apparently with little regard to expense. He [Mr. A. Eastwood] says of the men as labourers, that under a good foreman they work well, and are honest, unskilled at first, but quick to learn. There were drills, and carts, and other farm upholstery of the orthodox red colour about the premises, and every thing looked very unlike Connemara. He spoke in no despondent terms of their prospects, and seemed to think the worst was passed.

This 'worst' was probably 'Black '47'—but it seems that its lengthy aftermath wore out the Eastwoods' youthful energy and their capital, for in 1862, having expended £2,500 in building and £4,000 in fencing, drainage, etc., they had to put their 914 acres and their mansion on sale through the Landed Estates Court, the successor to the Encumbered Estates Court, set up to facilitate the sale of estates bankrupted by the Famine. The Particulars of Sale claimed that Kylemore was 'the most beautiful and picturesque part of Connemara,' while the accompanying engraving showed their triple-gabled house nestling in trees below conical mountains that aim at the sublime; nevertheless the property did not sell until 1868, when it was picked up for £1,590 by the man who would become synonymous with Kylemore.

The new factor in Connemara's history was Mitchell Henry, who had recently bought the nearby lodge and its lands from the sons of Robert Wilberforce and was beginning its transformation into Kylemore Castle. Absorbing the Eastwood estate, the Kylemore estate was soon to amount to over 15,000 acres, most of it what its new proprietor would have seen as 'rough shooting,' stretching from the coast at Mullaghglass to Barnanang in the heart of the Twelve Pins, and including lake and river salmon fisheries. 'The primary reason for Henry's purchase was its fishing and shooting rights,' says Kathleen Villiers-Tuthill, Clifden's historian, whose detailed account of Henry's career I lean on here. 'The fact that much of the land was uneconomical and that it brought with it dependent tenants, thrusting upon him the unknown hazards of landlord responsibilities, was of secondary consideration. However, once in place Henry faced his responsibilities with a businesslike efficiency tempered by a humane hand.' In fact for a quarter of a century and through one of the worst of times, the Land War of the 1880s, Mitchell Henry was a towering presence in Connemara and a lucid speaker for it in Westminster.

A. & S. Henry, traders in cotton goods, with headquarters in Manchester, branches in Bradford, Belfast, Leeds, Huddersfield and Glasgow, and family connections to cotton merchants of Philadelphia, was the money generator that funded the transformation of the Kylemore Valley. Mitchell Henry, son of the firm's founder and chairman, had pursued a medical career and at the time of his father's death in 1862 was a Fellow of the Royal College of Surgeons, with a surgical practice in Harley Street and a fine residence, Stratheden House, overlooking Hyde Park. He and his wife Margaret (of the Vaughans of Dromore in the County Down) may have honey-mooned at the Kylemore House Hotel, two miles east of Kylemore Lodge; in any case they knew the area from fishing trips, and had recently leased the lodge when Henry came into his immense fortune, became chairman of the family company, abandoned surgery and turned his attention to landownership and political reform. By 1866 he had acquired all the Wilberforce estate and the Eastwood estate, plus further land and fishery rights from Andrew Armstrong, the proprietor of Kylemore House Hotel. The new Kylemore estate, which had cost him over £18,000, became his hobby, brought him the satisfactions of lofty social status, and caused him a deal of heartache.

By 1866 work on a colossal scale was beginning on Kylemore Castle, which soon engulfed the old lodge holus-bolus. The architect was Samuel Ussher Roberts; the style baronial. A hundred workers earning seven to ten shillings a week laboured at transforming the landscape. What a clattering echoed across the valley, exorcizing the religious melancholy of the Wilberforce era! Hammering of rafters and floorboards, rasp of stone-saw, clinking of masons' chisels, rumbling of carts. The castle's six square-topped, battlemented towers and slender flag-turret thrust upwards against the wooded crags, their reflections sank deeper and deeper into the lake. Connemara had never seen such a building, a palace with over seventy rooms; who could have imagined that life might consist of so many functions each demanding its own room? Not the peasant with a large family, for whom a cramped living and cooking space doubled up as bedroom and cow parlour. There were four spacious halls for receptions, balls and family games, a drawing room, a dining room, breakfast room, morning room, library, study, billiard room, thirty-three bedrooms with dressing rooms, a boudoir (think of that: a room for sulking in!), gunroom, smoking room, school room, linen room, fish larder, vegetable larder, a boiler house on the roof with a crane to bring the coal up, lots of little rooms in the servants' wing at the rear of the castle with a close-up view of the mountain steeps; nearby, a Turkish bath, an orchid house, stabling for twenty-nine horses, a coach house, a fire station with tender drawn by two horses and manned by a helmeted crew, even a new public post office, with a darkroom above it for Mitchell's son Lorenzo. In the eight-and-a-half-acre walled garden, with its geometrical flowerbeds set in smooth lawns, were twenty-one glasshouses including vinery, fernery, palm house, fig house, nectarine house and banana house, heated by a boiler set over a limekiln that produced seventy barrels of lime a week, plus workshops, mushroom house, pot store, a young men's bothy with three bedrooms for six lads, and an elegant little villa for the head gardener. The Eastwoods' old house now accommodated laundry maids and dairy maids, ironing room, mangling room and drying chamber, churning room, washing room and cooling room, while their outhouses and stables became the headquarters of a model farm, with two courtyards and an arched gateway surmounted by a bell, calf shed, cow house, fodder store, boiling house, harness room, piggery, carpenter's shop, plumber's shop, yardmen's bothy, smithy, wheelwright's shop, gamekeeper's house with pigeon loft, fowl runs, duck pond and plucking house, iron-roofed dog kennels, a mill dam with a turbine to power a circular saw, a thrasher and an unsuccessful experimental apparatus for compressing peat. There were boathouses on the lake, and a salmon hatchery—a pioneering venture—on the Dawros River that drains it. In short, a luxurious fantasy of romantic days of yore married to modern industry was, over the space of a few years, dropped into the valley. Everything had to make way for it. A tenant had to be removed from his little farm where the walled garden was to be sited, and rehoused else-where, with compensation—a business that caused trouble later on. The public road, which ran along the north shore of Loch Pholl an Chapaill and passed in front of the old lodge, became the main avenue of the domain, while a new public road was built along the south shore and carried across the east end of the lake by a bridge, which is now often occupied by a tourist bus enjoying the most perfect, picturesque, indeed Tennysonesque, view along the lake to the castle. The estate sucked up the vast superfluous manpower of the locality; by 1877 there were 240 labourers on the gold-medal-winning drainage schemes that scored the mountainsides with vast webs of channels; even girls were earning ninepence a day in the turnip fields. Can it be true, as records suggest, that 300,000 trees were planted every year for several years? Exotics were planted too: the rhododendron that has multiplied out of hand and threatens the life of the great wood itself, the New Zealand flax that is now a familiar scarecrow sight along Connemara's laneways. Winding walks by the lakeside came into existence, and a lordly carriage sweep before the arched main entrance with its carving of a winged figure bearing the family coat of arms. Not all were pleased by this enterprise: the Martins of Ross blamed Henry's imported masons, carpenters and plasterers for introducing communistic ideas into Connemara. On the other hand the Joyces of Recess founded their more moderate fortune by selling *poitín* to them. After the annual balls in the Castle, 200 tenants and workmen would disperse 'with three cheers for Mr. and Mrs. Henry.'

Politics was Henry's other passion. His family background was Liberal, Unitarian and reformist, and to this he added a degree of Irish nationalism. Ireland was never really conquered by Britain, he announced in Manchester during one of his early and unsuccessful election campaigns; it cries out for free exercise of her religion, the established Church being solely for the benefit of the small Protestant colony. He also called for reform of landlord–tenant relationships; perhaps the astronomical disparity of wealth between himself and other inhabitants of the valley made this easier for him—he hardly needed their paltry rents—but on this he was consistent and principled throughout his career. In 1871 he was elected at last, unopposed, for Galway, and represented it at Westminster for the next fourteen years. A friend and steadfast, if later disillusioned, supporter of Isaac Butt, with whom he founded the Irish Home Rule Party, he opposed Parnell's policy of obstructionism, the use of voice-power and procedural quibbles to prevent all other work being done in the House and concentrate English minds on Ireland's grievances. At the same time he campaigned for amnesties for the 'misguided' Irishmen condemned for 'Fenian outrages,' and for repeal of the repressive Coercion Acts.

In 1874 Henry and his wife and several of their nine children holidayed in Egypt, and there Margaret fell ill and died of dysentery. He brought her embalmed body back to Connemara and laid it in a mausoleum by the avenue to the east of the castle. A few years later, in her memory, he had a lovely neo-Gothic church built, which raises its tower in a romantic gesture half veiled by trees near the mausoleum, at a point where it perfects the elegiac lakeside vista. Henry, left with his grief and his nine children, took some time to return to politics, which was becoming increasingly embittered as the Land War crisis approached. Reality was threatening romance in his realm. When he appeared at a meeting in Clifden in 1878 the Ballyconneely curate Father Conway attacked him as a Protestant and an evicting landlord, referring particularly to the tenant relocated from the site of the walled garden, and successfully proposed a vote of no confidence in him. The *Freeman's Journal* defended Henry against the people's 'dire ingratitude' and published a letter from 'the entire tenantry of the Kylemore estate' praising their generous and charitable landlord. Archbishop McHale, who had stayed at Kylemore, censured Conway, and the Ballynakill parish priest refuted his allegations, stating that the removed tenant was now 'a prosperous and contented man' in a fine slated house much superior to his former thatched cabin. But Henry had to defend himself against other complaints, unjustified in particulars but not without a kernel of general truth relating to the total dependence of the tenant on the landlord's goodwill:

> It is an absolute falsehood to say that I deprived any tenants of seaweed and sand. On the contrary I made a new road, the

better to enable them to obtain it, and I charge nobody for seaweed or for turbary, as is the case elsewhere. Doubtless there is still much misery on parts of my estate, but I cannot make people provident all at once, nor can I control the seasons, or build and improve houses faster than I am doing . . . One phrase common among them [the tenants] when the great sorrow fell upon my house, will never fade from my memory, and has often brought tears from my eyes—for when she who was their benefactress and their friend, but not their landlord, was taken away, these 'ill-used' tenants said—'It is not our mistress we have lost, but our mother.'

Nevertheless Henry continued in Parliament to speak for Home Rule and land reform, while still steadfastly opposing Parnell's obstructionism and being attacked by Michael Davitt for it. In 1879, a dire year of distress brought on by endless rain, he remitted a half-year's rent and criticized the government for relying on charity rather than employment on public works to counter the looming famine. After being returned for Galway in the election of 1880 he sat with Gladstone's Liberals, while Parnell joined the Conservative opposition. The petty terrorism of the Land War—cattle-maiming, arson, threats against rent-paying tenants—spread through Connemara as elsewhere; Henry admitted that his 'mercantile position' made rent-refusal less important to him financially, but he felt it personally, believing as he did that landlordism was a sustaining pillar of society. All the same he supported the Land Bill under which a Land Commission to arbitrate on rents was set up, and persisted despite his weariness and disillusion with the Irish Party to speak in Parliament for 'Ireland . . . stained with blood and crime.' Abandoning his Galway seat he was elected as Member for Glasgow. He opposed Gladstone's first and unsuccessful Home Rule Bill in 1886, on the grounds that it would have excluded the Irish Members from discussion in Westminster of many matters relevant to Ireland. As a result he was not reselected for the following election. Thereafter he spent more time in Stratheden House, living in great splendour, attending to the good things of life—'Wine is in truth the milk of old age'—using the castle only for the shooting and fishing seasons, and resigning as chairman of the family cotton firm. His finances worsened, partly through his vast expenditure on the Kylemore estate. Kylemore went on sale in 1894, and was finally bought for £63,000 by the Duke of Manchester in 1903. Mitchell Henry died in Leamington in 1910 at the age of eighty-four. His magnificent legacy to Connemara is Kylemore Castle, a pale granite dream afloat on its own reflection, in all the troubling moral ambiguity of aesthetic splendour founded on gross inequality.

William Angus Drogo Montague, Ninth Duke of Manchester, may be skipped over; the man was unserious, by Villiers-Tuthill's account of him, and unworthy of the valley of Kylemore. Playboy and gambler, a pal of the Prince of Wales, and bankrupt, he had made the necessary marriage to money in the opulent form of Helena Zimmerman, daughter of an Ohio oil and rail tycoon, and it was old Zimmerman who picked up the burden of the mortgage repayments for Kylemore. The new Duchess immediately set about 'improving' the amenities in expectation of a stellar guest. King Edward VII had visited Kylemore during his Connemara tour in 1903 in the latter days of the Henry era, and had been received there by Mitchell Henry's agent Henry Robinson of Roundstone; now there was talk of a second visit in 1904. Helena threw some bedrooms together into a royal suite, turned the Gothic ballroom into a kitchen, ripped out the delicate marble-columned arches of the entrance hallway and redid it in singularly morose Jacobean panelling. And then, the King was too busy to come. Perhaps the hoped-for glory of this visit—and a possibility of selling the place to the King—had been the summit of what she expected from Kylemore, for when her father died in 1914 and left her over a million dollars she did not redeem the mortgage. And so the estate fell into the hands of a banker, who visited only occasionally and eventually sold it to the Irish Benedictine Dames of Ypres, thereby bringing a new depth of seriousness to the valley.

There had been an enclosed Benedictine community in Ypres, Flanders, since 1655, and it had soon become a predominantly Irish foundation, educating the daughters of Irish nobility and gentry and maintaining its constant output of prayer. Their abbey had survived poverty at times, had been ransacked by French revolutionary soldiers in 1793, and had more recently seen apparently unending year after year of calm pass within the twenty-five-foot walls of its enclosure, until in October 1914 the thunder of artillery set the nuns to reciting the rosary in their choir. Columns of German troops marched past their gates, and a week later, columns of British. The nuns sacrificed veils and sheets to make badges of the Sacred Heart, which a faithful servant girl of the convent took out to distribute to the soldiers, among whom were many Irish. Precious old medallions, a gold crozier, ancient vestments, a piece of lacework made by Mary Queen of Scots, the famous Flag of Ramillies said to have been captured from a British regiment by the Irish Brigade in 1706 and many other invaluable treasures were walled up into recesses of the cellars. From the garrets the nuns could see the horizon smoking with war, and they thought of 'the hundreds of souls appearing before the judgement-seat of God.' The school was taken over by the British ambulance service; sheets and veils now went into making rolls of bandage. The Lady Abbess, who had not left the enclosure for sixty years, had to be carried by four nuns out to a cab and packed off into 'a world she knew not and had never wished to know.' There were some days of confused comings and goings between Ypres and the village of Poperinge nine miles away before the Mother Prioress made the final decision for the little community—fourteen or so in number—to abandon the abbey, carrying what necessaries they could. As the key was turned in the last door separating them from the outside world an explosion shook the building, and on reaching the street they looked back to see smoke streaming from its windows. Expelled from their walled paradise they trudged to Poperinge through a hell of slimy mud, rain, blood and terrified crowds. After some days they were taken by ambulance to St-Omer and then to Boulogne, and shipped to England. Throughout this nightmare, I doubt if they failed to observe the canonical hours once.

Having settled at first at Oulton Abbey with the Benedictine nuns from Ghent, the mother house to Ypres, then at Highfield House in London, the Dames of Ypres moved to Macmine in

Wexford and eventually opened a school in the castle there. One of the nuns was a niece of John Redmond, the Irish MP, and it was through him that an appeal was launched for funds to rebuild the abbey, but when it became clear after the war that it was ruined beyond hope, they looked about for premises. Kylemore Castle, empty and neglected, was on the market. The valley seemed propitious to prayer; the mountains could be their enclosure wall. Redmond's fund went to purchase the castle and its estate, at a price of just over £45,000, in December of 1920. Today, after the decades of labour put into revivifying the farm, remodelling the interior of the castle to make it into an abbey and a highly regarded girl's school, and more recently the prize-winning restoration of the walled garden and the development of the building and grounds into Connemara's prime tourist attraction, the future of Kylemore seems to be in the balance again. The last intakes of pupils are working their way through the school, the nuns are getting old and retiring one by one, and none are coming forth to take their place. Into what hands might this paradigm of the marriage of architecture and landscape fall?

In 1932 the nuns installed a statue of the Sacred Heart halfway up the mountainside above the abbey, in fulfilment of a vow thus to give thanks for their finding sanctuary here. From the valley bottom the figure of Christ with arms outspread looks like a sign of the cross made on the brow of the mountain—tiny, but powerfully distinctive. One of our summer neighbours in Roundstone told me that her mother had spent a year at Kylemore as a rebellious schoolgirl and remembered being made to climb up to the statue as a punishment. Since bad weather had stopped me from following the path up to it when I was making my map of Connemara in the 1980s, I arranged with my neighbour and two friends of hers— energetic hill-walking ladies with spiked hiking poles—to revisit the area recently. As we drove into the valley from Letterfrack the mountain tops were invisible, but the cloud base was well above the statue. I was amazed by the changes that had taken place since my last visit some years ago. There are broad and well-signposted entrance and exit roads to a huge parking space for tour-buses and another for cars; a shuttle-bus plies between the ticket office and the Victorian walled gardens; large placards instruct one on the history of the place, the prayerful calm of the Benedictine lifestyle, and the choice array of goods available in the craft shop. The nuns have obviously made an extremely efficient business out of Kylemore, but as everyone in Connemara agrees, 'Tourism is down again this year,' and the weather was against them too; here we were in mid June, and the coach park was empty.

A sharp shower persuaded us to tour the interior of the abbey first. A few German tourists were slumped on benches in the entrance hall, apparently overcome by the Duchess of Manchester's gloomy grandeur of oak panelling. In a display case on the wall we saw the faded flag of Ramillies (for it and other items of the community's precious heritage had been salvaged from the bombed-out Abbey of Ypres after the war). In the drawing room, with its elegant wallpapering of blue garlands on white, hangs a portrait of Margaret Henry: dark ringlets, snowy shoulders, voluminous silk. The room has been furnished as it might have been in her time; there is sheet music awaiting a player on the piano, a silver tea service ready to replenish delicate china teacups, books languishing unread in glass-fronted cabinets. One sidles past, not transgressing the stretched cords that protect this crystallized moment. Up a few stairs is the dining room, with a table elaborately laid for a dozen or so and separated from us again by cords that confine us to a narrow way along one wall. On a side table the worn and dully gleaming carving knife lies in an open case with its fork and sharpening iron; one can almost smell shoulder of lamb. We note the impressive array of glasses of various sizes and shapes at each place setting. But unfortunately their social superiority has rendered the diners quite invisible to us, the sideways-shuffling, ticketed creatures of twenty-first-century tourism. Corridors and stairs and galleries with portraits of timelessly similar mother abbesses, and big, black, locked doors marked 'Enclosure' through which plainchant softly seeps, lead us back to where we came in.

The sun was cautiously shining. We picnicked by the water's edge under splendid specimen pines and beeches, and then followed the lakeside avenue as far as the church, pensively solitary among trees as in some romantic tale of medieval England; the fact that it is cathedral-like in plan and proportions, but reduced in scale, adds to its air of unreality. Not far beyond that is the mausoleum, like a little one-roomed cottage, tucked away among damp shrubs, windowless except for three narrow slits on either side, its arched doorway bricked up in a way that induces morbid fantasies out of Edgar Allan Poe of imprisonment, death and decay. Imagine: a room for rotting in!

Then we returned to the abbey and took the path that plunges into the wood immediately behind it and zigzags up the hillside. In places one has to crouch and almost to crawl under tangles of rhododendron branches, or to climb through the forks of a fallen tree. The ground is muddy, one or two little stream-beds cut down across the way, there are occasional sagging concrete steps and where the slope is very steep the path has been reinforced with small stone revetments. The tangled rhododendron bushes cast such a dense shade that little grows on the forest floor except moss and fern; the tall trees, the ash, pine, beech and birch, are not giving rise to saplings, and I fear the ancient Coill Mhór is doomed unless a sustained programme of rooting out the lovely invader is undertaken—something beyond the resources of the abbey community, or of the National Park, which has charge of the hillsides south of the valley. As one climbs and the canopy thins out some flowers appear: wild strawberry, and a curious little creeping thing with leaflets like tiny coins, the New Zealand willow-herb, a rock plant turned weed, which has spread through north Connemara apparently since the 1950s. Then one steps out of the last of the woodland shade onto slopes of heather and bracken, dotted with yellow tormentil, and the statue of the Sacred Heart is seen some 200 yards ahead. At this stage of our climb the clouds had just cleared the nearest and steepest of the mountains opposite, Diamond Hill, so named from the quartz crystals that weather out of its rocks and that used to be sold by local children to tourists as 'Irish diamonds.' Behind it the heads of the further peaks were still lost as if in slowly shifting misty ruminations. In the valley the long lake lay as smooth as steel, gleaming dully, like that carving knife in its case. Steeply below us was the abbey, seen in plan, a toy castle. The weather-beaten statue, more than life-size and on a tall pedestal, spreads its arms to enfold all this immensity. Beyond it the path scrambles onwards and upwards, gradually fading out and losing itself among the streaming gullies and tussocky slopes of the mountains to the north. Looking at the hillside falling away below us and thrusting out bare stony shoulders through its ragged cloak of forest, I remembered with amazement coming over the hills from the north some years ago, missing the path here, and patiently unknotting my way down through endless complications of rhododendron thicket and tumbled rocks to the valley bottom.

There is a bench in front of the statue's pedestal, for the out-of-breath pilgrim to rest on while enjoying a view that had evidently been selected with artistry. Edmund Burke, in *A Philosophical Enquiry into the Origin of our Ideas of the Sublime and the Beautiful*, which would have been the source of those nineteenth-century travellers' ideas on the subject, associates the Sublime in nature with the terrible, with vastness, especially of precipices seen from above, with rugged and broken surfaces, obscurity and gloom, with 'Vacuity, Darkness, Solitude and Silence.' Here were all the components; this must be the Sublime, no doubt about it, I felt. The Sublime was invented to fill the glorious but terrible spaces left us by the evaporation—no, the exact term I'm looking for is the sublimation—of God. And then as we stood there and marvelled, a great bell rang out from below, and again, and again: the Angelus, reminding us that the toy castle is still a ceaseless machine of prayer. Burke deals with such repeated sounds too, under the heading of 'The artificial INFINITE,' which consists in 'an uniform succession of great parts'; the tension produced by the expectation and the shock of successive strokes, he says, 'is worked up into such a pitch as to be capable of the sublime; it is brought just to the verge of pain.' In foreign cities I tend to linger in those alleys around cathedrals where one is liable suddenly to be overwhelmed by a peal of bells as by a collapsing steeple of sound. It is from its bells rather than its sermons that I understand a little of Christianity. Now on the heights above Kylemore I lend myself to those few minutes in which the abbey turns the whole valley into a vast upturned bell, tolling to the tongueless bell of the sky.

Unfinished History

The inconstant sunshine of a Connemara spring fills Letterfrack as I call it to mind; it is a crossroads village, and one angle of the cross—between the main road to Clifden dipping southwards through little patches of woodland to the head of Ballynakill Bay, and the side road winding inland and upwards to the foothills of the Twelve Pins—holds a large open space with trees about it that filter the moody Connemara skies through their leafage. Leitir Fraic, two old and almost defunct words the crisp and fragile consonants of which have surely entered into my memory of this expanse of fluttering, palpitant sunlight: *leitir*, a hillside, and *fraic*, perhaps from *frag*, woman; hence, 'the hillside of the women,' a name that suggests the booley, the summer milking pastures. If that is the origin of the placename it carries a hint of the fun, the dance, the songs associated with the old times when the womenfolk would tend the cattle on grassy patches of the bog or mountainside while the men laboured in the potato plots by the shore or hauled nets out in the bays.

The façade of a two-storeyed building with a remorseless regularity of tall windows forms the far side of this open place; behind the long horizontal of its roofline rises the glistering cone of Diamond Hill, an outlier of the Twelve Pins and the heart of the Connemara National Park. Letterfrack is envied by other Connemara communities, for in addition to the normal complement of facilities—bars, a general shop, a Catholic chapel, a national school, several B&Bs, a hostel—it has the visitors' centre of the Park, five minutes' walk up the side road mentioned above, and the offices of an active cooperative development organization, Connemara West, and the highly regarded Letterfrack Furniture College, recently equipped with adventurous-looking new workshops on the south side of the open space; also, the headquarters of the local radio Connemara FM, an art gallery in building, and a film club, and a crèche . . . in short, Letterfrack seems able to create and recreate itself as no other Connemara village can do. Why? It is fortunate in having a few individuals of rare abilities and initiative among its residents, such as Michael O'Neill and Joe O'Toole, founder members and long-term energizers of Connemara West, but perhaps the roots of its positivity lie further back, in its early landlords and especially in the presence of the Quakers during crucial years of the Famine; in fact I believe that a Quaker air of civic responsibility and effectiveness stirs about the place still. Also, and paradoxically the most difficult part of its history, overshadowed by the Christian Brothers' Industrial School out of which so many terrible secrets have come to light in the last two decades, has left it an unrivalled legacy: the formidable institutional building beyond the open space, with its stables and outhouses and the associated farm up the hill behind it, which now accommodate nearly all the enterprises I have named. The brave new furniture college is part of an unfinished architectural project for the recuperation of Letterfrack's troubled past through the reshaping of these buildings and their purlieus; the confrontation of that past, through law cases, official enquiry and artistic mediation of memory, is ongoing. Meanwhile life in its glorious heedlessness and awful forgetfulness leaves no stone unturned to new use.

I will sketch the history of Letterfrack, starting from a change in its fortunes shortly before the Great Famine, prior to which time it was part of an impoverished and neglected estate belonging to absentee landlords, the Lynches, whose base was in Barna near the town of Galway. In 1841 the estate—6,000 acres in the south-western corner of Ballynakill Parish—was sold to a Francis Graham of Drumgoon in Fermanagh, and it was his son Robert Graham who became the first resident landlord of the villages of Letterfrack and Moyard, nearby to the south, along with another seventeen townlands and two islands. The Grahams, like the Armstrongs with whom they intermarried and who also figure in the microhistory of Ballynakill, were among the English Border clans settled in Ulster under Elizabeth I. By 1848 or earlier Robert Graham had built the family home, Ballynakill Lodge, by the head of the bay just south-west of Letterfrack. Soon the management of his estate was winning good opinions. John Bright, the parliamentary reformer, who visited the West of Ireland in 1849, commended him for giving permanent leases to his tenants, which secured him a return of 8 to 10 per cent per annum on his outlay of £15,000. This was in stark contrast to the surrounding dereliction, according to Bright:

> The proprietors are nearly all bankrupt, great numbers of farmers are gone away—thousands of peasants are in the workhouse or in their graves. I believe we can form no fair idea of what has happened in the last four years and I see no great prospect of solid improvement. Here we have to perfection the fruits of aristocratic and territorial usurpation and privilege, and unless these restrictions are removed, industry will be, as hitherto, impossible.

A few years later Sir William Wilde also noted the contrast between the poor condition of the Renvyle and Ballynahinch estates neighbouring it to north and south respectively, and the reclaimed bogland bringing forth corn and green crops on the Graham estate, with its several 'snug homesteads.' Although the Famine had hit the area hard and its population fell drastically, the village of Letterfrack was an amazing exception to this trend; its population remained steady, and went on to increase, the reason being a second and more remarkable stroke of fortune, the advent of a couple who, as another visitor, William Wakeman, put it, 'settled here with the sole object (we were told) of benefiting the people.'

The Ellis family had been members of the Religious Society of Friends of the Truth, or Quakers as they are commonly known, ever since the mid seventeenth century, when their founder George Fox was braving church and state to preach a drastic degree of honesty in matters spiritual and secular. The Quakers' solidarity in the face of persecution, their exclusion from public office and their bankable integrity in money matters had led to the development of a network of intermarrying families and mutually supportive businesses. James Ellis, born into a prosperous farming family in Leicestershire in 1793, served his apprenticeship in a north-Yorkshire corn mill owned by a member of another of the great Quaker stocks, the Priestmans, and was the last Quaker to be imprisoned for refusing to bear arms. At the age of twenty-one he became a corn miller on his own account in Hull, and married his former employer's daughter. A few years later he and his brother-in-law founded a malting and milling enterprise in Bradford, where they enjoyed a monopoly of the trade. When James became an apostle of the temperance cause the firm relinquished the lucrative malting business and took up that of worsted spinning. This proved even more profitable; as James himself put it, 'an outward blessing had followed the acting out of a conscientious duty.' When the life assurance company Friends Provident Institution (still with us, as Friends First) was formed by a number of Yorkshire Quakers, James became a director, and later served as chairman. His wife Mary died in 1832 leaving five young children, and in 1837 James married a Mary Wheeler, whose mother was of the Tuke family—and this is the clue to their later commitment to Ireland. Mary's relative James Hack Tuke had visited the most lamentable parts of the famine-stricken island in 1847 and published a moving account of its ills, which included extortionate landlordism, as witnessed by the observation of a government inspecting officer that 'all his efforts to keep the population from starvation and death had been baffled by the system of eviction which has been and is pursuing, as there is no shelter for them anywhere.' It was perhaps the Quaker-born William Edward Forster's observations on the Ballynakill area, which he visited to distribute aid and establish soup kitchens on behalf of the Quaker Relief Committees, and where he had been 'quickly surrounded by a mob of men and women, more like famished dogs than fellow creatures, whose figures, looks and cries all showed they were suffering the ravaging agony of hunger,' that directed James Ellis's thoughts to this particular pool of darkness. He was aged fifty-six when, in the words of a family history written by his niece:

> . . . believing that the accumulation of riches was a snare to
> parents and a source of great injury to children, in the year

1848 James Ellis retired from business, setting by this step, as well as throughout life by the simplicity of his establishments, a bright example of Christian moderation . . .

In the following year Ellis leased a thousand acres from Robert Graham and moved to Letterfrack with his 48-year-old wife and a son and a daughter, both of them in their twenties. Soon he was employing eighty men, draining bog, planting thousands of trees, building his family home, and establishing a renewed village of slate-roofed cottages focused on a school-cum-meeting house, a dispensary, a shop and a temperance hotel. In a letter to his brother he expressed a fear that he and his family had been 'but very unprofitable servants, and . . . have very imperfectly performed the most important objects of our mission.' Nevertheless he had seen 'delightful evidence that these children of our common parents are made of materials quite as plastic as any other family of our species with which we are acquainted, and I think naturally far more amicable and virtuous than those of the same class in any part of England where we are familiar . . .' Given their crowded living conditions, their chastity in particular impressed him, but he was sorry to say they were entirely ignorant of 'the one thing needful, a saving knowledge of our Redeemer . . .'

As to practical matters, he was delighted with the fertility of the soil, but saw that there was no easy livelihood to be made by its cultivation, given the expense of transporting the produce to England. And for their personal circumstances:

> Our house looks rather more imposing than I expected and will, when completed, be the best building in Connemara, our pleasure grounds (for James Ellis must needs have such strange things in the midst of the bog) are beginning to look very unlike Connemara—containing already about 300 yards of well laid down gravel walks.

As these quotations remind one, the Quaker way is not the Gospel council of perfection, 'Go and sell that thou hast, and give to the poor.' Such moral shock-tactics are out of date; capital is God's gift, to be invested in the social good, with due responsibility and care for its increase, rather than to be squandered in an unrepeatable fit of charity. James Ellis's wages were above the local norm of sixpence a day, but not sacrificially redistributive:

> These men work cheerfully from 6 in the morning to 6 in the evening, with proper intervals for breakfast and dinner, for wages varying according to their several capacities from 7d. to 9d. a day. They are paid regularly in money wages and they show themselves not only contented, but grateful.

One or two of the neighbouring gentry grumbled about these wage rates, but Letterfrack survived while other townlands faded. Census figures from 1841 and 1851 show the population of the Graham estate as a whole falling from 1,806 to 1,107, while that of Letterfrack changes only from 189 to 188. Since the Ellises only began their work after the worst year of the Famine, and the employment they offered must have drawn people into the village from the surrounding townlands, these figures are no more than a general vindication of their faith in capital and hard work.

Perhaps it was because these wages allowed their employees to pay their church dues that the Ellises encountered less opposition than they had expected from the Roman Catholic hierarchy. In a letter of 1850 Mary Ellis writes:

> It is in no way flattering nor of a good savour, but we seem to be getting into favour with the Roman Catholic priests. James got *highly* extolled from the pulpit about a fortnight since;—set, I believe, in contrast with the rest of the masters here, who 'keep back the hire of the labourer.' But one may see that we, in this, make them better 'sons of the church' by enabling them to pay their dues, which have dropped in very scantily of late. Yesterday, John of Tuam stopped his carriage to pay a visit to the school with two other priests, expressed his satisfaction in it; thought it was much better to be learning arithmetic, &ct., than spending the time over the catechism . . .

'John of Tuam' is her way of referring to Archbishop John MacHale, titles being taboo in Quaker parlance (elsewhere she jokingly pretends to find a difficulty in the placename of Mám, meaning a pass, which she misunderstood to be the English form of address, 'Ma'am'), and her letter sheds a truly astonishing light upon the dreaded 'Lion of the West,' a fierce nationalist and inveterate opponent of the national school system in which Catholic children might have found themselves sharing a bench with Protestant children. Dues may have had something to do with it, but the Archbishop's main fear was of the growing influence of the Episcopalian evangelists with their obsessive raging against the Catholic creed. Indeed it was with one of that sect that the Ellises had some trouble:

> Far more, we think, than Popery, Episcopalianism wants to lord it over all, and over us too; and we have had to wage a stiff battle just now against our clergyman taking possession of our schoolroom to deliver in it his controversial lectures, which we think have little tendency to promote real Christianity . . .

This makes it puzzling that when James Ellis's health began to fail and the family moved back to Yorkshire in 1857, the estate was sold to a John Hall of the Irish Church Mission Society. A bigoted anti-Catholic, Hall, when he let one of his buildings, stipulated that if any part of it were to be sublet to a Catholic the lease would become void. Hall was an absentee landlord; the Ellis house itself he rented to William Noon, the Ellises' schoolteacher. Five years later the Rector of Ballynakill, a Mr. Mollan, built a church and established a congregation at Letterfrack with the support of the ICMS; otherwise, the society does not seem to have been very active here, and good memories of James Ellis long outlasted its presence. James Hack Tuke revisited the area in 1883, and was moved to write of him:

> He combined in his character the qualities which always seem to me needed to govern Ireland and cure its maladies—justice,

kindliness, firmness, industry . . . I had not been long in the village before I heard this: 'The people still pray for good Mr. Ellis. He is always called "good Mr. Ellis".' Yes, he was a true friend to the poor; but he never gave anything to the men who could work, unless they did something for it. He employed the people in reclaiming the land, or he would set them to pick up the stones to build walls, or the children to gather flowers or roots for his friends. He was always teaching them the great lesson of work.

While the 'maladies' of Ireland were partly due to bad governance, Tuke, like Ellis, Bright and indeed most Quakers, would have had no doubts that Ireland needed to be governed; they did not consider that the problem of Ireland was in fact Britain, and they did not support Gladstone's Home Rule campaign. But Tuke's mission in Letterfrack was an indication that here, as elsewhere in much of the West, the ruling classes had utterly failed the poor, and now instead of offering them work was funding their passages to the New World—simply paying them to go away, as many landlords would have seen it, or financing a new start in life for them in more hopeful circumstances, in Tuke's view of it. As he had written, 'It matters not whether a tenant has fixity of tenure or being a peasant proprietor has no rent to pay; he cannot, unless he has some other source of income, live and bring up a family on a small farm of ten or fifteen acres.' Recent land legislation had not helped the small tenant, who could not afford to purchase his holding; land reclamation was too costly and the land too poor; and in Tuke's opinion the only remedy was 'emigration to a more favoured land.'

Unpatriotic, do you call it? It is the law written on the human race; the law which drew Abraham from his native land . . . the law which has impelled and is now impelling tens of thousands of people of all nationalities in Europe to surge forth with increased volume, in that great wave of humanity which breaks upon the shores of the western world, not to devastate, but to fertilise and bless.

As a result of Tuke's efforts a committee was formed and a large sum privately subscribed (the government approving but not at that stage contributing, as it did later on), and he was sent forth to enquire for ships in Liverpool, and then to proceed to the Unions of Clifden, Newport and Bellmullet, to select emigrants according to their fitness and circumstances, to supply them with clothes as necessary, to arrange for their transport—in their hundreds—by cart to Galway and for their reception by agents in Boston, New York and Philadelphia, and finally to see them safely on board. Over a period of some years the Tuke Committee, as it was called, expended £70,000 and oversaw the emigration of some 9,500 persons. 'The amount of detail in connection with the emigration work can hardly be estimated,' he wrote, 'and caused a strain and perpetual tension of mind and body, only made possible by the sense of the benefit which was conferred on these poor people, and which they so evidently felt and constantly acknowledged.'

In the second year of this task Tuke and his newly married wife Georgina were in Letterfrack, compiling lists of names, when the police sergeant and a constable called on them, and, as Georgina tells it, 'We had a curious interview!':

> The sergeant, very tall and thin, with a striking face and quiet manner, walked to the door, ran his thumb along to see that it was close shut, then the conversation began, carried on in whispers. The sergeant took from his breast pocket a list of persons who were suspected of complicity in some recent murders committed in this district. This list he handed to Mr. Tuke, who immediately compared it with his list, and noted any names that were on both. None of the names on the police list were to be sent abroad. No name was spoken, as few words as possible were uttered, and with the same silence and mystery the sergeant and his constable left.

These murders were part of a mysterious sequence of events on the Graham estate during the period of the Land War, and were perhaps connected with the assassination of the chief secretary Lord Cavendish and his under-secretary in Dublin by extremists of Fenian background. The local root of the trouble went back to 1877, when a small tenant, Stephen Walshe, having fallen behind with his rent, came to an arrangement with the Grahams' agent by which he gave up his land and moved into the village with his family, his arrears being written off. The land was then let out to John Lydon, a herd of the Grahams. One night in 1881, at about ten, when their daughter Margaret was out at a wake, six or seven men broke into the house and pulled John Lydon and his son Martin out of bed, dragged them outside and shot them; before they marched away one of them was heard to say, 'That will do—he will herd no more.' John Lydon died on the spot; Martin was badly injured, but was able to tell the police that Stephen Walshe's son Patrick had been among the gang. Martin died after a month or so, and during the night after the inquest on him, the house of another member of the Lydon family was burned down.

When Patrick Walshe was eventually put on trial in Dublin he swore that he had been at the wake all that night, and other witnesses said he could not have gone to the Lydons' house at the time of the murder, while Margaret stated that she did not see him at the wake till after midnight. An unusual 'Russian' gun had been found in the thatch of his house, the bore of which matched that of a bullet extracted from John Lydon's body. The jury failed to agree, and there followed a retrial, at which Walshe was condemned; he went to the scaffold protesting his innocence. His guilt was not accepted locally, and the newspapers regarded him as 'a victim of the crime of history.'

In the period between the two trials a Constable Kavanagh, who had been sent from Spiddal to investigate the crime and had arrested Patrick Walshe, was also murdered. Previously his house had been attacked by Patrick's mother, and he had prosecuted another Walshe for loitering with intent. Kavanagh had been drinking after hours in a pub near the barracks, and was shot as he left. Footprints found at the scene next day seemed to lead to the Walshe house, and matched a boot belonging to Patrick's brother Michael, who was arrested, and went on trial just after his brother had been hanged. He was found guilty but as he was only eighteen years old there was a recommendation to mercy, and at the last moment his sentence was commuted to penal servitude for life. He was transported, was later released in poor health, and died at home in Letterfrack.

These happenings further darkened the life of the little community. As Mrs. Tuke recounts:

> Mystery and anxiety were on every face, and men looked over their shoulder to see who was in earshot before they would answer a question! The bright-eyed, ragged little girl who was employed by the Post Office as telegraph messenger, was sister of the two young Walshes . . . The nice, gentle-looking maid who waited on us at our inn, and the man who drove the hotel car, were brother and sister of a very pleasant-spoken lad, who, now under suspicion of the murder of Kavanagh, was subsequently arrested and imprisoned, but full proof was wanting. This lad applied to Mr. Tuke for help to emigrate, but of course it could not be given at present, though he was sent out later on. A number of young men who had asked most urgently for emigration help were not forthcoming this time, and it transpired that on its becoming known, in the meantime, that James Carey had turned informer about the Phoenix Park murders, many of them who had belonged to the Patriotic Brotherhood, of which there had been a strong branch here, had scraped together some money and fled to America for fear of unpleasant revelations.

By this period another change in Letterfrack's fortunes was impending, though few knew of it then. In 1882 the estate of Mr. Hall, the virulent anti-Catholic, went on sale and was acquired for £3,000 by a buyer acting under a fictitious name, who, to the disgust of the Protestant faction, turned out to be Archbishop MacEvilly, MacHale's successor at Tuam. His intention no doubt was to counter the proselytizers' influence in the area by establishing a bastion of Catholicism, and in 1888 he signed an agreement with the Christian Brothers who ran the industrial school at Artane near Dublin, under which they were to set up and manage a similar institution in Letterfrack, in return for the rents and rights of the estate, funding towards new buildings and furnishings, and a grant of two shillings a week per boy. St Joseph's School for Roman Catholic Boys was certificated in 1886 'for the reception of male children, to be sent there under the Act of Parliament of the Thirty-first year of the Reign of H.M. Queen Victoria, Chap. 25,' and a big building comprising schoolrooms, refectory and dormitories, as unwelcoming in appearance as this mission statement sounds, soon arose in front of the former Ellis house, which was now the Brothers' monastery. The façade of the new building, an overpowering presence in the little village, was and still is of awful symmetry: on either side of a small central porch extends a row of five tall windows, their sills so high that no one can see out of them, or in; above them are the lesser windows of the dormitories; the gables of the two return wings, at either end of the central portion, seem to brandish their carved stone crosses aloft in a minatory gesture; behind, the central part of the building and the two wings form three sides of a rear quadrangle or marching yard, almost closed off by the Ellises' former stable block.

The institution housed not only boys judged to be delinquents, but orphans, beggars and strays, and aimed to equip them with a practical skill; it was also a profit-making enterprise. An advertisement terming the place 'a centre of industry' solicits orders for tailoring, bootmaking, carpentry, cartmaking, bakery, smithwork, wire and box mattresses, hosiery, hearth rugs, and 'boys placed out to the above trades. Also instructed in housework and farming.' In 1895 a recreation hall was built, for concerts and amateur theatricals; the school's band was also 'open to engagements during the summer months.' During the Great War the school farm was producing enough milk, butter and vegetables to avert destitution in the neighbourhood. A small hydroelectric installation on a stream flowing off Diamond Hill was inaugurated in 1925, serving both school and village. By the time the school closed, in 1974, 1,356 boys had passed through its doors. The main buildings were acquired by Connemara West, while most of the land and the farm buildings on the hillside above were bought by the Office of Public Works for the creation of the Connemara National Park.

At first it might have seemed that the memory of the Letterfrack Industrial School would moulder away in peace. Everyone knew that physical chastisement took place in it, but that was endemic in the educational system of the old days. The writer and playwright Mannix Flynn faced down his anguished past, as knee-high street bandit, juvenile tearaway and recidivist prisoner in various institutions including Mountjoy, through writing a semi-fictional account of his incarceration in St Joseph's, entitled *Nothing to Say*, and published in 1983; but even this ground-breaking and heart-breaking work describes just one case of persistent sexual interference with a boy, perpetrated by a lay member of the staff. A competent local history of Ballynakill Parish produced in 1985 by the Tully Cross Guild of the Irish Countrywomen's Association (which I have found very useful in compiling this history of the area) remarks that 'the discipline of the school was strict in the extreme,' and leaves the matter at that, while my own *Connemara Gazetteer* of 1990 merely notes that it had 'acquired a sad reputation for severity.' Since then we have had the testimony of many victims of the Letterfrack Christian Brothers. One was Peter Tyrrell, who did not live to see his tale made public and apparently burned himself to death on Hampstead Heath; his body was identified only through a bit of a postcard addressed to Senator Owen Sheehy Skeffington, with whom he had been in correspondence and who had encouraged him to write down his memories of St Joseph's. In a rare gesture of reconciliation, Mannix Flynn came back to Letterfrack in 2001 and stayed in the then deserted monastery while writing his play *James X.*, based on the cruelly indifferent documentation of his own case by the various authorities that blighted his childhood.

I once spoke to Mannix, a forthright man built like a clenched fist, at a meeting of Aosdána, the affiliation of Irish artists, to whose debates he brings a raw energy; he told me that he himself came to terms twenty years ago with his experience of St Joseph's, but that a wider process of reconciliation in Letterfrack has been frustrated by the order's refusal to engage in it. Meanwhile the slow apparatus of the courts of law and the Commission to Inquire into Child Abuse, set up in 2000, has forced a shameful truth upon us: at least in the latter decades of the Industrial Schools and other religious institutions sadistic paedophilia was rampant. There is no need for me to go into details: we have all dined out on horrors since investigative journalists and documentary makers broke open the matter. The commission has been struggling with a tidal wave of revelations, and with little cooperation from the religious bodies involved; according to an interim report in 2003, 'In the main Respondents have adopted an adversarial, defensive and legalistic approach . . . doing no more than complying with their statutory obligations and doing so reluctantly in the case of some Respondents, and under protest, in the case of others.' For their part, the Christian Brothers have insinuated that evidence given to the inquiry has been 'contaminated' by the prospect of financial compensation, without however identifying which claims they think to be fraudulent, or reporting such to the Gardaí. A further report expected from the commission may give us a more balanced view on this question. But it is horribly clear from the commission's interim findings that the simple and saintly West of Ireland was not exempt from a corruption spreading like the black webwork of dry rot through the structures of authoritarian clericalism. Neither state nor citizenry had tried to peep through those high-silled windows. Truly, churches make children of us all, the better to abuse us.

But what was the extent of this abuse in Letterfrack? The commission has received 126 complaints, many of them multiple allegations, against sixty-eight individuals connected with St Joseph's. In 2003 Brother Maurice Tobin was found guilty of sexually abusing twenty-five boys there, and at the age of seventy-one went off to gaol for twelve years; other court cases are pending. The order itself claims to have dealt with five cases between the 1930s and 1961, by canonical warnings and transfer to posts away from 'the occasion of sin'; the gardaí were not informed because, according to the Provincial of the Christian Brothers, sexual abuse was in those days regarded as a 'moral failure' rather than a crime—that is, concern was focused on the perpetrator rather than the victim. As to allegations of unreported deaths, the order claims that records of the one hundred deaths of boys during the entire history of the school showed that they died of illnesses such as pneumonia, TB and meningitis or from fatal accidents, and that each case had been fully accounted for. The toll of suffering will never be known, but when Mannix Flynn, in an interview with the *Irish Times*, says, 'The whole point for people to realize now is that hundreds of children were locked away in Letterfrack, hundreds of children were raped and murdered. It's a holocaust we're dealing with. In every bit of land around Letterfrack there is a child buried . . . ,' we are moving out of the realm of forensic truth into that of folklore, which has its own truth. The school's fields and turf bogs were worked by underfed, insufficiently clothed, frightened little exiles, and the suffering caused by this penitential regime for innocents has soaked into 'every bit of land.' What is to be done, to reclaim this tear-drenched land?

The opportunity to consider this arose in 1994 when Connemara West asked O'Donnell + Tuomey Architects, of Dublin, to submit a proposal for the redevelopment of the site. Connemara West had come into existence in 1971 as a local rural development group, and from the beginning had some exceptionally able and dedicated people among its voluntary directors. Its early enterprises were the group of thatched holiday cottages in Tully Cross, a few miles north of Letterfrack, and a 'Teach Ceoil,' a house for the enjoyment and passing-on of traditional musical skills, in the nearby village of Tully; both enterprises were crucial in the regeneration of this depressed locality, which was haemorrhaging its future through the emigration of its young. Having acquired the former St Joseph's on the departure of the Brothers, Connemara West was using its buildings to house all sorts of undertakings—a farmers' co-op, healthcare and resource facilities, a library, a hostel, an EC-funded anti-poverty project and, most significantly for the future of the site, a furniture-making course run in partnership with the Galway Regional Technical College. Sheila O'Donnell of O'Donnell + Tuomey has described visiting the site at that juncture with her life-and work-partner John Tuomey:

> We both knew the place slightly, having driven through the village on our separate childhood holidays; the grey

institution behind high gated railings, holding boys our own age, cast a temporary gloom over the occupants of the family car and left an indelible impression on the mind's eye. Arriving back in 1994 to meet the board of directors of Connemara West, much had changed; the railings were gone, a path led across the grass to the local pub, the building was open and in use by local people and staff and students of the furniture college. It was in a transitional stage. They were in occupation but they had not yet appropriated the buildings.

The coat of cream paint, with determinedly cheerful red details, only served to emphasise the forbidding character of the structure . . . Upper-floor drawing studios held memories of former use, dormitories with brown-stained boarding behind beamy trusses. The high ceilings of the ground-floor rooms seemed to have pulled the windows up with them so that they hung in the walls above eye-level, preventing views in or out, containing and enclosing the occupants.

The two architects spent much time getting to know the landscape's forms, textures and colours, and the community's needs, both practical and emotional. Demolition was an option soon ruled out; the fearful building had to be drawn into the village and go through the trauma of reconciliation, so that its clear and simple spaces could be cured of melancholy and adapted to house a productive future. And so, as well as designing the dramatic new buildings—machine hall, furniture restoration hall, library and cafeteria—that are now completed and in use, they formulated a second phase of development, a redemptive programme of subtraction for the old building. The secretive staircases and gloomy wainscoting were to be stripped out, the mean little central porch and the finial crosses removed and, in a profoundly symbolic deconstruction, the high windowsills cut down to floor level so that the building would be as open to its new forecourt and garden and the village green as what went on inside it should be to the local community.

The first-phase constructions have been well received—in fact O'Donnell + Tuomey was chosen to represent Ireland at the Venice

Architecture Biennale in 2004, and showed there an installation based on the project—but the second phase has never been implemented. My opportunity to find out why arose in 2007, when the two architects participated in a small conference in Folding Landscapes' studio in Roundstone and gave a public presentation of their Letterfrack work. Sheila and John are a well-matched couple, both being slim, dark and elegant, as well as being passionately dedicated to the creation of buildings not merely practical but beautiful and of metaphoric depth. Their presentation was in itself a work of art, almost dance-like as they alternated seamlessly between speaking and operating the projector; it had something of the traditional Irish form, the *agallamh beirte*, a dialogue, often between man and wife. That the project is unfinished was clearly a source of sadness to them as the symbolic power of the whole has not been fully revealed. When, some months later, I asked them to revisit Letterfrack with me and show me what had and what had not been done, they felt some reluctance, which I overrode in the interest of my book—and in fact I believe the experience was helpful to them as well as being indispensable to me in trying to decipher this palimpsest of a site. The new machine hall and restoration laboratory are quite simply the most dramatic buildings Connemara has seen since Kylemore Castle, and—but let me begin at the beginning, the approach from the village centre.

The old drive leading to the porch in the centre of the façade of the main building, which marched up to it as if under arrest with a constable on either side, is gone, replaced by a broad curve separating two levels of a lawn and opening into an informal space serving both the old building and the new ones to the right of it. Here the ground level steps down southwards by the height of a storey; the floors of the machine hall and restoration laboratory do not touch the ground but rest at one end on beams lying on the upper level and at the other on concrete pillars rising from the lower level. These pillars are like great haunches on which the buildings rise out of the ground below, and curve over to present a bowed back, in profile like the wind-shaped thorn trees of Connemara, to the open land to the south, and come down, in a strikingly protective gesture, in stages, with intervals for ranges of north-facing windows, onto the level of the main building. Both are mainly of wood, as befits a woodworking college, with emphatic triangular geometries of trusses visible inside, and claddings of oak planks that give the exteriors slightly undulant and natural-looking skins. Sheila and John pointed out some subtleties of design: a tall rectangular-sectioned chimney rises from boiler houses on the lower level between the two new buildings, to exactly the height of the small chimneys on either end of the old building, and at exactly the same spacing as them, thus gently decentring the formidable symmetry of the old and subliminally attuning it to the new buildings. The original intention had been to let the boggy ground to the south, and indeed the woodland just beyond it, to continue in under the two new buildings, but instead a playing field has come into existence there, and the undercrofts behind the concrete pillars have found new uses: a range of small classrooms or offices has been inserted like a drawer into one of these spaces, and John and Sheila were surprised and pleased to find part of their Venice installation stored in the other.

The new library, with a cafeteria below it, looks onto the courtyard behind the main building; and here the departure from the O'Donnell + Tuomey design has been less acceptable. Their scheme was to detoxify this grim marshalling yard by laying it out, right up to the glass frontages of the cafeteria, as an 'academic garden.' However, temporary buildings have been installed in it, and concrete pavements have been laid down around it. Inside the main building too, I gather, ad hoc solutions to access and storage problems have been imposed, and since they work 'well enough' stand as obstacles to a deeper reformation of the interior spaces. I think what has happened, as the Galway Regional Technical College matured into the Galway Mayo Institute of Technology over the years, is that it has turned to its own resources in architecture and engineering, and so the final realization and perfecting of the O'Donnell + Tuomey scheme languishes in a financial and planning limbo.

Having examined these and other aspects of what could well be termed a complex, being so densely self-intricated in space and time, we climbed steps behind the main building, between a row of cottages dating from the Quaker times and the former Industrial School workshops, leading to the former monastery and the church, which was opened in 1925 and largely financed by the Brothers. The front garden of the hostel was full of tents, and its little courtyard had been given a temporary-looking roof and seemed to be crammed with armchairs and sofas on which international youth was resting momentarily from its worldwide drift; the atmosphere was drowsy, oriental—one expected opium pipes and hookahs—and wonderfully carefree. Not so the church; near the altar was a highly realistic bronze memorial showing three small lads scrambling happily on a climbing frame, entitled 'To the memory of the boys—if only,' while the visitors' book was full of entries about the Industrial School, some of them long and deeply felt, some from former victims of the Brothers, some forgiving, or at least trusting in God to forgive.

Finally we visited the little cemetery in a clearing reached by a rocky path through the damp woodland over the road from the church, where there used to be just a cross with a large square pedestal bearing a long list of the names of the children who died while under the Christian Brothers' care. Now two lawns have been laid out in front of the cross, and an array of some eighty little heart-shaped inscribed stones at least give each child his own memorial space. But these are the ones that no process of reconciliation can touch. These are the dead.

Smuggler and Fabulist

Consider the coastline of north-west Connemara: with its deep and winding inlets running to the foot of trackless mountains, it was evidently drawn by nature with smugglers in mind. By his upbringing Captain George O'Malley, born in 1786 in Ballynakill, was as well adapted to that habitat as any scuttling crab or swooping seagull. Connemara in his early days was more prosperous than in later years, and this remote corner of it, patched with a mellower geology than the rest, with green hills of glacial till and sheltery valleys of lime-rich soils to soften its asperities, was, as it still is, favoured above the rest. It was not until the 1820s that new roads allowed the influence of civic authority into the region, and the inhabitants blamed the roads for the subsequent economic decline. The O'Malley ladies and those of their rival smugglers, and their financial backers the O'Flahertys of Renvyle, went in silks and lace-trimmed linen caps, and common boatmen sported swallow-tail coats and knee britches and extravagant high hats called 'coro-lines' (from King Charles I) brought in from Guernsey. The bad times succeeding upon the end of the Napoleonic Wars—ushered in by agricultural depression, the collapse of the kelp trade, and the coincidental desertion of the herring shoals that had brought the fishermen of all Atlantic Europe to Ballynakill—and culminating in the Great Famine, must have given the memories of Captain O'Malley's most active days a varnish of nostalgia even while he still lived, scribbling his memoirs in the poorhouse at Westport.

Two songs attributed to An Caiptín Máilleach, as he is known in Irish, are still sung in Connemara, one of them in praise of his boat, the *Slúipín Vaughan*, the other in praise of himself. The traditional singing of the West of Ireland called *sean-nós*, the old way, sounds strange to our ears, as it uses modes other than the major and minor ones we are familiar with, but it is worth persevering and learning to appreciate its expressive qualities. These are uniquely allied to the rich and complex phonetics of the Irish language. Hear the difference between 'Captain O'Malley' and, properly pronounced, 'An Caiptín Máilleach'—it is as if the syllables of Irish have more space inside them. In fact there are Irish words so spacious you could hold a *céilí* dance in one syllable and a wake in another, without mutual interference. The art that explores these spaces inside words is *sean-nós*. In print, and in translation, I can only explore the outsides of such words.

'An Caiptín Máilleach'is a series of scenes from a smuggling voyage. The first verse gives the course, by various islands and headlands, and the Captain rings fine music out of the placenames:

An chéad lá de'n mhí agus d'fhómhar a chrochamar ár seolta
Ag tarraingt ar na cóstaí úd tóin an Bhonnáin siar,
Thart anseo le Cliartha, Acaill Bheag taobh thiar dhe,
Is go hInis Tuirc dhá dtrialladh, bheadh aoireacht orainn
   ann. Thart le Rinn an haoile, síos 'un Crua' na Caoile,
An Cloigeann lena thaobh sin agus Trá Bhríde ina dhiaidh,
Nó gur dhoirteamar le fánaidh, thrí fharraige 's í ag
   cáitheadh,
Go ndeachamar don Ráithe, mar is ann a bhí ár dtriall.

On the first day of the autumn, our sails we quickly hoisted
While heading for the coastlands, by Bunaun's western
   waves;
Around here by Clare Island, and Achill Beg beside it,
To Inishturk we headed, as we were expected there.
Around by Rinn an Mhaoile, and down by Cruach na
   Caoile,
Cleggan right behind us, and Trá Bhríde not far away;
As southwards we were rolling, through seas all white with
   foaming,
Into Rath we sailed ashore, where our destination lay.

Then, as they come to Aran, the gale strengthens; they are heading for the shore, and it's no welcoming one; but they man the sails, and only just in time; the sea groans and the great waves flash, the sky quakes and fog thickens; if the planks could speak they would tell a dreadful tale of how only they stand between the crew and death. The crew are looking at the Captain's brow for signs of hope, but all he can do is to keep the boat under sail as long as it can float. His hands are torn from endlessly hauling ropes, the skin and flesh are pulled off the bones—but if the Son of God has decreed their death there's no avoiding it, and they'll all go to heaven in the same state of grace:

Tá mo lámha stróicthe go síoraí ag tarraingt rópaí,
Tá an craiceann 'gus an fheoil tóigthe amach on gcnáimh;
Ach más é an bás a gheall Mac Dé dhúinn, cén gar atá dhá
  shéanadh,
Ach a ghoil go flaithis Dé dhúinn ar aon stáid amháin.

The last two verses seem to deal with a different voyage. They have reached Ireland with a cargo of wine, brandy, tea, tobacco, Jamaica rum, long pieces of silk and the most expensive scarves; he'll put out his hand for whichever young girl he sets his heart on, his poor ship is battered from stem to stern, its bolts bent, and who can blame it; but now that the gale has weakened and they have a favouring wind, let them finish the song and drink their dram. Finally he relives the dangers they have overcome—water-guards on the lookout and police on their heels, the Revenue men and all their spies, cutters big and small, dirty rotten pilots, King George's ships on the hunt—and he ends with a triumphant boast:

Ach is mise Seoirse Ó Máille, fear maith de bhunadh
  Ghráinne—
Cuireadh i dtír mo lucht go sásta, agus ná raibh maith acu
  dhá chionn.

But I am George O'Malley, a sound man of Grace's family—
My cargo is safe ashore, and no thanks to them for that.

Years ago I came across an old reference to a manuscript auto-biography of Captain O'Malley said to have been written in the workhouse at Westport where he died in 1865. But, having heard the very groaning of planks and clapping of sails echoed in the words of his song, it was difficult to credit the existence of any such work; as a creature of stormy myth he seemed as unlikely as the Flying Dutchman to have left tangible documentation of himself. However, when I was mapping the Captain's haunts I made a point of asking the local inhabitants for any knowledge they had of him, and one day to my amazement Eileen O'Malley of Cleggan answered me by silently getting up from her chair, leaving the room and returning with an armload of paper—the Captain's memoirs in seven volumes, each of 300 or 400 closely typed pages. This huge and fascinating work has never been published; I subsequently learned that several scholars, including the late James Carney, had played with the idea of editing it for publication and had retired defeated by its verbose braggartry, as I myself have been. A Colonel Middleton O'Malley Keyes, who owned the original manuscript, had four typed copies made in about 1910, in collaboration with Tomás Ó Máille, the first professor of Irish in University College, Galway. The National Library has one copy, and one was passed down to the late Professor Tomás S. Ó Máille, his namesake's successor in the university and head of the O'Malley clan; this is the one I saw in Cleggan.

The next time I called in on Tomás, as I did now and again in search of counsel on problematic placenames, I discussed the document with him. He was dubious of its genuineness; he felt that the Captain was unlikely to have been able to write, and that much of it was inherently incredible. Indeed the Captain's adventures during the Napoleonic Wars—when he is pressed into the English Navy, captured by a French privateer, imprisoned in the Tower of St-Malo, and later with hundreds of other prisoners marched in chains hither and thither about Napoleon's collapsing empire—or in the Caribbean where, much against his conscience, he becomes a pirate and a slaver—might perhaps prove to have been lifted from other memoirs. But I can vouch for the accuracy of the references to people and places in the early chapters; his adversarial dealings with Captain Morris of the Revenue, his involvement with the Coneys family of Streamstown in the basking shark fishery and, above all, his father's relationships with his financial backer, Anthony O'Flaherty of Renvyle, place George O'Malley in the real Connemara of the early nineteenth century.

Since that first brief encounter with this ambiguous text I have failed to trace the original manuscript, and lost track of Professor Ó Máille's copy, but have located a copy (with quite different pagination) of the first half of the work, which is the most interesting part, and have had time to look at it in more detail. It begins in a painfully poetic vein:

> My first day at school happened in that season of the year when the corn fields wear the hue of pure virgin gold, and invite the sickle to reward the husbandman's toil . . .

Such passages occur here and there throughout, adorned with quotes from Lord Byron and Thomas Moore, but the actual narrative is crisply told; so it is easy to discount these embellishments as by another hand. But problems obtrude as one reads on. Could any single person have accumulated—and survived—so much experience? One's powers of belief are overthrown especially by some of his Caribbean adventures, such as the finding of a pocketbook containing a bank draft in the belly of a shark that had recently eaten a pirate, which enables him to restore the fortunes of the family of the fascinating Miss Penetho of Havana. But a striking constant in all his tales is a close attention to the sort of details that would catch a sailor's eye. For instance in 1812 he is incarcerated for a time at Givet, on the river Meuse, and meets some English sailors imprisoned there who tell him how Napoleon, on a tour of his northern fortresses, had come to Givet and found that the bridge there had been swept away by floods; the Englishmen had rigged up a travelling chair slung from a rope to get him across the river, and were rewarded by the release of some of their number. Now this odd incident is mentioned in memoirs of Napoleon, and in one of the magnificent gilded volumes of the *Correspondence de Napoléon 1er* is the Emperor's note giving orders for the release of 'eight or ten' of the men who showed particular zeal in the task. But O'Malley, in seamanlike terms, tells us exactly how it was done:

The great Napoleon crossed that river by means of a ridge rope and hauling lines from both sides [and] a chair suspended to a traveller backwards and forwards on the ridge rope, elevated many feet above the bed of the river. The rope was sent across thro' the help of a swivel gun, which drove a piece of wood tomkin [i.e. plug] like with a small line attached to draw it across the stout ridge rope and a note of instructions conveyed in that manner to an officer on the same side.

Now, where could he have got that? And his accounts of sea fights in the Caribbean are similarly precise concerning the handling of ropes, Here (much abbreviated) is how the intrepid O'Malley, at the helm of the *Rebecca*, outwits the *Saucy Jack*, the fastest ship of the West Indian coast:

I took the wheel, the owner was a seaman, and I told the old man to tell him that when I'd sing out to let go the after guys of the swinging boom and studding sail boom also the larboard side with the braces, and by doing so he might be sure I'd let the Yankee know that boarding us would be a difficult job for him . . . The guns were primed and loaded; boarding pikes, cutlasses and tomahawks were at hand; and all things requisite were put in their respective places. In a short time we came up so close to the Yankee that our flying jib boom was abreast of her quarter . . . He sheered his vessel towards us evidently to give us a broadside and board us on the quarter in the smoke. 'Let go the larboard guys and braces alow and aloft,' said the owner, 'and let every man lie flat on the deck.' The American was then close to our larboard main chains and clapped the matches to his guns. The Broadside went off: he put his helm to port to board us, and I clapped our helm hard a starboard; the booms and yards flew forward when the guys and braces were let go, which gave them room to clear his yards and not checking the vessel's way by fouling with her. When of a sudden I put the helm a starboard, and his being a port already, both ships closed. Our vessel fore reached on his, took in a moment his bowsprit, jib boom and flying jib boom, fore top mast, top gallant mast, royal sky sail pole and all their gear along his side in one confused mass. I righted the helm and kept the vessel again on her course. We were soon clear of his smoke. 'Come, boys, on your feet; up aloft, and in royals, top gallant sails, and studding sails also; brace up the main yard, and let her come to the wind; stick now to your going and make sure each shot will tell.' The word was given, and the broadside was fired with effect; down came the Saucy Jack's topmast, mainmast and nothing remained but her lower masts standing.

Having diligently read so many episodes like this in O'Malley's memoir I feel I could execute such a manoeuvre myself. They are the commonplace of pirate yarns, but while he might have lifted ideas from such books as the eighteenth-century best-seller *A General History of the Robberies and Murders of the Most Notorious Pirates*, attributed to Daniel Defoe, the obsessive detailing of the sailor's craft is perfectly consistent with the style of his Connemara and French recollections, and the personality revealed—pitiable in its boastfulness, helplessly given to passionate rages, progressively touched with insanity as his woes multiply—make the O'Malley of this stupendous text inimitably his own man. So, the results of my amateur prying into it are puzzling and raise problems beyond my power to resolve; I commend the matter to scholarship. Here, I will read it naively, as the memoirs of a small-time Connemara smuggler with the gift of a good deal more than total recall, and try to summarize his career.

George O'Malley was born in 1786, according to a note on the cover of one copy of his memoirs. George's father was himself a smuggler, whose 'well-armed merry little cutter' could outsail any of the Revenue cutters stationed along the coast. Once a month he would come in with a cargo of tobacco, brandy, gin, tea and silks, 'which, when landed, found their way to many other markets and caused a great circulation of money in that remote and backward place, the possession of which made the inhabitants lively, gay and prosperous.' On his first day at school the six-year-old George is accompanied by his sister, who wears a silk dress and a copper-coloured beaver hat ornamented with white ostrich plumes, tassels and a rich gold band, which is soon ruined as a result of the fights George gets into. From a rock behind the school he observes his father's outwitting of a Revenue cutter, and resolves to make the sea billows his hobby horse and ride over them in his 'race for life.' His childhood, as recounted, is a dreamlike jumble of stories involving the fairies, who had two dwellings nearby, and grotesque characters such as the thief, John Lee:

His wife took fever; John attended her faithfully, and she recovered. He caught the contagion himself. Their corner was a very poor one; he lay down with his shoes and stockings on and no mortal man, no, not even his wife, who acted most ungraciously in return for his kind attention to her; but God took pity on him, and after a very long fit he recovered. He made a fire for himself, as he always had flint and steel which were very useful on certain occasions. When the poor man had strength to take off his shoes and stockings he found that the flesh and sinews were completely rotten and in a few days fell off. He laid them on the hob to season; for he did not like the cat would take them away . . .

. . . and on it gruesomely goes: a creditor calls on him, John asks him to fetch a heap of stones with which to drive off the rats that are after his feet, and uses the stones to pelt the man until the debt is forgiven.

From an early age George shares his father's adventures in the basking shark fishery, and his truculent character is soon established by dozens of incidents. In Connemara lore the O'Malleys are always lightly built and limber (whereas the Joyces, their opponents in many a faction fight, are huge and soft, and the O'Malleys can always 'beat them like feather mattresses'); George too is slightly built and nimble, with an ungovernable temper and a ferocious energy in attack. He is also subject to nosebleeds, and is happy with cross-dressing—traits one would not have associated with a Connemara smuggler.

His preparations for the smuggler's career are meticulous. As a youth he has the run of his father's excellent nautical books, from which he learns all the spars and rigging of a first-rate man-of-war and the use of the compass, quadrant, sextant and Gunter scales. Then, 'to get acquainted with the rules on high ship board,' he joins a Revenue cutter employed in the Killaries in keeping order among the herring boats from Scotland, the Isle of Man and Skerries. The Revenue cutter also searches Clare Island and Inishbofin for illicit stills, and pursues smuggler vessels, but, as O'Malley notes, she has no chance against 'the beautiful Guernsey cutters and luggers.' The cutter is then ordered to Dublin for repairs, and while she is in dock there and O'Malley is on watch he finds a number of young women on board, who all scamper off except the youngest and handsomest of them all. He gallantly escorts her to her home, and her grateful parents invite him to call, which he does. Soon the father says he is expecting O'Malley to fulfil his promise to his daughter, and tries to march him off to church. O'Malley pretends to be taken short, leaps over a wall and makes his escape—the first of numerous unhappy experiences with the opposite sex. Then he ships on a cutter captained by 'a crab-catching sailor,' one who is too fond of nearing rocks. When they run aground on the Mayo coast the captain 'takes the fits' and has to be lashed to the cabin ladder, while O'Malley is swept overboard and washed back on again three times, and saves the captain from drowning by climbing the rigging and hoisting him up, ladder and all. George gets ashore and finds lodgings with a young man named Waters; one evening he dresses up in Waters' sister's clothes and they go to a dance where he flirts with a captain, steals his watch and then returns it, coming home 'well pleased with the frolic I had played on the love-seeking tar.' In Ballina he is impressed by the scale of the linen industry, and notes the wives and maidens 'as pretty as ever laid toe on a daisy.' Being ragged, he is taken for a chimney sweep, is entertained by the master sweep at the Cat and Bagpipes and has a wrestling match with the sweeps, 'the most jolly of all jolly traipsing professions.' Then he hears that his sister has been insulted, searches out the culprit and beats him with a bit of 'ship's trimmel'; the man dies soon after, and George is ever after sorry for 'the first and last blow of a stick during my life.'

His next berth is with the *Phoenix* of Dublin, a 'very heavy lump of a brig'; they sail to Oporto and smuggle some porter ashore with the connivance of the Customs House. He is seized by a British press gang and penned in a guardroom with many others until the gangmaster comes to see which of them are fit for the service of George III. All get drunk, make a mass escape and are recaptured. George is sent on board His Majesty's ship *Talbot* to accompany a convoy to Lisbon, where he escapes by swimming, but after innumerable adventures is caught again and makes his excuses: drink. They sail for England, escorting seventy transports (we are now in 1807, in the midst of the war with Napoleonic France). In Sheerness he witnesses bumboats full of Jews who come alongside with boxes of 'knick knackeries' to sell to the just-paid sailors, and are plundered by the crew, who hoist their boxes to the mast tops—'one of the most wanton and diabolical acts I had ever witnessed . . . neither the Bible nor the Koran troubled these English Rapparees.' The *Talbot* is then ordered to the North Sea to cruise against Danes and Russians, and chases 'everything our imaginative faculties could conjure up as enemies of England,' but can never take a prize. After a long and eventful cruise he is unjustly refused his pay because of his many acts of insubordination—'for gratitude from England "No Irish need apply"'—escapes with empty pockets, pays with his trousers for a lift in a cart, and after three days reaches Glasgow. In Greenock he ships on the twenty-five-gun *Caledonia* for the West Indies, leaves it when it calls in at Galway, signs on with a Captain Cottle of the *Liberty* of New York, bound for Cronstadt, where they take on a cargo of iron, tallow hemp and isinglass (a gelatinous stuff derived from the guts of sturgeon). In the town, which is built on piles, he is inveigled into a large building like 'some enchanted pigeon house' with two tiers of 'side berths' along each wall, closed off by slides; at the ring of a bell the slides are withdrawn and 'a very pretty female face projected out of each berth, and each waved very politely with her fair and pretty hand at the stranger wearing around her carmine lips a bland, bewitching smile, and dropped a rope ladder from the inside of each berth.' O'Malley, though, is mindful of 'a plain face, and more virtuous maiden' he knows elsewhere—one of many hints at some love interest that never quite reveals its secret.

The voyage back to Stockholm in the company of a convoy of 300 ships, including the *Victory* 'on whose deck the hero of Trafalgar often passed,' in a snowstorm, all the ships ringing bells or sounding drums so as not to run foul of each other, is dramatically described. O'Malley is the only man on his ship who dares to go aloft, and saves it from disaster. In the North Sea they suffer three weeks of storm, are driven far to the north, are reduced to a pint of water a day each, but always manage to spare some for a cup of tea for Mrs. Cottle, who becomes O'Malley's fast friend and rapt audience for his tall tales, in which, as she says, he rivals Captain Kidd and Sinbad the Sailor. Then the wind takes them south again and they make Yarmouth Roads. The gale has been the worst for fifty years; thirty ships of the convoy had foundered in sight of others, and another twenty were unaccounted for.

When they enter the Thames O'Malley reluctantly parts with the Cottles as he is in danger of the press gangs. He puts up at the 'Chicken and Swan' in Tower Hill, and finds it hard to resist the beautiful young daughter of the house who 'seemed to multiply her charms into a battery for discharging her love-pellets' at him in 'terrible broadsides.' He takes a coach to Liverpool, is assailed by another amorous young lady, borrows her clothes and has some transvestite and sentimental intrigues, before joining the *Emerald*, 'an old Guinea man' bound for 'Fyall,' which must be Faial in the Azores. Becalmed, they see 'heavy clouds begin to move as if they were sensitive objects labouring under mortal pain' and are struck by lightning. After numerous adventures, in which O'Malley escapes death by a hair's breadth and saves the day repeatedly, they return from Fyall to Liverpool. Narrowly escaping marriage to the young lady there, he joins a ship bound for Galway, and makes his way to Westport, where he lays out his money on perfecting his nautical education. Thence to Cadiz on the *Maria* of Dublin; they are pursued by 'a matchless French privateer,' the *Ferret*, and the captain bursts into tears at the thought of losing his cargo, while the crew sob for their sweethearts or wives. They are all taken prisoner and rammed down into the Frenchman's hold, where they are soon joined by the crew of another captured ship, nearly suffocate and barely survive on a gill of water and a biscuit a day. Having taken twenty-one prizes and scuttled all but one of them, but saving the ships' papers in order to claim prize money from the French government, the privateer sails for St-Malo. This is the beginning of his French captivity, in January 1811, of which he gives a truly terrible and rather convincing account.

After seven weeks in the tower of St-Malo the prisoners are 'marched and countermarched through many of the principal cities and towns of France . . . sometimes lodged in wide prisons at night, sometimes crammed up, sometimes huddled in the streets, the strongest in the middle and the weakest underneath or overhead.' To pass the time, as it were, a great English brute of a sailor, William Dick, fights with O'Malley as often as possible; when the gendarmes prevent them fighting, O'Malley is so frustrated he kicks off his shoes—'Fool and madman as I then was, I walked barefooted thro' the snow the rest of the afternoon'—and that night batters Dick into submission. Eventually they reach the receiving prison of Cambray, where about 5,000 men are being held and conditions are relatively indulgent; there are shops, public houses, a church, a chapel, a Methodist house, gymnasiums and schools for subjects ranging from reading to astronomy. Six hundred of the more unruly prisoners are kept in a long loft, and often break loose in the nude at night with their bodies soaped and carrying cudgels 'that could kill a hippopotamus,' to plunder their fellows and gamble their allowances. As a result of fights and an escape attempt, O'Malley is pronounced mad and made to join a group of criminals—handcuffed, with a chain rove through all the handcuffs, some with pitch caps on their shaven heads—for a 250-mile march to Givet, in the winter of 1812. There, after enduring unspeakable conditions in various cells on the way, they find themselves comparatively 'pleasantly situated'; there are even schools of fencing, dancing and boxing, navigation and astronomy, Freemason lodges and a smoking club. One man makes a fortune with a dog trained to swim across the river between the fort and the town, carrying money, avoiding the sentry and returning with two bladders full of brandy.

After six months at Givet the prison is 'broken up,' and O'Malley is one of 900 prisoners ordered to march to the Austrian frontier; on the way they fall in with the Napoleonic Guards on their way to the Rhine and to Moscow, 20,000 strong, a magnificent sight with their moustaches and lances, and 'mounted on entire [i.e. ungelded] horses having scutched tails with their hair plaited and turned up with knots of ribbons, and their manes same way.' O'Malley (writing here from memory, he says, having lost the hurried notes he made at the time) tells of the prisoners' ranks being thinned by cold and disease, in towns without provisions because of the enormous numbers of troops on the move. In a town within four days' march of Troyes the remaining 200 of them are put into a large room in an old building, shivering with hunger and cold, where they crowd round a fire of straw; when they find six rat-eaten corpses under the straw they burn the corpses and roast the rats. In another prison he gets a 'piglouse' in his ear that, he says, 'actually drove me to the point of madness.' Then in a street in Tours a beautiful young lady beckons to him from a window, and entertains him with food and champagne, because she feels an unaccountable warmth for him; she turns out to be a step-cousin; on parting she stretches out her lily-white hand and gives him two louis-d'ors.

A long zigzag march takes him to Fontainebleau, and then they are ordered back to 'Pirigue' in the south of France (Périgord, perhaps); it is the winter of 1813 and only thirty of them have survived, out of the 900 who left Givet. There he catches a fever, and in hospital is attended by the angelic sisters of Mercy. He loses his reason for twenty-four days, suffers a prolonged nosebleed and is restored by the prayers and remedies of a faithful sister 'fresh as a young blown rose.' After four months there he hears that peace has been proclaimed, and joins a few of his comrades in marching to Bordeaux. Somewhere within two days of Toulouse they see a triumphal arch in the street and French soldiers tearing the eagles from their caps, while an army whose commanders had not yet heard of the emperor's abdication plant cannons in the square and threaten to level the rebellious town. At last they see ships' masts in Bordeaux, an enchanting sight to O'Malley. Soon he is landed at Portsmouth, and eventually (and with many picaresque and amatory escapades on the way) reaches Westport, after a four-year absence. But his rich relatives there 'know him not,' and within a few weeks he is off again, shipping from Liverpool for Jamaica.

At this point, the beginning of his Caribbean career, although I have omitted scores of brawls and wild reckless incidents, we are only a quarter way through his 2,000-odd pages, and like all previous would-be editors or expositors of the inordinate O'Malley, I give up. I have already given a taste of his piratical adventures, which occupy him until 1818 and take him to and fro between the West Indies, New York (where he witnesses the first trials of Fulton's steamship) and the slave ports of West Africa. This episode ends when he comes to anchor under the castle of Clare Island, with a huge cargo of contraband—and then, he writes, 'begins the story of my real misfortunes. The sorrows of Werther were nothing to mine!' The theft of his cargo by the islanders launches him into labyrinthine and unsummarizable escapades among the hard-drinking gentry of Mayo and their gamesome womenfolk; much of this matter would suggest that his reason is tottering. He seems out of his element on land; his attempts at horsemanship are disastrous, and when he walks across a moor he falls in through the roof of a bog dwelling and is beaten up by its occupants; in fact the account of his sufferings verges on the masochistic. Then, as a preliminary to a more settled smuggling career, he disguises himself as a peasant and makes a survey of the nooks and crannies of the coast from Broadhaven north to Arranmore in Donegal. He also acquires a small sloop from another smuggler, Ned Vaughan; this is the famous *Slúipín Vaughan* of the song. He finally retires from smuggling in 1829. The vast work ends, or peters out, in some mention of his sickness, and a few loose papers, the very image of decline and death. A letter written in 1964 by a Mayo man preserves a local memory of the Captain's last years:

All I know about Captain O'Malley was what my mother often told me, that he would come down every other day to

her mother's house at the Quay, Westport, and receive some
kindness in the way of a drink or two and tobacco, but she
told me that he was always talking about the manuscript he
had written all about his life and adventures, and how he
would have money and fame when it was published. He was
as I told you in the Workhouse in Westport, where he died,
and I hope he was not buried in the Rocky Field without a
stone over his grave . . . No one paid any attention to the old
sailor when he spoke of his adventures and his manuscript.

The Captain's inordinate memoir is a buried treasure chest, and
I hope this partial account of it will encourage further unpacking
of its riches, for even if half of it is fiction, it is a creative achieve-
ment as a portrait of a self-haunted and storm-driven soul. But for
me, obsessive topographer, it is chiefly valuable for exactly situat-
ing the place of O'Malley's birth, which had eluded all my local
enquiries, and for the curious detour through the Otherworld by
which it does this. It was clear from various hints and conjectures
I had come across that the O'Malley home was near Keelkyle,
just south of Letterfrack, but nobody could confirm this, much
less identify the site of the house. The memoirs certainly point
to Keelkyle, though without naming it. George's early memory
of watching his father sailing into his home bay pursued by the
coastguard cutter, and turning his boat suddenly to dart through a
narrow passage between an islet and the shore and head out to sea
again, inscribes itself without difficulty on the map of Ballynakill
Bay. But a more precise clue (pointed out to me by the historian of
the O'Malleys, Sheila Mulloy, who has looked into the memoirs)
is the reference to a fairy hill on his father's land and 'within eighty
yards of the hall door.' Now, there is in the townland of Keelkyle
at the head of the bay a curious abrupt knoll between the coast
road and the sea (almost opposite a craftshop that used to adver-
tise itself as 'possibly the best craftshop in the west,' and is therefore known as the Possibly Shop). The knoll is called Dúinín Mór,
and although I never heard locally that it was regarded as a dwelling place of the fairies, this was formerly a familiar fact; indeed,
according to a story preserved in the Department of Folklore in

University College, Dublin, a Clifden man going by the spot on his way to Letterfrack intervened to stop a fight between two men, who turned out to be the respective kings of the Dúinín Mor fairies and those of Cathair an Dúin, the promontory fort on the Renvyle peninsula, also regarded as a fairy fort. The quarrel, like so many in Connemara, was over seaweed-gathering rights, and the traveller undertook to mediate:

'I'll settle the question for you,' said the travelling man, 'if you accept.'

'We're happy to accept,' said the pair of them.

'Well,' said the man, 'Let the people of Dúinín Mór come and cut seaweed from Letterfrack west until they come as far as Gob an Rosa, and let them go across the bay there and cut the seaweed opposite Gob an Rosa on the Leitir side and round by Damhros until they come back to Dúinín Mor again. And the Cathair an Dúin people,' said the man, 'they can cut the shore west of Gob an Rosa and then cross the bay to Leitir and cut that shore until they come to the Cora, the place where the Dúinín Mór people started to cut on the Leitir side.'

'We're satisfied,' said the two kings, 'We'll accept that.'

So Dúinín Mór was a well-known factor of supernatural economics (and tales about it no doubt had an ideological role in local power-politics); hence we now know pretty exactly where the Captain was born. It might seem odd to fix a human address by reference to a fairy dwelling, but the aura of the uncanny can outlast historical memory. In fact, although the knoll is no longer thought of as a fairy fort, it is still a locus of the numinous. In 1987 a statue of the Virgin Mary was installed in a little 'grotto' on its roadside face, and shortly afterwards reports that the statue was moving caused crowds to gather. Young men in suits of fundamentalist darkness materialized, I remember, to oversee the devotions and control the traffic jams. They were servicing a cult older than they knew.

Twilight on Old Stones

Lingering elegiac evenings of the summer solstice, when the parted day slips behind the mountains to the north like a child hiding behind a sofa, are the best for exploring the valley of Ballynakill Lake. Elements of this little world apart that might not be noticed at other times become quietly insistent on presenting themselves, and those prominent by daylight sink back into obscurity. The roofless gables of the medieval chapel of St Ceannanach (from which the parish is called Baile na Cille, the settlement of the church) are less distinguishable from the dark profiles of trees in the graveyard behind it, whereas by day the ruin, one corner of which touches the roadside wall, seems to rest an elbow on it and lean out like an old farmer eyeing the approaching passer-by; you know you will not get past without having to listen to some inconsequential local history. 'Did you ever hear of Strong Ned?' he might say. 'That's Éamonn Láidir in Irish. He was an O'Flaherty; his grandfather had the land round here until Cromwell hanged him and gave it to the Martins. Nimble Dick Martin used to come round for the rent with his servants, all armed, and Ned would drive them off all by himself. He was seven feet tall. When he died he was buried just where I'm standing now. People used to come and see his great big bones; they were on show in a sort of shelf in the church wall . . .'

But in the evenings the stories that make themselves heard are less easily understood and of much older origins. At the far end of Ballynakill Lake, which lies at the foot of the meadowed slope south of the chapel and stretches for over a mile to the west, the attention of the belated walker might be caught by two white shapes on a low hillock; at first glance they could be swans asleep. Two stones, in fact, strangely luminous in the gloaming, one of a pyramidal shape and about a yard high, the other a stubby block of the same size but fallen on its side. A little further on a lane leads to the south, climbing around some curious little hills, a moraine left by the glacier that once pushed through the Ballynakill valley to Cleggan Bay. It is because of these hills that the area is called Sheeauns, or Na Siáin, the fairy mounds; they are Sián Fada, the long fairy mound, Sián Mór and Sián Beag, the big and small fairy mounds, Conroy's Sián, topped by a circular cattle shelter which the long-departed Conroy built up out of the ruins of an ancient ringfort, and Sián na Cuaiche, the fairy mound of the cuckoo. When the crooked thorn trees in the hollows between these hills rake darkness out of the twilight, I have never seen a place more conducive to the fairy faith. The lane continues past a few cottages, then the sound of a stream hidden in an overgrown gully begins to accompany the way, and after a little bridge and a bend to the west, one sees another stone gleaming dimly, a stout pillar about five feet high, among gorse-bushes on a corner of rough land overlooking the stream. What are these ghostly stones that seem to come out at night?

Of course the archaeologists have noted them in all the daylight science can cast on them, and determined that they are Bronze Age monuments, dating from between 2500 and 1000 BC. I will approach the questions of their concentration in the Ballynakill area, their significance to our age, and the less answerable one of their significance to those who erected them, through an account of my first sight of one of their sort, in the townland of Garraunbawn, another maze of lanes and fields and little hills a mile or so to the east of the old chapel of Ballynakill. At the time of my visit I had already gathered into my mind a number of bits of information about this place, fragmentary but intriguing, like shards of some antique decorated vessel. According to the experts I had consulted at the Ordnance Survey, 'Garraunbawn,' the official townland name, is an anglicization of the Irish 'An Garrán Bán,' the white or fallow thicket, garrán, a shrubbery or thicket, being a common element in placenames. However, I had also dug out of the OS archives the 'field name books' kept by the surveyors who first mapped this area in 1839, and in one of these was a note saying that the Irish name of this place was 'An Gearrán Bán,' the white horse. Gearrán, a gelding or small horse, is close in sound to *garrán*, a shrubbery, and the difference between them—that subtle deflection of the *g* towards a *gy*—is lost, like so much else, in anglicization. Further, the old notebook stated that the townland took its name from that of a rock, although it did not record where this rock was. There was also a story I'd heard from a nonagenarian gentleman, formerly of Garraunbawn House, about a white horse that came up out of Garraunbawn Lake; a man caught it and saddled and rode it, and then took the saddle off and hung it over a rock, while the horse galloped away and plunged into the lake again. The mark of the saddle, my informant had heard, was still to be seen on the rock, but unfortunately he didn't know exactly where this rock was. Another hint had come from an archaeologist who told me that there was a Bronze Age standing stone on the top of a small glacial hill or drumlin in Garraunbawn; in fact such a hill occupies most of the area of the townland.

I remember that it was on a particularly beautiful evening that the thread of my explorations led me through Garraunbawn. I pushed my bike up the lane, sunk between banks rich with wildflowers, that crosses the hill, and just at the top of the slope I glanced through a gap in the hedge. There, in a meadow that fell away towards Ballynakill Bay and the vista of mountains beyond, was the standing stone. It was a stumpy boulder set on end, about five feet high, of milk-white quartz dappled with grey lichen, and in the half-light it looked exactly like the rump of an old white horse, peacefully grazing. I had previously noted a quartz vein exposed on the shore of an island in the bay below, from which big lumps of quartz had rolled out as the coast was cut back by the waves; perhaps some Bronze Age people rafted such a boulder across and lugged it up half a mile of hill to install it here. No doubt until the building of Garraunbawn House in about 1850 it was the most prominent object in the neighbourhood.

In fact I am sure that the stone is the mythical white horse itself, that the surviving version of its story, in which the man hangs the saddle over the stone, is an impoverished one, an attempt to mitigate the magic of an older tale, and that in the eclipsed version the horse was metamorphosed into the stone. So, at that moment, looking through the hedge at the old stone horse crop-ping the grass on the hilltop, I could tie together a geological and an archaeological strand of Connemara's prehistory, and follow the efforts of later generations to make sense of that mysterious stone, first by means of a legend of an otherworldly horse, and then by tidying up that story already half forgotten and fossilized in a placename, which itself was later to be misunderstood and gelded by officialdom. For this place is not An Garrán Bán, the fallow thicket, but An Gearrán Bán, named from its ancient, perhaps totemic, white horse of stone, which has been ridden over the millennia by various meanings we can only guess at. The stone itself is as it always was and as a physical object needs no restoration; the restoration of its meaning as a contemporary monument, an icon of the locality's specificity, is the task of the topographer and a touch in the restoration of our eroded modern consciousness of place. But what of its original significance in the life-world of those who set it up? If anything can be recovered of that, it is only in the context of a wider enquiry into the prehistoric remains of Connemara.

At the time of my beginning to map the region the prevailing opinion among archaeologists was that, compared to the riches of the Burren and the limestone plains east of the Corrib, not much was to be expected from these unwelcoming boglands beyond the half-dozen megalithic tombs and a similar number of standing stones recorded by nineteenth-century antiquarians, mainly in the area of Ballynakill. This view was soon to be confounded by the work of the Galway Archaeological Survey team, emanating from the National University in Galway, and in particular the discoveries made by one team member, the indefatigably enthusiastic Clifden archaeologist Michael Gibbons. The synchrony of the Survey's and my own campaigns in Connemara was productive; all the Survey finds went onto my own map, and the sites that I stumbled across myself or was directed to by local farmers or by placename evidence were all promptly visited, verified and recorded by the specialists. It was an exciting time for me, mentally and physically stretching. One day in the village street of Letterfrack I saw Mike Gibbons sitting in his car wrestling with the big sheets of the 1898 six-inch OS map; he told me that he had heard that turf-cutting had begun in an area of previously untouched bog, and he was off to see if any archaeology had been unearthed. I immediately abandoned the rather tedious sketch-mapping of houses and shops I'd been engaged upon and joined him. We took the main road south-westward for about four miles and left the car in a turf-cutters' track leading off to the east, in the townland of Crocknaraw (Cnoc na Rátha, the hill of the rath—and we had already checked out the dilapidated little cashel-like enclosure from which it presumably derives its name). After a few hundred yards the track ended in a welter of mud and we turned to climb the small bog-covered hill ahead; I soon diverted to go and talk to some turf-cutters at work nearby, while Mike raced for the summit. Soon he came striding down to tell me that there were white stones up there. We went up together. A fresh turf bank had recently been opened, a trench running across the rounded top of the hill, some six feet wide and a few feet deep, cutting down through the bog-stuff to bedrock—and there, gleaming in its blackish depths, were two massive chunks of white quartz. One stood on end, to a height of about four feet, and the other, a little larger, was prostrate and still partly embedded in the peat. Evidently they had been set up before the bog began to form, and had probably been lost to sight for thousands of years.

Elated by the discovery we looked around us, seeing the countryside as it were through the stones' eyes. Two miles to the north-east at the head of Ballynakill Bay was Rosleague (in Irish, Ros Liag, standing-stone headland), where we already knew of a standing stone now hidden in recent forestry and a stone pair in a gorse-grown field. In Roscrea a little nearer in the same direction was a well-known standing stone, a thin slab of schist set on edge, while just over a mile to the north was Garraunbawn and its stone. How many such monuments would be visible from the one we were standing by were it not for trees and hedges?

About a mile to our south-west, out in the bog on the further side of the road, was a small drumlin; we ran across and panted up to its summit—and there, just showing through the well-grazed heather and grass, was what looked like the top of a block of white quartz, still entombed in peat. Later on that summer I went up to the top of yet another drumlin three-quarters of a mile to the south of this last, and found the edge of a horizontal slab of rock showing in the side of a new turf bank there, a yard or so below the bog surface, which could well have been a thin standing stone like that of Roscrea, fallen or overthrown during the period of bog growth.

The current reckoning is that, west of the Corrib, there are about eighteen single standing stones like that of Garraunbawn, ten stone pairs like that of Crocnaraw, and five rows of four or more stones, including the prominent 'Finn Macool's Fingers' on a drumlin summit near Tully Cross, and the six-stone row I found on the crest of a moraine in Gleninagh, a valley of the Twelve Pins. A large majority of these single and multiple standing stones are in the north-west of Connemara, roughly between Clifden and Renvyle, and it is now recognized that they amount to one of the richest concentrations of such monuments in Ireland. This area is deeply penetrated by narrow bays reaching to the foothills of the Twelve Pins, cut by the sea into the lowland of soft schists and marbles. These lime-rich rocks, together with the drifts of till raked out of the mountains by the glaciers of the last Ice Age and deposited here, make this the most inviting part of Connemara to settlers; it was so in the late Stone Age and is so today. None of these sites have been excavated or accurately dated, and it is only because of their similarity to datable monuments elsewhere that they are assigned to the Bronze Age; however, studies of the pollen grains preserved in lake sediments in the area point to an increase in clearance, cattle-raising and crop farming in the later Bronze Age, and so it is not unlikely that most of these stones were set up in that period.

As to their purpose, both of the stone rows mentioned above are aligned with dips in the horizon into which the sun appears to set on the shortest day of the year, and no doubt some ceremony was involved in the observation of this phenomenon, which would have been of great practical and spiritual significance. While the standing stones perched on hilltops and glacial ridges, like the two mountain-top cairns also known in this vicinity, may have marked important burials, indicated boundaries or been the focus of religious rituals, their siting primarily suggests the outward gaze from a lofty centre, the eye of dominance—first cousin, I am forced to admit, to the eye of acquisitive enquiry and competitive discovery with which Mike and I swept the landscape that day from the top of Crocnaraw. To me it looks as if the Bronze Age people or peoples took mental command of territory through their highly visible monuments, triangulating their claims as tightly as the ordnance surveyors of the imperialist nineteenth century. If so, there is a sorry connection between the will to power these monuments hint at and the exploitation and depletion of the soil that contributed to the beginning of the formation of bog in about 1200 BC—the slow black tide that would swallow up their sacred stones, not to be revealed again until our own exploitative, turf-cutting times.

But if the world was already old in worldliness in those ancient days, it was as provoked by mysteries as it is still. What did the Bronze Age farmer make of the numerous structures like chambers or tables made of massive slabs of rock, which stood in his fields or by his paths just as one finds them in people's gardens or behind roadside walls in today's Ballynakill? In the nineteenth century antiquarians regarded them as druids' altars, and one or two are marked so, in the evocative Gothic print reserved for ancient monuments, on old Ordnance Survey maps. For country folk such a structure was Leaba Dhiarmada is Gráinne, Diarmaid and Gráinne's Bed, and everyone knew how Diarmaid ran off with Fionn Mac Cumhaill's betrothed, Gráinne, and how the tragic couple were hunted all around Ireland by Fionn and his warrior band the Fianna, so that they never slept in the same place twice and built a new bed for themselves every night. That was a legend from Celtic times, the pre-Christian Iron Age, and what theories or stories the Bronze Age, a thousand or more years earlier, had to explain those monuments is of course unknown and unknowable. Unlike the Bronze Age monuments, they occur mainly in valley bottoms and by the seashore, and we now understand them to be Neolithic tombs dating from the earliest days of settled, agricultural society, around 4000 BC.

No fewer than thirty-two such tombs have been found in north-west Connemara, nineteen of them recent discoveries of Michael Gibbons. I visited most of them with the Galway Archaeological Survey team, who were sometimes accompanied by more senior visiting archaeologists such as the late Seán Ó Nualláin of the Ordnance Survey. I became fond of Seán, a plain-spoken, practical-looking and unacademic man, though my first contact with him had not been auspicious. When I was mapping the Burren in 1976, and lugging with me the weighty County Clare volume of the *Survey of the Megalithic Tombs of Ireland* co-authored by Seán and Professor Ruaidhrí de Valera, I found I had wasted two days crashing around in dense hazel and bramble scrub looking for tombs which according to the map references in this magisterial tome were in certain overgrown fields, whereas in fact they were in certain other overgrown fields nearby. I wrote to the OS about this, and received a polite acknowledgement from Seán, regretting the mistakes and thanking me for my contribution to the pursuit of truth. During the Connemara campaign, Seán told me that he had been a humble clerk in the Ordnance Survey and archaeology had not entered his head until one day he had been detailed to assist 'this professor fellow' Dr de Valera with his Megalithic Survey, and found himself travelling round the country visiting every known megalithic tomb in most eminent intellectual company. By degrees he became a collaborator in the work and, after the death of the professor, standard-bearer for the Megalithic Survey and the theoretical classification of tomb types it had developed.

This theory recognized four types of tomb, which in those days were known as court cairns, portal dolmens, wedge-shaped gallery graves and passage graves, and nowadays are more crisply referred to respectively as court tombs, portal tombs, wedge tombs and passage tombs. Newgrange is the supreme example of the last type, with its long passage leading into a burial vault deep within a huge cairn; so far nothing like it has been identified in Connemara, though one or two hilltop cairns might conceal smaller versions. The other sorts of tombs were also originally covered in mounds of clay and small stones, but have largely lost this covering through the centuries of weather, and their now exposed vaults look like more or less collapsed chambers made of boulders and slabs of rock. Court tombs are so called because at one end, usually to the east, of the cairn was a semicircular open area defined by upright set stones, giving access to a vault of one or more chambers. Portal tombs have two tall stones flanking the entrance to the vault, which is usually of one chamber and roofed by a sometimes enormous slanting stone propped on the portal stones and a lower backstone. Wedge tombs have a vault that is wider and higher at the front, invariably western, end. According to de Valera each type is associated with a characteristic range of grave goods and has a particular distribution within Ireland. Court, passage and portal tombs are largely confined to the northern half of Ireland and may represent successive cultural influences or population movements from northern Britain, while wedge tombs are found particularly in the south-west and were considered to have been introduced from Brittany, late in the Neolithic period. Connemara was peripheral to this overview of megalithic culture, the few known wedge tombs there being seen as conforming to 'rather small and poor types' constituting 'a poor coastal diffusion of no great significance.'

This fourfold theory did not suit the Young Turks of Connemara excited by the discovery of a number of tombs that the de Valera scheme would relegate to the mongrel or anomalous classes, but that included some impressive and fairly well-preserved monuments. Their own emerging opinion was that the Connemara tombs, in their simplicity, variety and apparently ecumenical intermingling, represented indigenous and early variations of the Neolithic burial-cult, rather than the work of various cultures at various times. The finds of monuments were being paralleled by those of the Galway palaeoecologists, whose studies of the fossil pollen record in the Ballynakill area had revealed the onset and flourishing of settlement and farming during a 200-year period centring on 4000 BC; Michael Gibbons and his colleagues held that the wedges and some small 'unclassified' tombs, as well as the court and portal tombs, were built during that early and vigorous phase of the Neolithic. So it was an argumentative occasion when Seán Ó Nualláin was conducted on a tour of the recent discoveries by the Galway team. In the absence of radiocarbon dates or of funds for proper archaeological digs, all depended on visual inspection, mental reconstruction and stylistic categorization of the tombs; in each case the present position of every stone had to be accounted for in terms of the original form of the tomb and its mode of collapse. Seán was particularly physical in this exercise of the imagination; to see him miming the manhandling of a leaning pillar of stone back into what he thought should be its rightful place was to see the tomb builders themselves at work. Whether he succeeded in propping up the fourfold theory, I am not so sure. The final outcome of the Survey, the *Archaeological Inventory of County Galway*, employs the standard categories, listing twelve court tombs, four portal tombs and six wedge tombs for Connemara, sharing out eleven question marks among these determinations and noting that in a number of instances 'the classification lines are blurred' and that others 'cannot be considered as classic examples of their category'; another nine tombs, most of them robbed beyond recall of their stones, are left unclassified. Connemara has shaken but not yet overthrown the fourfold dogma, I think.

But however vague their theoretical status, the cumulative psychic presence of the tombs in Ballynakill is massive. Some, like the court tomb near the shore west of Cleggan House, with its thick tortoise-backed roof stone, on stubby stone legs, or the unclassified tomb on the opposite shore of Cleggan Bay in Knockbrack, which has a rather narrow roof stone eight feet long delicately poised, as if about to take flight, on the points of its few remaining uprights, stand in open land but seem to disassociate themselves from their surroundings and yearn towards the western sea horizon. Others have to be sought out in fields and thickets; one probable portal tomb in Ballynew, by the road that leads towards the chapel of Ballynakill, crouches as if it were seeking shelter under a gorse-bush behind the roadside wall, and the casual passer-by would not know it is there—but step over the wall and down into the hollow of the field, and the dozy weight and resigned slant of its displaced roof stone leaning against the darkly cavernous chamber will make you remember its presence next time you go by. Those who brought these great stones together thought much about death; they perhaps debated as to whether entrance to the house of death should be from the east or the west, that is, how the cycle of life and death interlinks with those of the sun, stars and moon. These were collective burial places; none of the Ballynakill tombs have been excavated, but elsewhere similar tombs have been found to hold the cremated remains, or in some cases the disarticulated bones, of a number of persons. The grave goods interred with them—pottery, tools, ornaments— indicate a belief in an afterlife in which such things would continue to be goods. Only the great would be accommodated so grandly and at such expense of communal effort. What of the common people? Their traceless burial places must be all around us, in every ditch and field and the foundations of our houses. Thousands of years of impious robbery and mindless weather have undone the forethought for survival of even the rich and famous. The dark hollowness of the tomb under the roadside gorsebush says, 'There is nobody here, and you shall be nowhere too.'

Perhaps the Bronze-Agers saw things differently from their Stone Age ancestors and placed their trust in monuments to life rather than death. They practised unobtrusive single burials; a Ballynakill farmer has shown me a box made of stone slabs, big enough to hold a crouched body, which had been torn open by a JCB in the side bank of a newly dug roadway—a Bronze Age 'short cist.' In general their standing stones are not known to be associated with death. At least some of the alignments of several boulders, and perhaps of the stone pairs, point out the midwinter sunset, but this event marks the winning-through to the halfway mark in the survival of the season of shortage, a cause of celebration. The quartz stones, which seem to radiate light and call attention to themselves from afar, may have been as territorial as birdsong: 'We are triumphantly here; this hilltop and this lowland it oversees are ours.' And sometimes in the hush of midsummer half-light the glimmering stones of Ballynakill whisper to the imagination, 'You cannot see us, but we are still here.' Ghosts and fairies are moods and modes of one's feeling for the Earth; they wax and wane with our desires and delusions. The glimmer of white quartz, dim afterlife of its daytime brilliance, may persist throughout a long summer evening, but will succumb to the black rainy nights after Hallowe'en.

In a little field not far to the east of Cleggan is a small heap of boulders with a broken fragment of a limestone cross lying on it, together with a lump of white quartz and a roundish stone streaked with what looks like dried blood. Its story, as I have gathered it in bits and pieces from elderly men met on the road, is this: St Gregory came from Inis Meáin, one of the Aran Islands, to preach the Word to the pagans of Ballynakill, and they, unregenerate, cut off his head; the little monument is the place of execution, marked by the saint's blood. But St Gregory picked up his head, carried it to a nearby spring, washed it and put it back on, and then, before returning to Inis Meáin, he cursed the people of that locality, saying that they would 'grow up like the ferns and do no good,' which has in fact been the case ever since.

St Gregory is also known as St Ceannanach, which is said to be from Ceannfhionnach, fairheaded; at any rate it contains the element *ceann*, meaning a head. The stone on the monument is of a breccia formed in a volcano's neck, a geologist tells me; it is not native to Connemara, but it could have been brought from Mayo, by glacier in the Ice Age, or by more recent hand. It not only has reddish veins of jasper in it, but it is roughly the shape and size of a head, which suggests that the story of his blood remaining on this stone is a slight rationalization of a legend according to which the head itself was preserved here. The townland of Cleggan, which comprises the promontory forming the north side of Cleggan Bay, is also supposed to be named from this beheading, *cloigeann* meaning a skull or head. The townland name has spread from there to the village of Cleggan, a nineteenth-century growth, on the south side of the bay.

The story has a certain gruesome medieval charm, but of course, as an explanation of the placename of Cleggan, it is nonsense. Look across the bay from the village: the promontory itself, with its bare, rounded hill that seems to lie on a low and narrow shore, is clearly a *cloigeann*, a huge stony head, weighty, reposeful. Once in an art gallery I found myself alone with five or six of Brancusi's sculpted marble heads, each lying on its side in its own glass shrine. There was no ugly truncation of their necks; they were rounded off as naturally as eggs, complete and content in themselves—and how profoundly they slept! One could imagine their taking perhaps one breath in a year, and turning over, gently, so as not to wake themselves, once in a thousand years. Similarly the huge bulk of Cleggan Hill is weighed down under sleep and the force of gravity, not a dead but a living weight, its ear pressed to the Earth, lulled by her breathing, her heartbeat, her snoring.

Seen from the south, Cleggan Head, as the promontory is called, is a smooth whole, scantily furred with low heathy vegetation, rising in successive bald foreheads to a domed skyline. But on climbing over this central hill (a height of just under 500 feet) and picking one's way down the steep and stony slopes of its far side, and then across gentler boggy descents draining to the shoreline, one finds that the northern and more exposed side of the headland has been savaged by the sea and its bedrock of quartzite exposed in ragged cliffs, from which long, deep and narrow clefts like hatchet-wounds run inland. The upper third or more of the highest cliff's 120-foot face is of glacial till that looks as if it were hanging on precariously, puckering into little terraces as it sags slowly but inexorably to a fall, an avalanche that will bury the fulmars endlessly circling in the gulf below. It is a wild place, this northern coast of Cleggan Head, not often visited, a stage for the performance of elemental rites. One winter evening when I arrived at the brink of that high cliff a peregrine falcon rose from a fang of rock down in the tumultuous bay and flew far out to sea before beginning a huge slow circuit pivoting on me, first over water and then over land, as if it were on an invisible tether, and, having satisfied itself that I was neither prey nor predator, settled to its rock again. A steady blast off the illimitable sea-spaces to the north was funnelling up the cliffs as I roved westwards and was brought to a stop by the sight of a hillside covered in tufts of deer-grass all bent double, combed and rippled by the wind so that they looked like thousands of glossy-furred little animals streaming up the slope.

There are four notable human structures on or around this hill. In order of antiquity they are: a megalithic tomb of massive slabs of rock, in a rushy pasture and just above the splash-zone of the southern shore; a holy well dedicated to the Seven Daughters, surrounded by a low squarish drystone wall just above the shingle bank of a little bay at the foot of the north-west flank of the hill; a ruined signal tower on the hilltop, built during the Napoleonic invasion scare to watch over the sea approaches; and Cleggan House itself, a Victorian gentleman's residence, with ample outhouses, steward's house and tree-lined avenue, set in a well-tended demesne that rises from the southern shore just east of the megalithic tomb. The shaggy grass and heather slopes of the hill itself look untouched by culture, but in fact have been created and maintained by human influence from the time of the megalith in the New Stone Age 5,000 years ago, through that of the holy well, which one could associate with Connemara's early Christian masters the Conmaicne Mara or their medieval successors the O'Flahertys, then the pre-Famine years that saw the building of the signal tower, and so down to the present, the lives and labours of the current landowners, the Musgraves of Cleggan House. The Musgraves' farm, with just under 500 acres of rough grazing on Cleggan Hill and shared use of a similar area of commonage east of it, plus about fifty acres of meadow, carries twenty or so suckler cows, fifteen Connemara ponies, and an average of 500 hardy little black-faced Connemara sheep, which produce about the same number of lambs for sale each year. And now the farm is one of the loci of a trans-European study of the potentialities and problematic future of landscapes shaped by low-intensity grazing, their associated ecologies and economics. But before going into that, I must set the local social scene.

It was only after the Famine that Connemara functionally became part of the British Empire, and even then the Empire was selective as to which parts of Connemara it took on, favouring the relatively fertile and welcoming landscape of Ballynakill as against the harsh granitic terrain of the south. Frederick Twining from

London, backed by the fortunes of the Twining tea-importing business (and billeted here by his family 'as he was not particularly steady,' said contemporary gossip), was one of the earliest of the new breed of settlers. He bought nearly 900 acres on Cleggan Head from the Law Life Assurance Society, mortgagees of the bankrupt Martin estate, and built himself a good-sized house. At that time the locality was swarming with squatters who had lost their little holdings in the Famine; according to one sarcastic reporter, 'The residue of the Occupiers now live almost in common, except as to the cultivation and cropping of the potato patches, and thieving is understood to eke out materially their security.' Twining tried to conciliate his poor neighbours, but when they 'became too familiar with his flocks' he shut himself up in disgust and 'had some trouble in persuading them that he was not a Communist.'

But Frederick, with the aid of house servants and coachmen and builders brought in from London, was constructing his own little empire, centred on a model farm and a well-connected family. He and his wife Elizabeth begat ten children, of whom two boys and a girl died young; of the rest, two boys emigrated to New Zealand and the five girls inherited various portions of the estate and its buildings. By their marriages three of these girls were to knit the gentry of Ballynakill into a mutually supportive 'neighbourhood,' in the Jane Austenish sense of the term, which to a surprising degree is still to the good today. The eldest sister, Charlotte, married into the Brownes, who had been granted Rosleague, south of Letterfrack, in the post-Cromwellian settlements and had a Georgian mansion there; her daughter Mary Browne did not marry but was responsible for the education of two girls of other Ascendancy families. Blanche, the youngest of Charlotte's sisters, married a William Bailey of Malaya, rubber-planter, and after his death retired to live in the steward's house at Cleggan. The main house and the bulk of the estate were inherited by Julia, the second-youngest of the sisters, who married a Dr Henry Holberton and retired to Cleggan at the end of his career in England. Soon after their arrival in the fraught year of 1921 they were driven out by threats from the local Republicans, who commandeered the house, but after the war the Holbertons returned to

Cleggan. Of their sons, one worked in forestry in Burma, another as a rubber-planter in Malaya, one was in the Navy and another was an army man. The last of these, Athelstan Leslie, reassembled the estate by buying out the relatives who had inherited parts of it. His daughter, Evelyn, became a doctor, and married another doctor, John Musgrave; their son, Hugh, is the present owner of Cleggan House and farm.

The pedigree of Hugh's wife, Nicola, brings several more land-owning families of Ballynakill into the equation. The Armstrongs had been in Clifden since shortly before the Famine. A youngest son of the family, William, had married a Kate Lushington and spent some years ranching in Buffalo, Wyoming, in the wildest days of the West. Kate inherited her aunt's fortune, on condition she take her name, Tulloch; so, for good measure, the couple became by royal licence the Armstrong-Lushington-Tullochs. In 1890 they sold up in America and bought Shanboolard Hall, just two miles to the east of Cleggan House, and later added Thomas Prior's estate and house at nearby Ross on Ballynakill Bay to their holdings. Kate became a respected horse-breeder and an improver of the estate. Her eldest son joined the Connaught Rangers and died in action at Neuve Chapelle, and another, Kinmont Willie, married George Doris, the land agent Henry Robinson's daughter and sister to Olive, chatelaine of Letterdyfe House near Roundstone. After a spell of tea-planting in Ceylon they returned to Shanboolard; their son Graham took over the estate, and their daughter Ann married into the Quaker milling family, the Goodbodys; Ann's daughter is Nicola Musgrave. That, in summary and with many cross-ties of cousinship and property transfers omitted, is the Book of Numbers of Ballynakill.

Two recurrent features in this, the Great Intertwining of Ballynakill's gentry from generation to generation, are the eager return to Connemara after fortunes made or lost elsewhere, and a devotion to estate management. Hugh—a slight, elegant and studious-looking man, who struggles gamely with a progressive eye disease—and Nicola—warm and hospitable, of a keen practical intelligence—are well aware what a treasure they possess in their land, which they generously keep open to ramblers despite occasional problems with the inconsiderate. Old photos show that their beloved house is structurally unchanged except that it has shed a Victorian facial growth of ivy and is now clean-shaven. Visitors are greeted first by the cawing of dozens of crows nesting in the sycamore trees of the avenue, and then by little dogs that jump out from the open doors of a Land Rover parked on the crunchy gravel sweep before the front door. At the rear of the house, with its sun-trapping glazed extension and wide outlook over the bay to Cleggan village and the hills beyond, are a geometrical pond set in a lawn and a shrubbery path curving down to the rocks of the foreshore. The barns and byres, of cut stone and slate, are in orderly array on the other, northern, side of the avenue, which continues to the west as a farm track, at first between meadows where cows ruminate and then over heathery sheep-land around the base of the hill, and delivers one to the sandy beach and shingle bank of the little bay called, simply, Port, where stands the holy well. Further west the headland rises into a lesser hill of unfenced rough grazing, also belonging to the Musgrave estate, and then shelves into the Atlantic, with a small automatic lighthouse perched on its last bare rocks.

I can imagine what it would be to love and to work this spacious but not overwhelming terrain, with its harmonious relationship to the house. But on the February day I last visited it, looking at the monotonous greyish vegetation gappily carpeting the hill, and the muddy cattle-trodden margins of the track, I could also imagine despairing of making a living out of it. However, the German ecologist I had gone there to meet, at the Musgraves' invitation, soon showed me that this was a rewarding territory for free-ranging grazing animals because of its variety. Here was a slope of young ling or *Calluna* ready to put forth tender shoots, draining through a gully feathery with *Molinia* or purple moor-grass, into a hollow full of sphagnum moss, bog-cotton and bog-rush; above it was a rocky steep with leggy old ling and a spreading stand of bracken; to the west was the wet hillside of deer-grass—actually a sedge, *Trichophorum cespitosum*—that I'd seen running with the wind, and a drier hillside of bell heather with St Dabeoc's heath growing up through it. Even the trodden mud was of importance, he explained: it afforded space on which seeds could settle and sprout, and light for the little rosette plants such as sundews and butterworts. The bracken could be controlled by increasing the number of horses and cattle, said my guide, but small patches on steep slopes should be left to provide snug niches for ewes and their lambs. The old ling was too woody to be grazed, but it afforded cover for grouse and golden plover and other birds that fed on the young ling shoots; most but not all of the old stuff should be burned off, leaving a patchy distribution of old and young. I was surprised to hear him talk so positively about burning, until he discriminated between the small, well-watched winter fires that on a cold dry day will lick through the heather so fast they don't even kill the beetles in the ground, and the uncontrolled summer fires that all too often rage across the bogs for a day or more, incinerating all life-forms. Some of these fires are lit with malicious intent, others are sparked by sunlight focused by discarded bottles, or by inexperienced farmers. (Hugh confesses that in his young days he put a match to some invasive gorse alongside the track, and in no time at all the hillside above was ablaze and he had to call in the neighbours to help beat it out with spades—dangerous work, when choking hot smoke could swirl around with a changing wind and surround one in an instant.) Proper and responsible burning demands planning and vigilance; the ecologist pointed out a quarter-acre of old heather that could be burned off safely, being surrounded by wet bog and areas of new and less inflammable heather.

Hill farming, clearly, was more than just putting a few sheep on the 'mountain,' as all rough land is called in Connemara, and although traditional knowledge of its strategies was dying out as old farmers retired and their offspring took up less laborious ways of life, there was still enough of it extant to be worth collecting and coordinating with scientific observation. The sheep mentality, for instance, was to be cooperated with, not struggled against. Sheep prefer to stay close to where they were born or first put onto the land; they learn every detail of the terrain and explore its amenities such as wallowing places and hidey-holes for resting up in, and their lambs acquire this flock wisdom at their mothers' heels. If they are moved to a neighbouring area cut off from the first by a fence, they will probe that fence until they break through it, or run up and down along it, reducing a strip of land to bare mud. At night they will congregate in high places, and may cause erosion there, but if the bare patches of peat are not too extensive they give heathers and grasses room to regenerate. Again, sheep will not eat the tough stems of deer-grass, but if there are cattle to bite off the tussocks then the sheep can get at the succulent roots in which the plant stores its winter nutriments. At every time of year there is pasturage on the 'mountain' for varying numbers of grazing animals: bog-cotton is eaten in early spring, and heather too if other food is scarce; by May the purple moor-grass is in season, and by August so is the ling, and lasts through the autumn; bog-rush and deer-grass, both called winter sedge locally, help bridge the midwinter deficit of fodder; nevertheless, to avoid trampling of the wet hillsides, stock should be moved to lowland meadows for a while.

Such was the mountain wisdom my guide had learned by talking to the farmers, and it is undocumented in modern textbooks. Its underlying theme is 'biodiversity,' the rude health of a complex ecosystem, and my ecologist was monitoring not just the welfare of the farm herbivores but of birds, beetles, spiders, etc. The previous spring and summer he had had lines of beetle-traps— plastic cups holding a bit of vinegar—set into the ground in nineteen different terrains, from the sand dunes of Omey Island to the squelchiest bogs of Cleggan Head, to trap ground-beetles, of which the number of different species, and the numbers of individuals of each species, are a delicate measure of biodiversity. He was particularly interested in a handsome inch-long predatory beetle with rows of golden dimples on its blackish wing cases, called *Carabus clathratus*, of which a western form is officially the special responsibility of Ireland, as it is now only to be found there and in north-west Scotland. It was flourishing on the lightly grazed wet heath and slightly eroded blanket bog of Cleggan Head but absent from areas of heavy erosion, old woody heather or rank *Molinia*, and what my mentor oddly but aptly called the 'squeezing' bogs, the waterlogged sphagnum-covered morasses. Thus a certain level of grazing, trampling and general patchiness is optimal for the beetle, and by implication for life in general. Overgrazing leads to erosion, undergrazing to invasion by bracken or rushes, and both to loss of pasturage; striking the right balance is a delicate matter.

All this detailed attention to the thought processes of sheep and the habitat preferences of beetles was obviously part of a wider discourse, in fact of a philosophy of the land, which I later read up in various reports on Cleggan Head and comparable terrains elsewhere. My wise man of the 'mountain' was Professor Giselher Kaule of the Institute for Landscape Planning and Ecology, in the University of Stuttgart, and his work in Connemara is one facet of a study of 'landscape development, biodiversity and co-operative livestock systems in Europe,' or lacope for short, covering seven regions in which extensive pasturage is still practised, from the North Cape of Norway to Gibraltar and from the Tatra Mountains to western Connemara. His concern is not just with the productivity of hill farms but with the conservation of open landscapes and the viability of rural communities, and, given the current flight from the farms and villages of Connemara, the loss to rushes or to gorse of thousands of its fields, the destructive exploitation of commonage and now its threatened abandonment, it is time we had a more intelligent and informed dialogue on the symbiosis between people, stock, wildlife and the land. The 'hypothesis' of lacope is that beautiful and productive open landscapes have evolved hand in hand with pasturing systems deriving from the grazing patterns of wild herds, and that self-organized grazing produces a mosaic of habitats on all scales, from the hillside over which sheep can pursue their daily migrations to the mud-patch the beetle can scuttle across; a proper husbandry system including improved grassland as well as large unfenced areas of rough grazing would maintain biodiversity and landscape quality. Over half of the vegetation of lowland Connemara depends for its flourishing on grazing and the mowing of meadows; nearly a third, including many endangered species, depends on the extensive grazing of unimproved land and will disappear if hill farming dies out. But hill farming in such areas of low natural productivity as Connemara cannot compete in today's global market—Hugh tells me that ewes are selling for €5 at Maam Cross these days—and social engineering is required, in the way of fair prices to the farmer and the encouragement of shared use of the land by farming and the tourist industry. At present farming and tourism are at loggerheads over the question of public access to open countryside, and practices such as the fencing and subdivision of commonage are inimical to both interests. Similarly, there are many points of conflict between the farming organizations and the state-appointed guardians of the natural heritage; official interventions such as the Rural Environment Protection Scheme and the designation of Special Areas of Conservation are overly bureaucratic and do not rest on a holistic understanding of countryside life, a vision of how shared landscapes, tended by the local population, could offer recreation to the urban visitor, stability to local economies, and refuges of biodiversity in a shrinking world. In fact official policies are often contrary and obstructive, and although there are some progressive thinkers in the bureaucracy, as Giselher Kaule puts it, 'There are too many fences in the mind.'

The remains, ravaged and truncated as they are, of open pastured landscapes here and there in Europe, are, according to Giselher, a model for the regeneration and sustainable development of the countryside, in the interests not only of humans but of all creatures. And there may be deeper reasons to cherish these most ancient habitats of humanity. *Heimatgefühl*, the sense of a homeland, is the term Giselher uses for the feeling induced in us by semi-natural landscapes that are at once open to the hugeness of the sky and rich in their detailed accommodation to human purposes. They evoke a nostalgia of the genes for the great savannahs in which the human species was born, while a good half of our culture fondly recalls the nomadic and pastoralist setting of revealed religion: Abraham was 'very rich in cattle,' Christ was the Good Shepherd, and more recently Man has become the Shepherd of Being. In more intimate and less patriarchal terms, these landscapes are the epitome of what I have called the Echosphere, the zone in which a balance is maintained between culture and the wild, so that, through daily frequentation and the communal memory of placelore, nature answers to the human voice. Ireland still holds such areas; Ballynakill, with its subtle gradations of scale from the bare mountainside and mountain-reflecting lake to the stone-walled meadow holding a ditch full of meadowsweet and a 5,000-year-old tomb, is among the most appealing. But preserving them is a tightrope-walking task, as Giselher's work shows in detail; it calls for attentive listening to the breathing of the Earth. He hopes to bring together local farmers and representatives of the conservationist movement, including the personnel of the National Park, to discuss the future of the land in terms of the co-development of community and its habitat. Previous attempts to do this have failed, but Giselher Kaule is a remarkable personality, with the academic standing to compel the attention of officialdom and the modesty and tact to win over the alienated Connemara land-user, and in the Musgraves he has found generous and open-minded supporters. It is a tiny initiative in terms of the world crisis of population growth and resource depletion, but 'somewhere and at some time, a beginning must be made . . .'

However, there is one monstrous contradiction at the heart of this caring programme, and that is the slaughter of the innocents, exemplified by those 500 Cleggan lambs torn from their mothers, packed into lorries and taken off to an abattoir every spring. (I am complicit in this, since I sometimes eat meat—not often, but not never.) Is there no way back to Arcadia without leaving blood on the stones of Cleggan Head? On the contrary, it may be that only by abjuring its carnivorous ways can humanity come into equitable balance, morally and practically, with our cohabitants on earth. The peregrine falcon and *Carabus clathratus* have no choice in this matter, but we omnivores do.

Fate

On the south side of Cleggan Bay are a number of small rounded hills of a hundred feet or so in height that lie together like a clutch of eggs, their longer axes aligned east-north-east, parallel to the shoreline. They are difficult to count as their smooth forms tend to blend, but a geological study distinguishes eleven of them. A few of them have been eaten into by the sea and so are cross-sectioned by cliffs from ten to forty feet high, and here one can see that they are composed of clay studded with rounded boulders; hence, perhaps, the name of one of them, Knockbrack or Cnoc Breac, speckled hill, which is conspicuous when seen from a boat heading out of the bay.

The glacier that crept out of the mountains, excavating the long valley that now holds Ballynakill Lake and Cleggan Bay itself, deposited some of its scrapings here and moulded them into these drumlins, as such hills of glacial till of boulder clay are called. I believe the mechanism of this moulding is not well understood, but it must have been a wave process like the formation of sand dunes or of sand ripples on a beach. In a broad belt across Ireland from Fermanagh through Leitrim to Down thousands of close-packed drumlins interspersed with boggy or lake-filled hollows constitute a landform of national historical agency that has opposed the march of armies and sheltered rebel bands. In Connemara the drumlins occur in a few swarms near the coast—at Renvyle, at Tully (An Tulaigh, the hill), here by Cleggan Bay, on the peninsulas west of Clifden, and near Ballyconneely; there are also some isolated ones like beached whales out on the brown levels of bog south of the Twelve Pins. It is because they are such a well-developed phenomenon of the Irish landscape that the Hiberno-English word 'drumlin' (from *droimnín*, little back) has been adopted by geographers internationally. In Connemara, however, the usual term is *imleach*; hence the townland of Emlagh, occupied by the westernmost of the Cleggan swarm. In comparison to the sour boglands underlaid by harsh metamorphic rocks the drumlins offer fertile pasturage; characteristically an *imleach* is divided into good big fields by a wall along its spine and a small number of walls down either flank.

The glacier having provided both a deep bay and fertile land beside it, a village naturally came into existence, and took its name from the relatively huge hill of Cleggan Head to the north on the opposite side of the bay. In the early nineteenth century this might have been a reasonably prosperous community, balanced between good farmland and the bounteous shoals of herring and mackerel that visited the bay periodically and the well-established basking shark fishery off Inishbofin, had not the institutionalized extortions of landlordism worn it down into generational poverty. This area was part of the neglected estate of the Martins of Ballynahinch, and, as the Blakes of Renvyle remarked in one of their letters in 1825, it was vessels from Scotland and the north-east of Ireland that profited from the fishery, the natives of 'the large straggling village' of Cleggan being too badly equipped to do so.

> It was only last season, that the benefit of an immense shoal of herrings arriving unexpectedly after a lapse of some years, was almost lost to them by the very dilapidated state of their boats and tackling . . . This spot, instead of presenting the pleasing picture of legitimate employment, and prosperous industry, is the scene of smuggling and illicit distillation, bearing all the outward marks of that poverty and wretchedness which is so generally the lot of the poor underlings in the traffic. The *seigneur du village*, a middle-man, is himself one of the most active and persevering agents in both branches.

All the same, by that date a proper harbour was in building in the townland of Cnoc Breac, under a famine-relief scheme of public works funded by the charitable Mansion House Committee. Alexander Nimmo, engineer to the Western District, had chosen its site and designed it in 1822, as he reported four years later:

After examining the shore of the whole bay, I adopted a small bight on the south side, where a cut might be made into a little bog hollow, so as to form an inner dock out of the swell, the entrance to which might be covered by a small pier. This work, and several of the neighbouring piers, I placed under the management of Mr. Alexander Hay, a young architect of talent and good character, though not of great experience in such works, which indeed it was then difficult to obtain. His excavation and pier progressed with tolerable success, until a heavy gale in October, with an unusually high tide, filled part of the entrance with gravel, and damaged part of the pier. I then sent one or two workmen of more experience, to make up the pier in the most substantial way the case admitted; but the grant for that pier was now exhausted, and the work had accordingly to be suspended until additional funds could be obtained. This was only agreed in January 1824, when I found the storms of that winter were likely to destroy all that had been done, unless immediate steps were taken to put it out of danger; Cleggan pier being particularly exposed. I therefore deemed it necessary to employ a person of skill and experience on this service, and sent for Mr. Alexander M'Gill from Dunmore, who having been for twenty years constantly and successfully employed in that kind of work, was one on whose judgement I could rely . . . To his skill and exertion it is owing that these works have been preserved.

Cleggan is now a stout pier of two hundred feet long . . . rough but substantial work, and had stood the gales of two winters without injury . . . It affords a very convenient landing-place to the boats of Bofin and the western fishery, and having an excellent road from there to Clifden, is very much frequented. The adjoining farm being in lease, buildings have not yet been undertaken at this place, but there is little doubt of its becoming a thriving village.

Nimmo was too optimistic in this, as appears from an enquiry into the fishing industry held in 1836:

All the male inhabitants of Claggan [*sic*] are more or less fishermen. They are destitute of every convenience; they live in the most wretched hovels that can be described; they are yearly tenants, generally holding land under freeholders, who are themselves miserably poor. The condition of the fishermen is so wretched, that any change must benefit them. The aged are supported by their neighbours, and the widows by begging.

And shortly after that, Cleggan, like all the rest, fell into the common pit of the Great Famine. The Martins were swept away, and their cold-blooded mortgagees the Law Life Assurance Society, after many evictions, sold most of the estate to the Berridges, but parted with outlying scraps of it around Cleggan to minor landlords who have not left much trace in local history and were eventually bought out by the Land Commission: thus a retired Catholic clergyman, the Revd Anthony Magee, who lived near Streamstown, had Knockbrack; and the neighbouring townlands of Moorneen, Rossadillisk and Emlagh belonged to a supporter of the Irish Church Mission Society, Sir Christopher Lighton, Bt., who, although an absentee, was reported by a *London Times* correspondent to be an 'improving landlord,' taking care of fencing and charging moderate rents (even if some of his tenants were 'still obstinately slovenly').

In 1900 there were about eighteen sailing craft and forty-eight rowing boats working out of Cleggan Bay, and the fishery employed 480 people. Fish from Cleggan could be in Billingsgate Market the morning after it was landed, thanks to the rail link from Clifden. The Congested Districts Board had the pier extended in 1908, when the herring and mackerel fishery was at its peak, and introduced a new type of boat from the Isle of Man, the nobby, which was typically about forty-five feet in length, with two masts and a pointed stern. But, with a rise in freight charges to the UK, competition from steam drifters and season after season of poor catches, by 1919 the nobbies were rotting skeletons and the fishermen had reverted to their big rowboats and to the small type of hooker known as the *púcán*. Lobster fishing became more important with the establishment of a Breton exporting firm in Aughrus, the promontory two miles to the west, in the 1920s. In general, then, the 'straggling village' scattered throughout these townlands suffered the same story of penury, survival, development and setback as the rest of coastal Connemara, and did not catch the eye of any peculiar fate until 1927—but I will return to the Cleggan Disaster shortly.

Nowadays there is a distinctive little settlement tightly bunched around the harbour, which itself has been improved and enlarged over the years. There is a tall white ice-plant like a gigantic old refrigerator, a gaggle of lobster boats, and the usual heaps of lobster pots, nets and rusty tangles of gear, incomprehensible to non-fishermen, on the quays. The daily mailboat service to Inishbofin, inaugurated in the 1930s, has grown into a chief part of the village's economy; there are several sailings a day in summer, and therefore groups of tourists investigating the four pubs and the seafood restaurants or filling in time in the coffee bars and postcard shops, while every available space becomes a carpark. There are also a national school, a post office, and an apartment block made out of the former coast-guard station. To see what has become of the rest of the 'straggling village' one can turn up the lane by the Pier Bar, passing a house that Richard Murphy built himself out of pink granite stones from the ruined cottages of Aughrus. From the top of the hill, Cnoc Breac itself, one can survey the treeless drumlin-land, its smooth green swellings dotted with white buildings: farms, B&Bs, holiday homes; it looks a cheerful and companionable neighbourhood in summer, but lonely in winter when the holiday homes are empty, and bleakly exposed to the winds off the ocean. The way now leads down to the fine crescent beach of Sellerna Bay; the name is from *sailearnach*, a sally garden, that is, a plot in which willow rods were grown for making baskets and lobster pots. In a meadow by the near end of the beach is a magnificent tomb that I mentioned in connection with the Neolithic landscape of north-west Connemara, with a long capstone, craggy but serenely poised; presumably it is the burial place of ancient nobility. In extreme contrast, by the far end of the beach is a not-so-long disused burial ground for unbaptized children, a humble scattering of small set boulders in a rough field, with just one more noticeable stone of white quartz, which I am told was brought there from a nearby house to mark the grave of twins. White stones are to be found in several graveyards of Connemara, such as St Colmán's in Inishbofin and at Kill near Clifden, and even in prehistory seem to have been associated with death; conversely it was thought unlucky to use a white stone as ballast in a boat.

There is a little stream to be crossed here, forming the boundary of Rossadillisk, the nearer part of which is called Cloghacorra, probably from *clocha chora*, stepping stones. Sellerna House, the most substantial house in Cloghacorra, was the home of a Samuel Freyer, of an English family, who farmed over 200 acres in the vicinity and whose son Peter had a remarkable medical career. Sir Peter Freyer, as he became, was born here in 1851, studied at Queen's College in Galway and then at Dr Steevens's Hospital in Dublin. He gained first place in the exam for the India Service, rose to the rank of Lieutenant Colonel and became surgeon to a hospital in Benares, where he practised a recently devised treatment for gallstones. (I have been told by one of his descendants that he operated successfully on a rajah, who rewarded him with the storybook 'lakh of rupees'; when the Army tried to claim the money he resigned, and used it to set himself up in Harley Street.) His speciality was urology, and as surgeon to St Peter's Hospital for the Stone, in London, he originated an operation for the relief of urine retention by removal of the prostate gland. During the First World War he rejoined the India Service but was appointed consulting surgeon to the Queen Alexandra military hospital in London, and finally retired with the rank of Colonel and a KCB. He died in 1921 having devoted his life to the cure of humdrum but anguishing complaints, and is buried in the Protestant graveyard in Clifden, Cleggan's worthy knight of the scalpel.

Rossadillisk is in Irish Ros an Duilisc, promontory of the dulse, an edible seaweed that grows on rocks exposed near low water; no doubt the inhabitants of this townland, which lies between the open sea to the north-east and a marvellously complex inlet of sandy shallows and mudflats to the west, were very familiar with its sweet and salty chewiness. The Ordnance Survey six-inch map of 1898 shows a settlement of about thirty houses on the north-east side of the promontory, most of them close together along the shoreline of a little bay called Trá Bhríde, Bridget's strand. When I made my own map a hundred years later there were nine houses in all, just two of them by Trá Bhríde. Looking at the slumped stonework of ruins in the dank rush-infested pastures and bramble thickets by the path along the shore, from which a few gable ends rise infirmly and crooked window-spaces peer out to sea, one senses some irreparable woe. And indeed the little village of Trá Bhríde was widowed by the Cleggan Disaster of 1927. This is how it came about.

The fickle herring shoals had returned to seas within range of the Cleggan men's big wooden rowboats and *púcáin* by that date. On 28 October, in an evening of flat calm and light rain, four boats from Ros an Duilisc were shooting their drift nets for mackerel within sight of the crew members' homes. No doubt the drizzle they were grumbling about was the effect of an incoming front; but they were not to know that beyond the horizon, out in the Atlantic, a vortex of wind was spinning towards them. It would have originated in the Caribbean as a depression, a rising column of air warmed by the tropical sea, sucking in more air to its base from surrounding areas of higher pressure. The mysterious Coriolis force, an effect of the earth's rotation, twisted these winds and the clouds they bore into a cyclone, the sort of galactic whirl so familiar to us from weather reports and which of course no human being had seen as a whole until our own times. The weather system of the North Atlantic is a chaotic regime in the sense that, while it is entirely determined by the laws of physics, a small fluctuation can have huge and incalculable consequences. Back near its origins, a cloud shadow here, a puff of breeze there, and the cyclone would have developed differently, arced across the globe a degree or two to the north or south, or would have faded out entirely. But things were exactly as they were.

That evening Dr Holberton of Cleggan Farm, now retired and living in a cottage on the estate, happened to pick up a storm warning on his homemade wireless system, and sent a horseman galloping round the bay, who reached Ros an Duilisc just too late to stop the boats going out. Some of the villagers were reciting the rosary in the parish church, the Star of the Sea, in Claddaghduff, when the storm struck suddenly, tearing slates off the roof, darkening the sky, flinging the door open and blowing out the candles. People looked round and, seeing young Michael Laffey from Ros an Duilisc standing inside the door, gestured at him to close it. When he didn't move, a girl got up to do it, saying to him, 'Isn't it a wonder you didn't close the door?' but he didn't reply. And why was he wearing his fisherman's oilskins, and why was he dripping wet? But it can't have been him because by then Michael Laffey was drowned or drowning, along with the boat-owner John Cloonan and the four others in his crew, on Black Rock, only a couple of hundred yards from the safety of the beach they had been making for at the head of Cleggan Bay. Meanwhile two other boats from Ros an Duilisc were smashed on the rocks of Cleggan Head, and the two crews, each of five men, all lost. Festy Feeney of Ros an Duilisc managed to save himself and his crew, keeping his boat afloat until a freak wave threw it onto Sellerna beach. (Festy's granddaughter Mary Feeney recently wrote a detailed book on the disaster, from which I have most of these facts.) The total of the drowned from Ros an Duilisc was sixteen.

Two boats from Inishbofin were wrecked too, with the loss of nine lives, and nineteen men in boats from Inishkea and Lacken Bay, further north in Mayo, were also drowned. Pat Concannon and his Inishbofin crew famously survived; accounts of their experiences differ widely, but it was Pat's own version that became the basis of Richard Murphy's famous poem on the Cleggan Disaster. Instead of cutting their nets loose as other boats did when the storm burst, Pat held on to them by a rope all night so that the ebbtide dragged them out from the shore of Inishbofin, and he kept the men rowing to hold the boat's head to the wind. When the tide turned at two in the morning they were near a rock called Codú, two miles west of Ros an Duilisc, where they cut away the nets and began to row, backwards, bows to the wind. Eight hours after the beginning of the storm they reached Cleggan pier, their hands torn and swollen from the oars, and Pat himself temporarily blinded by salt spray.

The next day a dreadful fishery of corpses began. John Cloonan's was the first to be found, half buried in the sand at the head of Cleggan Bay; Michael Laffey and the rest of that crew were never found. The following day an old man went looking for his son, saw a hand sticking up out of the water, pulled in the body and found that it was that of another man. On the following Sunday four coffins were carried from the Star of the Sea church across the sands to the graveyard in Omey Island, and another was taken out to Inishbofin on a patrol boat. A week later another Ros an Duilisc victim's body came ashore on Cleggan beach, and after a further ten days, a second. A month after the storm a man gathering seaweed on a little island, Inis Brúin, off the point of Renvyle, found another Ros an Duilisc body, that of John Murray, who left a wife and seven children.

Newspaper correspondents arrived soon after the event, and wrote with horror of the dreadful hovels of Ros an Duilisc, pity for the distraught widows and orphans, and anger at the state of the boats in which the menfolk had to risk their lives every day. President Cosgrave appealed for subscriptions to a relief fund, and over the next few months £36,719 came in, and a hierarchy of national and local committees was set up to administer it. The Honorary Secretary of this West Coast Disaster Relief Fund visited Ros an Duilisc in December, and found that so far £20 had been granted to each bereaved family irrespective of their loss, and that this aid was in the form of orders on local shopkeepers to provide value in kind; in many cases it had merely paid off part of what the families already owed to the shopkeepers. Another inspection in the following January found that matters had not progressed, and the officer of the fund brought back with him the cheque he had been given to cover the commitments of the local committee, who, he reported, had proved hard to reconcile to the fact that no further allocations could be made without the sanction of the General Committee and due inspection of bills. A schedule was drawn up for the payment of pensions and allowances, but in January 1930 the drowned fishermen's dependants wrote to the National Committee demanding 'a general distribution of that enormous fund to be made before February 7th, 1930,' which understandably did not take place. Instead the money went into general and long-overdue improvements of equipment and services that should have been funded by the state. Fifteen fully equipped small boats were supplied to the dependants of victims, and nine to other fishermen who had lost their boats. There were suggestions that the Department of Fisheries should provide larger boats, but the Minister of Fisheries was of the opinion that they could not be kept with safety in the little harbours of the West, and, if used only intermittently, would soon fall into disrepair; in short that nothing should be done without further trials. In fact six motor vessels for herring fishing were sent to Cleggan in 1928,with Donegal crews to instruct the local men, but failed to locate any herring. A smaller motorized lobster boat proved equally disappointing in the following year. Consequently the Fisheries Department was unable to recommend the Disaster Committee to fund motorized boats. However a medium-sized motorboat was commissioned in 1931 to provide a daily service to Inishbofin, carrying passengers and freight, delivering the mail three times a week and, over subsequent decades, with the increase in tourism, binding the two poverty-stricken communities ever closer together.

There were also some ameliorations of farming and home life. The Lady Dudley nursing scheme received a grant for the provision of district nurses in the affected areas. Soon after the disaster Monsignor McAlpine of Clifden and others had called for the available grasslands in the vicinity to be bought out by the Land Commission and divided between the landless fishermen's families, to lift them out of perpetual poverty; three years later three families were moved into new houses on lands acquired from the Freyer estate, and others had extra land from the Lighton estate in Ros an Duilisc allotted to them.

But if the Cleggan Disaster was a stage in the irregular and backsliding development of the port of Cleggan into the ramshackle little hub of activity it is today, Ros an Duilisc never recovered. Emigration has sucked the remaining life out of the hamlet by Trá Bhríde. Perhaps the sea, just one low stone wall and a few yards of foreshore away from their windows, was too immediate a presence for the bereft and orphaned, as insufferable as a neighbour eternally perturbed by a bad conscience. For it was believed that the sea will never be at rest until it has given up all its drowned.

Refloating Inishbofin

The foundation myth of Inishbofin may seem ancient foolish-ness, unfounded in reality, but it is well and wisely founded in the unfoundedness of reality itself.

Ages ago there was an island that floated to and fro hidden in mist. Some fogbound fishermen came across it one day, landed and lit a fire, or, some say, shook the ash out of a pipe onto it. As soon as the island was touched by fire—by technology, that is; by a wild element tamed by humanity—it became fixed. The mist cleared, and the fishermen found themselves on a shingle bank between the sea and a lake. They saw an old woman driving a white cow down to the water; she struck it, and it became a rock. One of the fishermen ran to strike the hag, and both she and he turned into rocks too. The cow has occasionally been seen since then, its appearances foretelling some disaster. Hence Inis Bó Finne, the island of the white cow.

That is what John O'Donovan was told in 1839, during his topographical work for the Ordnance Survey of Ireland, that great mission of fixing and naming. A similar legend of the disenchantment of Inishbofin was recorded in the same year by Caesar Otway, a traveller in the West. Otway was rather given to picturesque embellishments of the tales he purported to recount verbatim, but no doubt the more prosaic details—which are the more arresting ones—of his version derive from local lore. Inishbofin, he was told, was part of Hy Breasail, the Celtic Atlantis, and 'it was invisible like all the others, in the far western sea, and was only spied at times, and then passed away again like a fog bank.' An Omey Island man and his son, fishing for mackerel, had in their boat a glowing sod of turf on a lump of blue clay, to broil fish on when they got hungry. Far out at sea they found themselves in a mist, and heard birdsong and the lowing of cattle. At that moment the father happened to hook the finest mackerel he had ever seen.

He says to his son Darby, 'Boy, jewel, we'll just have this fine fellow for our dinner;' and, with that, he takes the coal of turf off the clay between a clipstick, and begins to blow to light it up, when, as it happened, some of the fire fell overboard, and, would you believe it? all at once, a beautiful island burst on his view, just within five fathoms of his boat, and he had nothing to do but push on shore, and look about him.

They took a bit of the glowing turf with them wrapped in a handful of seaweed, and had not gone far when they saw a beautiful lady 'all dressed out in a gown and petticoat of green,' driving a white cow down to a lake. The younger man caught the cow by the tail, which came off in his hand and turned into a stem of seaweed, while his father pursued the lady, who seemed terrified of the fire he carried and fled into the lake, where she disappeared. The island has been disenchanted ever since, and 'from this tradition, the people all along the coast expect, that some time or other, greater and finer islands will be disenchanted.'

Inishbofin, now that it is fixed on its base, named, disenchanted and so made amenable to reason, turns out to be situated five miles north-west of Cleggan, to measure three and a half miles from east to west and two miles from north to south, to have a rough, heathy interior rising to a central height of 288 feet, and a shoreline mainly of jagged cliffs, with a good natural harbour on the south, where the principal settlement is, and a stretch of dunes on the east. It has a sister island, Inishshark, nearby to the southwest, about a third of its size and of similar topography. Shortly before the Famine the population of the two islands was 1,612; Inishshark was deserted by its last inhabitants in 1960, and there are now about 180 living in Inishbofin, sustained by tourism, lobster-fishing and sheep-rearing.

Perhaps something of the island's original ungraspable nature can be imagined to beset its coastline still, which is armed with shoals and reefs the sea breaks over, and gashed with deep, cliff-sided chasms that gape at the ocean and narrow into sea-caves, some of them with great ragged openings above, left by the foundering of their roofs. A sailing vessel, the *Royal Oak*, helplessly adrift before a north-west gale, having lost its rudder head in a race against a steamship, rammed herself into one of these creeks on the western shore and was held upright between its walls, so that the mariners were able to swarm up the masts and out along the spars to the cliff-tops. When did this happen? Paddy O'Halloran of the North Beach village in Inishbofin, who told me the story, was born around 1900 and heard it when he was young from men who were then old and claimed to have witnessed the event when they were themselves young; since the creek is named as Royal Oak Cove on the OS map of 1839, perhaps the wreck took place not long before that date. Of another such windfall ship and its dreadful welcome to Inishbofin, we have the date, 27 January 1780, but not the ship's name. In the preceding year two army officers had been recruiting in Newfoundland, and in mid December they set out with 196 men in a hired boat to Halifax or New York. Unable to make way against a tremendous gale, they let it carry them across the Atlantic, and were dashed onto the rocks of Inishbofin. A sergeant and fifty-five recruits were lost, the wreck ignited, or was set on fire by the natives, and the survivors nearly starved as the islanders demanded exorbitant prices for food. Official records show that a few days later sixty men had made their way to Galway Harbour (where they were refused entrance to the town for fear of plague), twenty-seven had died in the island and another thirty-one were lying sick there, while eighteen had deserted (and were soon to be rounded up by Lord Westport's Volunteers). The last we hear of these unfortunates, in a 'memorial' to the English authorities drawn up by the two officers, is that they had no food, no money and no orders, that the men were in rags, and that they requested leave to march to some port or come to England for equipment and pay; what answer they received, if any, is unknown.

Wrecks were part of the living of this open-jawed island. I am told that craftsmen used to go looking for bolts and the like around Carraig na dTáirní, the rock of the nails, the tallest of the three great teeth of rock known as the Stags of Bofin that rear up out of fierce tidal flows off the north-west head of the island, where a ship with a cargo of such ironmongery went aground.

And if night, fog and wind did not serve the island rightly in this matter, they could be assisted. In 1741 the Royal Exchange Insurance Company in London offered £30 for the arrest of various O'Flahertys charged with the wrecking and looting in Inishbofin Harbour of the *Kitty Brigg*. (Their names, 'Edmond Flaharty the elder, John Flaharty, Edmond Flaharty the younger, Anthony Flaharty a reputed Popish priest,' suggest that the elder 'Edmond' might well have been the famous Éamonn Láidir of Renvyle, and the next two, his sons.) The brig, bound from Antigua to London with a cargo of sugars, cocoa and other valuable goods, had been in distress and the O'Flahertys had conducted it into the harbour, where they 'wilfully, maliciously and feloniously' made a hole in its bow, slipped its anchor so that it was wrecked, and plundered its cargo—'facts so treacherous, detestable and barbarous in their nature, that they cry aloud, and justly demand the resentment and abhorrence of every fair trader and honest man.'

Death by drowning also haunts these coasts. In the Catholic church by the harbour are stained-glass windows commemorating two young Americans who walked out to the Stags at low water, were cut off by the rising tide and swept away when they tried to swim ashore. The ghost of an Englishman who vanished together with his little boat on his way from Cleggan to the island, one night in the 1950s, is said to have been seen several times. Three men came over from Inishshark in their currach to hear Mass on Easter Sunday in 1949, stayed on to have a few drinks, and, against all advice, set off for home in worsening weather from the treacherous beach of shifting sands called Trá Gheal, bright strand, and never arrived; a tombstone-like memorial to them stands on the cliff-top of Inishbofin overlooking the straits between the islands. A sailboat with four Inishbofin men was lost in a sudden storm on their way back from Cleggan; their oars and rudder came ashore in Clare Island, but their bodies were never found. The father of one of these victims had been among the nine Inishbofin men lost in the Cleggan Disaster of 1927. And so on, back through time beyond all memory or inscription.

The first settler to arrive in Inishbofin whose name has been preserved was one Colmán, later St Colmán, who sailed in with his
followers in about AD 665. His predecessors—the Bronze Age
folk whose cooking sites have been found in Inishshark; the Iron
Age builders of the so-called promontory forts, the scant traces of
which can be seen on several headlands of the islands—have left
nothing of their histories or personalities. But Colmán came as
an intransigent individual with a freight of history. He had spent
thirty-seven years as a monk in Iona before becoming Abbot of
Lindisfarne, both foundations representing steps in the advance of
Christianity from Ireland into Scotland and northern England that
had been spearheaded by St Columba or Colm Cille. At that same
period the Christianization of England from the south, initiated
by St Augustine's mission from Rome, was spreading northwards.
However, the two missions were in disagreement as to the correct
way of calculating the date of Easter, for in the centuries since
St Patrick left Rome for Ireland the astronomers of Alexandria
had been at work on the problem and the Universal Church had
adopted their solution to it. Southern Ireland, more in contact
with the continent, had long conformed, but the Columban north
and its Scottish outposts had not. Now the situation had arisen
that King Oswiu of Northumbria and his Kentish wife were cel-
ebrating Easter on different dates. The King proceeded to hear
witnesses from both sides at a synod held in St Hilda's Abbey in
Whitby, in AD 664, as the Venerable Bede tells us in great detail,
in his *Ecclesiastical History*:

> King Oswiu . . . then commanded his bishop, Colman, first
> to declare what the custom was which he observed, and
> whence it derived its origin. Then Colman said, 'The Easter
> which I keep, I received from my elders, who sent me bishop
> hither; all our forefathers, men beloved of God, are known
> to have kept it after the same manner; and that the same may
> not seem to any contemptible or worthy to be rejected, it is
> the same which St John the Evangelist, the disciple beloved
> of our Lord, with all the churches over which he presided, is
> recorded to have observed' . . .

Then Wilfrid [a priest of the Roman faction], being ordered by the king to speak, delivered himself thus: 'The Easter which we observe, we saw celebrated by all at Rome, where the blessed apostles, Peter and Paul, lived, taught, suffered, and were buried; we saw the same done in Italy and in France, when we travelled through those countries for pilgrimage and prayer. We found the same practised in Africa, Asia, Egypt, Greece, and all the world, wherever the church of Christ is spread abroad, through several nations and tongues, at one and the same time; except only these and their accomplices in obstinacy, I mean the Picts and the Britons, who foolishly, in these two remote islands of the world, and only in part even of them, oppose all the rest of the universe.'

And after entering into involved expositions of what, according to St Peter, should happen 'if the Lord's Day did not fall the next morning after the fourteenth day of the moon, but on the sixteenth, or the seventeenth, or any other day till the twenty-first,' etc., he delivered a knockout blow:

'But as for you and your companions, you certainly sin, if, having heard the decrees of the Apostolic See, and of the universal church, and that the same is confirmed by holy writ, you refuse to follow them; for, though your fathers were holy, do you think that their small number, in a corner of the remotest island, is to be preferred before the universal church of Christ throughout the world? And if that Columba of yours (and, I may say, ours also, if he was Christ's servant), was a holy man and powerful in miracles, yet could he be preferred before the most blessed prince of the apostles, to whom our Lord said, "Thou art Peter, and upon this rock I will build my church, and the gates of hell shall not prevail against it, and to thee I will give the keys of the kingdom of heaven"?'

When Wilfrid had spoken thus, the king said, 'Is it true, Colman, that these words were spoken to Peter by our Lord?'

He answered, 'It is true, O king.' Then says he, 'Can you show any such power given to your Columba?' Colman answered, 'None' . . . Then the king concluded, 'And I also say unto you, that Peter is the door-keeper, whom I will not contradict, but will, as far as I know and am able, in all things obey his decrees, lest, when I come to the gates of the kingdom of heaven, there should be none to open them, he being my adversary who is proved to have the keys.' The king having said this, all present, both great and small, gave their assent, and renouncing the more imperfect institution, resolved to conform to that which they found to be the better.

But Colmán, unreconciled, decided to take himself back to that 'corner of the remotest island' so despised by the Romanists. With his 'Scots,' i.e. Irish, monks, and about thirty English followers, he withdrew first to Iona, and then 'to a small island, which is to the West of Ireland, and at some distance from its coast, called in the language of the Scots, Inisbofinde, the Island of the White Heifer.' In a slight valley by a little lake near the more sheltered, eastern end of the island Colmán and his monks built a monastery; it has long vanished, but some mounded stones in the graveyard of a ruined church of late medieval date there are thought to mark the spot. But his 'Scots' and his 'Saxons' did not agree, 'by reason that the Scots in the summer season, when the harvest was to be brought in, leaving the monastery, wandered about through places with which they were acquainted; but returned again the next winter, and would have what the English had provided to be in common.' To end this dissension Colmán bought a site on the mainland, south of the present town of Castlebar, and established the English contingent in a separate monastery, which prospered and continued for a long time to attract English monks. Colmán ruled over both communities until his death, probably in 674; the inland one went on to become famous as Mag nÉo na Sachsan, the field of yews of the Saxons, and left its name to what is now the county of Mayo, while the island monastery fell out of history. Old tales have been recorded of a chieftain, Guairim, who quarrelled with Colmán over a question of tithes and had six of his monks massacred; blood used to seep from the earth at the site of this deed on its anniversary. Guairim is said to have been tried in Renvyle and condemned to be chained to a rock and drowned by the tide. The names of four of Colmán's successors in Inishbofin are known from *The Annals of the Four Masters*, but after that little is heard of the monastery until 1334 when it was destroyed by Sir John D'Arcy, who was appointed Lord Justice of Ireland by Edward II and whose concept of justice led him to sail down the west coast of Ireland burning and looting as he went.

In 1380 Inishbofin was captured by the O'Malleys from the O'Flahertys, and like Clare Island, Inishturk and other islands became part of their 'upper territory' or Umhall Uachtarach, anglicized as Upper Owle. In the mid sixteenth century Grace O'Malley herself is said to have had a castle on the headland still called Dún Ghráinne on the west of the harbour, while an ally of hers, Don Bosco (who is supposed to have been a Spanish pirate, but is untraceable in written record) had a castle too, just east of the harbour, their respective fleets being protected by a chain stretched between the two strongholds. Whether all this is more than a flourish in the romantic iconography of the island is more than our days can tell.

The most dramatic times in Inishbofin's history were at the bitter end of the fighting between the Confederate Catholics and the forces of Oliver Cromwell. In 1651 the victorious Parliamentarian army was closing in on the town of Galway, and the Confederate leader, the Marquis of Ormonde, had slipped out of Galway Bay in a sailing boat to try to call up help from the Continent, leaving the Earl of Clanrickarde to defend the town. In answer to appeals from Clanrickarde, the Duke of Lorraine sent two frigates with cargoes of guns and ammunition; one of them, commanded by a Colonel Synnot, came in to Inishbofin. After the surrender of Galway and the strategically important Aran Islands commanding the entrance to Galway Bay, Colonel Synnot led an expedition from Inishbofin of 600 men to retake the islands; the Cromwellians reacted forcefully, shipping 1,300 soldiers out to Aran from Galway with a battering ram, and dispatching another 600 men along the south Connemara coast to back them up. Aran soon surrendered, leaving Inishbofin as the sole hope of the loyalist cause. A loyalist pamphleteer describes its situation as being:

> Kept for the duke of Lorraine, whoe furnished the same with all things conducent unto its defence, provision, and ammunition for two yeares seidge, extraordinarie good workes with abondance of great ordinance, beside a world of armes . . . In this brave posure of defence did stande this machine; many Irish, both ecclesiasticke and laitie, did thither flocke, some for safetie, others for loyaltie, to see things well carried, and others contrarie. Amonge the rest that soe thither retired was the bishop of Clonferte, Roger Moore and Donogh Oflahertye.

In early February a Cromwellian force of 270 foot, on its way to combine with a naval expedition to crush Inishbofin, was ambushed and routed near Renvyle Castle; nevertheless on 17 February the island surrendered. Perhaps this last bastion of revolt was carried by bribery rather than military might, as the same aggrieved author claims:

> This forte was an itch in the enemie arme, makinge, therefore, all the shewe possible with shipps and otherwise to leager the ilande, though well perswaded, consideringe the posure and strength therof, to be in vaine, unlesse a waye was founde to corrupt the commander by inticinge angells, which was an easie taske in the opinion of seuerall witts, as being one George Cussacke, leutenant colonel to late Generall Preston, and one of his hatchinge . . .

In fact the commander, Colonel George Cusack, was rewarded on his surrender and allowed to sail away with up to a thousand of his men to France, together with the Bishop of Clonfert; while the O'Flaherty leader was beheaded, and 'Roger Moore,' better known as Rory O'Moore, one of the initiators of the rising of 1641, had to go on the run again and died soon afterwards, it is not known where.

The victorious Cromwellians considered having the harbour entrance blocked, but soon changed their mind and began to build a massive fort overlooking it, on the site of Bosco's castle. Perhaps one reason for this was that it had been decided to use both Inishbofin and Aran as holding camps for the Catholic priests who were being hunted down and imprisoned, prior to transporting them to the Barbados. Orders were given for the payment of £100 to the governor of Galway for the 'maintenance of such popish Priests who are or should be confined to the Isle of Buffin, according to six pence dayly allowance, Building Cabbins and the like.' This allowance compares not too badly with the soldier's pay of eight-or ninepence a day; other sources say the captives nearly starved on twopence a day, subsisting on herbs and water, so perhaps most of the money went into the pockets of their captors. It seems that at first about fifty priests were held, some in Aran and some in Inishbofin; later on there were only five in Inishbofin. Some of them were still imprisoned for a time after the restoration of the monarchy in 1660 and even after Ormonde's triumphal return to Dublin as viceroy; a Father Brian Conny, formerly the Franciscan Provincial, died in captivity in Inishbofin as late as 1663. Island lore says that the priests were held in a cave on the north coast known as An Priosún, where the sea spouts spray up a blowhole, but the idea seems impractically Gothick, and the placename is not uncommon in Connemara, where I have found it applied to a number of natural features such as quaking bogs and narrow inlets that are easier to get into than out of.

The fort was kept manned and saw some action during the wars with France and Holland that ended in 1667; the garrison was withdrawn in 1684, but in 1690 during the War of the Two Kings, as the Irish called it, there was a Jacobite military force in the island, which surrendered to the Williamite army in the following year. For thirty years or so thereafter the fort was kept up as a discouragement to French privateers, but then was abandoned. Over the years it has suffered slow dilapidation as the limestone blocks used to dress it were crowbarred out and carried off to be burned for lime, leaving its walls of dark local schist ragged-edged and gapped. Nevertheless it is still a commanding presence looming over boats coming into the harbour. It encloses a roughly oblong area some sixty yards long, with a projecting bastion at each of its four corners, those at either end of the inland, eastern curtain wall being symmetrical and diamond-shaped, and those on the west, where the ground falls irregularly and becomes a sea-cliff, themselves more irregular, adding to the whole's resemblance, as seen from a boat below, to a surly old crab, menacingly still on its rock, armed with heavy claws.

Like many other formerly ecclesiastical properties Inishbofin had belonged to the Clanricardes since the dissolution of the monasteries, and they regained control of it in the post-Cromwellian settlements. In 1689 the ninth Earl, John Bourke, was made Baron of Bophin, but in the next century the island passed to the Brownes of Westport, one of whom later became the Marquis of Sligo. The Inishbofin fisheries were immensely productive, although the islanders themselves profited little from them. Up to ninety sailing vessels assembled from as far away as the Claddagh in Galway, and a fisheries report of 1837 tells us that 'contentions frequently happen during the herring fishery, especially at Boffin Island, which is considered a neutral ground, where each party meet in strong force, and dreadful conflicts ensue; which are injurious to the fishery, as the weaker party must keep at a respectful distance from their more powerful adversaries, and generally lose their chance of fish.' Clearly the weaker party was that of the fishermen of Inishbofin itself, who had only rowboats, and sold their catch to the sailboats, which sold them on to 'cadgers' and to Westport merchants, who cured the fish in bulk. The landlord's agent, Henry Hildebrand, was much complained of. The island curate denounced him to the Devon Commission in 1844; he monopolized the sale of boats and equipment to the fishermen and charged extortionate prices; he would not permit them to sell their fish to any buyer but himself, and since they had no leases on their land, they knew the consequences of defying him. He was later to encourage the Protestant missioners to come into the islands, which made him even more unpopular. By chance we have a portrait—almost worthy of Thackeray—of this petty tyrant, written by a young Scottish surveyor whose manuscript memoir of a visit to Connemara came up for auction and was published a few years ago. The setting is a meeting of the Poor Law Guardians of the Clifden Union in 1853:

Mr. Scully, the deputy Vice Chairman,—perched on the mantlepiece, with his feet resting on the back of a brother Guardian's chair,—while Paul Hildibrand [*sic*] lashed the table, within an inch of the Chairman's nose, with an immense horsewhip, while advocating the Protistant side. This man is known in the district as the 'Sea wolf ,' and I could easily imagine the thong he wielded, sufficient to chastise a wayward walrus, or a 'wanton Whale'!

Hildibrand is certainly as fine and open a specimen of a 'rough diamond' as I ever beheld, his black curls fell in bunches on his shoulders as he shook his immense head and twinkled his sparkling eyes at the opposing party. A homespun blue frock coat enveloped his body to the knees, a leathern belt encircled his expansive waist, and his feet and legs were encased in dreadnought sort of Fisherman's boots. He is a descendant of a faithful Dutch retainer of an ancestor of the Earl of Sligo, who accompanied William of Orange on his world glorious mission to our regenerated land . . . Such are the men necessary to cope successfully with insinuating Romanism, bearing all retorts with dogmatical good humour, but striking openly and fearlessly home to the truth as he sees it—tearing the flimsy mask from slimey tongued Jesuitism.

In the 1850s the Irish Church Mission Society opened a school in Inishbofin, and a soup kitchen, which, according to one orally transmitted version of history, attracted all but seven of the island's families; but according to another tradition the soupers were driven into the tide with sticks and stones, and in the words of a priestly historian of the island writing in 1920, 'in after years, souperism looked in vain at the islands from the opposite shores of the mainland, and never succeeded in planting one blade of heretical-cockle in St. Colman's or St. Leo's patrimony.' In any case it seems proselytism was of short duration in Inishbofin, and an astonishing change in its religious circumstances took place in 1860 when the two islands were bought from the Sligos for £11,000, by a Catholic convertite and embattled journalist on behalf of the Catholic cause. The Hon. Henry Wilberforce (whose brother Robert we have met in Kylemore) was the youngest son of William Wilberforce, the evangelical philanthropist and parliamentarian most famous as a campaigner for the abolition of slavery. Henry had studied at Oxford and been deeply affected by the Oxford Movement associated with John Henry Newman, Keble and Pusey, which sought to redefine the Church of England as a spiritual institution not subordinate to the state and looked back for inspiration to the High Church tradition of the seventeenth century. He had been ordained in the Church of England, but then had followed his friend the future Cardinal Newman into the Catholic Church. In 1852 he had organized the Catholic Defence Association in response to the proselytizing campaigns of the ICMS, and his denunciations of the 'demoralising system of wholesale bribery' deployed by the Protestant missions at work in Dingle and on Achill Island awoke controversies that were further embittered by the fact that the founder of the ICMS, the Revd Alexander Dallas, had been among those who had laid hands on him at his ordination.

It seems that Henry Wilberforce did not reside in Inishbofin—in fact Hildebrand stayed on as a considerable tenant and perhaps as agent—but let the island to a Mr. Black, for £600 per annum, on condition 'that he should expend a sum of £200 yearly in the improvement of the island.' A succession of poor potato harvests followed by a spell of rough weather in 1873, cutting the islands off from the mainland and curtailing the fishing season, brought the famine back again. The island had been mortgaged to a London company, and on Wilberforce's death in that distressful year the debt was discharged by another convertite, who thus became the landlord. Thomas William Allies, a Church of England vicar and High Church theologian, had been regarded as of a 'peevish and querulous disposition' by his superiors, who sent him off to the obscure parish of Launton in Oxfordshire 'to learn sense.' On a holiday in France he had then been overwhelmed by his encounter with the Catholic ethos, and came to see the Church of England as 'a monster with two heads and no feet.' In this crisis of faith he sought out the most eminent of all those that made the doctrinal journey through the Oxford Movement into Roman Catholicism, John Henry Newman, and was received by him into the Catholic Church in 1849. Later he became the first professor of modern history at Newman's foundation, the Catholic University of Ireland, and passed the islands to his son Cyril, who became the island's last owner, and, in 1876, the first to live on the property.

An 'improving' landlord, Cyril Allies rearranged holdings and relocated tenants, mainly to clear the way for his own expanding sheep farm. He also undertook the modernization of belief systems by offering £50 to anyone who could show him a fairy, and £100 if it could be photographed. He is remembered as a most beneficent landlord, but he was soon faced by the social contradictions of the 1880s, a time of 'distress' in Inishbofin as in other west-coast communities, and of increased politicization of local resistance to all authorities. This unrest was countered by a strange mix of welfare and coercion, as Sir Henry Robinson, a civil servant concerned with the distribution of relief, describes:

> The multifarious functions of the gunboats on the West coast were very puzzling to the islanders. The same vessels which came with food supplies for the people and departed with bonfires blazing on the beach in their honour would return in a few days with bailiffs, process servers and police to sweep the island bare for rent or rates. Then, after a pitched battle, away would go the bailiffs with their seizures, and back again would come the gunboats after a few weeks' interval with tons of meal to help the people to tide over the further distress caused by its previous visit!

The *Illustrated London News* carried reports and depictions of both phases of such operations in Inishbofin in April 1886:

Inishbofin seemed even nearer to starvation than Achill; but the arrival of H.M.S. Banterer, one of three gunboats sent by the government to this part of the coast, with supplies of meal and potatoes, was a happy reprieve. In our Artist's sketch of this scene, the vessel is entering between the rocks, her boat is putting off to land, the people are cheering . . .

It was during this same period that, through the intervention of the Congested Districts Board, the modernization of the island began, with the building of the pier in the inner harbour in the 1880s, a fish-curing station beside it, and another on an islet in the harbour pool. A second pier and a curing station at the hamlet called the East End and a curing station at the North Beach soon followed. The CDB also provided loans enabling the fishermen, who were dependent on rowing boats, to buy the stout two-masted sailing boats called nobbies, inaugurating a boom time for the fisheries that lasted until the 1920s. In 1907 the Land Commission bought out the estate, and the CDB proceeded to rationalize the tangle of tiny fields by dividing the cultivated land into 'stripes,' and to settle the tenants on their own farms in decent stone-built, tin-roofed cottages, thus tending to break up the pattern of nucleated settlement of immemorial days. Cyril Allies contributed largely to the building of a fine church completed in 1914, and lived on, a widower, and no longer a landlord, in Inishbofin until shortly before his death in 1916. Bofin House, his residence overlooking the harbour, later became Day's Hotel, the social hub of the island. But by the 1920s the fishing industry was failing, and the Cleggan Disaster virtually ended it. Emigration has steadily reduced the joint population of Inishshark and Inishbofin from about 1,200 at the time of Allies' arrival to 248 in 1961, when the last residents of the relatively inaccessible and undeveloped island of Inishshark were ferried out and resettled in Land Commission cottages on the mainland at Claddaghduff. It was not until the 1990s that the development of the tourist industry stabilized the population of Inishbofin at around 180. Since then—but perhaps the most recent, drastic, indeed almost convulsive, transformations of the island are best told in another mode, as below.

Carrying this heavy burden of circumstance, and being so widely rooted in the history of the British and Irish islands—from the Synod of Whitby to the Oxford Movement, from the Catholic Confederation to the CDB!—can the island be refloated? To find out, or, more modestly, to find the sense of the question, I revisited Inishbofin in 2007. My travelling companion was Fidelma Mullane, whose mission was to document the island's one remaining thatched house. As well as being an expert on vernacular architecture Fidelma is an enthusiast for poured concrete—she was eloquent on the perfection of the material as used in the new Louvre in Paris—and, as it turned out, concrete was to be the determining characteristic of our findings. We took the morning ferry from Cleggan; it was early May: playful weather and few tourists. The voyage took only half an hour in the powerful, two-storeyed motorboat. As we cleared the mouth of the bay and the steeps of Cleggan Head in their tattered-looking spring vegetation fell back, mountain after mountain was revealed to the north: the gaunt domed skull of Mweelrea, then the silvery cone of Croagh Patrick—sacred because symmetrical, and vice versa—then other peaks we could not identify far off in Sligo, and the fierce blade of Achill slicing into the ocean; all these linked by a muffled drum roll of misty hills around half the horizon, to which the vessel danced across the waves.

As Inishbofin grew towards us I told Fidelma a legend of a St. Scaithín, to whom one of the island's holy wells is dedicated. He was known for his ability to walk to Rome in a day and come back in another day. On one of these journeys he met St Barre (the famous saint of Cork), who was travelling by boat. 'What is the cause of thy walking on the sea?' said Barre. 'It is not sea at all, but a plain full of clover-blossom,' said Scaithín, and he picked a flower and threw it to Barre in his boat. 'But what is the cause of a vessel swimming on the plain?' he asked, whereupon St Barre put his arm down into the sea, pulled out a salmon and flung it to Scaithín. This magic interchangeability of land and sea seemed to me to have some special relevance to the fundamental question of Inishbofin, but before I could capture it we were already passing under the distrustful inspection of the island's Cromwellian fort. The harbour, on the south coast of the island, is entered between scattered reefs and shoals; the navigator has to keep two beacons in alignment, cylindrical white-painted towers dating from the late nineteenth century, one of them on the cliff that carries the shore road west from the principal settlement, and the other a little further inland behind it. We were astonished by the scale of coastal protection work going on below this cliff, which is of glacial till and has been eaten back by cliff-falls until the tower and the road are threatened with imminent collapse. Part of this fifty-foot-high cliff had already been armoured with gabions, cuboid parcels of stones, six or seven feet long, in stout wire mesh, stacked in course upon course. Further west a zigzag Berlin Wall of concrete panels twenty feet tall was being constructed below the cliff, and the space behind it filled with silt dredged out of the inner reaches of the harbour and pumped through a fat blue tube that lay like a monstrous snake along the foreshore. A variety of bright yellow lifting, shifting, digging and concrete-mixing vehicles were barging in and out of the tidal pools, and one might have thought that the indigenous dress was fluorescent yellow jacket and hard hat. Refloating Inishbofin looks an increasingly remote possibility, said Fidelma, as we gaped at this titanic welding of the island to its base.

We disembarked at the New Quay (new since my last visit, in the 1980s, and approachable at nearly all tides, unlike the original pier further up the shallow and silt-logged harbour, where passengers had to be transferred in small boats to and from the ferries waiting offshore) and shouldered our bags along through a chaos of traffic and the contents of what looked like a hardware yard for Titans. To my surprise, Day's Hotel, which I remembered as a plain, long, whitewashed building with its roof modestly drawn down close to the tops of its small first-storey windows, had been transformed into Inishbofin House Hotel and Marine Spa, with architecture in the current global-travel style. It had two full storeys and lots of dormer windows and sharply triangular gables above them, a spacious foyer, a gleaming restaurant with acres of glass wall and an impressive head waiter. Our rooms, we found, opened onto a broad terrace enjoying the view of the inner harbour, where a rusty landing craft was disgorging a crane vehicle, which after some hesitation came sliding down the ramps and roared ashore through the muddy fringes of the tide. The scarp behind the hotel had evidently been cut back to accommodate this startling apparition of elegance, which looked as if it had been dropped into position from another planet, leaving the rest of the village staggered, taken aback, knocked sideways.

That afternoon we worked to and fro in the lanes on the hillside behind the seafront, Fidelma examining every building, however banal or ramshackle, and pointing out a host of details I would not otherwise have noticed. There were some pretty white-painted single-storey houses with blue or green reveals round the doors and windows, but also many empty and derelict CDB houses, redolent of the sadness of emigration, their window-places blocked with concrete, leaving pale eye-patches on the blind exterior. An islander told us that in the old days people rarely wrote down their wills and the lack of clear title made it difficult for these houses to be sold off as holiday homes; Fidelma surmised that, in these days of environmental regulations, the cost of dealing with the asbestos tiles most of them had at some stage been reroofed with was another obstacle to refurbishment. Many of these houses, which are of a standard linear layout with a central kitchen, a room off it to one end and usually two small rooms off it to the other, had a small extension to one side under a continuation of the roof slope, open to the kitchen and near the fireplace, just big enough to hold a bed for the old lady of the household. This is a feature of vernacular architecture associated with the northern half of Ireland and probably introduced to Connemara by the CDB, and referred to as the *cailleach*, literally 'the hag.' Some experts would derive the term from *cúl*, back, and *teach*, house, but as Fidelma pointed out, there is no reason to expect *cúltheach* to mutate into *cailleach*, a word perfectly familiar in both of its applications. (Also, *cailleach* is not always as derogatory as the English 'hag'; in fact it can be used fondly.)

Interior partitions of concrete were a more unusual feature of some ruined houses we peeped into. Stone-canopied fireplaces were absent too; the chimneys must have been of wattle and daub, or reduced to a mere smoke-hole. Concrete seemed to be lavishly used to compensate for deficiencies in stonework; the corners of some houses and barns were of big stones with curved surfaces that hardly engaged with each other, and loosely built walls were supplemented by thick smearings of what Fidelma said was the worst of damp-retaining concrete. Even some field walls were patched with concrete, and there was nothing here to match the artistry of the walls of the Aran Islands or many other country areas. We understood this better when we found walls that still carried their original covering of sods so that the haphazard construction of their stone cores hardly mattered and they were bedecked with ferns and wildflowers. But even these had fences of wooden posts and wire mesh implanted along their tops, more for the sake of the grants available for fencing than for any real need to keep the sheep in, Fidelma surmised; I have rarely seen such distressing tangles of wire. Another feature of the outskirts of the settlement was the prevalence of rusty and battered cars, some of them still on the go and others too far gone to go; according to Fidelma the gargle and spit of old car engines is an auditory cultural specific of islands, where second-hand cars are imported, run into the ground and then discarded. Eventually we found the last thatched roof she was in search of, on yet another abandoned house. It was a sad sight, caved in and reduced to separate peaks of blackish mould draped over the gables and interior walls, with the fishing net that had held it down still spanning the empty gaps. The net was weighted at the eaves with saucer-sized stones from the shore, neatly tied on and evidently chosen with care; the sight of them somewhat heartened us, and Fidelma photographed them with loving respect.

Above the settlement, where turf-cutters' and farmers' roads run out into the treeless, rocky, uninhabited interior, we saw on the skyline the busy silhouettes of machines at work flattening knolls and filling glens to make the runway from which Aer Arann's ten-seater Islander planes will soon be commuting to another runway just inland of Cleggan. Having campaigned against the Clifden Airport Company's proposals for a much larger strip on what should be the inviolable terrain of Roundstone Bog, I had felt I could hardly oppose their more modest Cleggan scheme, especially as it would primarily serve Inishbofin's community, rather than the wealthy patrons of Clifden's hotels and the Connemara golf course near Bunowen; also, from my years in Árainn I knew the comfort and reassurance an air link provides to islanders. Nevertheless the sight and sound of yet more of nature going under concrete made me uneasy. The dilemma is this: each individual development may be justifiable in terms of the welfare of some community as against the preservation of the environment, but the sum total of such developments is the death by a thousand cuts of the natural world, and the thinning of the human spirit.

To round off the day's explorations with a medieval touch, we followed the coast road westwards until it became a grassy track, in search of a children's burial ground I had once been told was the site of St Scaithín's retreat, and his holy well nearby. The burial ground is a vague overgrown hummock in a field; the well I could not locate at first, but a man living in a house nearby, who remembered directing me to it on one of my previous visits, pointed out a large stone by the roadside, which had formerly stood behind the well and had now been laid flat over it, to prevent passers-by stumbling into the little hollow. This islander, a young family man, had heard that people once brought 'some good-looking women' to try the saint's chastity. He had nothing further on this legend, but fortunately a literally wonderful old book by one of the eighth-century ascetics known as Culdees or Céilí Dé (clients of God), *The Martyrology of Oengus*, has the titillating details:

> Now two maidens with pointed breasts used to lie with him every night that the battle with the Devil might be the greater for him, and it was proposed to accuse him on that account. So Brénainn came to test him, and Scothín said; 'Let him be in my bed tonight,' saith he. So when he reached the hour of resting the girls came into the house where was Brénainn, with their lapfuls of glowing embers in their chasubles; and the fire burned them not, and they spilled the embers in front of Brénainn, and go into the bed with him.

'What is this?' asks Brénainn. 'Thus it is we do every night,' say the girls. They lie down with Brénainn, and nowise could he sleep with longing. 'That is imperfect, O cleric,' say the girls: 'he who is here every night feels nothing at all. Why goest thou not, O cleric, into the tub of cold water if it is easiest for thee? Tis often that the cleric, even Scothín, visits it.' 'Well,' says Brénainn, 'it is wrong for us to make this test, for he is better than we are.'

The man who pointed out the site of the well to us had also heard that the saint was said to have visited Rome, but he thought that doubt had been cast on that story; it did not seem that the miraculous aspects of the journey were still remembered locally. I went back up the road to photograph the stone concealing the saint's well, thinking, 'At least they haven't filled it in with concrete!' With archaeological advice no doubt something of the original structure could be brought to light. Although I cannot yet translate it out of the obscure language of legend it seems to me that Scaithín's familiarity with the mystic dialectic of land and sea has something to say to this island in its travails with concrete reality.

Coming back from the day's explorations along the coast road we stopped to peer over the cliff-top at three grasshopper-sized, yellow-jacketed men far below splashing about in tidal puddles and coaxing one of the huge concrete panels into position as it dangled from a crane; dangerous, strenuous and comfortless work. Finally they shoved a stone under one corner of it; a lorryload of concrete would then be poured to fix it in place. By this stage we were accustomed to the rough energies, the bustle and roar of this island in transformation; even the clutter of empty oil barrels and stacked concrete pipes had become homely, familiar and indeed full of interest. A minute or two further on, we were impressed by the parish church, which turned out to be the apotheosis of concrete-work on this concrete-obsessed island. This is St Colmán's church, built by the munificence of Cyril Allies, the zeal of Father Rhatigan, PP, and the voluntary labours of the parishioners; it was dedicated in 1914. The numerous stepped buttresses—four of them against the west gable wall alone—and the rounded heads of the windows and doorways give it the defiant air of a fortified Romanesque cathedral; it is, in the big elements, simple, but it has attractive details in an Arts and Crafts style. The exterior is beautifully dashed with rather large sea pebbles, some of them white quartz, and incorporating the odd periwinkle shell, all unified by a thin spray of light concrete; this highly textural finish gives it a comfortable presence, like that of a hand-knitted sweater, at odds with its church-militant stance. Even the little grids of the ventilation openings are coated with concrete, moulded as fine as fretwork, and all in perfect condition.

That evening we strolled out of the village again, this time taking the little road leading eastwards to the site of St Colmán's monastery. Once past another big new hotel and a hostel, we were in the most beautiful part of the island, a shallow valley of rough little pastures and field walls harbouring treasuries of wildflowers, which opens out onto a broad sandy plain, a beach, the ocean, and a horizon that to the left was a dream of far-off unvisited hills and to the right pointed straight as a signpost to infinity. The old cemetery lies between the lake, with its reed-beds that were a glowing russet in the last of the daylight, and the machair, where yellow irises were flowering in a damp dune slack. I remembered being here a long time ago, alone on an autumn evening, when thousands of starlings swept in to settle among the reeds, which bent under their weight with a sigh. There is a roofless medieval church among the graves old and new, and a holy well associated with St Flannan in a small enclosure like a cylindrical tower, leaning towards collapse, in a corner, and a few ancient altar-like stone platforms on which lie dozens of large white pebbles from the seashore. All is quiet, secluded and con-templative (but even a saint might be excused a spasm of anger over the laxity of a planning process that has permitted a new house and a white plastic polytunnel to spring up between the cemetery and the seashore). Grass and wildflowers flourished knee-high around the old stones, and on the cemetery gate was a notice apologizing for this untidiness and explaining that this year the corncrake has selected the cemetery area to nest in. The

Inishbofin Conservation Initiative, it seems, is working together
with local farmers, BirdWatch Ireland and the Heritage Council
to restore old fields worn down by sheep or overgrown by rushes,
to produce hay for cattle and habitat for corncrakes; in 2006 six
corncrakes were heard, the first for twenty years. In general corncrakes have become so rare, as the meadows they used to frequent
are cut at the beginning of summer for silage instead of at the end
of summer for hay, and the Sahara they have to venture across in
their astonishing migrations laps further southwards year by year,
that the few little corners of the world where their call, a subdued,
repetitive creak-creak, can still be heard are places of pilgrimage to bird-lovers; the next day I was to meet two ladies from
Galway who remembered the sound from their childhood—as I
do from magical midsummer evenings in the Aran Islands thirty
years ago—and had come to Inishbofin out of pure nostalgia. So,
while it might seem that the ear-rending construction work and
the discreet self-advertisement of the corncrake represent opposite poles of the island experience, in fact this plump, speckled,
furtive little creature could be central to the economic future of
Inishbofin, a partner in the risky symbiosis of airstrip and expensive hotels. Whether or not there is such a thought behind it, I
am heartened to know that care is being taken of this shy survi-
vor of the world-wide abuse of grasslands. I am minded to imagine a time when the storm of construction will have abated and
the island community can catch its breath and look to the details
of its own nesting site, clear up the detritus of this neglectful age
and bandage the wounds inflicted on its fragile habitat. However,
that evening the corncrake uttered not a syllable in support of
such a hope.

That night, over-stimulated by the long, rich, contradictory
day, I could not sleep. At midnight, disturbed by lights moving
outside, I stepped through the glass door of my hotel room onto
the wide terrace overlooking the harbour. The tide was far out;
the lights belonged to a big caterpillar-tracked digger, a dino-
saur with long swaying neck and spastic head, which was making its slow way down to the water's edge. There its neck became
a two-elbowed arm with a clawed paw, which it stretched out

as far as it could reach to scoop up mud and, swivelling, put it aside into a giant mud pie. I watched this strange sight for some time, then slept, and shortly before dawn woke to view the other phase of these tidal harbour works. Now the tide was full, the top of last night's mud pie showed as a conical island, and a long, low vessel with a cabin and an obscure mass of machinery above deck was manoeuvring around it, agitating two fussy little paddle-wheels, one on either side of its bows. Ahead of this curious boat was a line of buoys that supported a length of the same fat blue pipe we had seen on the foreshore nearly half a mile down the coast; suddenly the buoys began to buck and shudder, a tall whale-spout arose from a loose connection on the pipe, and I guessed that the boat was a floating pump, now delivering mud to the coastal protection works. The paddle-wheels whirled first one way and then the other, sometimes they turned in opposite senses, and then mysteriously vanished underwater; the boat nosed forward and backed off again; the buoys wallowed and spouted, the light of day began to outline the hills ringing the harbour, twelve big off-white geese browsed the hotel lawn.

It was too late to go to sleep again. I dressed, made my way down through the pale silent glassy space of the foyer and strode out of the village in the direction of St Colmán's monastery. Sunlight was just beginning to flood the golden beach beyond the old graveyard and galaxies of daisies were about to open their flowers in the meadows, enough little propellers to levitate the island imperceptibly under my feet. The saint's valley was so brimming with nature's sun-worshipping matins—lambs bleating for their mothers, robins establishing territory from perches on fence posts, wrens in bushes singing as if they would burst themselves, skylarks soaring above the dunes, sandpipers trilling on the tideline, seagulls shrieking over the wave tops—that I despaired of hearing the introspective little rattlings of the corncrake; but then it came, that old-fashioned sewing-machine noise, a precise seam of so many stitches, a silence, so many stitches, and so on. Soon it stopped. Perhaps the bird had flown. Perhaps its stubby little wings had given the island enough of a lift to float it into Scaithín's world, where salmon swim beneath the clover blossoms. But I would not like to force anything on the moment. The quality of wonder should not and cannot be constrained, for 'it droppeth as the gentle rain,' etc.

In the Mist

Aughrus—Eachros, horse peninsula, in proper Irish—is the broad, low-lying lobe of land at the head of the peninsula south-west of Cleggan Bay. Its main topographical feature is a large lake set centrally within it, so that its flowery hay-fields and marshy pastures form a rim only 200 or 300 yards wide between lake and sea; quiet country lanes serving a scattering of small farmhouses and holiday homes make a loop around this rim, which I would think a horse could trot in less than half an hour. I connect Aughrus with childhood and have wanted to write about it with that theme in mind ever since, a decade or so ago, an elderly lady from there called on me with the typescript of her autobiography, looking for my advice on its publication. Mary Walsh, *née* de Lappe, had had a successful and serviceable professional career, and to her this was the most interesting part of her story, whereas to me its most valuable chapters were the first few, rich in details of life in a Connemara cottage in the early 1920s. I must have suggested some ways in which she could bring the work up to a publish-able standard, for she went off encouraged; but I heard no more about it, and when I tried to get in touch with her not long ago I found that she had died, and that the fate of the typescript seemed to be unknown. I had looked forward to learning much more from her about her childhood; now all I have is a few pages of her reminiscences that I photocopied, with her permission, at the time of her visit.

With its three-foot-thick walls of stone, plastered inside and out and lime-washed white, its tiny windows, its roof of thick, rough trusses and rafters and wooden slats, covered by a heavy layer of sods, grassy side down, and then a layer of thatch, fastened down with *súgán* ropes of plaited straw tied to heavy stones lying on the ground, and old fishing nets thrown over it to keep the wind from plucking at it—Mary's cottage reads, in her account of it, as if it were designed by the elements themselves.

We could hear the roar of the ocean day and night. We would watch the massive white waves from the gable end of the house. Sometimes a storm at sea would throw up the whole ocean into a wild turmoil and the whole ocean would be rolling and gleaming in the moonlight, like a sea of molten silver . . . The house was always at the mercy of the elements: storms, thunder, lightning and torrential rain. Whenever storms arose my father would struggle to throw some heavy rope across the roof to hold it in place. He would secure the rope to stones or pegs in the ground.

When the thatch began to leak and the rain poured down, the kitchen floor would be an obstacle course of pots and pans placed to catch the drips; when the storm raged, holy water would be shaken against its direction, out of one of the many bottles of it kept in the house; when the chimney would not draw and the kitchen was full of black smoke, it was 'the will of God.'

The kitchen, centrally placed in the house, with a big straw mat hung against the back door to keep the wind out, its earthen floor strewn with white sand or lime in which her mother would stroke squiggly patterns with the broom, its wide-open fireplace with a stone bench inside it on either side, was indeed the living space, never without a cradle, for 'new arrivals came in rapid succession.' If anything was missing—odd shoes, cutlery, school satchels, the grandmother's bone corset—the cry was, 'Did you search the cradle?' Crickets chirped by the fire; visitors who liked the tiny melody would take a couple of them back to their own hearths in a matchbox. Mary's mother, who had spent time in America, kept books and magazines sent by her kinsfolk there in a little arched recess over the kitchen window, and struggled to beautify the place:

I remember coming home from school one day to find she had painted the kitchen wall half way up a lovely shade of pink, complete with shamrock symbols to give it a pleasing effect. She had put white frilly curtains trimmed with pink and pink tie-backs in the little window. I thought the kitchen had been converted into a small palace.

In fact Mary's mother was always at work 'making something out of nothing.' She would pluck the geese and ducks to stuff a pillow, lay flour bags out on the grass for weeks to bleach out the company's name, 'Palmers,' and turn them into sheets, or dye them pink to make them into dresses for the children. Thanks also to a hard-working father and relatives in America who sent parcels, Mary's family was not among the most deprived of the locality, and she describes with disgust a cottage she used to visit in which the cow and its calf occupied one end of the house, separated from the kitchen only by a filthy drain.

Mary's father was both farmer—sowing the potatoes, turnips, cabbages and onions, tending a couple of cows and a mixed gaggle of fowls—and fisherman, out in his wooden currach after herrings, mackerel, white fish or lobsters. In winter the seas were too rough for his little boat and his fishing nets hung on a timber projecting from the loft into the kitchen roof space. When the grandfather died, and his ten-shilling-a-week pension with him, and then one of the cows died and was towed out to be sunk at sea, as was the custom, the family's situation was bleak; but then a French firm trading in shellfish turned up looking for a site for holding tanks for their lobsters, and gave Mary's mother ten pounds for a bit of land behind the nearby pier. Her father had some building and diving experience, and was offered the job of manager of the new lobster ponds. The site was perfect: the pier already closed off one end of a narrow and deep channel between the mainland and a long islet lying parallel to the shore; all that was needed was another wall with sluices across the other end of the inlet. In the company boat, a small single-engined vessel called the *Nugget*, Mary's father would range around the coast from Slyne Head to Clew Bay, bargaining for lobsters. More locally he would travel on his bicycle, coming home late at night, guided by a little carbide lamp, often soaked to the skin, having to empty out his boots and to warm them with cinders from the fire before putting them on again in the morning.

Mary's reminiscences of this amphibious life in the raw edges of Connemara—the piglet that used to go swimming with her sister, the geese with quills from their own wings pushed through their beaks to stop them rooting up the potatoes, the white-faced baby calves 'with an almost angelic quality,' her mother taking off her coat to cover a badly mutilated corpse retrieved from the sea—are precise and evocative, and I was sad to have missed the opportunity of calling on her in Aughrus before writing about the place for the present book, for it was many years since I had explored it in the course of making my map of Connemara. But the connection with the lobster ponds makes it easier to shift my focus to another former child of Aughrus with whom I had a slight acquaintance, one who was brought up there in the 1950s, her father being the then owner of the business itself.

The idea of walking Aughrus, or walking through her childhood memories of it, with this daughter of the lobster ponds had intriguing and intimidating ramifications. Olwen Fouéré is an actress at the height of her career; she has starred at the Abbey Theatre and the Gate, in the UK with the National Theatre and the Royal Shakespeare Company, and in Becket and Pinter festivals in New York; she also co-directs an enterprise called the Operating Theatre with composer Roger Doyle, and figures in several works by the conceptual artist James Coleman. Moreover her art is not just cerebral but of demanding physical intensity; I have seen little of it, apart from a video performance, because of my rather retired life in the western margins, but I have been given breathtaken accounts of Steve Berkoff's version of Wilde's *Salome*, in which, it seems, she did a dance of the seven veils that was at once extremely erotic and perfectly chaste, without shedding a stitch. Her performance-theoretical pole star is Antonin Artaud, originator of the Theatre of Cruelty, the aim of which he summarized as being:

> . . . to restore to the theatre a passionate and convulsive conception of life, and it is in this sense of violent rigour and extreme condensation of scenic elements that the cruelty on which it is based must be under-stood. This cruelty, which will be bloody when necessary but not systematically so, can thus be identified with a kind of severe moral purity which is not afraid to pay life the price it must be paid.

My connection with all this was that I had written a few pages on the visit Artaud made to the Aran Islands in 1937, when he was already on the cusp of madness. He was in search of the last descendants of the druids, and also wished to return to Ireland a staff that he believed to have belonged to St Patrick. Harassed by the island children, he had left without paying his bill, then got into street fights in Dublin, lost the staff and was deported, arriving in France in a straitjacket, to spend years in the asylum of Rodez, where he was subjected to fifty-one electro-shock treatments without benefit of anaesthetic. My bit of writing had attracted the notice of a Cinzia Hardy, one of the directors of the Dialogues Project, a UK-based organization that pairs up artists who otherwise might never make contact. She wrote to me proposing a collaboration with Olwen Fouéré on some Artaudian theme. As it happened I was then nursing an obsession with the labyrinth of strange, high-walled fields in Inis Meáin, one of which, called Balla an Tairbh, the bull's wall, had the layout of a stage, on which no one ever appeared but which seemed to hold some theatrical experience in suspension in its emptiness, such as, perhaps, an Artaudian treatment of the legend of the Minotaur's labyrinth in Crete. I therefore began to write an outline of a film with nobody in it, and for which Olwen Fouéré seemed the right protagonist:

> An actress known for the mysterious gift of presence, for an accentuated and baroque corporeality, would surely fit the role I have in mind for her—not even Nobody, who might be an allegorical figure, or A Nobody, who might keep a diary, but nobody at all—the ultimate challenge. Whether she could make the part her own would depend solely on our awareness of her past successes in embodying a bizarre range of passions . . . Her non-appearance in *The Bull's Wall* draws its strength from all her past appearances, her commitment to the art of immediacy, the ambiguities of the physical. Set among a thousand featureless little fields, with its title supplied by one of them, this film directs Fouéré as inexorably as a jigsaw puzzle outlines and locates its one missing piece.

Olwen lent herself (or her name and fame, at least) to this notional outcome of Cinzia's initiative, and even wanted to be there when the film was being made, although her presence was not required. But in the event we decided that an actual film would be no advance on my proposal, so the outcome is merely a non-existent film of a non-appearing person. This wispy conceit was all that connected us when I contacted her to propose a walk around the fields and shores of her childhood. She immediately replied that she would be down in the West shortly, and a date was arranged.

The Roundstone man who drove me up to Aughrus had been a fisherman and like almost every man of the Connemara littoral had had dealings there, first with a Frenchman they knew as Samson, and later with Mr. Mauger, Olwen's father. He remembered incidents from the early and illegal days of the French presence in Irish waters: a French fishing boat approaching a Roundstone boat one day and asking the crew to take their catch on-board for a time as the Irish Coastal Protection vessel was after them, which the Roundstone men gladly did; and a French captain pulling crayfish pots saying in broken English, 'Goldmine—off Slyne Head—Irish not know!' Later on when it was realized that there was a market on the continent for crayfish the Fisheries Board supplied the Connemara fishermen with tangle-nets to catch them; unfortunately these were so efficient, compared with the pots, that crayfish have now been practically fished out. Mr. Mauger he remembered as a fair dealer, always ready to advance the fishermen the price of new nets or lobster pots against the coming season's catch. In fact the lobster ponds of Aughrus were for some decades a mainstay of the Connemara economy.

So discoursing, we drove through the town of Clifden and then the disseminated suburbia that has spread across the flat coastal region of Claddaghduff, to Aughrus. My driver pointed out the house of a branch of the Coneys family, to the east of the lake. These Coneyses were formerly middlemen, leasing Eachros Beag, the northern portion of Aughrus, from the Martins of Ballynahinch and then from their successors the Law Life Assurance Society, and subletting it (in the 1850s) to some forty subtenants. In *Connemara: Listening to the Wind* I quote a contemporary denunciation of the desperate state of those subtenants and the famished horde of unrecognized occupiers of land here. Mary's grandfather had been threatened with eviction at that time, and the bailiff had refused the ten-shilling note that was all they could offer towards the rent—a bitter family memory her mother tried to dissuade Mary from recounting in her book. The Coneyses were reputed to give lavish parties and to have been extremely rich, and no doubt in comparison with the subtenants they were so; Mary's mother used to tell her that when the lads played at skimming flat stones on the lake, the Coneys boys used fistfuls of silver two-shilling pieces. At that period the family lived in what amounted to the local Big House, near the sea and west of the lake, but it seems Anthony Coneys must have defaulted on the rent for he had to move into a smaller one nearby. One of his daughters married a brother of the celebrated surgeon Sir Peter Freyer from Sellerna near Cleggan and in Mary's time was living at the east end of the townland (where they had the only clock in Aughrus, and anyone needing to know the time would call in on them).

A little further to the west from the Coneys house, a sign for the Cleggan Lobster Company directed us down a little road that passed the Maugers' small house and terminated among large sheds by the shore. Olwen was sitting on a stone outside the house; with her long silvery-blonde hair, little white shorts and T-shirt, she looked as if she had already slipped on the role of child for the occasion. I noted her serenity, the Easter Island repose of her face. Her brother John, who now runs the company, soon joined us, and led me down between the packing sheds and freezer rooms to view the ponds. It was a peculiar day: a sea mist had come into existence and annulled all distant prospects, while overhead the sky was full of August sunshine. A narrow, unrailed, concrete walkway led between two deep tanks perhaps fifty yards long; looking back from the dam wall and sluice gates at the far end, the sheds loomed large, slightly dematerialized by the mist. The lobsters were all lurking in bits of drainpipe laid out for them on the bottom of the tanks, among which a big greyish crayfish like the ghost of a lobster strolled stiffly to and fro, and a blackish conger eel

writhed into sight and vanished like an evil thought. It was pleasant to come out of the premises to the sun-washed strand below
the house from which Olwen and I proposed to make a clockwise
circuit of the locality.

I was unsure how to begin my enquiries, having met Olwen
only once before, when she and her partner the actor David Heap
called on us at the time of the non-film project. I did not want to
interview her, least of all about her father (who, to cram the matter
into a winkle shell, had been prominent in the Breton nationalist
movement during the Second World War, was accused of collaboration, fled to Ireland, where he took the name Mauger, returned
to stand trial in the 1950s and was cleared of the charge). There
was a touch of shyness in the air, though perhaps it was only visible
from my point of view, for Olwen was perfectly unconstrained,
trotting nimbly before me down narrow sandy paths between
rounded hummocks of sparkling granite, paddling across the shallows in the bay she used to swim in every day, and talking readily
about whatever it was we talked about—for I must admit I have no
mental or physical record of this. The mist lay in vague tufts and
wads just offshore; the sun, high behind us, produced a low-arched
bow of colourless light in it, which accompanied us for a while.
Olwen pointed out a great anchor bedded in the sand, which raised
a fluke in a gesture of greeting or drowning; I remembered from
Mary's book that it came from a cargo ship called the *Verity* which
had been abandoned with some loss of life in a mid Atlantic storm
in 1879 and had eventually drifted onto the rocks west of Aughrus.
Mary's grandfather and other fishermen had salvaged what they
could from it, and towed the anchor to its present position on the
beach below Mary's family house. To her it was a shrine at which to
leave offerings of sea pinks and pray for the souls of the drowned,
a landmark to be danced around and climbed up, and a toy, with a
huge ring that gave a musical sound when turned. What it meant
to Olwen as a child, I now realize, I do not know.

Where the sea dwindles away into the branching inlets and salt-
marshes that separate Aughrus from Ros an Duilisc, invisible to the
east, we left the shore and took to the road that rounds the lake. The
first house we passed, she told me, was built by Tony White, the

English actor and writer whom Richard Murphy met on Inishbofin, where they had both gone to be alone and to write; they had become the closest of friends, until Tony's early death. Olwen added that he was buried in Omey graveyard in the same corner as the cross commemorating the Cleggan Disaster victims, and her own two children—thus alluding, calmly, to a tragedy I knew of, but not about, from a TV film about her life. Further along, down in a steep hollow full of brambles by the roadside, we saw an elderly man collecting blackberries in a milk carton; how he was to get out seemed a puzzle. Olwen introduced us; he was Mary's brother. When I told him that his sister had shown me her writing he said, 'Was that book ever published?' I took it from this that the work had gone astray; but shouting down into a blackberry bush was not the way to pursue the question, so I let it drop. Olwen offered to come back with her car and drive him home when he had finished blackberrying, but he had already arranged for another sister to pick him up, and so we walked on. Soon the lake appeared on our left, a great pool of stillness, its margins precise among green meadows grazed smooth by cattle. Mary used to have to fetch bucket after bucket of water from it on washdays, but in fine weather the washing would be done by the lake; water would be boiled in pots and pans on turf and wood fires, the clothes rinsed on a flat stone in the lake and then spread to dry on the stone walls or on the grass. She also describes putting hairs from a horse's tail under rocks in the lake to see if the common belief that they would turn into baby eels were true—her first scientific experiment, which came to nothing. And she preserves some truly Arcadian lakeside hours:

> On beautiful calm summer evenings we frequently sat by the lake while my mother played the accordion. The sound of the music would travel across the water. On a few occasions I remember accompanying her in a small canoe on the lake playing not only Irish music but classical as well. Whenever I hear Handel's Water Music it brings back happy memories of those far off days . . . the tranquillity of the place broken only by a dog barking, a bird singing or the sound of the swans to keep us company.

And what were Olwen's memories of the lake? I must have forgotten to ask her.

At the westernmost point of the circuit we hopped over a field wall to the right and climbed a little hill between the road and the shore. I have never seen a pasture so rich in wildflowers. I named some of them for Olwen: yarrow, devil's bit scabious, eyebright, wild carrot, tormentil . . . 'Tormentil? From torment?' queried the Artaudian (and indeed the old herbalists thought tormentil could cure most torments); but otherwise I felt her interest in them was perfunctory. The hill is called the Gazebo; we could find no trace of whatever little lookout place or summerhouse it was named from, but the name itself is a last trace of the Coneys's 'Big House,' of which it would have been an appurtenance. The house itself was doorless and windowless when Mary used to play hide-and-seek in it as a child, and by Olwen's time it had totally disappeared. From the vanished gazebo we looked out to sea, or rather into the mist, which still surrounded the land with a soft obscurity, so that it felt as if we had been walking around the interior of a diorama, or were ourselves mere projections onto an illusory and depthless background. Below the hill we looked down through the collapsed roof of a sea-cave at dark water languidly shifting to and fro; in wild weather this would be a blowhole, spouting foam onto the meadow. Olwen used to be able to slither down into the cave, but now the hole was almost smothered in brambles. From there another few minutes brought us back to the lobster pond, the circuit completed, and we went into the house for tea.

The Mauger house was built by Olwen's father in 1950–53 after he took over from 'Samson,' whose proper name, I learned from Olwen's brother, was Marcel Samzun. It felt well-worn and comfortable, familial and bookish, seasidey and snug. The fireplace in the living room was tiled with flat scallop shells painted brown; above it hung a colourful map of Brittany with the place-names in Breton, and a large wooden cross of traditional Breton craftsmanship. I was surprised to learn that Yann Fouéré, to give him his proper name, was still alive, in his nineties, and living in Brittany. Olwen showed me his attic study, where his big tweed jacket hung on the back of his chair, a powerful fatherly presence.

She got up on the chair to reach me down a copy of one of his books from a stack of them, on a high shelf: *Towards a Federal Europe*, evidently not much in demand. Published in 1968, this is a recipe for a Europe of region-states, 'life-size' states with their own cultures, to which one could feel a personal loyalty; its main thesis is that such an arrangement of mutual accommodation can only be achieved if the big, centrist, nation-states, which he identifies as the sources of fascism and dictatorships, delegate power upwards to an external federation, and downwards to an internal federation of their regions—to Brittany, the Basque Country, Sicily, Scotland, the Tyrol and dozens of others, each of which, one can see, posing its own problems. Not mentioned, of course, is the great fact of more recent times, the vast immigrant populations in the big states; nor are the Jews, a nation central to a cultural definition of Europe but denied even a region in it; nor those of us who do not want to be defined by the culture we were born into, or by any other. Olwen also gave me an old recording of an interview her father gave on one of those terrible country telephone lines of the 1960s to a *Times* correspondent, whose metropolitan accent cut through storms of static but who failed to make anything of Yann Fouéré's gentle, French-accented, affable-sounding voice. From this recording I later made out that he had been campaigning for the teaching of Breton in the state schools of the region before the war, and then had become General Secretary of a Consultative Council for Brittany set up by the Vichy regime. He was at pains to distinguish between the Council's purely cultural activities and the independent actions of the Breton Nationalist Military Movement which seceded from the Breton Nationalist Party and fought with the Germans against the French Resistance. Arrested after the Liberation ('when everyone was getting arrested,' as Olwen put it) and given a temporary release, he had taken the opportunity to flee, and was condemned *in absentia* to lifelong penal servitude. He was sheltered by Welsh nationalists and taught French at Swansea University College for a while before coming first to Dublin and then to the West, eventually acquiring Irish citizenship under the name of Mauger, so familiar to all Connemara fishermen. He returned to Brittany in 1955, stood trial in a military court and was cleared of all charges. He went on to found the Mouvement pour l'Organisation de la Bretagne and to edit a monthly newspaper, *L'Avenir de la Bretagne*. Her father's latest book, *La Maison du Connemara*, sent to me by Olwen later on, describes his travails as a fugitive in Wales, struggling to support his wife and three very young children and always in fear of deportation, and his more settled life in the remotest west of neutral Ireland, where Olwen, the last of his offspring, was born. Ironically, in his encounter with the raw Celt in the form of the lobster-pond workers, the passionately regionalist Yann Fouéré evinces a rather Cartesian regard for exactitude in space and time. He soon found that it was up to him to know about funerals, races and religious festivals, and not to expect people to turn up for work on the following day. It irked him to find tools mislaid and rusting out in the fields; but when he had a board made with an outline of each tool under its peg, the hammer would still be hung in the place for the saw. The use of the spirit level and plumb line was virtually unknown, and 'the walls of the pond were as sinuous as the minds of those that had built them, or the dry stone walls that marked out the fields.' Nevertheless the book shows that he came to love and respect his neighbours as he adapted to Connemara ways, while sinuous Connemara still speaks well of Mr. Mauger's straight dealing, and the ponds, whatever shape they were, served the local economy well, as they do to this day.

These books and the recording gave me some idea of the cauldron of ideologies out of which Olwen's family had been blown like a bubble to this Atlantic shore. But, trying to under-stand afterwards how it was that I had come home with little or nothing of interest about her own childhood in Aughrus, I realize that my concept of a walk, which almost precludes talk except of the immediate data of landscape-consciousness, had imposed itself. And it was as if Olwen had literally gone along with this determination of the occasion, leaving me as free within it as if I had been alone (which was in fact my abiding impression of the afternoon). That she was able to do this, without having to think about it or make any effort, demonstrates that she is neither self-effacing nor overbearing; she exactly occupies her own space. Perhaps she had brilliantly performed the role of nobody, as in my first conception of her. Looking back on our circuit of Aughrus and its central lake, I only know that I had felt the presence of a lake of stillness within her.

What is the connection between that great calm and her theatre life? I remembered Diderot's *Paradoxe sur le comédien*: the great actor who can reproduce the passions convincingly and movingly is not the person who is overwhelmed by them but the one who studies them dispassionately and subjects them to the discipline of art; '*les larmes du comédien descendent de son cerveau.*' But that seems inadequate. Olwen is no Enlightenment automaton or cold encyclopaedist of the emotions; also, she is not just an actor but a disciple of Artaud. At the time of our walk she was soon to appear as Artaud in a documentary on his life, and was regularly performing her 'Artaud Installation,' a gruelling piece in which she appears as Artaud incarcerated in a glass box. When I mentioned that, after leaving Aran for Galway, Artaud had sent off a telegram that compressed extremes of sadism, misogyny, blasphemy and anti-Semitism into a dozen words, which I did not quote in *Stones of Aran* (and do not quote here) for fear they would burn a hole in my page, she immediately quoted it from memory without turning a hair. Artaud himself could not handle those passionate, convulsive and cruel theatrics in his head; they turned on him, became external forces, broke into his mind. What would be the Paradox of the Artaudian? That only the deeply sane can present extremes of the instinctual and irrational convincingly and without being harmed by them. The body fluids of the Artaudian spring from her well-planted feet.

I am guessing, of course; I don't know her well enough to do more. In *La Maison du Connemara* there is a rather misty photo of the handsome family group, with little Olwen between an evidently fond father's knees, her eyes narrowed, as if in curious and confident dialogue with the camera, or with the viewer of the photograph. Her broad cat-face is immediately recognizable, but I cannot read the sense of her long Cheshire-cat smile.

Plague and Purity

In AD 664 there were already too many people in Ireland. The joint High Kings Diarmaid and Blaithmac held an assembly at Tara to consider the problem. The nobles proposed asking God to send a pestilence to cull the lower orders. St Féichín approved this plan, and he and his party 'fasted on God,' that is, they went on hunger strike to coerce Him into granting their wish by the public spectacle of their sufferings. And the 'yellow plague' duly broke out, carrying off not only multitudes of superfluous peasants but also many nobles and clerics, including St Féichín himself. Humanity is a pollution of nature, and society a distraction from the eternal. Even before this date holy misanthropy, like a centrifugal force, had scattered monks and hermits throughout the desert places of Ireland and its surrounding seas. For St Féichín it was not enough to quit his celebrated foundations at Fore and at Cong and travel across the mountain passes and wooded valleys of Connemara to Omey, which is subject to twice-daily tidal occlusion from the mainland; he went further, four miles out into the ocean, to establish a hermitage on the rough little cliff-sided plateau of Ardoileán or High Island. Such, at least, is the legend, and that there was indeed a monastic settlement on the island is attested by a roofless chapel within a ruined cashel wall, stone huts and carved crosses. Similar if less elaborate remains, of which similar tales are told, can be seen on half a dozen Connemara islands and many others off Atlantic shores; some of their foundation tales—St Colm Cille on Iona, St Colmán on Inishbofin—have at least a toehold on history.

In 1984 I visited the long-uninhabited High Island in the company of some archaeologists from the Galway Survey, led by Mike Gibbons. Our boatman, Pascal, was a jumpily energetic merman with massive pectorals compressed into a wetsuit that seemed to be his natural integument. We found him outside his mobile home in Omey with two elderly islanders; their gossip was of an abortive attempt by some entrepreneur to blast a huge propeller—twelve tons of phosphor-bronze—off a First World War wreck to which he 'didn't *exactly* have a claim,' and winch it onto a trawler for a discreet passage to Northern Ireland, where unfortunately the businessman who was to buy it had gone bankrupt at the wrong moment. At last we got free of this subplot, and Pascal's diving dinghy with its 25 HP engine shot us out past the low jagged profiles of Cruach and Friar Island—both alluring unknowns to me—to High Island in a mere quarter of an hour of splashing and bumping. Steering into a cove under the cliffs on the south side of the island, Pascal said, 'Now, this is tricky, and it isn't tricky. When you jump out onto the rock jump straight away, don't hesitate with one foot on the boat and one on shore. The climb up the cliffs looks hard but it isn't.' So encouraged we stormed ashore and rabbited up seventy or eighty feet of rock to where a cross-inscribed slab stood in the short turf as if to greet us with a sobering reminder of the island's unworldly ethos.

The inmost point of the cove we had landed in and that of another one opposite it on the north coast are separated only by nine paces of land and between them almost nip the island in two; they have both been eaten by the waves out of the soft rock of a copper-bearing vein that traverses the island and once gave its pre-Famine owners, the Martins of Ballynahinch, hopes of reviving the family fortunes. Close by was the ruin of the miners' long cottage, one end of which had been given a flat roof and converted into a one-room dwelling by a more recent owner, the poet Richard Murphy. The monastic settlement was located by a little lake half a mile away over rough, hilly pasture and close to the south-western tip of the island, as if to get full penitential advantage of storms coming in from that quarter. The one upstanding feature in a choppy sea of fallen stone and grassy tussocks was the west gable of a little rectangular chapel, with a narrow, flat-topped doorway we had to bow to creep through. We could make out traces of the wall of a squarish enclosure immediately around the chapel, and a largely shattered but more massive wall, like that of a cashel or stone fort, surrounding the chapel enclosure and two dilapidated beehive cells. Here and there in the vicinity were other obscure heaps of stone, perhaps collapsed huts or rude altars, and two or three small slabs set in the ground and carved with crosses. A rivulet flowed out of the lake to the cliff edge and dropped into the sea far below; on the very brink were remains of a stone building, evidently a mill, and of particular interest to the archaeologists.

The team's study of the old stones took a long time; after following them in criss-crossing the terrain in all directions for a while I wandered off to chat to a few fishermen from Claddaghduff whose custom, they told me, was to come ashore here to eat their lunch, have a crap and stretch their limbs. Their exercise was to try lifting a boulder of granite lying near the chapel, an almost perfect sphere about eighteen inches in diameter. Later I rejoined Pascal, who was sunning himself on the cliff-top at a place from which he could keep an eye on the boat, moored in the waterway between the shoreline and a huge rock in the landing cove; 'Boats get contrary if they're left alone too long,' he said. As we watched a seal appearing and disappearing in the dizzy cleft below us, he told me about his career as a stuntman, the dreadful trade he had abandoned for the sea after a colleague of his was killed in a jump from a high building when he missed the pile of cardboard boxes he was supposed to land on. Then we pondered an infection of the island's sea-scrubbed purity by the modern world's impurity: the dozen or more gull corpses I'd noticed on the cliff-tops, dead of botulism acquired through feasting on the contents of plastic bags in rubbish dumps on the mainland.

Meanwhile the declining sun was raking through the grass and Mike, striding by, called out to us in delight that new finds were 'popping up everywhere': a particularly fine incised cross had been revealed on the apparently plain back of a cross-slab by a holy well near the highest point of the island. But the archaeologists were flagging, the sky was beginning to think of the coming night, and it was time for us to gather up our Thermos flasks, cameras and measuring rods and scramble down the cliff to the boat. The sea was blue milk and every now and then a shoal of mackerel brought a patch of it to the boil as they surged up after sand eels. High Island became a black silhouette against the sunset; our wake was tumultuous gold. Over the roar of the engine we could only smile at each other, sharing our delight in speed, the salty blast and the hour's astringent splendour.

Since that hasty survey of 1984 a great deal of research has been done on the island's history, and published in a fine book, *High Island: An Irish Monastery in the Atlantic*, by Jenny White Marshall of UCLA and Grellan D. Rourke of Dúchas, the Heritage Service. The resulting picture of the monastic community in its heyday is very different from my romantic image of spray-lashed penitents barnacled to the naked rock. Long before the monks came, and as early as the late Bronze Age, the island could offer settlers good grazing, fish, seals, flocks of meaty seabirds, and patches of pine and hazel scrub for fuel; there may even have been some arable farming, as the palaeoecologists from NUI Galway have found barley pollen preserved in the depths of the peat on the hillside east of the settlement. The pollen record for the Iron Age (from about 540 BC to AD 640) suggests the clearance of scrub and the growth of grass and weeds, and possibly the cultivation of rye. The massive cashel wall may well date from this period, and its position in a dip of the hillside indicates that its purpose was residential rather than defensive. Many legends and pseudo-histories of the early saints tell of local rulers donating land and even cashels to these exigent and terrifyingly convincing emissaries of the new religion, in the hope of eternal bliss and enhanced worldly standing. Perhaps one of the Conmaicne Mara, the rulers of Connemara at the time of the coming of Christianity, handed over the island and the cashel to enable the monks of Omey Island to establish another foundation a few miles offshore; the cashel wall itself may have been seen by the first monks, in a hurry to shelter themselves before the onset of winter, as a convenient stone quarry for their own chapel and beehive cells.

The Omey foundation is attributed to St Féichín or Féchín; according to two seventeenth-century Latin *Lives* of the saint compiled by the Franciscan monk John Colgan and based on earlier Irish manuscripts that have not survived him, 'At the angel's command Féchín goes into the west of Connacht to Omey, and he blessed it, and built a cloister therein, and brought those tribes under a yoke of belief and piety. 'The tradition that he then went on to found a monastery in High Island has just one sentence of written basis, in one of the Latin *Lives*: 'The man of God founded another monastery in a nearby island, which today is called Ardoileán.' It need not be taken literally; the evolving story of St Féichín would have been the thread on which the monks strung their own understanding of how they came to be where they found themselves, long after the supposed travels of the saint in the mid seventh century, the great days of monastic sea-voyages and island foundations. There are no records to confirm it, but that High Island was rooted in Omey is most likely, from practical considerations: Omey would be the natural assembly point for pilgrims to High Island, a place of retreat for the island contingent of monks during dire winters, and conversely, High Island, protected from worldly influences not only by a rock-strewn and storm-prone sea but by its tall cliffs, would have attracted the most radical members of the congregation, who were perhaps scandalized by the growing power and wealth of the great mainland foundations with their profitable pilgrim trade. The standard elements of the earliest monasteries, the little narrow-doored oratory, the simple repertoire of patterns of the crosses incised on slabs of stone, retained their primacy in the conservative West; from the point of view of a cross-slab set on the brink of the known world, the elaborate high crosses evolving at Kells and Clonmacnoise might have seemed showy, attention-grabbing innovations. If those famous monasteries had their dormitories and refectories, High Island had a rectangular building just outside the cashel wall that is thought to have been a guesthouse, and probably attracted pilgrims. There may even have been a nautical pilgrims' way along the Atlantic coast, taking in, among other holy ports of call, the Skelligs, St Enda's Aran Islands, Inishbofin and Caher Island off Mayo. But perhaps the monks of High Island saw the sails of one of these pious ocean cruises on the horizon with mixed feelings. Money offerings, news of the profane world, distraction from contemplation, indulgence in food and word, would have to be atoned for by mortification of the flesh; there is a low chamber in the thickness of the cashel wall, where perhaps the monks imitated their spiritual forefather:

Generous Féchín of Fore loved this
—It was no false piety—
To lay his wretched ribs
In the hard cell, unclothed.

Nevertheless, such was the lure of the eremitical fashion that High Island became the home of a substantial and settled community. Its main business was prayer, but St Féichín's successors were not unrealistic about the prayerful body's need of food and shelter. The monastery's site is not so mortifyingly exposed to the elements as I had supposed on first seeing it, being set into a slight hollow that gives some ease from most winds. And there is plenty of evidence of the care the monks had for their power supply: the lake that functioned as a millpond, and a shallow hollow above it on the hillside that was originally a feeder pond. There are traces of a substantial dam of earth and stone that retained the feeder pond, and the stream-bed from it down to the millpond was partly quarried out of bedrock. The millpond itself is partly natural but has been extended and its sides revetted with large stones. Sluice gates would have been set into the dam of the feeder pond and in the millpond's outflow, which has also been cut into the bedrock. This stream divides into a headrace that drops steeply to the mill itself, and a bypass channel that conducts excess water to the cliff edge.

The archaeologists have drawn deep conclusions from the presence of the mill, the building, maintenance and operation of which must have called for a considerable commitment of resources. It was of a type having a horizontal waterwheel mounted on a vertical shaft that directly turned the uppermost of the two millstones between which the grain was ground. Traces of such mills are known from many other sites throughout Europe, and in Connemara one or two were still in use until the late nineteenth century, but it seems that in early medieval times the West of Ireland was more advanced than anywhere else in this technology, and the trade of millwright was a specialized one. The mill itself was housed in a stone-built, gable-ended building on the brink of the cliff, straddling the mill race, with the waterwheel below it in an undercroft and the millstones, which were probably a yard or so across, in a room above. Grain was fed into a hole in the upper stone by a hopper, and the spacing of the two stones was controlled by a lever acting on the millwheel, the drive shaft passing through the centre of the lower stone and being directly connected to the upper stone. All these constructions, together with the necessary stores for grain and for flour, a kiln for drying the grain and a threshing floor, suggest the existence of a community large enough to operate it and to make it a worthwhile investment of effort; the authors of *High Island* estimate that the island could have maintained a population of fifty to seventy, which the mill could easily have served.

No hermitage, then, attentive only to the spirit, but a busy, organized settlement, full of the sound of iron against rock. Its lasting art form was the inscribed cross-slab, of which about thirty-six have come to light, including two now in graveyards of Omey and Kill near Clifden and known to be from the island, and four recorded by earlier visitors but now missing, perhaps stolen. These slabs are all of the mica-schist of which the island is composed, except for one tall and elegantly proportioned limestone pillar, which probably came from the Aran Islands. Some are themselves shaped into short-armed crosses; others are rectangular or taper downwards to a tenon that would have fitted into a socket on a base. Some bear simple incised crosses of single lines; others are more or less elaborate and deeply carved. The cross and the circle, symbols of salvation and eternity, are juggled with grace and finesse; the meanings of certain configurations—the linear crosses with forked terminals, for instance, similar to ones found in Coptic Egypt and other nurseries of Christianity, or the short-armed crosses with D-shaped terminals—are unknown, but their deep seriousness is unarguable.

The chapel whose remains can be seen today is perhaps the third or fourth to have arisen and to have been replaced during the lifetime of the monastery; it certainly post-dates the mill, which seems to have gone out of use and to have been robbed of stone at this last stage. Perhaps the attempt to grow a hermitage into a monastery had been over-ambitious and the majority of monks had withdrawn to Omey when the island proved too small to sustain a larger population through periods of drought or endless Atlantic rain. Nevertheless this late period was that of the island's fame. From the time of St Féichín three prayerful centuries had passed before its first mention in the monastic *Annals*; in 'the Age of Christ, 1017,' *The Annals of the Four Masters* record the death of 'Gormgal of Ard-Oilean, chief *anmchara* of Ireland.' An *anmchara* (literally 'soul-friend') was a confessor or spiritual director, and Gormgal must have been widely venerated to have drawn such notice upon a remote little monastery. According to the seventeenth-century hagiographer John Colgan he 'ennobled' the island by 'his anachoretic habits, and most exact life.' The High King Brian Bórú himself may have made pilgrimage to consult Gormgal; at least, the well near the top of the island is named from him and is said to have run red as blood at the time of his death in the Battle of Clontarf in 1014. Colgan possessed a copy of an old and divinely inspired poem by a St Corcrán, a younger contemporary of Gormgal, concerning the Abbot's virtues, and, what was more important to a monastery looking to attract the pilgrim trade, his relics. Sadly this work of piety has not survived, but Colgan does quote from it the names of other hermits buried in the island alongside Gormgal; to read these solemn-sounding latinized Irish names—Maelsuthunius, Celecharius, Dubthacus, Dunadach, Callechus, Tressachus, Ultanus, Maelmartinus, Coromachus et al.—is to catch an echo of ancient ritual.

A century or so after the flourishing of Gormgal, it seems that all such voices had fallen silent, the chisel had ceased to ring against the stone and the island no longer attracted pilgrims. Why so is not known; monastic reforms may have made life on the mainland more acceptable, the climate may have worsened, a combination of factors may have led to a fall-off in recruitment and to the spectacle of a last few ageing monks creeping rheumatically down the cliff to the currach for Omey. Thereafter the island is undocumented for six centuries; no doubt it still belonged to the monastery in Omey, and, when that faded out, came into the hands of the O'Flahertys, the secular rulers of Connemara until their defeat and dispossession by the Cromwellians in 1652. I do not find it mentioned in the *Books of Survey and Distribution*, which summarize the changes in landownership from before the Cromwellian confiscations to the post-Restoration settlements, unless it is the anonymous island listed as 'Iland in ye Sea not found in the plott' at the end of the section on the Parish of Omey; but even if it escaped the eyes of the compilers of these documents it would not have been unnoticed by Nimble Dick Martin, and was probably disposed of to him, along with the greater part of the O'Flahertys' former territory. At all events its name next turns up in an agreement dated 1794, by which Richard Martin (Nimble Dick's grandson, Humanity Dick, of Ballynahinch Castle) leased High Island and nearby Friar Island to a John Bodkin, of a middle-man family later of Omey House in Omey. It seems to have been unoccupied and only used for grazing thereafter, until the copper miners came in the 1820s, bearing Thomas Martin's delusive hopes of mending the family fortunes. They were probably a team of eight to ten, locally recruited and captained by an experienced miner, perhaps from Cornwall. Robbing stone from the monastic ruins, they built a large cottage for the men and a small one for the captain, in the partial shelter of the central height and close to the mineshaft at the north-eastern neck of the island. It is probable they were only there for one or two summer seasons, but perhaps a few years earlier than the date, 1828, suggested by Marshall and Rourke, for the Blake family of Renvyle mention in one of their letters that, while becalmed during a sailing expedition in August 1823, they had ample leisure to observe 'the remaining traces of the copper-mine, which had been opened in High Island, with tolerable prospect of success, but which failed in consequence, it is supposed, of letting in the water, while carrying on the works under the sea.'

Then came the Famine, the collapse of the Martin estate and the sale of High Island, together with neighbouring Friar Island, an islet near the latter called An Meall Thuaidh, the north hummock, and the island of Cruach, off Omey, to the Revd Anthony Magee, a retired Catholic priest who came to live in Streamstown near Clifden at that period. For over a century to come High Island was to mean nothing more than grassland for sheep to its owners, but the monastic remains had begun to attract the antiquarians and their descendants, the archaeologists. George Petrie, father figure of Irish archaeology, visited in 1820 in company with Henry Blake; John O'Donovan, for the Ordnance Survey, came in 1839; and George Henry Kinahan, of the Irish Geological Survey, in 1869. The last-named reported that while the Martins had protected the ruins, the more recent absentee proprietors had allowed persons hunting rabbits to destroy them, and that the carved stones had been knocked about or even carried off. In 1895 the steamer *Caloric* (a name redolent of a new age) came by, carrying members and guests of the Royal Society of Antiquaries of Ireland on their way from Belfast to the Aran Islands; the learned excursionists, led by Robert A. S. MacAlister, later to become president of the society and of the Royal Irish Academy, made a hasty, scrambling survey of the antiquities, and came to the conclusion that the ancient stones had been pulled about in the pursuit of the seabirds nesting among them, by 'boys condemned to the monotony of solitary sheep-tending.'

After this long neglect the island was to be blessed with a happy and improbable change in its ownership. In about 1899 High Island, Friar Island and An Meall Thuaidh passed to the Joyces of Lenaboy Park near Galway, and were sold by their descendants in 1951 for £300 to Graham Lushington-Tullagh of Shanboolard, in Ballynakill. Mr. Tulloch found sheep-rearing on this scatter of salty acres unprofitable, and in 1969 sold them for £1,200 to the poet Richard Murphy, who found buyers for the two lesser islands, and himself became, for over twenty years, the Prospero of High Island.

It was not long after my own brief visit to the island that I first met Richard Murphy, who had by then left Connemara, when we were both in the audience of a *Late Late Show* devoted to islands and islanders—a demeaning occasion, a swash of puerility and exhibitionism, out of which Murphy and the poem he contributed stood like a sea-stack of self-possession. Afterwards I approached him; we spoke of Connemara and exchanged copies of our books. Richard is tall and lean, with the elongated patrician elegance of a thoroughbred stallion or a champagne glass; his delivery, both of poetry and of gossip, is similarly distinguished, deliberate, leisurely and nuanced. He is keenly and uneasily conscious of his standing, his relative shining, in the constellations of poetry—he told me ruefully of how Michael Longley once greeted him with, 'Ah! Richard Murphy: Ireland's best . . . looking poet!'—and much of his courageously frank memoir, *The Kick*, is devoted to his relations with his elders and contemporaries in the literary world. The rest is devoted to love, of men and women and places. A Festschrift entitled *Richard Murphy, Poet of Two Traditions* lays emphasis on his Anglo-Irish background (on his mother's side he is descended from General Thomson of Salruck House and the Bowen-Millers of Milford; his father was in the Ceylon Civil Service and became the last British Mayor of Colombo), and Richard himself has written of a division in his mind between his English education and his feeling for the coast-folk of the West of Ireland. But if that tension powered his creativity in his early narrative poems and sparked off some rueful comedic moments for his autobiography, the deeper dialectic of his life is condensed into this delicate and yet brutally frank poem, 'Moonshine':

To think
I must be alone:
To love
We must be together.

I think I love you
When I'm alone
More than I think of you
When we're together.

I cannot think
Without loving
Or love
Without thinking.

Alone I love
To think of us together:
Together I think
I'd love to be alone.

Here what concerns me is the High Island phase of his career, as revealed in the memoir and the poetry. This naturally tends to the solitary pole of his existence, the self-questioning self—'Buying an island, even with the intention of creating a wild life sanctuary, is a predatory act among predators, much easier than writing a book'—but it does not exclude the social; for instance he tells how, before he ever stayed by himself on the island, he had an ecumenical Mass celebrated in the ruins of St Féichín's chapel, the communicants kneeling on cushions of thrift. Nevertheless it was the island's own and aboriginal predators who became his confessors. In clearing stones off the floor of the chapel he came across storm petrels' nests, and later when sleeping, or rather keeping a vigil, on hearing the storm petrels slipping into their nest burrows under the holy stones—'Quietly as the rustle / Of an arm entering a sleeve'—he jotted down in the dark:

Not lonely here, I have the companionship of thousands of birds rearing their young . . . a life I never knew existed.

More isolated than the monks of old ever were in their busy little community, he noted for himself:

I feel more affection for everyone when I'm alone on High Island than when I'm among a crowd. Love, the supreme good, the redeeming harmony in every person, in all of nature, needs detachment and space as well as intimacy. Simply by being alone in this place I feel its force.

Richard, who at that time lived in Cleggan village and owned a *púcán*, a small traditional sailboat, had the miner's cottage partially roofed with the intention of sailing out to spend four or five nights on the island now and again. As the poems in his collection *High Island* attest, these solitary retreats were profoundly rewarding; nevertheless, after one spell of five days during which he saw the sun for twenty minutes only, he gave up spending more than a few hours there at a time, 'being neither a hermit nor a saint.' In 1985, having left Connemara for Killiney near Dublin, he offered the island as a gift to the people of Ireland and called upon the Office of Public Works to preserve it as a wildlife sanctuary—it has been estimated that a thousand pairs of storm petrels nest there, as well as Manx shearwaters, fulmars, peregrine falcons and ravens—but it seems that the state's response to this was so laggardly that the gesture was withdrawn, and eventually the island was sold to a trusted friend of Murphy's, Feichín Mulkerrin of Claddaghduff, who preserves it as an unpolluted wildlife sanctuary and whose piety towards its legend and history is profound.

Imagining the island now, left to the seals that mysteriously sink from sight in its deep coves, the silently circling fulmars, the screaming gulls, my thoughts tend as if by gravitational attraction to that granite globe the fishermen were testing their strength on. George Petrie noted it as lying in the cashel when he investigated the ruins in 1820, as did Kinahan in 1869. When I visited, it was outside and to the south of the cashel, and no doubt it gets moved around. Richard Murphy in a poem boasts of lifting it to his thighs; I saw the fishermen getting it to chest height, and, to spare their toes, casting it from them a little as they let it fall, and they told me of a John King who once carried it up to a little cairn on the hill to the east and back down again. Kinahan wondered if it had been used for grinding corn in a rock basin, but that seems very unlikely, and no such rock basin has been found. It is a natural water-smoothed stone such as one finds on storm beaches or in creeks where crashing waves grind rocks together, shaping them over millennia, unusual only in being so nearly a perfect sphere, just a little flattened from pole to pole as is our own globe, the one whose weighty cares we cannot cast from us. Omey Island is part of the nearest granite emplacement; the stone could have been brought across by ice in the last glaciation and shaped by wave action at the foot of High Island's cliffs, or perhaps it was found on the Omey shore and shipped here by the monks; but wherever it was born it had to be hoisted up the cliff, and so its presence is proof of its weighty significance. Perhaps then it was part of the symbolic furnishings of the monastery, as it is now part of my emblematics of Connemara. From St Féichín's invocation of the plague to Richard Murphy's love affair with loneliness, the dangerous equations argued by High Island are those between humanity and pollution, society and contamination, companionship and distraction from the eternal. Even if we feel that the eternal can well look after itself—for it has time on its hands—we might be made uneasy by that sterile orb, glinting in the harsh light of High Island's associations. Is it a prevision of the Earth's future? In St Féichín's time, that pool of medieval darkness, things may have seemed clearer, but nowadays we cannot distinguish plague from people, there being so many too many of us.

Sometime Island

Omey, an irregular low-lying square mile of granite, sand and pasturage, is nipped off from the south of the Aughrus peninsula by a pincer movement of each rising tide and reunited with the mainland by a wide sandy beach at every ebb. On suchlike tidal islands, claimed and relinquished twice a day by the sea, the alternation of high water and low water is as pressing as that of night and day, the two time patterns do not harmonize, and since the modern world wags by the twenty-four-hour clock the antediluvian rhythms of the sea become an inconvenience. Because of the importance of getting children to school in Claddaghduff or Clifden on time (as measured by the time of the land) all the island families have now moved out and Omey's only full-time resident is Pascal, the boatman whom I met there over twenty years ago, and who is sometimes seen wading through the inswilling water on his way home from Sweeney's bar in Claddaghduff, holding a final pint high above the splashes.

I revisited Omey recently in the company of a French friend, Sophie, to call on Giselher Kaule, who rents a small farmhouse there for some months every year as a base for the researches I have described apropos of Cleggan Head. The crossing place is at the foot of a road that runs down to the shore from the church in Claddaghduff and delivers you onto the sands. The island is nearly half a mile away; a row of posts marks the route, which, depending on the weather and the time of year, is passable for six or eight hours around the time of low water. Our car drummed across the hard sand-ribs, the sea hardly visible far off to right and left. Omey is low-lying, treeless, and on that day, although it was the middle of August, rather greyed by a damp mist. Its one narrow road starts where the line of posts ends, climbs a rocky shore and turns south between small stone-walled wind-tousled hay-fields and a very few one-storey houses. The ruins of a more substantial two-storey dwelling appeared on the left; this was the home of Henry Kearney, who some seventy years ago owned half of Omey as well as Aughrusbeg and Shinnanagh, a tract of land now largely forested, on the Clifden–Cleggan road. Richard Murphy, who had a little hideaway on Omey in the 1970s, heard that Kearney was remembered as a rich miser too mean to get married.

Kearney used to walk to cattle fairs wearing a raincoat belted with a rope of straw and with newspaper stuffed in his boots to save the price of socks. During the 'Emergency' of 1939–45, when news was as scarce as the tea and the sugar, it was often said, in reply to the question, 'Where did you read that?,' 'I read it on the paper in Kearney's boots.'

Soon the road turned westwards, and the broad sandy-shored lake that occupies the middle of the island appeared on our right, and opposite it, the house Giselher rents. There we were overwhelmed by welcome; Giselher's wife Brixi and her cousin Traudi, two ladies in lacy Bavarian tops, brimming like steins with joy and fun, had a quite unexpected and un-Irish meal ready for us, with slivers of smoked lamb, the grainy breads that we suppose have been introduced by immigrant workers into the Clifden bakery's formerly restricted repertoire, and a craggy apfel strudel. Then Giselher showed us the map on which he had anatomized, or atomized, Omey into no fewer than thirty different vegetational associations, as an aid to predicting what the effect of the fall-off in farming will be on the cultural landscape and the biosphere. As soon as the meal was finished we roved out to view the island's discreet wealth, led by Giselher's far-focused blue eyes and floaty white prophetic beard.

The Irish names of Omey's five little townlands are indispensable. Guairín, small dune, which the local people call simply Guairí, dunes, is the wide-open tract of dunes and machair stretching from the lake to the north-western corner of the island. An Cartúr Beag, the small quarter, is the north-eastern portion, mainly of small walled pastures. An Storraicín, the small pinnacle, includes a miniature mountain range of surprisingly sharp summits, east of the lake. An Chluain, the meadow, is the south-eastern quarter, of grazing land that was 'striped' when Mr. Kierney's holding was bought out by the Land Commission and divided among his sub-tenants; on the OS map of 1899 one can see the pattern of long, almost straight walls radiating from the lake to the shoreline. And lastly, Guairín an tSionnaigh, the fox's small sand dune, partly of striped meadowland and partly of open sandy commonage, occupies the south-western corner.

The reason the fields of the last two townlands were looking shaggy is that corncrakes were breeding in them and the farmers are paid a grant to delay cutting the grass for silage until the fledglings have left the nest (and then the mowing is to start from the middle of each field and work outwards so that the birds are not driven into a last stand and finally killed by the machinery). We saw no corncrakes—they are shy, skulking birds reluctant to take wing when not on their fabulous migrations to and from Africa—but as we walked northwards across the commonage we did see eight or ten choughs, the small red-beaked crows only to be found nowadays in the western fringes of Ireland; the little flock fluttered with surprised shrieks as if it had been tossed into the air by an invisible hand, and settled again to strolling on the thin layer of herbage carpeting the sandy plain. Choughs eat the beetles that eat cowpats; they are an indication of the health of the machair, said Giselher. In 1841, a few years before the Famine, the population of Omey was an amazing 396; the island must have been as worn-out as an old mat beneath the footprint of that gigantic cohort of humanity. The only way to keep it going was to heap seaweed on it, and the only food it could grow for that hungry multitude was the prolific potato; when the potato succumbed to disease the population was, by 1851, reduced to 205, and it has continued to fall ever since. There were thirty-two households here in 1856; when I first visited in 1988 there were three, and now Pascal, in his battered mobile home where the road peters out near the western shoreline, is alone with the seagulls for much of the year.

However, a dozen farmers now living on the mainland raise some or all of their suckler cattle on the island, and the grazing pressure of between thirty and a hundred beasts, depending on the time of year, keeps the commonage in good condition, so that, ecologically, it seems that the sandlands of Omey are in their prime. And their openness, their gently undulating sward nibbled down into a flowery carpet out of some rather ascetic Persia, make it a joy to wander to and fro, changing direction at random, diverting to look at every little eye-catching feature. Perhaps rabbits are a problem—it is a long time since there was a fox in 'the fox's small sand dune' to keep them in check—because their tunnelling breaks up the consolidated dunes and exposes the sand layers for the wind to rip. A storm will spread a layer of sand from the eroded dunes or from the sandy tidal zones over the machair, through which the buckshorn plantain and other sturdy little rosette plants quickly push their way up to spread their leaves in the sunlight again; in the more exposed areas it looks as if the sward is composed of the smallest number of plants that can just cover it by stretching out to touch each other leaf-tip to leaf-tip. Burrowing rabbits, birds rooting for grubs, the heavy tread of cattle, the discarding of oyster and winkle shells in middens by prehistoric seafood-gatherers, and the scattering of these middens by the tearing wind, are all part of the endless upsetting and resettling of this land under the lash of the sea. The sand is rich in the ground-up shells of creatures that extract dissolved calcium carbonate from seawater to house themselves; on land these break down further, sweetening the pasture with lime and nourishing both the cattle and the land snails one sees in colourful plenty cruising the machair, which build their own shells of it, and in turn die, dissolve in rainwater and seep back into the sea. There are three main springs draining this slightly domed, rain-sponge land of Guairín, Giselher told us. Each is fed by a flush, a long shallow depression full of watercress, at the lower end of which the water bubbles up through lush grass or forms a pool among stones coated with limey deposits and furred with a curious greyish moss that has crunchy, lime-stiffened fronds, the rare *Cratoneuron filicinum*. One of these springs flows out to the northern shoreline, another to the west, and a third feeds into a small bay to the south of the townland. This last outflow is a holy well, Tobar Féichín. We became antiquarians, or pilgrims, and diverted to visit it.

The real name of Omey is Iomaidh Féichín, St Féichín's bed. 'On a certain night, the holy man being in the monastery of Easdara was by an angel admonished in his sleep, that it was the divine will that he should go to a certain island of the ocean,' says John Colgan in his *Acta Sanctorum*, and in my first volume I mentioned the holy wells in the pass of Mám Tuirc and at the ford of Ballynahinch, and a 'bed' of stones he left by the shore of Fountainhill, on the mainland just east of Omey, that seem to mark the way he took, coming from Sligo to here. His well on the island used to be visited on his feast day, 20 January, and according to Roderick O'Flaherty, writing in the mid seventeenth century, 'of late proves very miraculous for restoring of health.' There is a little recess in the low stone wall that surrounds it, containing some white pebbles which perhaps were used for counting the 'rounds.' When each of us had paid his or her own form of homage to the sacredness of water we crossed the sandy hillocks to see the saint's church, or at least the ruins of a medieval parish church that occupies its site, close to the north shore.

It seems that Féichín was not made welcome on his first coming:

But the inhabitants, by the suggestion of the Devil, endeavoured by all means to exclude him; whence, at night, they, several times, cast into the sea the spades, axes, iron tools, and other instruments which his monks used in the work of building; but as often as they were thus cast, so often, being cast back on shore, were they found by the monks in the morning. But when the man of God and monks, thus meeting with the opposition of the people, persisted in continual labours, watchings and fasts, and the people, hardened in malice, denied them all nourishment, at length two of the brothers perished, being worn out with want. But St. Féchin, having poured forth for his servants a prayer to the Lord, in complying with whose will those who were thus exhausted had perished, merited that they should be recalled to life.

Perhaps the Omeyites have always been resistant to conversion; when I come to Clifden and the history of the Irish Church

Mission Society I shall tell how the evangelical schoolmaster of Omey had to pile his family into his coach and flee across the sands from their resentment. Not a stone of his church remains; or rather, they have all been put to good use here and there about the island. More recently Féichín's church too had a narrow escape from the islanders' best intentions. Over the years since it became disused, which was perhaps in the seventeenth century or earlier, it had been almost entirely drifted over with sand so that only the tops of its gables were visible, and in 1981 the parish priest organized a restoration effort, and a JCB was brought onto the island. But if the parishioners acted with benefit of clergy they did not have benefit of an archaeologist, and as the body of the church was emptied of sand so the pressure of the sand outside began to force its walls inwards. Work was stopped before the church collapsed, however, and the damage was repaired. Now the roofless, simple little church—rectangular, with a lancet window in its east gable, a doorway in its north wall and a blocked-up flat-topped doorway in the west gable—lies in a broad sand pit, and its confident rugged stonework is a pleasure to contemplate. Stretches of stone walling can also be seen in the sides of the pit, the remains of a surrounding rectangular enclosure about twenty yards long by nine wide, within which graves, less deeply buried than the church, have been found.

This was once the hub of a sizeable and long-lasting religious community, which was presumably motherhouse to the hermitage on High Island. Fifty yards or so inland of it the sappers of the first Ordnance Survey in 1839 recorded the site of a graveyard in which it was said only men could be buried. No trace remains of that, at least on the ground surface, but many other graves have been found in pits around the church enclosure, and to the north-west of the church a previously unsuspected monastic site was brutally thrown open in January of 1991 when a storm ripped away a low cliff face of sand, and skulls and skeletons spilled out. An archaeological dig-against-time there in 1993 found remains of three houses dating from the 1800s, below which was an enclosure with a wall nearly two yards high, partly already lost to the sea, with a mass burial of about forty-five bodies within it. Two *leachta*, low stone altars, with white quartz pebbles on them, were found too, one on top of the other, and two cross-inscribed slabs have subsequently been found among the masonry tumbled on the foreshore below the sand cliff. Three hundred yards to the east, to complete this brief necrology of necropolises, there is another long-disused burial ground by the shoreline called Cnocán na mBan, the hillock of the women, which was reserved for women only. The saint's mother is said to lie in it—but bones are surfacing here and melting away under the rain in the course of the sand's restless workings, so perhaps the good lady has already contributed her mite to the endless recycling of material between land and sea.

Having poked reverently around these boneyards we moved on eastwards and looked at the former national schoolhouse, opened in 1883, closed in 1973 because of the dwindling number of scholars and now made into a holiday home. Near it is the odd little flat-roofed one-room house Richard Murphy built in 1974, sitting like a hexagonal nut bolt upright on a little height, as a scriptorium for times when it was too rough for him to sail out to High Island, Omey offering a compromise between hermetic inaccessibility and car-borne convenience:

> The bed filled one of the six walls opposite a golden-rectangular window facing north with a view across a shallow sound to Aughrusmore. A sink and a gas cooker filled the wall under a window looking down across the strand, where, on a rising tide, I could watch the two arms of the sea join to embrace the island for five hours and part to release it from isolation on the ebb . . .Whenever I entered, harassed by rain, wind and the anxieties of life on the mainland, the figure of the hexagon, repeated like a musical theme with variations in the walls, the table and the ceiling, calmed me with a sense of concentricity and gave me the centripetal energy I needed to sit down, take out a notebook, and write.

By this stage of our walk the mist was beginning to veil all distances; a group of riders out from a pony-trekking centre on the mainland seemed at a loss, motionless grey silhouettes on a near horizon, and it was certainly going to rain. But Giselher was anxious to show us the little hay-fields and abandoned potato plots of An Storraicín, so we clambered over unsteady drystone walls and bulges of bare granite in the little Rockies just east of the lake. The commonage we had now left had been designated as a Special Area of Conservation, which gives it some legal protection, but these old fields should have been included too, he said, for they are extraordinary in their botanic richness. And indeed the crazily humped and hollowed, wriggly-walled plots—like a basket of broken crockery—tucked in between and around great slanting rock outcrops, were rank with wildflowers: red and white clover, ox-eye daisies, common sorrel, devil's bit scabious, as well as various grasses Giselher named for us. The margins and fissures of the granite were equally alive, brimming with bell heather, ling and tormentil. A magnificent sheet of the glinting rock thirty or forty feet across lifted us to the topmost point (which is less than a hundred feet above sea level; one must adapt one's scale of heights and sizes to the terrain in order to appreciate its dramatics), and looked around us, but the view was gone, and the mist was thickening into rain.

So we crossed fields down to the road, tramped the half mile or so to base through an increasing downpour, fleeing the great process, the run-off from the hills, the soaking of the sand-plains, the brimming of the holy well and secular springs, the necessary mouth-to-mouth resuscitation of the land by the sea, and turned in at the gate with relief. Traudi and Brixi were as effervescently generous as before; they plied us with cakes and tea in front of a splendid fire. Then Sophie and I bethought ourselves of the rising tide, that overriding quasi-insular consideration, and said goodbye. The rain had stopped by the time we reached the edge of the strand. We were in plenty of time to cross; in fact another shift of ponies and riders was just heading out to Omey, and a few local lads in their cars were practising handbrake turns and drawing doughnuts with their tyre tracks on the patient sands.

Controversial Pitch

Main Street and Market Street, the two broad thoroughfares of Connemara's little çapital, form a west-pointing angle; Hulk Street, narrower and rather crooked, completes with them a slightly bent triangle; one guesses that, if the site had allowed, Clifden would have been a perfectly regular triangle, that a geometrical inspiration has been thwarted by the underlying irregularity of the terrain, and that, in terms of the ideologies of its founding in the early 1800s, an Enlightenment and Protestant will has been subverted and humanized by aboriginal, Catholic and recalcitrant wilfulness. A turf-brown and foaming stream off the Twelve Pins, a sequence of rowdy cascades and slow-turning pools made for salmon poachers, cuts down through a glen to the head of Clifden Bay, leaving the southern face of the town, the backs of the houses and shops, the old ruin of the gaol and the new supermarket along the outer side of Market Street perched precipitously above a steep, rocky and overgrown slope and, according to the state of the tide, a broad oval of mud or of sheltered seawater; while bare rounded heights of bogland loom above the roofs of the hotels, the post office and the tourist shops of Main Street. There are two spires: the taller, that of the Catholic church, is prominently displayed on a rise near the eastern end of Main Street, with the former convent, now adapted to various civic purposes, behind it; while the more modest spire of the Protestant church rises from a leafy, genteel and private-feeling little quarter of lanes climbing northwards from the busy junction of the two broad streets, the focus of market-day hubbub and traffic jams. (The hostilities, now long allayed, between the two institutions these spires stand for will be my theme, after this brief preliminary orientation.)

Of recent years it has seemed that development, particularly of holiday apartments, would eliminate every spare inch of open or underused space around this triangle of streets, but for some reason the interior of the triangle remains unregenerate, almost derelict; one narrow lane winds through it from Main Street, climbing between back premises and neglected corners to a little patch of open ground and dipping again to emerge through an archway onto Market Street. A few years ago there was much talk of a project for Mexicanizing this rundown enclave to celebrate Clifden's connection with Mexico (which amounts to the fact that in 1846 a John Reilly, thought to have been born in Clifden, led a group of fellow-deserters from the US army to join the Mexicans; they became the core of a brigade called the San Patricios and their courage so impressed the Mexican general that he said that if he had had a few hundred more of them he would have won the war). This fantasy was enthusiastically forwarded by Daniel Dultzin, then Mexico's fun-loving ambassador to Ireland, but since he was posted to Brussels to take up more mundane EU responsibilities the idea seems to have lapsed, which is a pity; we Roundstoners were looking forward to seeing the Clifden folk dozing through long afternoons here, booted and spurred legs stretched out across the alleyway, sombreros tilted over their noses to keep off the fine Connemara rain.

Roads to various elsewheres depart from each vertex of the Clifden triangle. Carrying straight on eastwards from the end of Main Street one passes a hotel and shopping 'complex,' a building supplier's yard, and a cattle mart out into open countryside and the main road to Galway. The signpost for Cleggan and Letterfrack directs one up the hill by the Catholic church past a proliferation of new holiday homes, the entrance to a hidden-away housing estate, then St Anne's Home for the Aged and, on the northern fringes of the town, Mike and Patricia Gibbons's hostel, Dún Gibbons, which was built with hill-walking tourists in mind but to date has functioned as a direct-provision centre for asylum seekers. From the junction of Hulk Street and Market Street, where the triangle is already sagging into the valley of the Owenglin, the road for Ballyconneely twists southwards and crosses the river, passes the leaf-hidden Franciscan monastery on the left and the Community School on the right (giving me a chance to thank Brendan Flynn, until recently the vice-principal here, for his creation, Clifden Community Arts Week, which brings artists of international standing to the town each September for a festival that still holds to its initial commitment to Connemara's children as well as to us grateful adults). Finally, from the western vertex of the Clifden triangle goes a road that soon forks; the left-hand way down to the harbour with its old warehouses, one of which is refurbished as a restaurant, and Alexander Nimmo's old stone quay, the right-hand fork climbing to become the Sky Road, the famous scenic drive around the peninsula west of the town. On the left is the Abbeyglen Castle Hotel with its green lawns and flowery shrubberies slanting down to the harbour, and its battlements, which, if flimsier, are I suppose not much more anachronistic than those of Clifden Castle, *circa* 1815, a mile further on. Before it acquired its battlements and became the Abbeyglen Castle Hotel it was simply the Abbeyglen Hotel; the abbey is historically and physically non-existent, but the place's even earlier name, the Glenowen House Hotel, was less advantageously situated in alphabetical lists. Of most relevance to the history I am working my way into is the first avatar of the building, or at least of its oldest part, as Glenowen, 'the Female branch of the Connemara Orphans' Nursery.' (Gleann Eoghain was the name of the area it stands in, but who this Eoghan or Owen was is forgotten.)

Here I will introduce Honor, a child of the Famine. Her (Catholic) parents having died or abandoned her, she had been brought up in this Protestant institution, and was therefore stigmatized as a 'jumper.' (This disparaging term was originally applied to members of a mid-eighteenth-century Welsh Methodist group who jumped about in their religious excitement, and later came to refer to other Protestant sectaries; in Ireland it became an insult thrown at Protestants in general and missioners and their convertites in particular; perhaps the similarity of sound with the Irish *iompú*, 'turning,' from one religion to another, for example, may have eased its entrance into common speech.) Honor was staying with relations in Clifden before going to join a brother in America, when she was approached by the nuns of St Joseph's Convent, which had been set up as part of the Catholic Church's response to Protestant proselytizing. This is the story in the words of Miss Gore, Matron of Glenowen:

Here the nuns got round her, promising her great things if she would go to the convent as their servant. After a great deal of ill treatment from her relatives, she unhappily yielded. Last week I saw her on her way to the convent, and beckoned to her to come to me. I then spoke to her of the fearful sin she was committing in forsaking Jesus for the Virgin Mary, and in bowing down to images of saints, etc. I entreated her to consider what she was about, and to examine her heart by that blessed Word which she had been taught in the Nursery, and to pray to the Lord for the Holy Spirit to convince her of the evil course she was about to pursue for the sake of the gain of this world. During the time I was speaking to her thus, one of the girls from the convent came up to us, and began to whisper Honor to leave me; however, she remained, and the other went, and reported the conversation to the nuns. When Honor returned to them, they taxed her with speaking to a jumper, and said they would send her to a good place where she would never see a jumper, warning her, at the same time, not to go near the Orphan Nursery. Instead of obeying their orders, Honor came up to the Nursery on Saturday last. I had another talk with her. After a little while she burst into tears, declaring she had not had a happy moment from the time she went to the convent; the teaching there was quite the opposite of the Bible teaching, which she knew to be the truth; and that she was acting now quite against her conscience. The next day, Sunday, she was expected to appear at mass at the chapel, and Father K— endeavoured to get her consent to take away her two little sisters from the Nursery, and to get them to the convent. Poor Honor seemed greatly grieved at what she had done, and she resolved not to return to the convent. On Sunday she felt so happy to be again in her class and at church, praying to God in her own tongue, instead of attending mass, and hearing Latin prayers.

So that was one-up to the Protestants in the soul-count. There are several such accounts of 'brands plucked from the burning' in an ICMS publication, *The Story of the Connemara Orphans' Nursery*, some of them involving a degree of physical tussling as well as threats of eternal damnation. As a correspondent for *The Times* who visited Clifden in 1850 noted:

> That the ladies and gentlemen embarked on this crusade are most earnest and sincere, none dispute; whether they could, or could not, carry on their operations less open to the accusation of bribing converts, by feeding them, I cannot say: that they have raised the utmost hostility of the priests, is only natural; that they must cause much domestic division, is inevitable. That they feel themselves justified in this, I do not dispute . . . But I will say nothing further here on the subject; to touch any of these matters in Ireland, is to handle a sort of controversial 'pitch'—you are sure to be blackened.

Nevertheless, I will delve a little deeper into the pitch. And it is only fair to the memory of the religious disputants to begin by describing the alternative accommodation provided in the workhouse for girls like Honor by the secular authorities. Here is the correspondent for *The Times* again:

> Here I have the painful task of recording a state of things most disgraceful to a Christian, civilised land. The parent house was built for 300. There are now 759 in it!! The total number of inmates in all the houses was 2,439 . . . There was a yard, with a day ward in it, of about 30 ft. by 15 ft., with an open roof, in which were about 160 small children; in one corner there was a child with the small-pox out upon it; at least 30 of the others had not been vaccinated. The state of these children's clothing was quite shameful. Many of them were mere skeletons. They were walked out into the yard for me to see them better; as they passed us, one child actually, whether of herself, or by order, put her hand across to hold the rags together in front of the poor thing that walked with

her, that we might not be more shocked than she could by such ingenuity prevent; they looked in the yard so cold, so comfortless, so naked, and such a libel on humanity, that I was glad to have them called in again to the close and infected atmosphere of the crowded day room . . .

And so on; it gets worse, but I have quoted enough.

The establishment of Glenowen together with an archipelago of other soul-saving enterprises, mainly in the west of Connemara, was due to a collaboration between an English cleric, the Revd Alexander Dallas, and Hyacinth D'Arcy, the landlord and son of the founder of Clifden; I will associate each of them with a building on the Sky Road circuit.

Clifden Castle arose out of wilderness early in the nineteenth century, to the admiration of visitors such as Henry Inglis in 1833:

Let no traveller be in this neighbourhood, without visiting Clifden Castle, the delightful residence of Mr. D'Arcy. The walk from Clifden, by the water-side, is perfectly lovely; and the distance is not greater than two miles. The path runs close by the brink of a long narrow inlet of the sea, the banks of which, on both sides, are rugged and precipitous. It was an evening of extraordinary beauty when I sauntered down this path; the tide was full, and the inlet brimful and calm; and beyond the narrow entrance of the bay, lay, in almost as glassy a calm, though with a gentler heaving, the wide waters of the Atlantic. After reaching the entrance of the bay, and rounding a little promontory, Clifden Castle comes into view. It is a modern castellated house; not remarkable in itself; but in point of situation, unrivalled,—mountain and wood rise behind; and a fine sloping lawn in front, reaches down to the beautiful land-locked bay; while to the right, the eye ranges over the ocean, until it mingles with the far and dim horizon. Twenty years ago, the whole of this was bog: and now not a rood of bog-land is to be seen.

Within twenty years of this calm and lovely vision, another visitor, on another day of calm, saw the castle on the eve of its desertion by the D'Arcys:

> As I entered the park, I saw how busily the hand of improvement had been at work; a melancholy feeling stole over me, and my deepest sympathy was, you will allow, very naturally excited . . . The view was indeed beautiful, but a melancholy stillness pervaded the whole. Not a ship—nay, not a boat was to be seen. The blue waves broke on the shore unvaried by any tokens of human existence. Under the idea that the house was deserted, I entered a spacious hall; then a room, in which, close to the window, was a harp, betokening at any rate recent occupation. Alas! thought I, melancholy doubtless were the last strains that proceeded from those strings. I crossed the hall, and entered another room; it was yet early; the windows were open, and a gentle breeze had sprung up from the sea. The table in the centre exhibited preparations for the morning meal. I therefore made good my retreat, fearing lest some of the family were resident, perhaps still lingering to the last moment, amid scenes that must naturally be so dear to them.

Although the Irish sept O'Dorchaidhe anglicized its name as Dorcey or Darcy, and then aspired to the use of the apostrophe and became d'Arcys, the D'Arcys of Kiltullagh in eastern Galway claimed a pedigree stemming from Sir John D'Arcy, the fourteenth-century Justice of Ireland, a descendant of the genuine Anglo-Norman d'Arcys. They were a Catholic family; the lawyer Patrick Darcy, eminent among the Confederate Catholics assembled at Kilkenny in 1647, was commissioned to raise an army in support of King Charles I, and as a result lost his estates once the Parliamentarians had defeated and executed the King and Cromwell had suppressed the Irish rebels. In the *Books of Survey and Distribution*, which list the previous owners of lands seized by the Cromwellians and those in possession of such after the restoration of Charles II, a James Darcy appears as proprietor of many townlands, formerly O'Flaherty territory, in the Clifden area (the town itself, and the name, Clifden, did not yet exist); it seems likely that this was Patrick's son James, the family having been 'transplanted' further west under Cromwell, and like many transplanters managed to avoid actually making the terrible journey but hung on unobtrusively until they regained some or all of their former estates after the Restoration. Four generations later, in 1804, another Patrick D'Arcy, husband of Humanity Dick's sister Mary Martin, died without issue, and his estates went to his second cousin John D'Arcy. He too was a direct descendant of James Darcy the transplanter, and he was visited by the idea—which must have seemed foolhardy to his contemporaries—of genuinely transplanting himself and his family and making something of this tract of bog and rock on the edge of the Atlantic. Nothing could be further from his background and European connections. His aunt Jane D'Arcy had married his great-uncle, another Patrick D'Arcy, a mathematician and philosopher who as aide-de-camp to Maréchal de Saxe had fought at Fontenoy and became Count D'Arcy, while Jane, as Countess D'Arcy, became a lady-in-waiting to Marie Antoinette and the hostess of a brilliant Paris salon.

John D'Arcy, like Humanity Dick's father Robert Martin and many another landlord of Catholic background, had conformed to the established Church in order to save his inheritance, consisting of the Kiltullagh estate near Athenry and lands in Mayo as well as the Clifden, Sillery (i.e. Omey Island and its hinterland) and Kylemore estates in the far west of Connemara. Shortly after the death of his first wife, Frances (*née* Blake), in 1815 he leased out Kiltullagh and started on the building of his fantasy home between the Atlantic foam and the cloudy mountainside. It was, and is, even in its present state of sorry neglect, rather grander than the description quoted above indicates. An extravagantly sinuous half mile of carriageway, flanked by four standing stones (not genuinely prehistoric, but lending an antiquarian tone), leads from the gatehouse to a fine Gothic-arched portal flanked by two slim round turrets in the centre of the southern façade, which commands the view of the bay; a massive square tower rises over the central hall, and there is an attached round tower at the east end of the frontage. The whole is generously castellated. Nearby are the wrecked remains of a grotto through which a stream flows, with a shell house or 'marine temple.' Of all unlikely people, Asenath Nicholson, the doggedly itinerant American Bible-reader, was charmed by it:

> I saw here a fairy castle, with variegated pillar and open door, made of shells of the most delicate shades, arranged in stars and circles of beautiful workmanship. These showed exquisite taste in the designer, and must have been done with great cost and care. A labouring peasant, still working for eightpence a day, was the architect of this wonderful fabric.

At the same time as the castle, the town of Clifden was coming into existence. The area was known as An Clochán before it was, as James Hardiman puts it, 'fashionably anglicized' as Clifden; the Irish *clochán* covers various sorts of stone structures, and here referred to stepping stones across the Owenglin river (the '*ch*' becoming '*f*' as in many placenames involving *cloch*, a stone). At first the spelling was variable; the Blakes of Renvyle spelled it Cliefden, and the acidulous scholar John O'Donovan could still sneer about it in 1839, scribbling in one of the Ordnance Survey name books, 'Why did not Mr. D'Arcy call this clifftown, i.e. town on the cliff which could be descriptive enough, cliff-den! den in the cliff.' At first progress was slow because of the lack of a quay and of a road from Galway, but after the failure of the potato crop in 1821 the government, in response to D'Arcy's representations, put money into public works, and soon the rapidity of Clifden's growth was astonishing all reporters. Where there had been only one slated house (belonging to a Walter Coneys) and a few thatched cabins, by the 1830s the principal streets, seventy feet wide, unpaved but clean, were lined by two-and three-storey slate-roofed houses; the population was variously reported as 1,100 and 2,000; there were two hotels, twenty-three public houses, an Episcopalian church, a Catholic chapel and monastery, three schools, a police barracks for twenty and a gaol for a hundred; there was a courthouse in which Mr. D'Arcy as magistrate presided over quarter sessions and petty sessions; there were quarterly fairs and Saturday markets, a distillery, shoemakers, tailors, carpenters, blacksmiths and linen weavers. The quay, designed by Alexander Nimmo, had not been completed and was inaccessible at low water; nevertheless good stores had been erected and merchant vessels were bringing in iron, pitch, ropes, earthenware, etc., and taking away fish, corn, kelp and marble, and this place, 'heretofore only remarkable for smuggling and illicit distillation,' was now paying a considerable amount of excise duty.

This hopeful venture soon fell on bad times again. In 1831 John D'Arcy wrote once more to Dublin Castle:

> I consider it my duty to acquaint you that great distress pre-vails in this neighbourhood in consequence of the failure of the potato crop last season, being one half deficient of its usual produce and the quality is so bad that disentery & fever has already made its appearance to an alarming extent. There is sufficiency of oats in the country but the poor are unable to purchase it. The object of my present communication is to request you will order that the people shall be employed in finishing the publick works already begun in this part of the country, and that those funds which are applicable to that purpose . . . should be timely applied to relieve the poor & enable them to earn the price of provisions & to make a sowing for the next year . . .
>
> The prevention of illicit trade is absolutely necessary for the protection of the merchant & trader. A corps of Revenue police were for some years stationed at Clifden (without whose aid I should probably have failed in my undertaking). Under their protection a distillery was established. They were removed about three years ago, and the distillery & spirit retailers were much injured by illicit trade. Restoring the Revenue Police to Clifden would effectually protect those embarked in the spirit trade who expended their capital on the faith of that protection. The next is to have a proportion of the money granted for public works expended in improv-ing the different approaches to the town (as the barony is too

poor to do so) and it must be admitted that the first object should be to open communication to the country & to enable the people to bring their produce to market. There is one thing more, a daily post. We suffer great inconvenience from its being only three times a week . . .

Mr. D'Arcy had this appeal followed up by a petition from the townsfolk, as a result of which the pier was finally completed, while another missive from him to Dublin Castle in 1834 at last brought about the completion of the roads to Galway and to Westport.

John D'Arcy, it seems, was well regarded as a landlord, and, unlike Thomas Martin at Ballynahinch and Colonel Thomson at Salrock, was not inclined to interfere in his tenants' religious practices. When the Protestant Archbishop of Tuam sent in the Connaught Home Mission Society to evangelize in the area, and the Catholic Archbishop of Tuam transferred two Franciscan brothers from the recently established monastery in Roundstone to inaugurate one near Clifden, D'Arcy was concerned to preserve peace between the two confessions. Two assault cases came before the magistrates in 1837, in pleasing symmetry: an evangelical curate, the Revd Brabazon Ellis, was alleged to have assaulted a Catholic woman, and the Catholic parish priest, Revd O'Malley, was alleged to have assaulted one of his flock who had converted to the rival faith. John D'Arcy, still close to the Church he had been born into and concerned that reports of religious conflicts might injure the reputation of his tender young town, drew his fellow magistrates' attention to the Catholic Church's efforts to put down the spirit of dissension, and contrasted them with the Revd Ellis's conduct, which 'seemed directed to the inflaming of the minds of the people, disturbing them from their peaceable avocations . . . first to exasperate and them calumniate them.'

D'Arcy may have been a conscientious and benevolent landlord, but the economic decline of the times, and the recurrent potato failures, were against him, while his vast expenditure on the castle cannot have helped his personal finances. In 1837 he mortgaged all his estates, and on his death two years later (which at the early age of fifty-four seems to have been unexpected), his eldest son

Hyacinth inherited his father's debts, but not his wisdom. I have read somewhere that Hyacinth suffered from some painful disability and found his best comfort at sea in a small sailing boat; perhaps pain lay at the root of his notoriously contentious disposition. In 1843 Daniel O'Connell held one of his 'Monster Meetings' in Clifden as part of his campaign for the repeal of the Act of Union, and a crowd estimated at 100,000 heard Hyacinth denounced by one of O'Connell's supporters for having tried to forbid the meeting: 'I said before that the men of Connemara would not sell their consciences nor be deterred by the imbecile threats of any despotic landlord from engaging in the struggle of their country . . . Can the contemptible wretch now dare assert that he could prevent his tenants from coming here to manifest their patriotism and prove their attachment to Liberty?' Shortly after the Clifden meeting O'Connell was arrested on a charge of conspiracy and spent some months in prison. His release was greeted with nationwide celebrations, to which Clifden's parish priest and his flock wanted to contribute a peaceful demonstration around a bonfire and a triumphal arch; D'Arcy, as magistrate, forbade this, had a confrontation with the local temperance band and behaved as if he were dealing with an insurrection, arming the crew of a steamer in the bay and issuing the police with sky rockets to call on the sailors for aid if needed. Some shots were fired, but the town remained calm, and later on D'Arcy had to defend himself to Dublin Castle against a memorial from the townsfolk claiming that his actions were intended to excite a riot rather than prevent one.

During the Famine, though, it seems that Hyacinth did his best, as chairman of the Board of Guardians and of the Clifden Relief Committee, to alleviate the sufferings of the people through the distribution of Indian meal, the provision of public works, and the operation of the workhouse, all these initiatives being repeatedly thwarted by the government's parsimony. By 1848, with the town the D'Arcys built being drained of its population by starvation, sickness and emigration, Hyacinth D'Arcy was bankrupt, and two years later his castle and lands were put up for sale through the Encumbered Estates Court. Nearly all of the estate went to the principal mortgagee, Thomas Eyre of Bath, for £21,245, and the Eyres were to be Clifden's landlords, absentees apart from occasional holidays, for the next eighty years. The castle was abandoned in the early twentieth century, the demesne was let out to local shopkeeper graziers, and after some disgraceful squabbles was striped by the Land Commission and distributed among tenants with holdings nearby, who also held the castle in common—an arrangement which led to its being stripped of its roof and windows and left in its present abject state, with a barbed-wire fence attached to a corner of it as if it were no more than a cowshed.

About three miles west of the castle the Sky Road—that standing invitation to the contemplation of sunsets—having climbed along the steep slopes above Clifden Bay, falls almost to sea level and turns north to cross the peninsula and then east to return to Clifden along the shore of Streamstown Bay. For that short stretch of the road between the two turns we are in the townland of Ballymaconroy or Kingstown Glebe. A glebe is the land attached to a clergyman's residence as part of his benefice, and the forlorn ruin visible 300 yards to the west of the road was indeed a Church of Ireland rectory once. But first, why 'Kingstown'? Long before the rectory existed this area was Baile Mac Conraoi, the settlement of the Conroys, a clan immemorially associated with Connemara who became tributary to the O'Flahertys when the latter moved into the territory in the thirteenth century; their name has been confusedly rendered into English as King, the Irish for 'king' being rí. There are records of a Mac Conraoi leasing a half-cartron of land near here for six shillings and eightpence a year from Murchadh na Maor O'Flaherty of Bunowen in 1615, and tradition says that Dubhdara Mac Conraoi, who built the now-ruined chapel in Kill, by the shore to the north, was murdered by the O'Flahertys of the castle of Doon, on the opposite side of Streamstown Bay.

The rectory was built in 1809 at a cost of £400, by a clergyman who 'sadly disgraced his profession,' according to the Blakes of Renvyle:

The barren unprofitable spot which had been purchased as glebe land, in order, from its vicinity to the sea, to facilitate an intercourse with smugglers, and on which the parsonage house was built, whose too ample offices testified the same unhallowed purpose, is situated at the distance of four miles from the church, and from the nearest protestant parishioners . . . who are indeed as a few scattered sheep in the wilderness.

But in 1819 the neglected Diocese of Tuam got a new archbishop, Dr Power le Poer Trench, an energetic evangelizer who soon dispersed a squad of like-minded curates—Trinity College men trained in the Irish language for this purpose—to wake the West out of its religious slumbers. The Revd Charles Seymour took in hand the inchoate expanses of the Union of Ballynakill, which contained not only the parish of Clifden but most of Connemara, including the Joyce Country. One of his weapons in what he saw as a holy war was the Bible translated into Irish:

I have found my Irish sword (Irish testament) of singular service in clearing away the obstacles that opposed my English weapon (the English testament). I am every day polishing, sharpening, and, I thank God, in some degree successfully brandishing my Irish sword . . .

Seymour's swordwork was vigorously parried by the Catholic clergy, who prohibited their flock from sending their children to the mission school in Clifden, but the D'Arcys, the Martins of Ballynahinch, the Blakes of Renvyle and other gentry supported him and his successor at Ballynakill, the Revd Anthony Thomas. Two of the Archbishop's zealous curates, the Revd Mark Anthony Forster at Roundstone and the Revd Brabazon Ellis at Moyrus near Carna, founded the Connemara Christian Committee in Clifden in 1836, with Hyacinth D'Arcy as its treasurer. Both the proselytizers and their converts faced such denunciations from the Catholic altars, and even physical violence—Ellis and his wife finding themselves almost prisoners in their own house in

Clifden—that the committee, inspired by the success of the Revd Edward Nangle's famous settlement on Achill Island, bought a bleak stretch of blanket bog in Sionnanach near Cleggan with the idea of founding a Protestant colony. That scheme came to nothing, but with the aid of General Thomson of Salrock a settlement of convertites was housed in Moyrus and another on the little headland called Ross near a new Protestant chapel in Kill on the south shore of Streamstown Bay, and similar little enclaves took shelter behind rectories at Ballyconneely and elsewhere in western Connemara, as well as at Castlekirke near Mám. All this fostering of division (which was not to the taste of many of the regular Protestant clergy living peaceably among their Catholic neighbours) can be seen in hindsight as a straightening of the way for the coming of the Revd Alexander Dallas, whose messianic self-confidence and millenarian delusions added another dimension to the sufferings the Famine was to inflict on Connemara. The old rectory at Kingstown Glebe was to become his campaign headquarters.

Alexander was a soldier, first under Wellington and then under Christ. He served as a commissariat officer in the Peninsular War and at Waterloo, became a man of fashion and author of a French farce in a brief *Vanity Fair* period of life, almost decided to go with his cousin Lord Byron to Greece, married unhappily and had several children, studied divinity at Oxford, was ordained, and after financial and emotional crises surrendered himself to the Holy Spirit, which he now realized had been 'moulding the heart of His servant for a vessel unto honour prepared for His own use.' As Rector of Wonston, near Winchester, he bullied his flock for their own spiritual good, but after ten years' labour he had to admit that their tendency to relapse had defeated him; however, a pamphlet of his, a 'little work of prophecy' concerning the conversion of Jews and the soon-to-be-expected Second Coming of Christ, gave him some standing in evangelical circles and led to a fateful meeting with the Revd Anthony Thomas, the incumbent of Ballynakill, who was also concerned with the conversion of the Jews. Thomas invited Dallas to address the Irish branch of the Jews Society (as the interfering body concerned with their conversion was called) in Dublin, which he did, and he was enthusiastically heard. In 1845 he was offered a gift of £3,000 by a wealthy English gentleman towards the task of bringing the elect out of the bondage of popery before the onset of Armageddon, and was enabled to begin his personal mission to the benighted Irish. Using the new 'penny post' service, he arranged for 90,000 copies of his modestly titled tract, *A Voice from Heaven*, to reach 'respectable' Roman Catholics in miraculous simultaneity; as he himself put it, 'The military manoeuvre of the soldier was now brought into full exercise in the Lord's work.'

Later in that year of famine, 1846, Dallas toured Ireland soliciting patronage from influential Protestants such as the Duke and Duchess of Manchester and Lord Roden, and visiting mission stations, including Castlekirke. (This name is the anglicization of Caisleán na Circe, the hen's castle, so called from a legendary defence of the nearby island-castle by Grace O'Malley; it is said, perhaps disingenuously, that Protestants were first drawn to the spot in the expectation of finding a kirk there.) In Clifden Dallas was welcomed by Hyacinth D'Arcy, who had established a school at Ballymaconroy and was holding prayer meetings there; their subsequent collaboration was, according to Dallas, 'the confluence of two rivulets of prayer for Ireland.' Thenceforth he was particularly concerned with the western fringes of the Diocese of Tuam, where the minor clergy were already engaged in preliminary skirmishes of the millennial battle:

> Not more surely did the British army fight the battle of all Europe on the plains of Waterloo, than do the spiritual clergy and laity of the Church of Ireland fight at this moment the battle of God's truth against the apostasy of Rome, for the Christians of England as well as for themselves.

Soon Dallas had seven ordained missioners, sixteen scripture readers and a dozen schoolteachers at work among the peasantry, in the spirit of his exhortations:

> I know what miserable, grovelling, ignorant, superstitious creatures they are. You must learn to love them in the midst of

all their degradation. If their filth, and folly and superstition and passion repel your love you are not fit to go among them. You must be able to see the jewel of God in the midst of that dunghill, and condescend to be the scavenger to get it.

That God was on his side was evidenced by the Famine; starvation and cholera were the instruments by which 'many hearts were being prepared to receive those consolations which the glorious Gospel of God can alone impart.' During one of his visits, in 1848, he saw this work for himself:

> We walked across Mannin Bay, and on our way we saw about a dozen poor famished creatures attempting to work, but too weak to do anything. It was impossible to lose the opportunity of telling the gospel to these apparently dying men, as they stood or sat around me like living skeletons. They listened with fixed attention, as if they were pausing on the brink of the grave to receive a message from heaven as to their journey beyond it . . . As I stepped into the boat I prayed for them as for those who had heard the call of the gospel probably for the first, still more probably for the last time.

But his adjutants, more permanently faced with the realities of suffering, could not match his heroic indifference to the body; an element of famine relief crept into their ministrations, which naturally favoured those who attended to their preachings, and so, with a certain inevitability in this world of impure motives, the practice of 'souperism' took root.

In 1849 Dallas's web of activities was formalized as the Society for Irish Church Missions to the Roman Catholics, with headquarters at Exeter Hall in London (a venue already known as the Vatican of Evangelism). For some years the ICMS rode a tide of anti-Catholicism among English Protestants reacting against 'papal aggression,' as they called the campaign of Pope Pius IX to impose the ancient authority of Rome throughout Christendom, fearful too of revolutionary unrest in Europe, including Ireland,

and of the influx of disaffected Irish Catholic labourers, and agitated more immediately by the Oxford Movement and the apostasy of such high-minded men as Newman and the Wilberforce brothers. Funds flowed in from Dallas's devoted English followers (one of whom, Fanny Bellingham, married Hyacinth D'Arcy), and western Connemara was garrisoned with missions. A sixpenny guidebook for 'parties who may be desirous of inspecting for themselves the operations of the Society' suggests this exhaustive itinerary: the Galway mission house, Sunday service at Barna, the mission school and orphanage at Spiddle, and the mission schools at Inverin, Casla, Clynagh and Lettermore in south Connemara; then, returning to Galway and taking the Bianconi car towards Clifden, the enlarged church and a school at Oughterard, schools at Glan and Glengowla and a detour to the Castlekirke mission; at Clifden, the new church, male and female schools and girls' orphanage; the boys' orphanage at Ballymaconroy; then south to the new mission church at Errislannan and the school at Ballinaboy, the parsonage and school at Derrygimlagh, schools at Aillebrack, Doohulla and Roundstone; thence by boat across the bay to the church, parsonage and schools for boys and girls in Moyrus; then north from Clifden to schools at Streamstown, the church, parsonage and school at Sellerna, schools in Cleggan, on Omey and Turbot Island, at Barnahallia near Claddaghduff and Fakeragh near Clifden Castle; finally north again to the new church, parsonage and school at Moyard, schools at Tully and Cloonlooaun, the church and school at Salrock—and so on to another almost comparable constellation of institutions in County Mayo.

In 1852 the society was claiming that 1,659 children were attending its schools, and that the congregations of its churches totalled 2,030. This was a new Reformation, and it brought forth its own church music. Here are the first and last verses from the Hymn of the Omey Islanders, as the Revd W. C. Plunkett, chaplain to the Lord Bishop of Tuam, heard it on his admiring visit in 1863:

And shall we shut the Book of Life,
And shall the sinner die?

Then every Omey Islander
Will ask the reason why!

And never more shall priests of Rome
Beguile us with a lie,
For every Omey Islander
Will know the reason why!

At Ballymaconroy the Connemara Orphans' Nursery was opened in 1849, in the old glebe house with its suspiciously spacious outhouses, which D'Arcy had leased for the purpose. The second Mrs. Dallas (the first having died in 1847, a few years after the break-up of their marriage) wrote an account of this 'nursery for Heaven' to a ten-year-old niece of hers who was fund-raising for it:

> I have often told you the dreadful state these poor children were in before they came to the Nursery. Their arms and legs were perfect sticks, their faces and jaws had scarcely any flesh upon them, and their heads were covered in sores—all from the want of food. As to clothes, many whom I saw last summer had but a mere rag that did not cover their bodies; now they are looking well and healthy, and have clean clothes, though their food is very different from yours: and they do not have meat or bread very often, only a mess made of Indian corn; and their clothes are provided according to what kind friends in England may send. These orphans have now other food beside that which their bodies require. Their souls are fed with the knowledge of God's holy Word. Formerly they were left in ignorance of God, and knew nothing—growing up like wild goats upon the mountains. If they picked up any knowledge from the poor people around them, it was the knowledge of evil—to worship the Virgin Mary, and practise idolatry, like the heathen . . . Mr. Dallas asked the boys of what trades they would like to be; and one chose to be a tailor, another a shoemaker, and another a carpenter; and five little boys cried out, 'I will be a Scripture

reader.' . . . The girls are learning different kinds of household work, and I hope, in time, there will be some good little servants among them.

More details of the boys' regime are given by the orphanage's director, the Revd Roderick Ryder:

There are 11 employed in digging for two hours in the morning and two hours in the afternoon; and the strength and activity that some of them display, although but twelve years old, and without shoes, in very severe weather, in digging land that has not been moved these 20 years, is truly wonderful . . . On Tuesdays and Fridays, when I meet my people for prayer at Ballyconree School-house, subjects are appointed for discussion, such as, 'Justification by Faith,' which was our last.

In 1853 the girls were moved to Glenowen, next door to Mr. D'Arcy's rectory (he had been ordained in 1851), while the storm-battered old glebe house was replaced by a larger building with farm outhouses, so that the boys could be trained in agriculture.

When, a few years later, a Catholic convent and then an orphanage were set up in Clifden by the Mercy nuns from Galway, as part of Archbishop MacHale's counter-reformation, some disgraceful tussles took place over undernourished little bodies and their bewildered souls. The Revd Hyacinth D'Arcy in his pulpit railed hysterically against the priests, associating them with the Jewish priests we read of in the gospels:

Oh, what have these priests to answer for? Who bribed Judas to betray him? THE CHIEF PRIESTS!! Who, I say, PERSUADED THE MULTITUDE THAT THEY SHOULD DESTROY JESUS? The Priests!! THE CHIEF PRIESTS!!! Yet, who persuaded the multitude in Clifden market, on Saturday last, to stone the men that said the Son of God was sent from heaven to make satisfaction from sin . . . THE PRIESTS!! THE PRIESTS!! . . .

Within a few more years the supremacy of the ICMS was in doubt: with the Crimean War raging, interest in its activities had waned and donations had fallen off, while the Indian Mutiny had suggested that the Christianizing of India was more urgent than the Protestantizing of Ireland. By 1863 the ICMS had withdrawn from west Mayo to concentrate on west Galway. The income of the society was no longer enough to pay its ministers, who therefore were open to the temptation to leave the wearisome field of battle, especially as the prospects of a reasonable pension to reward their decades of struggle and keep them out of the workhouse faded. The broad body of Irish Protestantism had long regarded the missioners as troublemakers, while an imminent Second Coming was a fading dream. Dallas made his last tour of the missions in 1869, the year of the disestablishment of the Church of Ireland. Shortly after his return to England:

> . . . a severe cold fell upon his lungs, and after three days of great suffering he entered into the joy of his Lord . . . No fear or doubt beset his dying pillow. When Psalm xxii, 4 was read to him, he said, 'I don't fear; what have I to fear? My sins are more in number than the hairs of my head; but the blood of Jesus has covered them all.'

With the death of Hyacinth D'Arcy in 1874 the ICMS lost its local chieftain, and then in 1879, the year of hunger and unrest that saw the foundation of the Land League, its hold was further shaken by an astonishing outburst of physical confrontations, a sectarian parallel to the secular campaign against landlords and their agents. The first victim was William MacNeice, schoolmaster of Omey, known locally as Croisín, little cross, it is said, from his being 'a little martyr of a man.' One day at the end of February Father Rhatigan, the newly appointed Catholic curate at Claddaghduff, crossed the sands to Omey, burst into the school 'in search of his lost sheep' and was hit over the head with the soup ladle, by whom is unknown. MacNeice and his wife ejected him, and the school was stoned by an angry crowd. Father Rhatigan in his sermon the next Sunday gave it to be understood that he had his bishop's backing for 'seeking satisfaction' from jumpers. Soon afterwards the mission school at Belleek near Streamstown was burned down, and the MacNeices were attacked on their way to church at Sellerna and had to be rescued by armed police, one of whom was beaten unconscious by the mob. The family then left the island, fleeing across Omey strand in their coach. Sixteen persons were charged with riotous and unlawful assembly. In April the school at Rossadillisk was set on fire, a hundred extra police were brought in by Bianconi car from Galway, and a temporary police station—a twelve-foot-square, four-and-a-half-ton prefabricated box, with portholes—was erected at Claddaghduff. Mr. MacNeice came down from Dublin under police escort for the trial, as a result of which most of the defendants were transported to Galway to await the quarter sessions there in July. Father Rhatigan and another local priest, Father Flannery, set up the Connemara Anti-'Jumper' Defence Fund to cover their legal costs. Meanwhile the mission school at Ballinaboy had its windows and door smashed, and another temporary police station was installed there. Questions were asked in Parliament about the Clifden situation; two more temporary stations were erected, in Kingstown and Errismore, and a permanent one at Moyrus where there was ongoing hostility to the ICMS and its 'jumper' community. In the event it seems no one went to jail for the 'Clifden disturbances'; released on bail, the defendants melted away, most of them probably going to America. Mr. MacNeice never returned to Connemara, but his son, a child at the time the family fled Omey, later taught at Ballymaconroy and went on to become Bishop of Cashel and Waterford; he married an Elizabeth Clesham, daughter of a matron of the Glenowen orphanage (and one of their sons was the poet Louis MacNeice).

By this period the ICMS was an anachronism; its like had faded out of existence elsewhere, but in Connemara the poison persisted. In 1880 widespread famine in Ireland was averted largely by the efforts of a charitable body, the Mansion House Relief Committee, working though local committees, as explained in its subsequent report on the crisis:

Within the parish area alone were found all the elements of such an organisation: the Roman Catholic and Protestant clergy, the dispensary doctor, the magistrates, traders, and Poor-Law Guardians, daily face to face with the actual aspect of affairs; with interests, sufficiently divergent to create a wholesome check without lessening the bond of a vital interest in the unhappy people . . . In only three instances throughout Ireland, was there found the slightest difficulty in combining the Catholic and Protestant clergy in hearty brotherhood, on the Committees. The exceptions were parishes in Connemara where the Protestant clergymen happened to be also members of the Irish Church Mission Society. It was agreed on all hands that a union of the conflicting elements in these three localities was impossible, and that it was equally impossible to withdraw grants from places literally threatened to be devoured by famine. The sage council of the Protestant ARCHBISHOP OF DUBLIN was, under the circumstances, cheerfully followed; and the Distribution Committee were authorised to put an end to the difficulty, by making grants to two Local Committees in the same neighbourhood in those special cases. It was the only occasion on which, during six trying months, any shadow of religious division vexed the plain course of charity.

A sad distinction for Connemara, the ICMS's heritage of hate; but it faded in the end. The pathetic little outcast settlements of convertites, huddled near the Protestant strongholds of rectory and mission school, were eroded by emigration and relapse, and dwindled away, though the hurt of ostracism and the demeaning name of 'jumper' remained with some families for generations. By the 1900s Glenowen, or the Bird's Nest, as such orphanages came to be called, was housing waifs from Dublin and other cities rather than from Connemara; the Protestants still preached the gospel in the street every Saturday 'and nothing comes of it except that once in two years or so there is a trifling riot,' according to Stephen Gwynn. Glenowen lasted until 1955, but the Ballymaconroy orphanage was burned by the IRA during the Civil War; forty-five bewildered boys were driven out and locked in the gate lodge while their only home went up in flames, before the matron, who was out shopping at the time, returned to march them into Clifden. From there most of them were taken by gunboat to Plymouth, and travelled on to London, and eventually to Fagan's Homes in Australia. A few remained at Glenowen; here is a last glimpse of them, as remembered by a member of the Heather family of Errislannan, kind patrons of the orphanage:

> Once we had two of the small boys in the back of our car. A woman with three children stood on the pavement in Clifden, and one orphan tugged at the younger one and said, 'Look, Jimmy, *that's* a mother, see?' Jimmy peered through the window until the family were out of sight.

Perhaps history runs shallow for certain periods, leaves little changed. For a time the Evangelicals were a resource for a small proportion of the children of the Famine. Hypocrisy was part of the pragmatism of the Connemara folk in their struggle for survival, and the missioners taught them no better. What was required of them in return for bodily food and shelter was not a surrender to a soul-shaking conversion-crisis or the adoption of a demanding personal ethic, but merely an ability to parrot formulae—the Kingstown boys particularly excelled at 'Twenty-four Reasons for Leaving the Church of Rome,' complete with supporting texts. Perhaps even some of the missioners took their own sermons with a pinch of salt. The Revd Roderick Ryder, for instance, had been ordained as a Catholic priest and would never have lost the deep-rooted organic relation to rural society granted him by that irrevocable fact. Neither his conversion nor his subsequent marriage were enough to strip him of the aura of magic that invested a priest in those old days and country places (and if a priest had something supernatural about him, a priest's wife was an even rarer and more wonderful phenomenon, on whom some of her husband's powers would be expected to rub off; I have heard that after Mrs. Ryder died the 'priest's wife's shift' was kept locally as a relic for sick people to come and touch in hope of a cure). Ryder was also a native

Irish speaker and it is said that when he had to conduct some evangelical preacher around the locality he would stand behind the visitor and undermine his pious outpourings with a murmur of, 'Ná bac leis, tá tú ceart go leor mar atá tú'—'Don't mind him; you're all right as you are.' The Bible-thumpers may even have convinced a few of the hollowness of all dogma; the ICMS journal, *The Banner of the Truth in Ireland*, quite exceptionally records one outburst of truth, from a Moyrus woman harassed by missioners and priests: 'God help us between ye. I think we should all stay at home and go near neither of ye, and let ye fight it out between ye.' And the reams of documentation left by the ICMS, their pamphlets full of smug self-justification and humble professions of unworthiness by those conceited enough to think themselves the elect by grace of God, not to mention the mind-numbingly repetitious recitations of their puerile beliefs—all of this stuff, heaped into a mound, goes up in an inglorious smoky bonfire at the touch of one spark of wit, still relished in Clifden, from a man who said, as he passed the Catholic chapel on his way to the Protestant meeting house, 'Slán leat, a Dhia, go dtagann na fataí nua!'—'Goodbye God, until the new potatoes come!'

From Ballinaboy

Tá mo mhac le cur, is tá do mhacsa le crochadh—'your son is to be buried, and mine is to be hanged'; the words of the mother of a lad arrested for killing another in a faction fight, spoken in shared grief with her neighbour. Their heavy fatalism has scored them deeply enough into the folk memory to survive when all their context has been worn away. I cannot even remember who gave the saying to me, but I know its mention was prompted by our talking of the rebel friar known as Father Miley, who in his old age was called out of hiding to administer the holy oils to a dying man after a fight at Ballinaboy Fair, and announced that that would be his last act as a priest. But that story itself, even if it does refer to the same incident, says nothing more about the victim or his killer. Dates are unfittingly vague: Father Miley came to Connemara as a refugee from the massacres in Mayo after the failed insurrection of 1798, and died worn out by years (how many years?) on the run in the bogs and mountains; Ballinaboy Fair probably faded away soon after a licence to hold a fair was granted to John D'Arcy for his newly founded town of Clifden, a few miles to the north-west, in about 1820. I will leave the brawlers' epitaph to stand alone in its grand rhetorical symmetry, undated.

Ballinaboy is nowhere nowadays. Everything seems to hurry through it: a little river out of Roundstone Bog meeting salt water as soon as it passes under the bridge, the traffic on the coast road zigzagging awkwardly before and after the bridge and making it hard to loiter and unpick the involved topography. The Bog Road from Tuaim Beola comes in from the east immediately north of the bridge, and just past that junction the coast road, making for Clifden, dips across the head of the sea inlet, isolating a damp hollow on its inland side walled by tall rhododendron bushes. Sometimes the road is interrupted here by high spring tides for an hour or so, and the Irish name of the place comes into its own: Béal

Átha na Báigh, the opening to the ford of the bay. The locality is shadowed by sycamore, ash and, on the steep southern bank of the inlet, shaggy Monterey pines, one of them fallen, that make wide scything gestures. Such plantings in Connemara invariably mark the conjunction of shelter with the former presence of gentry; in fact the Morrises, descendants of Ballinaboy's landlords, are still the owners of a trim eighteenth-century villa hidden from below by the brow of a steep knoll rising behind the great pines. Their driveway curls away into privacy from the south end of the bridge, and the few other houses nearby are also discreetly treed about, protecting the retired status of their occupants; I used to call on a former RAF wing commander here, and there was a German ex-pilot, but who lives here now I do not know. Ballinaboy is the empty hub of a web of ways that formerly converged on the fair, some of them long foundered in bog. I will take it as a starting point and follow out two of these routes. One leads north-eastward to melancholy, the other west-north-west to mirth.

The Bog Road mentioned above was one of Nimmo's works of the 1820s; before it existed, if Thomas Martin of Ballynahinch wanted to go to the fair he would follow a winding bridle-track lying a mile or two further north, and I am told that whenever his coach got stuck in a slough he would climb onto its roof and sound his horn to summon the tenantry from the scattered cottages along the route to come running and drag him out. The western few hundred yards of this way is now a minor road branching off the Bog Road close to Ballinaboy and serving a few isolated houses, beyond which it degenerates into a track along a slight ridge and then becomes scarcely traceable. A privately owned stretch of bogland alongside the track, from which the land falls gently northwards to a stream valley, was the site proposed for Clifden Airport in the 1980s, and logistically it would have been very suitable since the town is only a mile or two away along a little road on the opposite flank of the valley. But this is part of the environmentally precious and beleaguered Roundstone Bog, and after a contentious campaign (some absurd but bruising moments of which I have described in *My Time in Space*) the Clifden entrepreneurs had to look elsewhere, and there is now a possibility that an airstrip on a less ambitious scale will be built on bogland north of Clifden, by the road to Cleggan.

So much for the intrusion of modern anxieties into this otherwise ignored and bypassed corner of the bog, this quiet bottom-land with its scattered lakelets and patches of badgery old woodland. My immediate object here is something ancient and sacred: a boulder, an erratic, torn out of one of the strata of marble that traverse the Connemara lowlands just south of the mountains, and left by the ice fields some 12,000 years ago on the schists that underlie the bog here. It has split and fallen apart into three or four cuboid fragments and weathered into rough ledges that house little ferns and herbs, and in its size and shape and its isolation, on a dry patch out on a very wet bog, it is all that could be required for its role of mass rock. In the days of the Penal Laws such a rock might have served as a makeshift altar for an oppressed community that could not afford to be surprised at their devotions by the authorities; a century later the people had their mass houses and little chapels, but the priest was proscribed, a man on the run, so they went out from their homes in secret to meet him here. Father Miley was the celebrant; his ministry was a secret one, for as a fugitive from justice, a prison-breaker and murderer, he was an outlaw.

In 1798, for ever known as the Year of the French, General Humbert's expeditionary force landed at Killala in Mayo in support of an Irish rebellion against English rule. After an initial success at Castlebar the Franco-Irish forces were crushed with great brutality. Many of the rebels fled from Mayo where the English yeomanry was hunting for them; some got away to France with the help of George O'Malley's father and other smugglers, and others lurked for years in the mountain fastnesses of Connemara, where Father Miley became their leader. Father Myles Prendergast, to give him his full name, was an Augustinian friar from Murrisk in Mayo who had long supported the United Irish cause and in 1798 had hurried to Castlebar to welcome General Humbert. When the rebellion was suppressed he went on the run and became the leader of the Connemara outlaws. There was talk of fully a hundred armed men drilling in broad daylight under his captainship, drawing their supplies locally and from plundering expeditions into Mayo, and, when that failed, being 'resolved to levy a "black mail," even on their hospitable friends in Connemara.' In the aftermath of the rising the chief prosecutor of the United Irishmen was the Honourable Denis Browne, brother to Lord Altamont of Westport House, and he went about his task of having people hanged with such enthusiasm he earned the nicknames Soap-the-Rope and Donncha an Rópa. The blind poet Raftery, the most famous itinerant rhymer of his time, curses him in a song about the men on the run in Connemara. The verse is very fierce: he says he'd like to shake hands with Denis Browne, not out of friendship but to string him up with a hempen rope and stick a spear in his big belly—and threatens that many of the fine lads he drove overseas would be returning with help, in red uniforms and lace-trimmed hats, and a French drum will be beating for them:

A Dhonncha Brún is deas chraithfinn láimh leat
agus ní le grá duit acht le fonn do ghabháil,
cheanglóinn suas thú le rópa cnáibe
agus chuirfinn mo spiar i do bholg mór.
Mar is iomdha buachaill maith a chuir tú thar sáile
a thiocfas anall fós is cúnamh leo,
faoi chultaí dearga agus hataí lása
is beidh an droma Francach ag seinm leo.

In another verse he names some of the men on the run, describes their sufferings out in the bogs 'under thirst and dishonour, and the cold of night,' and cries 'shame' on those who didn't help them, for unless Christ wills otherwise, they will succumb, and others with them.

Tá Johnny Gibbons is ár nAthair Maol're
agus iad á gcaomhúint amach faoin móin,
faoi thart is faoi easonóir is fhuacht na hoíche
is níl fiú an braon dí acu ná dram lena ól.
Ní mar sin a chleacht siad ach fuíoll na bhfuíoll
agus shoraidh díofa nach dtug aire dó,

is rímhór m'fhaitíos mura bhfuil ag Íosa,
go mbeidh siad síos leis, agus tuilleadh leo.

The Johnny Gibbons whom Raftery mentions in association
with Father Miley (an tAthair Maoil're) was the son of Lord
Altamont's land agent John Gibbons, an elderly gentleman who
became treasurer to the Connacht branch of the United Irishmen.
John senior was captured after the defeat of the rebellion but
escaped to France where he joined the recently established Irish
Legion in the hope of participating in another French expedition
to Ireland, which never materialized, and he died in Antwerp a
ruined man, his family back in Ireland having been hounded by
Browne. His son Johnny, a close relative called Affy Gibbons and
Father Miley had been captured and imprisoned in Castlebar after
the failure of the rebellion. The story of their escape was recorded
in the 1930s from an Irish speaker in Carna:

> When Father Miley was in prison he and the Gibbonses cast
> lots to see which of them would knock out the gatekeeper.
> It fell to Father Miley, but he didn't intend to kill him. The
> gatekeeper was asleep. They had no weapon but a sledge-
> hammer and he hit him on the head with the sledgehammer
> thinking not to kill him but put him into a deep sleep or a
> faint. It happened that he killed him with the blow. They
> took the key off him, opened the lock, and the three of them
> escaped.

Mayo being infested with redcoats, Affy fled to Inishbofin,
where he got work as a tutor, but quarrelled with one of the
Coneyses in a drinking house there and was murdered. Meanwhile
Johnny Gibbons and Father Miley got away into the mountains of
Connemara. Johnny's hideout was a recess among huge fallen rocks
on the forested steeps of Léim na hEilte near where the Mitchell
Henry mausoleum now stands. (Almost inaccessible nowadays
because of the dense understorey of rhododendron, Scailp Johnny,
as it is still called, was used by the IRA in the 1920s, and perhaps
more recently, I have been told. Its roof is a 21-foot-long block, and

in the rear of the cave is a small iron grate with a flue pipe.) Johnny was captured in 1800 with the connivance of the O'Flahertys of Ballynakill, who wanted the £300 price the government had put on his head. He was imprisoned in Galway, but escaped and rejoined his comrades in Connemara. Valentine Jordan, an important rebel leader who had returned from exile in France, was another of the Connemara outlaws causing anxiety to Denis Browne:

> This Province is not safe while Connemara is a secret asylum for outlaws of all descriptions. It has a great extent of coast, fine bays and harbours, and people are in the habit for the smuggling trade of running over to France. Thirty or forty French officers might live there in perfect safety, communicating with the enemy, organise a thousand rebels within it, set up there the standard of rebellion and make a material division of the forces of the country if there is to be a war.

Despite Browne's offering considerable rewards for the rebels' capture, in 1803 he had to report that:

> . . . there are still in the mountains of Connemara John Gibbons (Jnr.), Fr. Myles Prendergast and Valentine Jordan, whom it would be very desirable to arrest and send away. Gibbons is mad, Jordan feeble and penitent, and the friar the only one that could again do harm, being a most daring character of desperate courage and some influence arising from his sacred function.

But by degrees the rebels were worn down. Johnny Gibbons foolhardily went back to Mayo to attend a wedding, and while he was resting after the journey someone soaked his pistols in water and sent for the redcoats to deliver him into the hands of 'Soap the Rope.' When he was about to be hanged, he cried out, 'Ah Connemara, my five hundred farewells to you; no treachery would have come to me had I stayed with you!' Father Miley, through many trials and alarms, remained almost alone in freedom, a sad reminder of the hopes of 1798. It seems that he was recognized by the Catholic Church as the parish priest of the western parish of Moyrus, and the first parish priest of Clifden; so the rough block of marble out on the bog should be recognized as the spiritual foundation stone of that community. There are caves and dwellings, or their ruins, associated with his many escapades scattered over the region from Clifden to Carna, and one can still pick up fragments of his story from living mouths. According to the Carna folklore quoted above a spy once tracked the priest to a house in Doire Bhrón, a tangled bit of woodland and scrub a few hundred yards west of the mass rock, in which remains of a village and a mill can be made out in the undergrowth. Father Miley, guessing that this man's intentions were not friendly, shot him. Recently a Clifden man who was looking into the legend of this unusual parish priest enquired locally about some stones sticking up in the bog close to the old road from Clifden that passes by Doire Bhrón, and got the reply, 'That's the grave of the man the curate shot!'

The many stories of Father Miley's sojourn in Connemara add up to a tale of mounting weariness and despair. Always fearful of treachery, at any rumour of strangers he would shift from valley to mountainside, from house to cave. When he was in Mweelin near Kylemore Lake he heard of gentlemen who were ostensibly on a fishing holiday there, and immediately took himself off to Moyard, and then to a cave on Binn Bhán, the highest and most central of the Twelve Pins. From there he shifted to Derryclare, where he slept in a cottage but spent the days on the mountainside, and a girl brought food out to him. It seems that he and three other outlaws were captured once, but managed to escape from Galway Gaol by night; in the dawn a woman beetling her washing in the river saw them under an arch of the Galway bridge, where they were trapped by the tide. She told her husband, who came with a rope to rescue them, and they got away to Connemara again, where the priest continued this purgatorial life of alarms and harelike startings. Early one morning when Father Miley was asleep in a house up in Gleann Chóchan in the Twelve Pins, a young woman who had gone out for a bucket of water ran in to say that men wearing little gold caps the like of which she'd never seen before were approaching. He just had time to leap out of bed and run out of one door while the yeomen were coming in at the other. They chased him a long way through the mountains until they came to a river. Father Miley managed to jump it, but he slipped on the frosty ground and an icicle pierced his knee. Fortunately the soldiers could not cross the river, and he limped away to safety.

The yeomanry was quartered at Ballynahinch, but it was Ballynahinch that held his only hope of peace. Richard Martin, who was the largest landowner in Connemara as well as being the Colonel of the local Volunteer regiment and Galway's representative in Parliament, offered to get Father Miley a pardon from the government, for although the Martins were by that period anglicized gentry, their relationship to their tenantry was still coloured by the ancient mutual attachment of clan and chieftain, and their Protestantism was skin-deep, a cover adopted a generation earlier in order to be able to hang on to their estates at a time when Catholics' lands were being expropriated. But Father Miley would not accept a pardon unless his fellow outlaws were included, and that could not be done, so Martin could only advise him to move on, to the peninsula of Iorras Aintheach in south Connemara. There he had a remarkable escape—but that is a long story rooted in local topography, and I shall save it to tell when I come to write of south Connemara, that topography of tales.

Eventually, it is said, Lord Mayo got a pardon for Father Miley, who lived on into the 1840s in a cottage south of Ballinaboy, making a living by playing the bagpipes at weddings. He used to write out the Gospel according to St John for people to wear around their necks as a charm. He was once seen taking off his hat when caught in a hailstorm, to let the hailstones strike his head as a penance. Perhaps the story of the pardon is incorrect, for it is also said that he was living in a little cottage in Gowlaun, by the bridge two miles east of Clifden, when the yeomanry found him at last. Hearing them approach he took up his pistol but found that some traitor had damped it. 'Ní raibh mé i mo nead lachan ariamh go dtí inniu,' he said ('I was never in a duck's nest till today'); but the yeomen found him so pathetically decrepit that they left him to die in his own good time. His colleagues in the rebellion of 1798 had by then long gone abroad or died or vanished into obscurity. A verse from a lament for Affy Gibbons by an unknown Connemara poet, said to be Affy's uncle, can be their epitaph:

Is gurb as Cill Alaidh a ghluais an dé-smál
A dhíbir sinn ó chéile,
Na Francaigh a thíocht go hÉire,
Mo léan agus mo chrádh!

From Killala came the cloud of smoke
That drove us asunder,
The Frenchmen's coming to Ireland,
My grief and my sorrow!

Ballinaboy forms the root of a narrow, four-mile-long, high-ridged peninsula: Errislannan, Iorras Fhlannáin, named from St Flannan. The quiet country road running along it departs from the coast road a little south of the bridge and climbs steeply up Ballinaboy Hill. Stopping for breath on the slope and looking back to the south one sees, a mile and a half away out on Roundstone Bog, the footprints of a cluster of buildings: Marconi's telegraph station, burned down by the Republicans at the height of the Civil War in 1922, as I will tell when I come to that historic site. Looking the other way an alert traveller might notice a small stone cross in a field at a little distance to the left of the road. An inscription on it has been defaced and rendered illegible; it used to tell whose blood was spilt here, on Sunday, 29 October 1922. In July of that year, having destroyed the telegraph station, the workhouse and other large buildings around Clifden, the Republican forces had ceded the town to the National Army, and three months later retook it in fierce street fighting, before withdrawing to the surrounding heights. Two young IRA snipers from Ballina, Morrissey and Jameson, were stationed on Ballinaboy Hill to cover the coast road and the way to the Marconi station, the habitable buildings of which were still in the hands of the Nationalists. McDonagh, the officer in command of the Marconi unit, happened to be in Clifden during the Republican attack. Disguised in a long raincoat and an old *cáibín* or peaked cap, he mingled with the crowd coming out of Mass and came dodging down the road to Ballinaboy, where he got a sight of the snipers, produced a rifle from under his coat and shot them both as they were eating their sandwiches. (That is the story as I heard it in Roundstone from my old friend the fiercely Free Stateist John Barlow.) Despite this little victory McDonagh soon had to abandon the Marconi station, telling his men to go home, and himself taking a boat from Ballyconneely to Galway, where he narrowly escaped court martial. He fled to the States for a time, where it is rumoured he always carried a revolver, and then returned to live in Doohulla near Ballyconneely. He is remembered as a short, sturdy, vicious-looking man. Some IRA men from Mayo came down to kill him, I am told, but were dissuaded by their local colleagues. When, in about 1924, it was proposed to erect a memorial to 'the brave young Volunteers who died fighting for Ireland,' a letter to the *Connacht Tribune* newspaper protested that the burned-out ruins of the Marconi station and the Railway Hotel at Recess, and the destruction of rail and road bridges from Maam Cross to Clifden, were a fitting memorial to the 'short period of Republican rule' in Connemara. And when the little cross was installed, it was soon rendered wordless. Such are the brambles that infested, and to some degree still infest, that tiny fraction of an acre on Ballinaboy Hill.

A little further west at the top of the hill is a tall, slanting monument of limestone in the shape of an aircraft wing or tailfin; it commemorates the first transatlantic flight, in 1919, and is directed towards the actual landing place, marked by a white beacon like a tall beehive, a mile and a half away near the Marconi site on the lowlands now widely outspread to the south. Too many crossed lines of history here! Again, I shall write of the two heroic aviators, Alcock and Brown, in my next chapter apropos of the Marconi station. *Tá a ngaisce greanta ar chlár na spéire*, it says on the monument; 'their deed is graven on the face of the sky'—a fine line, and if it is not literally true one can admire its aptness to the aftermath of that deed, for from this windy height on a bright day the sky's vast forehead is furrowed with contrails, which are still feathering out and fading into haziness when the airliners, miles high, are well on their way to the New World.

Look around you from this viewpoint; never mind the crummy car-parking space with its bust-up benches and tourist litter. Ahead, Errislannan, virtually treeless, a blade damascened with the pattern of little stone-walled fields, sinks into the Atlantic. To the north is Clifden Bay, narrowing into the small harbour below the town of two spires perched up on its eminence, from which the long, bare, almost mountainous peninsula circuited by the Sky Road rises, stretches out and similarly comes to rest in the ocean. North of that again, glimpses of the further headlands or at least the hills on them, and the north Connemara islands, and then the mountains and islands of Mayo veiled in the distance. To the south, the broad waters of Mannin Bay with its gleaming beaches, and then the last of the western promontories, Errismore or Iorras Mór, turning away to the south-west and the last stand of land, Slyne Head. Nearly every one of these headlands and islands has its saint. I have written of St Roc at Little Killary, St Colmán in Inishbofin, St Ceannanach at Cleggan, St Féichín in Omey and High Island; yet to come is St Cáillín of Errismore. Then there is St Coelann of Deer Island off Roundstone Bay and his rival of St Macdara's Island, and the saints of the tangled archipelagos east of Carna, Bearchan, Breacán and Enda, and (I nearly forgot him) the obscure Mocán or Smocán of Barr an Doire near An Cheathrú Rua, and finally the great St Colm Cille, who has all the south Connemara coast under his protection. These names speak to me of the wonders of this world; the acts of the saints are inward and invisible signs pointing us to outward and visible graces; their interventions in topography—passes opened through hills, rocks sailed from one geology to another, springs summoned forth, pot-hole fonts hollowed out of granite—stand for the extra dimensions human histories have grafted onto places, particularizing and dis-criminating them, bringing a supplement of spaciousness to space, a treasure that is lost if memory is allowed to die and place reverts to the relative flatness of its three dimensions.

And here we have St Flannan; what of him? Son of Turlough, King of Thomond or North Munster, he entered the monastery of St Molua, which has given its name to Killaloe in Clare. There he laboured so diligently that a miracle was vouchsafed: after thirty-six hot hours in the bakehouse a heavenly light shone through his left hand, so that he could carry on working in the dark. This persuaded the Abbot to resign so that Flannan could take his place, inaugurating a legendary period of peace and plenty:

> The fields waved with the richest crops, the sea poured almost on the shore an abundance of large whales and every kind of smaller fish, and the apple trees drooped under the weight of the fruit, woods abounded in acorns and hazelnuts, the most restless nations were at peace, and the poor of every description experienced open-handed hospitality.

Flannan then went to Rome (sailing on a stone, according to one source) to be consecrated Bishop of Killaloe by Pope John IV, in AD 640. On his return a vast concourse of commons and nobles assembled to hear him preach. He is said to have travelled widely, bringing the good word; perhaps he even reached western Scotland, where the Flannan Islands may be named from him. There is an Inis Fhlannáin in Lough Corrib, and a holy well, Tobar Fhlannáin, in Inishbofin. He is the patron saint of the Parish of Ballindoon, which covers the area from Clifden south to Errismore (and is now, in the Catholic divisions, amalgamated with the Parish of Omey into the Parish of Clifden). In the townland of Kill (from *cill*, a chapel), three miles further down this peninsula of Iorras Fhlannáin he has both a well, where there used to be festivities, with tents selling food and drink, on his feast day, 18 December, and near it, a chapel, or the ruins of one. Local tradition credits him with an alteration to the geography here, to provide a site for his foundation, as I shall tell when I come to describe that area. This chapel 'admits no burial within the walls of it,' says Roderick O'Flaherty; it was believed that any corpse buried within it would be found above ground the next morning. The Morrises, landlords of Ballinaboy, broke this taboo to bury a daughter of the family within the ruined walls, and thenceforth had their vault there, without bad consequences that one knows of.

Errislannan, which was anciently O'Flaherty territory—it seems to have belonged more immediately to their hereditary doctors the O'Leys—came into the hands of the Frenches after the Cromwellian disaster. In the early eighteenth century Mathew French left the estate to his four daughters to hold in common, an arrangement that lasted until 1843 when the lands were divided between descendants of the four gentlemen—Lynch, Lambert, Skerrett and Burke—whom the daughters had married. The Lynch share, Ballinaboy and Maum, which lies along the road a mile or so west of the Alcock and Browne memorial, came by marriage into the hands of the Morrises, descendants of one of the mercantile families known as the Tribes of Galway. Captain Anthony Morris we have met: when he was in command of a Revenue cutter Captain George O'Malley gave him many a good run even though Morris knew the ways of the smugglers, having been one himself, as Captain George tells us. It was Captain Anthony's grandson, another Anthony, who obtained Ballinaboy and Maum in the 1843 division, and built the elegant little Ballinaboy House, tucked away out of sight to the north of the Errislannan road. Family tradition proudly recalls that he was a responsible landlord in the Famine times that came so hard upon his settling in Ballinaboy; he kept his tenants' cattle and sheep for them, and, as Barony Constable, when the government warehouse in Clifden received a cargo of corn but red tape was delaying its distribution, he broke down the doors and distributed it himself. But the Famine ruined him and the estate was leased to the Kendalls, an English family (I am told) who had a house at the west end of the Bog Road as well as the now obliterated Derrygimlagh Lodge. (Looking inland from the coast road a mile or so north of Ballyconneely one sees a big cashel-like structure on a low hill near the site of the lodge—a famine-relief folly the Kendalls had built to enclose their rose garden.) When John Kendall died in 1890 the next generation of Morrises, in the person of James Morris, bought out the Kendalls' lease, and re-established the Morris presence in Ballinaboy House. James was 'one of the last Irish-speaking J.P.s in the west' according to Kathleen Villiers-Tuthill, and his son, also James, was both British Navy man and an Irish patriot; he retired from the Navy in protest over the burning of Clifden by the Black and Tans, and later, under the name Séamus Ó Muiris, became the director of the fledgling Irish Navy. His nephew, Colonel Anthony Morris, retired to Ballinaboy in 1968; he it was who lent me the family documents from which I have reconstructed some of this history, and whom I used to meet occasionally, rather infirm but still militarily trim, going to see to the welfare of his beloved trout streams and lakes, until his death some years ago.

The other three co-heirs of Errislannan and their descendants we shall meet further west. Following the road as it falls gently through Maum and leaves Morris territory one soon sees a sturdy little stone-built Victorian church half-hidden in low windswept trees—a contemporary document notes 'the style of the building admirably suited to the surrounding scenery—from a plan drawn by Francis Farrell, Esq., architect.' It has a steep slate roof, Gothic windows, a Gothic-arched doorway in a square porch like a stunted tower, topped by an incongruous modern belfry of four tall blades arranged in a stook around the bell. A splendour of cream and purple Japanese anemone covers a large grave plot beside the neatly kept gravel path inside the gate; here lie the Revd Richard Henry Wall, died 1889 in his seventies, and Mary Anne Wall, 'relict of the above,' died 1890 aged eighty-five. The Revd Dr Wall had the church built, with the help of the Irish Church Mission Society, in 1853–5; he raised most of the money through a circular addressed to:

> All ye who feel a desire that Protestantism should take root in our land,—all ye who would wish to see the blessings of civilisation, industry, contentment, loyalty and peace grow up in this remote and unvisited peninsula, instead of barbarism, sloth, discontent, disaffection and turbulence . . .

As the society faded out later in that century and the general Protestant community dwindled in the aftermath of Independence, so the church fell into disuse, and in 1960 might have been demolished but for the devotion of a group of parishioners, the Friends of St Flannan's. Now it is open for Sunday evening services in July and August. The Revd Richard and his wife lived in Errislannan Manor, a little further on. The manor was begun in 1839 by a

James Lambert of Dublin, descendant of one of the four co-heirs of the Errislannan estate; he was brought low by the Famine and sold up through the Encumbered Estates Court in 1850. (It is chilling to read in the documentation of this sale, 'It will be seen by the above rental that three-fourths of the Lands are untenanted, and it may be fairly assumed that, if all were tenanted, they would produce an annual rental of £400.') The Revd Dr Wall purchased both the house and the lands, and advertised them for sale again a few years later—although for some reason the sale did not go ahead—having in the meantime completed the 'staunchly built and commodious' house and its extensive offices, planted 'upwards of 20,000 trees' and formed a garden full of thriving fruit trees. Of the next generation two sons were lost on active service with the army in India and a third with the navy in Jamaica; the Revd Wall's daughter inherited, and married the Revd George Heather—the first marriage in the little church, and the last for over a century. Two daughters of this marriage, two fond maiden aunts to the next generation, lived in the manor to a good age, until the land went to the Land Commission for subdivision among the tenants, and the house and its grounds were sold in 1958, after over a century of familial inhabitation. A granddaughter, Alannah Heather, a talented artist, has written a fond book about the place and its history, as well as her own wandering bohemian life. The writing of the book was precipitated by the collapse of a loft over the coach house, an avalanche of memory:

> All the beams gave way at once and down came sacks of letters and diaries, trunks of clothing and linen, crates of honey, boxes of china and broken furniture. Regimental flags wrapped in old corsets, dozens of sermons, my great-grandmother's will and a huge block of wood on which mutton had been chopped up.

The manor now belongs to Mrs. Brooks (her husband Donald died a few years ago), who runs a pony-riding school there, and it is still replete with the past and fresh with life, and wears its considerable privileges with grace and modesty. It is perhaps built on the site of an ancient religious foundation, for bits of medieval stone-work have been found in its walls during alterations, together with a small limestone carving of a robed, saintly looking figure that could be St Flannan himself. I revisited the lovely old place one recent summer's day. From the road (where in summer the ditch is sumptuous with purple loosestrife and creamy meadowsweet, and the stony roadside bank with spires of bright yellow gorse, purple bells of St Dabeoc's heath and the lingerie tints of honeysuckle) one sees the manor's mellow plastered façade—two-storeyed, with three dormer windows, a gable window at the east end and a central, ivy-covered porch—some way off across herb-rich pastures, looking down a slant of lawn to a small lake. A billowy crescent of mature trees is gathered comfortingly around the house to the rear, and a green hill rises steeply behind. One enters the grounds by a gate with tall cylindrical stone-built gateposts surmounted by small, silvered, prancing horses, and follows the curves of a shrub-lined drive. On this occasion, charming children were playing on the lawn in front of the house, white doves were pecking about, girls were overseeing tiny riders steering sedate ponies in a circuit around a paddock ('Tommy! Your left rein is longer than your right!') and a peacock and his hen perched on the lofty wall of the stable yard were winding their necks to and fro as if delighted by the view. After taking tea with Mrs. Brooks I visited the holy well, a natural bowl of water purslane in a stone-lined hollow with a few steps down to it, on the brink of the lake, and invested a coin in a small collection of them in the lap of a roundish stone lying on its surround. The old part of the graveyard, close by the well, is almost a thicket; one ducks under branches to enter the mossy rectangle of low broken walls of the medieval chapel, which itself has a fat-trunked ash and a fair-sized sycamore rooted in it. Two Morris family slabs, hard to read in the leaf-filtered light, are propped against a wall. The saint's bed, an uncomfortable boulder, lies outside the graveyard, to the east. The traditional tale as Alannah Heather has it is that the saint arrived from the Aran Islands driving a cow, and asked where he could spend the night. He was directed to an island in the lake, which was larger than it is now and lapped the foot of the hill behind the manor. In the morning the lake had shrunk to its present level, and the saint had a conveniently accessible site for his foundation—and, a dozen centuries later, so did the Revd Richard Wall for his manor.

Beyond the manor and the townland of Kill lies the westernmost townland of the peninsula, Drimmeen or Droimnín, literally 'small back,' so called from the green and grassy drumlin that terminates the point. Most of this townland belonged to the Skerretts, but a northern portion of it, Boat Harbour or Caladh an Bháid, belonged to the Burkes, these families being direct descendants of two of the four co-heirs of the Errislannan estate. Boat Harbour is a shingly bay with a small quay dating from 1869, near which is a curious house like the standard two-storey dwelling of a substantial nineteenth-century farmer, but given the airs of a villa by a flight of steps up to a porch and doorway on the upper floor, and adorned with two heraldic shields in plasterwork. The arms on the shield, with the boastful motto *Certavi et Vici*, 'I have fought and conquered,' are those of a John Byrne, who I was told locally was a retired collector-general of rates in Dublin; he bought Boat Harbour from the Burkes in 1865, and had the quay built as a famine-relief project. It is remembered in the Byrne family (who no longer own the house) that when Mr. and Mrs. John Byrne came to view their newly built residence, he went up the front steps and she, saying she would meet him upstairs, went in by a ground-floor door, only to find that the architect had forgotten to provide an indoor staircase, which is why its present staircase is so narrow.

So much for the grandees, saintly and secular, of Errislannan, on whom the existence of copious documentation tends to focus attention, leaving the *cosmhuintir*, the smallholders and landless folk, in shadow, glimpsed at best as the lamentable victims of famine, at worst characterized by 'barbarism, sloth, discontent, disaffection and turbulence.' But as it happens we have some report of them too, valued according to their own lights, and in their own language:

Amach tráth ghabhainn,
Níorbh eagal dóibh mo ghlaodhach isteach.

Baile bradach an Druimnín thuas,
Gan tréan ná truaigh a bhuain as.

[Any time I went out there, / No fear of them inviting me in,
/ That scoundrelly village of Drimmeen, / Neither strong nor
weak get anything there.]

This is from an *aor* or satire called 'Eascainne Mhic Suibhne
ar Iorras Fhlannáin,' MacSweeney's curse on Errislannan. Mac
Suibhne, the best-known of Connemara's vernacular poets, was
born near Cong in Mayo in about 1760 and died in Fahy three
miles west of Clifden, in about 1820. He was small and plain, he
had a little Latin and some knowledge of classical myth, worked
as a blacksmith, wandered, drank, sang of women and drink. His
'Amhrán an Phúca,' a comic proposal to his neighbours to hunt
the *púca* out of its lair in the ruined castle of Doon on the north
shore of Streamstown Bay, is well known; 'Muirnín na Gruaige
Báine,' 'The Fair-haired Darling,' praises a daughter of Richard
Martin's, whose kisses, he cheekily claims, were sweeter than
honey or beer; he also wrote a lament that he, a learned man,
has to go mending roads, and a commendation of 'fuisgi Mhister
Slóper,' whose stillhouse was, I guess, close to Sloper Cliffs,
below the Sky Road just east of Fahy. The song quoted above was
his revenge on Errislannan—and a harsh one, the poet's word
being feared and respected in those days—after he was looking
for lodgings there one night and nobody would let him in. Here
are a few more verses:

Do siúil mé Iorras Dún Dónaill ó thuaidh,
Iorras Mór agus Iorras Beag.
I n-Iorras Fhlannáin nach bhfuil cóir
O! mo bhrón, atáim anocht.

[I've walked Erris in Mayo north-west, / Errismore and
Errisbeg. /In Errislannan that lacks largesse, / O! my sorrow, tonight I rest.]

Anocht féin agus go bráth
Nár ba fearr a bhéas a sliocht,
Dream dorcha na malaí gruama,
B'olc a ngnúis 's níor mhaith a ndreach.

[This very night and for evermore / May their progeny no
better be, / Dark folk of the cheerless brows, / Bad was their
face and not good their mien.]

Dreach ba duibhe go mór ná an gual,
Dreach fuath do ghráin Dia,
Dreach nach raibh ar aingeal ná ar Naomh,
Ná ar an té roinnfeadh go cóir an bia.

[Their look was blacker by far than coal, / A ghastly look
that God did hate, / A look that was never on angel or saint,
/ Nor on anyone willing his food to share.]

Ar maidin nuair a chonaic mé amharc an lae ghil bhreá,
D'éirigh m'aigne is do bhreathnaigh mé uaim go hard,
Dhá fhuaire an mhaidin níor theasc orm theacht sa snámh,
Ach d'fhág mé mo mhallacht i mbaile na gruamacht thall.

[By morning on seeing the light of the bright fine day, / My
spirits rose and I viewed the distant shore, / Though cold the
morning I willingly swam the bay / And I cursed that village
of gloom for evermore.]

An exactly opposite impression of the people of Errislannan
is given by an extraordinary work that Mrs. Brooks showed me
during my recent visit; it was published only a few years ago but
dates from the mid nineteenth century, and at first glance reads
like *Finnegans Wake*. It begins:

Noar a cholee a Hack– soh harrick fied aun agas Crunnee a
tees oag astach agus beagan gun Hack– Croppo Soas agas
noar Veen teach reah hussee a fara vus agas a far haul lagan

amach a mead ibra a hurach Shea diess gun Hack– agas vee
ahas more air mar Vee Sule eggah Sheashure mah a yeeue fee
Claddach Sol a diech Shea Wallah . . .

—which, when one realizes it is colloquial Irish written out pho-
netically according to a mixture of the English and Irish spelling
systems, may be rewritten thus:

Nuair a chuala an Haicléara seo, tháinig foighid ann, agus
chruinnigh an t-aos óg isteach, agus b'éigean don Haicléara
crapadh suas, agus nuair a bhí an teach réidh, thosaigh an
fear abhus agus an fear thall ag leagan amach an méid oibre
a thabharfaidís don Haicléara, bhí áthas mór aige mar bhí
súil aige séasúr maith a dhéanamh faoi chladach sula dtéadh
sé abhaile.

[When the Hackler heard this, he relaxed, and the young
people gathered in, and the Hackler had to sit back; and when
the house was ready, a man here and a man there started to
lay out the work that they would give to the Hackler, and he
was delighted, because he hoped to do a good season's work
on the coast, before he went home.]

Its title is *An Haicléara Mánas*, 'Mánas the Hackler'—and here
we need to know a little of the nineteenth-century technology of
flax, the basis of linen. Flax is a plant a few feet high with a fibrous
stem; to remove the woody outer layer it had to be soaked for eight
days or so in a pond or pit, spread out to dry, softened by pounding
with a beetle, and finally hackled, that is, dragged through a comb
like a little board closely set with nails, until it was as smooth and
soft as silk. Because the cultivation of flax impoverished the soil,
the crop liable to failure in the damp climate of the West, and
the hand-preparation of the fibre very laborious, the country craft
of linen, unable to compete with the Ulster industry, died out in
the nineteenth century. But as the frequency of such placenames
as Loch an Lín, the flax pond, and An Tuairín, the bleaching
green, shows, it was once widespread in Connemara. The story of

Mánas's adventures in and around Caladh an Bháid was written most probably a decade or two after the Famine, and describes a bygone time perhaps shortly before it; the landlord Skerrett makes an appearance. The author was a Patrick Lyden, born in 1832 in Fakeeragh near Clifden Castle, who emigrated to the States at some date before 1872, when he became an American citizen, and died in 1929. To the linguist studying the evolution of dialects the manuscript is treasure trove, but I think it has not yet been read as the portrait of a neighbourhood at work and play, a self-sufficient and self-confident way of life. The first four pages are missing, but it is clear that they covered Mánas's arrival from his native Joyce Country in search of a season's employment. The mood throughout the narrative is one of cheerful sociability. When Mánas is persuaded to give a party for the local tradesmen he agrees, reckoning that he is the only tradesman in the vicinity, but soon he learns differently (and the text breaks out into a sort of poetry) when he hears who is to be invited:

> Bring with you the mower, and the gardener, and the
>   sweet-sounding fiddler,
> the thatcher and the lobsterman, and the fine turner.
> May the smith of the big sledgehammer come with you,
>   and the white miller,
> the baker and the piper, his wife and his children.
> Bring with you the thresher, and the beater, and the keen-
>   eyed valuer,
> the cooper and the joiner, and even the sawyer.
> The travelling fishmonger, and the cattle-jobber, and the pilot.
> Bring the boatwright along, and the young doctor,
>
> the basket-maker and the boatman, who is an expert with
>   the sail.
> Bring the slater, and the glazier, and the neat painter,
> the weaver, and the drover, and the cogger from the south.
> Have the cobbler of the awls with you and the humorous
>   tailor,
> the coachman and the sailor, who climbs the masts.

Bring along the plasterer, and the weatherman, and the
  impoverished haulier,
  the blaster and the butcher and the butler of the wine . . .

. . . and so on: cook, bailiff, ploughman, miner, huckster, stone-
mason, surveyor, saddler, crane-operator, baker, dyer, moulder,
gelder, farmer, Jew's harpist, priest, steward, merchant, knitter,
tinker and seamstress. Of course, to the Hackler's relief, only the
village pranksters turn up—but the passage does give some indication of the complexity of the economy of the growing town of
Clifden and its environs, into which that of Errislannan would
have been integrated.

The matter of the narrative is comic: gleeful banter; simple practical jokes mainly at the expense of an itinerant beggar, an outsider;
and macabre larks involving the clothes of a drowned sailor whose
corpse has been washed up (perhaps the one said to be buried by
Cloch an Mhairnéalaigh, the boulder of the mariner, a hundred
yards west of Caladh an Bháid). When a house is to be built all the
villagers come to help, as was the customary way, and each man
works so enthusiastically at laying stones to raise up the stretch of
wall in front of him they forget to put the doors in, and those inside
have to scramble out with the aid of a plank; then, as the house
owner hasn't noticed the error, they quickly roof it with rafters and
sods. The next day the owner and his mother come to move into
their new home, bringing with them a glowing turf from the old
house as was the tradition, and 'the devil of a door can they find.'
The neighbours protest that he had only asked for a house, without
stipulating doors, but they promise to put in two doors if he treats
them to a gallon of poitín. When he provides only a half-gallon
they put in one door only, and so the house remains.

By the end of the season Mánas has done so well he comes
back the following year with twelve assistant hacklers, and they all
make pocketfuls of money. The Errislannan folk arrange a marriage for him with a young respectable girl; he stays in Connemara
thenceforth and gets on 'reasonably well' in life. The author ends
by telling us that he himself is now old and grey, and contrasts the

people of these his latter days—'sharp and sarcastic, each man out to gain the advantage over the other, with litigation, wrangling and summonses'—with those of his youth, 'full of enjoyment, companionship, and everyone making fun of the other, without legal action or trouble.' Well, we are all exiles from the past, willing or unwilling, and can allow for the nostalgia of those exiled in space as well as time. So we need not grudge Errislannan this good memory of itself:

> . . . everyone happy and prosperous, potatoes piled to the rafters, and herring in their thousands running in shoals onto the land, and butter and sour milk available to all the people of Ireland . . .

and we can nod along to the author's final words:

> . . . but it's no use talking, my dear friend. I suppose that's how life goes.

Photons in the Bog

One day in 1907, out on the western margins of Roundstone Bog, there was a noise, a tremendous crack, as if the sky had flapped like washing on a clothes line. Photons more numerous than all the sands of all the seas streamed westward, headed for Nova Scotia, and were there in a trice, while a spillage of them bombarded everything animate and inanimate in the vicinity, causing electrons to hop. This surge of radiation was different from sunlight, starlight, lightning flash or any previous such visitation of the bog, for it had a meaning, bore a message; the first such intelligence to be transmitted across the Atlantic by wireless, it marked a step in the globalization of talk. Marconi's Wireless Station in Derrigimlagh was a huge installation; the output of hundreds of turf-cutters and wagonloads of coal powered its generators. Fifteen years later the station was torched and shot up, and today only ragged bits of masonry remain of it.

Guglielmo Marconi was born in Bologna in 1874, just one year after the attainment of that summit of nineteenth-century mathematical physics, James Clerk Maxwell's theory of electromagnetism. Since the 1820s it had been known, from observation and experiment, that there were deep connections between the mysterious forces of electricity and magnetism; for instance that if a current is passed through a wire near to a compass needle, the needle will be deflected. Maxwell captured the basic facts of these interactions in four equations of elegant symmetry and brevity; two of them state that currents and changing electric fields produce magnetic fields, and that changing magnetic fields produce electric fields. It follows from these equations that an alternating current in a wire, causing an alternating electric field in its vicinity, produces an alternating magnetic field that in its turn produces an alternating electric field, and that this double disturbance will spread out like waves in water. When Maxwell calculated the speed of propagation of these waves he found to his amazement that it matched the speed of light as determined by experiment; thus light was shown to be a phenomenon of electromagnetism. Also, since his reasoning did not depend on the frequency of the waves, he was able to predict the discovery of waves of greater or lesser frequencies than those of the visible spectrum. Fifteen years later the existence of the low-frequency waves we now call radio waves was demonstrated experimentally by Heinrich Hertz, although the nature of the 'ether,' the hypothetical medium in which these waves were propagated, remained a mystery.

Hertz died in 1894; Marconi, then studying physics at the University of Bologna, read his own professor's obituary of Hertz, and was inspired to use the wonderful and invisible 'Hertzian waves' to transmit a pulse of energy, a signal; soon he had an apparatus that could switch a bell on and off from a distance of ten metres, with no visible connection between them. Professor Lodge at Oxford was pursuing the same idea, and had transmitted a Morse signal over a distance of 150 metres—but it was Marconi who saw the commercial applications of this 'wire-less telegraphy,' and in no time at all he was set up in business by his wealthy family, came to London, filed a preliminary patent for a wireless telegraphy system and demonstrated it to the General Post Office, the armed forces and an enthralled public. An immediate application was to communication with ships at sea; Marconi's Wireless Telegraphy and Signal Co. established coastal stations in Bournemouth (from where he flashed news of Gladstone's dying moments to Fleet Street, when snow had brought down the telegraph wires the journalists were reliant upon) and the Isle of Wight (where the dazzling young genius and celebrity entrepreneur was granted an audience with, or vouchsafed an audience to, Queen Victoria during Cowes Week). The triumph of the first cross-Channel and international transmission followed in 1899, and in 1900 came a crucial technical improvement: the ability to tune a receiver circuit so that it would resonate to and be sensitive to just one frequency of signal, thus solving the problem of messages interfering with each other.

A transatlantic telegraph service was, to the bold, the obvious next step. More cautious scientists thought that the curvature of the Earth would make this impossible, since radio waves, like light waves, travel in straight lines; but in 1902 Oliver Heaviside had postulated the existence of a layer of charged particles high in the atmosphere which would reflect radio waves, and by that time Marconi knew from experience that his signals could be picked up by ships far out to sea. Marconi came to Ireland in 1905 (and married Beatrice O'Brien, daughter of Lord and Lady Inchiquin) to look for a site for a huge telegraphy station. He stayed in the Zetland Hotel in Cashel, carried out some experiments with kite-born aerials in Leitheanach Theas and Ros Rua, two peninsulas just south of Cashel, and eventually settled upon a site in the townland of Derrigimlagh or Deirg Imleach, on the western edge of what we now call Roundstone Bog but which then had no name, being regarded merely as a vague stretch of commonage attached to a dozen or more townlands. An *imleach* is a hill of glacial till (the *deirg* probably means 'stream' in this context), and apart from the low rounded drumlin that gives the townland its name it offered an uninterrupted outlook to the Atlantic horizon, as well as lakes full of fresh water and bogs full of turf for the boilers that would drive his generators. The Morrises of Ballinaboy sold his company the 300-acre site, and within two years the first messages were flying across the Atlantic.

The appearance of the station on its opening for business in October 1907, seen from far away on that level landscape, must have been something like a flotilla of schooners riding out a storm. The transmitting aerial wires were carried on eight wooden masts 210 feet high, each held in place by four stays, in an array that stretched for a third of a mile eastwards out into the bog; to celebrate the occasion one mast carried the flags of Britain, the USA, Canada and Italy. The noise of the sparks made visitors cover their ears, and flashes as of lightning were visible, especially by night. The first few days of operations were accompanied by torrential rain, which according to a Galway newspaper local people blamed on 'the penetration of the clouds by the electricity which gives impetus to the Marconigrams.'

The buildings—the boiler house with its six tall cylindrical smokestacks, the big galvanized-iron condenser house, the receiver house, the brick-built staff housing, the blacksmith's forge, the chief engineer's cottage, the stores, etc.—formed what looked like a shanty town scattered around the shores of a small lake and ringed by a high barbed-wire fence. Three little steam locomotives puffed to and fro on a two-foot-gauge railway bringing in turf from the cuttings to monumental turf stacks, as well as coal, equipment and supplies from the road at Ballinaboy. Passengers could be carried too, on seats facing outwards as on a horse-drawn side-car. (When Lord Aberdeen made an official visit in 1906 upholstered seats were quickly nailed into place; photographs show the Viceregal party perched high, Lady Aberdeen's voluminous hat and ample skirt reducing the train to funfair proportions.) But reporters and casual visitors were not permitted to enter the technical buildings, such was Marconi's fear of rivals stealing his secrets. Photographs from that period show elegant little gadgets of mahogany, brass and ivory, and transformers like elephantine wind-instruments. The interior of the 350-foot-long condenser house must have been spectacular. The condenser, on which electric charge was accumulated before being allowed to surge through the aerial, consisted of an array of 1,800 sheets of galvanized iron suspended vertically a foot apart from porcelain insulators, each sheet being thirty feet high and twelve feet wide. The earth system consisted of two sheets of heavy copper mesh, four feet wide and 600 feet long, partly buried on land and partly on the bed of the lake.

On that first day of private and commercial transmissions in 1907 the ether demonstrated its political neutrality by carrying Lloyd George's congratulations to Marconi in Nova Scotia—

Every improvement in the communications between various parts of the British Empire helps to consolidate and strengthen it. All well-wishers of the Empire will welcome therefore, every project for facilitating intercourse between Britain and the great Dominion across the Atlantic . . .

—as faithfully as it did County Councillor H. M. A. Murphy's to President Roosevelt:

On the opening of the Marconi station here, allow me, on behalf of the country, to congratulate you on the success of your Presidency in the United States and hope Ireland, in her struggle for a just measure of self-government, will have the encouragement and support of yourself and your liberty-loving people.

Marconigrams cost fivepence a word for ordinary messages and half that for the press; rival companies operating by transatlantic cable were charging twice those rates, and soon saw their shares wilting. When the Marconi station was at its strength, with three eight-hour shifts a day, it employed 10 engineers, 25 operators and 50 additional station staff, plus 70 male turf-cutters who were joined by another 140 casual labourers in the summer months; there were even a few women, employed as housemaids. Clifden prospered in particular, but men from Roundstone worked there too, threading their devious eight-mile way over the hills and between the lakes of the bog twice a day. Because transmission and reception could not be carried out simultaneously, a separate receiving station was opened near Letterfrack in 1913, with a workforce of over a hundred; but this did not prove economical and it was closed three years later, many of the workers being transferred back to Derrigimlagh.

In June 1919 an unimaginable gift of publicity dropped down upon the station from the heavens: a great gleaming light-yellow bird that roared out of the western horizon, circled around the amazed town of Clifden, turned south and alighted behind the condenser house, tripping along lightly for a while before burying its nose in the bog. Two men struggled hastily out of the contraption, fearing a fire. 'I'm Alcock—just came from Newfoundland,' said the captain of the Vickers Vimy biplane to the operatives who ran out to greet the apparition, and the navigator, Lieutenant Brown, added, 'That's the way to fly the Atlantic!' What an extraordinary fact, that these two emblematic events in the transformation of the world by technology—the first faint transatlantic radio messages, and this first frail and courageous transatlantic flight, an unknowing intimation of so much that was to come, from intercontinental mass tourism to thousand-bomber raids—should have happened within a hundred yards of each other, on the western fringe of Roundstone Bog! Extreme westernness is their common feature, apart from which it was largely coincidental that the plane pitched down by the wireless station and so ensured maximum immediate news coverage of its arrival. The intrepid pilots had aimed generally for Galway Bay but had not expected to 'hit it off,' as they put it, so nearly; and after sixteen and a half hours of deafening noise, thick cloud and freezing fog, having glimpsed the ocean only half a dozen times since leaving St John's, apart from when they became disoriented and nearly spiralled down into it, they were glad enough to land on the first flat area they saw, mistaking the bog for firm pastureland, although they had plenty of fuel left and could have gone on to Galway, where a *Daily Mail* reporter was awaiting them. The Marconi station transmitted their story to London, and provided them with a 'railcar,' like an open sports car, to run along the track to Ballinaboy. In Clifden they were welcomed by the parish priest and the chairman of the District Council, who hoped that their triumph was the prelude to the establishment of regular services from America to 'the nearest point on the European side'—which, broadly interpreted, would surely be Clifden. Crowds besieged the Marconi station but were refused admission; however, some people managed to wade ankle-deep through bog to get to the plane, bits of which were on sale as mementos in town that evening.

During the First World War the station was garrisoned by British troops, and in 1916 the government took steps to ensure that no word of the Easter Rising could reach the United States through Marconi's operatives; in the event, word was got through clandestinely by their rivals at the cable company in Valentia, County Kerry. When the War of Independence brought the Black and Tans to Clifden in 1921 they were known to have enjoyed the hospitality of the station's social club. In the Civil War of the following year the Republicans, who held the Clifden area, regarded the station as a nest of hostility, and indeed most of the workforce was of the Free State persuasion. These seem to have been the reasons behind the Republicans' attack on it, shortly before their withdrawal from Clifden in the expectation of the Free State forces' advance; at any rate the station suffered the same fate as other large buildings that could have become strongholds of the Free Staters. Three local Republicans, probably led by Gerald Bartley, set fire to the receiver house and other buildings and fired shots into the condenser house. As a result 250 people lost their jobs, which caused great hardship in the region. Workers arriving the next morning were turned away by company officials, who did nothing to repair the damage or even clear away the debris. The truth was that Marconi, when establishing the Derrigimlagh station, had been working at the outer edge of what was possible in the detection of wireless signals and had to minimize the distance over which they were to be transmitted. As the sensitivity of his receivers was improved through theory and experiment, distance became less of a deter-mining factor; westernness in itself was no longer an advantage but a disadvantage, as many a business has found it to be since then. He had only with difficulty been dissuaded by local appeals from phasing out the station even before the attack; and so, when peace came at last, it was not rebuilt, its operations were transferred to a more up-to-date station in Wales, and the electromagnetic field that pervades Roundstone Bog fell into aphasia.

I revisited the site of this adventure into modernity several times a few years ago, in connection with a campaign against a projected airstrip there. On one of these occasions a Roundstone friend, Jacky King, and I walked across the bog from Murvey Wood, following the linear features—a mile or so of turf-cutter's track, then a stream, then a reed swamp, then a series of long narrow lakes—that mark the Murvey fault. As we turned west-wards towards the end of this traverse I picked up a couple of what the geologist might have called xenoliths, stones strangers to their surroundings: a nugget of red brick and a smooth curved shard of a white porcelain insulator; how they had strayed so far out into the bog from the station I cannot tell. Soon afterwards Jacky said, 'I smell bogs!,' which momentarily puzzled me since we had been trudging across bog for two or three hours. But to a Connemara man a bog is a place where turf is cut, and the rest is commonage or 'mountain'; and indeed there was a pleasantly tarry zest in the air as we climbed the gentle slope from Loch Fada (long lake) towards the Marconi site and began to pass carpets of machine-cut turf sods laid out to dry. Soon we were kicking about in the tussocky grass to find the overgrown mast footings and the sunken concrete blocks to which the stays had been attached, and then splashing along a sodden track towards the Marconi Lake, as it is called, and our goal, a monument recently inaugurated at a ceremony I had missed, by Marconi's daughter from his second marriage, the deliciously named Princess Elettra:

PRINCESS ELETTRA MARCONI GIOVANELLI
UNVEILED THIS PLAQUE ON THE
28TH JUNE 1995 TO COMMEMORATE
THE 100TH ANNIVERSARY OF THE
DEVELOPMENT OF WIRELESS BY
HER FATHER
GUGLIELMO MARCONI

Standing at the monument and scanning the site of this great enterprise that day, I found it dispiriting: the bogs ravaged for decades to feed Marconi's boilers and criss-crossed by blackish waterlogged turf banks, the rutted track where the railway once ran, the rat-grey teeth of broken-down concrete walls; perhaps the plaque should have read, 'Look upon my works, ye Mighty, and despair!' But on other occasions the place has been idyllic. On closer examination one finds that the old turf-cuttings are filling in with a luxuriant vegetation; in fact the botanist Micheline Sheehy-Skeffington once identified fifty-five plant species for me in the course of an hour or two here, a list duly presented as evidence in the anti-airport campaign. I also conducted a politician around the site one day, and it put on an irresistible show: there were mute swans dreamily adrift on the lake, waterlilies in flower on the ponds and ravens croaking overhead, and as we strode westwards to see where the airstrip was planned to run out into the untouched parts of the bog, we found *natura naturans*, nature behaving naturally, as exemplified by extraordinary numbers of the luxuriantly furred caterpillars of the Northern Eggar moth sunning themselves on the heather—one or two visible at every step—so that when at last the politician, who had remained non-committal and tight-lipped throughout the inspection, sank back into his car, he announced, 'I think that would be a dreadful place to put an airport!' All the same I have to admit that symbolically, because of the Alcock and Brown precedent, Derrigimlagh would have been just the place for a Clifden airport; but happily ecology has won out over symbology, and the Marconi site will, I hope, remain as it is now, a tranquil antechamber to the great airy palace of Roundstone Bog.

So, what was the nature of that strange event, the first crack of Marconi's whip over the bog? Was it alien to nature, hostile, inimical? First, the physics of it. When Newton was investigating the properties of light he was of the opinion that it consisted of streams of particles, and as it has turned out, he was right, if for the wrong reasons. In the nineteenth century it seemed easier to account for such phenomena as interference and refraction in terms of waves that could in places reinforce each other and in others cancel each other out, as particles presumably could not. Marconi was working in the concept-world of Faraday and Maxwell: radio waves were like visible light waves but of a lower frequency. In the 1900s came the multiple crises of modern physics; delicate experiments seemed to show that light was indeed made up of particles—a very feeble beam directed at a sensitive detector does not cause a feeble continuous buzz, but a series of separate clicks—while on the other hand streams of atomic particles such as electrons could behave exactly like waves and produce interference patterns. Quantum mechanics, the theoretical response to the anomalies of particle physics, was developed in the 1920s and was soon extended to deal with electrodynamics, the interactions of light and matter. Richard Feynman, the Norman Mailer of theoretical physics, has tried to explain his 1950s version of quantum electrodynamics (or QED as it is called for short, as if it really could demonstrate *quod erat demonstrandum*, that which was to be demonstrated) to the unmathematical; but mathematics, and of a level I can only scamper after like a forgotten dog behind a car, is the only way of describing this level of reality. According to QED, light is definitely particulate, and all its wavelike properties can be explained in terms of one strange feature of the subatomic world: that there is and can be no way of predicting with certainty whether a certain event, say the movement of a photon from Derrigimlagh to Nova Scotia, will or will not happen, the most information nature vouchsafes us being no more than the probability of the event. And the twist that makes the world at that level utterly different from the one we have been born into, and which has formed our expectations, is mathematical: those probabilities are calculated using complex numbers rather than the ordinary numbers that suffice for considering odds on horses, for example. This introduction of complex numbers is at the root of such mysteries as the notorious Uncertainty Principle, and at the subatomic scale it undoes our innate framework-conceptions of space, time and causality. QED is counter-intuitive, many of its results are apparently paradoxical, and yet it is the best-tested and most successful theory physics has ever invented, and it covers all phenomena other than those of gravity and nuclear physics. In terms of just three basic actions—a photon goes from here to there, an electron goes from here to there, an electron absorbs or emits a photon—and the uncountable repetitions and compilations of them, a vast range of phenomena—the flicker of lightning in the bellies of clouds massing above the Twelve Pins, the rainbow sheen of turf oil on water in the bog-holes, the sunshine-yellow of the daffodils that still bloom by the ruins of the chief engineer's cottage, the drifting pheromones that will guide the Northern Eggar moth across miles of bog to its mate—are in principle made comprehensible. This doctrine is an unnervingly precipitous reductionism, and needs to be accompanied by a converse study of how new laws, calling for new terminology, emerge at every step of the ascent from particle physics to chemistry, to biology and so to psychology and sociology. But basically this is how nature works, it seems; physics does not presume to say *why* this is how it is, and perhaps the question has no meaning or addresses one of those matters 'whereof one cannot speak.' As Feynman says to his readers, 'I hope you can accept Nature as She is—absurd.'

The Marconi event was no exception in terms of physics. Electrons in unimaginable numbers flooded to and fro in an aerial; they emitted photons of which a tiny proportion flocked to another aerial in Nova Scotia and were absorbed by electrons, which moved to and fro in a receiving apparatus. The new element was the multiple involvement of mentality in the process. The flux of photons was switched on and off by an operative tapping out Morse code, a surrogate for natural language, which brings into play the mysterious relationship of word to thing—and, at fivepence a word, implicates those photons and electrons in economics and so in all the structures of human society. This might make one think that something utterly different, something not subject to or explicable in terms of the laws of physics, had entered into the situation, rather as the soul is supposed, by those who suppose such things, to be breathed into the body at some stage or other of the smooth development from sperm and egg to morally conscious human being. But perhaps we need not think so. To take one strand in the web of mysteries linking thought with reality, the way in which a name refers to the object named, some contemporary philosophers have postulated a purely causal theory of reference: in brief, that a chain of usages, of followings of example, links my use of a name back through time to the original bestowal of that name; thus my correct use of a name is a matter of my time-and-space-bound embeddedness in the world, and, more generally, intentionality and meaning are no more fundamentally mysterious than any other aspect of the loom of cause and effect.

Nevertheless, and to extract myself from the bogs of philosophy, it is a curious realization that we are all now suffused by messages, in a way that did not obtain in the past. Marconi in Derrigimlagh represents a crucial step in the filling of the bath of invisible communications we are all immersed in today, the electromagnetic fever and silent cacophony of words and images passing through us at every moment. The most common message, the one we are most urgent to impart, is and has been since the days of the megalith-builders, 'I'm here . . . ,' wherever that may be; 'I am here, now—therefore I exist. And you know it, so I belong to the human race.' The ubiquity of the mobile phone with televisual capabilities heralds or threatens an ideal or a nightmare: the total communicability of immediate experience between any and all of the worldwide family. One can foretell the reduction of such devices to implants or corporeal rejiggings, making any individual's phenomenological world accessible by anyone, anywhere, instantly; that is, our becoming one organism.

But, stepping aside from the science-fiction fantasy we seem condemned by the might of technology to live out, when I'm roaming the photon-drenched spaces of Roundstone Bog and suddenly feel like sending a love-note to M back at home, it is simply a wonder the way the complex numbers dance together, the photons flit, the electrons run and the world folds like a map for one point to kiss another.

The Kingdom of Manannán

Once when the tide was far out and the sleek black mud bottom of Roundstone harbour was revealed, two little girls poking around down there hailed me as I passed by on the quayside and told me to come and see what they had found. So I went down by the slip and trod warily out to them. What they had was a slimy brown clump of something stringy, which they were trying to untangle. A bootlace worm, I pronounced, and suggested that when they had finished looking at it they should put it back where they found it. 'Oh, I know!' said the elder of them, casting her eyes up to heaven with heavy sarcasm. 'It has just as much right to life as I do . . .' 'Good girls,' said I doubtfully, and left them to it.

Back among my books I looked up the bootlace worm. *Lineus longissimus* is its name, and it is often five yards long, while specimens of thirty or more yards have been unravelled, though it tends to tie itself in knots when handled and breaks very easily. It is usually about a tenth of an inch across, but can contract and thicken itself or stretch itself out thinner. It is an unsegmented worm or nemertine, and it lives on small segmented or bristle worms. It exudes slime and lives in a coiled mass under stones, but can progress smoothly by means of ripples passing along its body from tail to head. It has ten to twenty obscure little eyes.

I saw the elder girl again later on. 'Did you put that worm back?' I asked. 'No!' she screamed fiercely. 'We dropped rocks on the yucky thing!'

If some marine life-forms are repellent in their strangeness, others appal by a beauty that chills, being so evidently not addressed to us. When I rang the ecologist Cilian Roden to ask him something about the bootlace worm, he told me there was an image on the NASA website I should look at, a satellite photograph of an algal bloom in the Atlantic off Slyne Head. I called it up on my screen: a milky-blue curdling 500 miles long, curled and combed by sea-currents, consisting of quadrillions of coccolithophores. I knew something of the coccolithophore, a single-celled planktonic plant. Once when I called in to the Marine Research Centre of the University in Galway to ask about the foraminifera found in Dog's Bay, which I was writing about at the time, the researchers there agreed that 'forams' were mightily abundant and quaintly shaped entities—but had I ever seen the coccolithophores? And they got out a coffee-table-format book of electron micrographs to show me. These less-than-dust-sized organisms—of which half a million could fit on the head of a pin—have spherical shells made up of plates of calcium carbonate; some species grow these plates or 'coccoliths' in large numbers and shed them constantly, while others produce just the twenty or so needed to cover themselves, which are released when the plant dies. It is the lime-white clouds of coccoliths swept together in a gyre of the ocean and reflecting the sun's rays as they drift down to the seabed that turn vast stretches of water into milk now and again.

Leafing through the hundreds of illustrations in this book of different species of these plants and the distinctive coccoliths each species produces, I was moved as never before, both frightened and overjoyed, by nature's fecundity of form. The coccolith in general has the shape of a tube, shorter than it is wide, with a broad flange around either end, like a hat with two brims, the outer end of the tube being open and the inner end closed by a grill of radial elements. The details are endlessly varied, each specimen, when enlarged a few hundred thousand times, looking like a caprice of the ceramicist's art. And yet it seems that these extraordinary confections come into being quite automatically. A vast deal of research has gone into studying this process, which takes place within the plant cell and uses the lime dissolved in seawater: a ring of calcium carbonate crystals is laid down, each of which then grows at different rates in very specific directions, to build up the two-flanged tube with all its never-to-be-seen detailing. When complete the coccolith is extruded onto the surface of the cell, where by random jostling it fits itself in among the others, all interlocked by means of their flanges. Presumably the initial ring of crystals is formed on a template of some complicated protein, which in its turn has been precisely engineered by the genetic machinery, directed by DNA, of the coccolithophore species—but all this fantastic collaboration of crystallographic and biochemical processes remains to be figured out. Nor is it known what the coccoliths are for! Perhaps the whole structure, the 'coccosphere,' enclosing the cell retains some water between the two layers of flanges, surrounding the plant with an environment the chemistry of which it can control; perhaps the plates protect the plant against viruses or make it less attractive to plankton-eaters; perhaps they adjust the buoyancy of the plant and keep it within some range of depths; perhaps like lenses they deflect sunlight into the cell to further photosynthesis. Nobody knows; the answer probably involves some or all of these possibilities, and others, evolution by natural selection being so efficient an exploiter of what is to hand.

And in the end the coccolithophore, however well adjusted it is to its environment, dies, and its armature breaks up and falls like a slow snow into the ocean ooze, which over millions of years is compressed into rock. All that ingenious geometry is compounded into bulk material. The Downs of southern England, the White Cliffs of Dover, are built of coccoliths.

Now, of all Connemara's shores by which one might meditate on the alterity of sea-life, one in particular proposes itself, by its name, as the most suitable: Mannin Bay, a mile or so north of Ballyconneely. Manannán mac Lir, whose patronymic, meaning 'son of the sea,' shows him to be a sea-god, was (or is) the Celtic Poseidon. Like the Greek god he is a shape-shifter, an ungraspable master of disguise. He makes several appearances in the lore of the Fianna, Fionn Mac Cumhaill's warrior band; sometimes he is helpful, sometimes a tease, and sometimes both. For instance when the Fianna are challenged to a race by a stranger called Caol and Fionn is looking for a champion to represent them, he meets Bodach an Chóta Lachtna, the grey-cloaked lout, in the forest, who offers to take up the challenge. The course set is from Howth Head to Sliabh Luachra in Kerry, and back again. Caol sets off at a great pace, but the grey-cloaked lout overtakes him despite stopping for huge meals. When Caol tells him that he has left tatters of his cloak on a thorn-bush the lout thanks him and goes back to collect them and sew them on again, before passing Caol with the speed of the wind and winning the race. When the wind and the sun light up the lout's face Fionn recognizes him as Manannán mac Lir.

In another complicated and rambling story the god plays the role of the Ceithearnach Caoilriabhach, the narrow-striped kern or soldier, a joker and conjuror in striped clothing, who among other tricks casts a silken thread up into the air so that it is made fast to a cloud, takes a hare out of his bag and sends it running up the thread, takes a dog out of the bag and sends it in pursuit of the hare, produces a little serving boy and sends him after hare and dog, and finally a beautiful girl to follow after the rest. When a commotion breaks out in the cloud he hauls in the thread. On finding that the dog is chewing the bones of the hare and the lad has 'gone between the two legs of the lady' he strikes the lad's head off and puts it on again back to front, but then relents and twists it around to the right position.

> And with that the man of tricks vanished, and no one saw where was he gone. That is the way Manannan used to be going round Ireland, doing tricks and wonders. And no one could keep him in any place, and if he was put on a gallows itself, he would be found safe in the house after, and some other man on the gallows in his place. But he did no harm, and those that would be put to death by him, he would bring them to life again with a herb out of his bag.

But it is on the sea that the god appears in his true majesty. The story of St Scaithín walking across a flowery plain and meeting St Barre sailing in a boat, which I told in connection with Inishbofin, is a brief Christianized echo of a meeting with Manannán described in an eighth-century wonder-tale, *The Voyage of Bran*. Wandering near his royal house one day Bran hears sweet music, and falls asleep to it. When he awakes he sees a silver branch bearing white blossoms, and takes it home with him. There a woman in strange raiment appears and sings fifty quatrains, explaining that the silver branch is from the apple tree of Emhain, an incomparably beautiful island 'without grief, without death, without sickness.' Then she disappears, taking the silver branch with her. The next day Bran, with three companies of nine of his followers, puts to sea. After rowing for two days and two nights they see a man in a chariot coming towards them over the sea—Manannán mac Lir, who sings them thirty quatrains, beginning:

Caíne amra laisin mBran
ina churchán tar muir nglan;
os mé, am charput do chéin,
is magh sccothach ima-réidh.

Scholars have rendered the beautiful obscurities of Manannán's song in irreconcilable ways; I condense their efforts freely, in the wake of the concise antitheses of the original:

Bran delights in sailing his currach on the pure sea, which
for me is a flowery plain my chariot crosses from afar.
Bran sees numberless breaking waves, where I see perfect
red blossoms.
Sea horses glisten in summer as far as Bran can cast his eye.
In the kingdom of Manannán rivers flow with honey.
You see speckled salmon leaping from the sea's white
womb; they are calves and particoloured lambs peacefully
at play.
Men and gentle women at wine under a bush play a
delightful blameless game.
From the beginning of things we are ageless, facing no loss
of fresh-ness, exempt from original sin.

Manannán goes on to predict that he himself will lie with a queen and father a son, Mongan (who is a historical figure; he was a prince of Dál nAraid in Ulster and died in AD 624, according to the *Annals*). Bran and his crew then sail on to blissful adventures in the Land of Women, where there is a bed and a bed-companion for each of his thrice-nine followers. After what seems like a year but must have been centuries they return to within shouting distance of Ireland; one of them leaps ashore and immediately crumbles into ashes. Bran tells the people there his name, and they say they don't know him but that *The Voyage of Bran* is among their ancient stories. Bran tells them his adventures, and leaves an account of them in ogham. He then sails off again, 'and from that hour his wanderings are not known.'

When gods became obsolete and reinvented themselves as heroes Manannán became a sea-trader from the Isle of Man, which was anciently called Mana; according to a ninth-century glossary 'he was the greatest navigator of this western part of the world, and used to presage good or bad weather from his observation of the heavens, and from the changes of the moon.' Manannán has especially close connections with Connemara. The Conmaicne sept of Leinster, who later moved into Connacht, knew him under the name of Oirbsiu and regarded him as their ancestor. Presumably it was the branch of the sept known as the Conmaicne Mara, the Conmaicne of the sea, from whom Connemara is named, who brought his cult to the lands west of Galway. Their traditions held that he was killed in a battle at Moycullen, was buried standing up, and that the great lake, Loch nOirbsen, now corruptly known as Lough Corrib, burst forth from his grave. This flood is not the only example of the sea-god's mastery of geography; like Poseidon again he is an earth-shaker. There is a little island called Oileán Mana off Cill Chiaráin in south Connemara that according to local folklore was called into existence by Manannán to save his daughter when her boat was caught in a storm there. Mannin Bay too is named from him, says James Hardiman, the Galway historian, writing in the 1840s, but exactly why this should be so is, I believe, unknown.

Mannin Bay, then, would seem to be a privileged site for a consideration of the strangeness of that zone disputed twice a day between the strange but familiar land of Connemara and the strange and unfamiliar realm of Manannán. Having talked with Cilian of such extravagant entities as the numberless coccolithophores and the immeasurable worm, I suggested we go down to the sea at Mannin to defamiliarize ourselves with some of the more familiar creatures in its margins. We left it till late in the summer, when the rock pools should be hopping with sun-fuelled life, and chose a day of spring tides and the hour of deepest ebb. I persuaded some other friends and mentors along too: Cilian's partner Sabine Springer, marine biologist and illustrator of seashore life, the poet Moya Cannon, and Máirtín O'Malley, whose dealings with the sea are so multifarious we call him the Ambassador of the Ocean. Mannin is the widest of Connemara's west-facing bays; about three miles of water separate Errislannan, its northern shore, from Errismore or Iorras Mór, the big peninsula, to the south. The Coral Strand is the finest of the beaches that line the head of the bay, with the coast road passing immediately inland of them. When we stood out of our cars in the carpark above the sea wall there and stretched ourselves it was around midday (spring high waters being affairs of dawn and dusk in these parts, and low waters in between them). The wind was light and the waves, *caiple Mhanannáin*, Manannán's horses, as Irish folklore knows them, were pasturing peaceably far out in the bay. A long hazy sector of horizon stretched between the rockbound point of Errislannan and the little hill of Knock three miles away to the west where the Iorras Mór coastline turns southwards and runs out to the last lonely land's-end of Connemara, Slyne Head. Beyond that lay, we knew, the coccolithic bloom seen from space as a milky way, and the Porcupine Bank, teeming with fish, and the recently discovered sea mounts about which Michael Viney has written so eloquently, submarine pyramids and towers of coral hosting fantastic worlds of creatures barely known to science. However, our appointment was not with those unreachable wonders, but with the little everyday, every-tide doorkeepers of the near waters, the ebb and flow. There was a note of celebration in the sea breeze, perhaps because Moya, gentle creature of gold dust and heather pollen, had sufficiently recovered from illness to be with us, perhaps because beaches bring us back to a primal time of life. We tumbled onto the sands like the children of her poem 'Shells':

We used to hunker on the Silver Strand,
sifting the shells after a storm, hunting for cowries.

The pink, furled nuggets were stored in jam jars,
hoarded in jacket pockets, on windowsills,
with pelicans' feet,
razor shells,
scallop shells,
turret shells
and the rare, white wentletrap.

Ignorant of how Venus had sailed ashore,
we were already intrigued
by all the felt asymmetries of the small sea-beasts' growth,
all the dizzy architecture
of the first flesh.

The Coral Strand too is silvery, glimmery, moon-pale, and
it crunches underfoot pleasantly; pick up a handful of its beach
and you see it is composed of tiny twiglike bits of something like
unglazed pottery, white, cream-coloured, pale green or faintly
violet-flushed. This is not strictly coral, which is an animal product, but fragments broken off a coraline alga, a seaweed that
draws on the calcium carbonate dissolved in seawater to stiffen
its fronds with a limey deposit. Further down the beach one finds
bigger branchy pieces like stag's horns and, near the low tide mark,
roundish bushes of it an inch or two across that have been floated
ashore attached to the holdfasts of the big kelp seaweeds thrown
up by storms. There are a few such coral beaches in Connemara,
of which this and An Trá Choiréalach near An Cheathrú Rua
are the finest. The offshore, deep-water thickets of living maerl,
as the several sorts of coralline seaweed are known collectively,
provide nooks and crannies for an abundance of lurking, glid-
ing, tube-building, tunnel-boring and sedentary sea-dwellers—I
have seen an impressive list of the species recorded from Mannin
Bay—and a vast fractal surface area for encrusting algae to col-
onize, and for specialized prostrate seaweeds to peg themselves

onto, helping to storm-proof the maerl beds on which they depend for security.

Down at the water's rippling fringes we gathered around a boulder draped in dripping seaweed on which brightly coloured winkles were slowly cruising to and fro licking up the surface film of bacteria, and listened to Cilian proclaiming the priority and superior multiformity of marine life over terrestrial life. The genetic froth of evolution investing every possible habitat the sea offered eventually threw a splash of foam onto the shore, a few species, a few Venuses, from which all land-dwellers and their loves are derived. Thus only four phyla or major categories of many-celled animal species are represented on land, while there are about thirty-five phyla in the sea. Radial symmetry is unknown in terrestrial lifeforms, but there were several exemplars of it for Cilian to point out, stuck to the boulder at hand: beadlet anemones, plump blood-red sacks with one central aperture above, encircled by 200 or so short tentacles and necklaced with twenty-four blue spots—the beadlets only visible when the creature is under water and open, for when the tide withdraws it swallows its tentacles and purses itself up, perfectly justifying its Irish name, *bundún leice*, arsehole of the rock.

In the water around the foot of the boulder Sabine pointed out a beautiful snakelocks anemone, grey-green with tinges of many other colours; she bade me put my finger to it and feel the soft clinging of its long wavy tentacles, to let it investigate us as we were investigating it. We looked at limpets clamped to rocks; to survive the hours of exposure they have to keep water within their shells, and therefore they always return to the same spot on their rock after roving around and grazing, and fit themselves onto it exactly. Where the rock is soft, as in the limestone Aran Islands, it is the stone that is worn into a perfect fit for the shell, but here on the hard metamorphic rocks of Connemara it is the shell that has to adapt itself to the stone. Then Máirtín wrestled over a big hunk of rock in a pool and exposed various disparate sea-beings. Soon I had, lying on my hand for Moya to photograph their 'dizzy architecture,' four sea-beasts that differed as much from each other as they did from me: a cushion starfish, like a plump little pentagonal badge; the well-named sea gherkin, finger-long, whitish, with ten feathery tentacles at one end; a purple heart-urchin, heart-shaped indeed and covered in pale spines; and a reddish periwinkle Cilian said was unusual, for what reason I have forgotten. Meanwhile Sabine, who has micro-sharp eyes as her delicate drawings of sea-creatures witness, roved among the rock pools and brought back curiosities to show me, so fine as to be transparent: a bryozoan or sea-mat, like a patch of velvety net appliquéd onto a seaweed frond, each compartment of the net containing a tentacular Charybdis too small to see without a lens; and a hydroid, which looked like a tiny plant rooted on a bit of seaweed, but was actually a 'ramified animal' with numerous anemone-like polyps on slender branches. This latter sea-wonder practises 'alternation of generations,' Sabine told me; the hydroid produces buds that become detached and float off like jellyfish, and breed sexually, discharging their ova and sperm into the water, the offspring settling to the bottom and growing into the next generation of attached hydroids like their grandparents.

Enough! There is no end to the weirdness of Manannán's subjects. The incoming tide was beginning to lift the seaweed tresses; billions of hungry little arms were reaching out into the flux of rotting seaweed dust and plankton. We returned our finds to their niches, pocketed our lenses and guides to the seashore, and turned inland. But before we left the intertidal zone we had to stop and consider the barnacle, how it grows. Thousands of them—30,000 or more per square yard, say the reference books—armour the rocks with their sharp, hard studs. Barnacles, though fixed in place like rivets, and hermaphrodite, still manage to interbreed, reaching their neighbours by means of penises up to an inch and a half long. The sperm and the ova come together within the little tent of limey plates that immures each individual, and the result, four months later, is a host of microscopic larvae that bear no obvious resemblance to their parents, clearly being crustaceans rather than molluscs, as barnacles were long assumed to be. They swim off, feed, grow, moult a few times and eventually fix themselves to a rock by means of a cement exuded by glands on the head. Then they create their protective plates of calcium carbonate, which they extract from seawater as do so many other marine life-forms. Inside this drought-and predator-defying castle, with its roofplates that can be opened like the dome of an observatory, the animal totally rearranges its bodily parts so that its ten legs become feathery feelers it can wave out from its roof aperture to trawl through the drift of sea-dust for edible particles.

Barnacle larvae are apparently a main constituent of the plankton pullulating in rock pools in summer, along with swarms of the sperm, eggs and young of hundreds of other species. Each sperm and ovum is as intensely alive, as unique, as the individual to which they may, against millionfold odds, give rise if they happen to pair up. Each bears a half-burden of genetic specification from parental to filial generation; it makes as much sense to say that the generations of individuals exist to produce the intermediate generations of 'dividuals' as the other way round. We too swim in such a continuous stream of life; ethicists and legalists have to inscribe divisions in it as best they may, but this is for our own debatable purposes; there is no 'fact of the matter' written in the stars to guide us. And it is equally important for us to feel this continuity, feel how it reaches back generation by generation to the rock pools, to the primeval slimes of self-replicating chemicals and perhaps to some extraterrestrial spawn of earth-life, blowing in the solar wind.

Finally, how is it that such minute creatures can be so complex, that such almost impalpable parcels can hold so much—anatomies, senses, instincts—and in their short lives can go through such profound reorganizations of themselves? The answer, I think, is that seen in the right perspective these creatures are huge. This perspective is not that of atomic physics, though that already makes the barnacle larva elephantine, an atom being so very much smaller than it, say a million times smaller, while an atomic particle such as a proton, millions of times smaller than an atom, has its own elaborate and dynamic interior structure. No, there is a deeper perspective that opens up from an idea of the quantum theorist Max Planck. He showed that there is something like a least length, below which the concept of a length is meaningless; this 'Planck length' is a naturally arising unit with which to measure greater lengths—and it is small beyond all imagining, being a million million billion times smaller than a proton. In terms of this unit the size of one of the rock pool's motes of life would contain so many zeros that the difference between that and our own size could easily be missed. So the simplest larva and even the single-celled coccolithophore have room for a universe of complexities. And since there is also a matching Planck time (it is that taken by a photon of light to travel the Planck length), the lifespan of the barnacle as measured in those units is of scarcely conceivable length and allows time for almost endless reactions and reconstructions.

So, having recognized some of these strange little creatures—recognized them from their descriptions and photographs in our reference books, and recognized them in their strangeness as our sea-cousins—we adapted our eyes once more to a human perspective, and turned for home. As Sabine remarked, we didn't have to make a long journey to see such marvels; we were only a hundred yards from our cars. And the beach watched as we, perhaps the strangest of all creatures, with glacial slowness lifted our gigantic heads out of the seaweed, blinked our meagre allowance of eyes, balanced ourselves on towering appendages, locomoted by a succession of arrested fallings forward, communicated by waves of agitation of air molecules, pairwise brought the lateral surfaces of our heads into centuries-long brief contacts (a behaviour the purpose of which is unknown), bent our spinal cords to coil ourselves into our waiting coccospheres and, rolling on wheels, a device unknown among the people of Manannán, departed—strange to each other, strange to ourselves, fit denizens for this strangest of all impossible universes.

Who Owns the Land?

One bright afternoon some years ago a geologist friend and I stood on the bare top of Doon Hill, the 213-foot height of which was enough to let us see how the promontory of Errismore gesticulates in lesser promontories and throws out archipelagos as if to spend itself in splendid complexities before dwindling into the western ocean like a rocket into the sky. The waters of Bunowen Bay lapped the base of the hill steeply below us, and the old Bunowen pier and the fishing village of Aillebrack (Aill Bhreac, the speckled cliff), with its clustered cottages and long, two-storeyed coastguard station, now converted into holiday apartments, lay in a sheltering crook of the land half a mile away across the bay to the south-west. Close by us to the east the head of the bay had taken a spoon-shaped bite out of the sand underlying green rolling pastures, and left a little beach. The roofless, teetering hulk of Bunowen Castle, a nineteenth-century Gothic mansion, stood on a low ridge a few hundred yards upslope from the beach. Beyond it a stream came down to the sea out of the glinting filigree of lakes and bogs inland of us to the north; and at its mouth, we knew, though it was too obscure to see from the hill, was a mound of grassed-over stone, remains of the original medieval castle the site of which has given its name to the whole area, Bun Abhann, river-foot. But among all these and countless other features of the scene my attention was on one, a car standing on the green grass in front of the ruined mansion. In it, I felt sure, Sailor MacDonagh was sitting, watching us—two tiny twig-figures upstanding against the sky—to see if we were going to trespass further upon his territory.

Sailor, so named from his earlier nautical career, having abandoned the sea, was now passionately possessive of the land; in fact his vigilance bordered on obsession and he was notorious for his treatment of tourists who rambled over his fields—sometimes, no doubt, leaving gates open through which his cattle might have escaped onto the roadway—to poke about the castle and perhaps endanger themselves in the ruins. On previous visits to Bunowen, in the days when I was in and out of every corner of Connemara making my map, I had called in at the farmhouse, which is behind the castle, and had got a grudging permission to explore. But on this occasion I had neglected to do so; we had clambered up the hill after having looked at the little holy well of the Seven Daughters near the roadside north of it, rather than going the long way round via the farmhouse. So, when my friend headed off down the slope to investigate a basalt dyke previous geological visitors had noted by the beach, I followed with trepidation. And as soon as our intentions were obvious, the car started to move, honking its horn, flashing its lights and with an arm waving madly from the driver's window. By then we were tumbling through gorse-bushes down the butt of the hill. As soon as we emerged onto the grassland I walked up ahead to greet Mr. MacDonagh and to make our excuses. He didn't recognize me, in fact he was incoherent with rage. He said he'd blast us out of it if we didn't fuck off his land; I told him I would call the Gardaí if he threatened us; he said he wouldn't mind that. Trying to placate him I reintroduced myself, but at that period I was not universally popular in Connemara, having been busy in the campaign to protect the various sites successively proposed for the Clifden airport, including most recently the machair commonage west of Bunowen. Sailor therefore associated me with interfering environmentalists and faceless bureaucrats who unbeknownst to the landowner draw red lines around his property on the map, declare it an Area of Scientific Importance and presume to dictate what can and cannot be done with it. The fact that I was English made the imposition all the more intolerable. However, I asserted my right, as a long-time resident who actually knew something about the place, to express my opinions, and suddenly he changed tune and said that in fact he agreed with me about the airport! This was probably out of some local wrangle between users of the commonage and the airport entrepreneurs, rather than any ecological concern, but it let the conversation settle into amicability, and we parted in peace, with me saying that we were just going down to the foreshore to look at the rock my companion was interested in. Sailor started to drive off, but as we reached the shore he stopped the car and began honking and waving again. I went back up to him, and he said, in the most reasonable manner, 'I think, just for the principle of the thing, you should fuck off my land!' I appreciated this memorable formulation, but I repeated as weightily as I could that we were going down onto the foreshore (there is a perhaps mythical right enshrined in the eternal law of Ireland that anyone can walk on the foreshore), and took myself off with dignity.

Of course we were in the wrong, and I apologize to Sailor's memory. I feel territorial enough about my garden to empathize with the atavistic drive to defend the approaches to the nest. But nearly all the interesting and beautiful items of my close-up view of Connemara lie on private land or on commonage, access to which is controlled by the group of farmers who use it and who can decide to fence it off. England's fiercely defended network of rights-of-way and the well-developed right to roam open land have no parallels in Ireland. However, there was in general no difficulty about crossing farmland until the enormous increase, over the last decade or so, in the numbers of ramblers, some of them ignorant or careless of the practicalities of working the land. Now we need dialogue, mutual understanding, sensible legislation, etc.—rare panaceas—and, much deeper, a shared sense of the Earth's surface as a palimpsest, the compiled and over-written testaments of all previous generations, which it is our right and duty to read. When I come to enquire into the monuments and marks that have been set on this little facet of it, and note how consonant the history of Bunowen is with that of Ballynahinch or Renvyle, for example, I realize how much of the history of Connemara is covered by the question of who owns the land. It is a story of interventions—the O'Flahertys thrown into the West by the tidal advance of the Norman conquest, the Elizabethan attempt to impose the Composition of Connaught, the Cromwellian transplantations, the bankruptcy of estates by the Famine, the spread of Land League agitation and consequent land reform—rather than a story generated by Connemara itself. Those interventions are the generalities that impose a periodization on the story—but humanity is in the details, and to read it properly we need to attend to the small print of that vast document.

Doon Hill is so called from what Roderick O'Flaherty, the only early source to mention it, refers to as 'an old fortress of a down on the top of the hill.' This *dún* or cashel, a circular enclosure with a rampart probably of piled stones and earth, was scarcely traceable when O'Donovan looked at it in 1839, and I can make out no sign of it today. Its fine situation gave it a sea-hawk's view of all approaches, and it would have been within mutual signalling range—say, by fire or smoke—of Dún na bhFál, a small cashel on one of the islands off Slyne Head to the west, and of the Aran Islands' hilltop forts on the horizon to the south, but whether or not it was contemporaneous with any of these remains unknown. It seems possible that in early medieval times the Conmaicne Mara, having come into Iar-Chonnacht from what is now north Galway, occupied it, if not residentially then on occasions of danger or of ceremony. Perhaps the O'Flahertys wrested it from them when they in their turn were driven into the far west by the Normans; or it could have been won from the Conneely sept, if the local legend of their near-extermination by the O'Flahertys has any truth behind it. But whoever its successive owners were, its site proclaims its power over Errismore.

By the Elizabethan era the old *dún* was out of date and the O'Flahertys had built a tower house in the Norman mode, at the eastern end of the sandy grasslands below the *dún*, by a footbridge over the stream (known locally as the Brandy River—a name redolent of smuggling). Within the gapped walls of a rectangular bawn or courtyard, head-high in places, totally gone in others, all draped in vegetation—I remember trailing stems of ground ivy several yards long, and a clump of sea-beet, a rarity in these parts, growing in a crevice of the stonework—a mound some ten feet high marks the footprint of the vanished tower. What ferocities nested or were fledged here! In the mid sixteenth century the castle was owned by a descendant of the senior branch of the O'Flaherty clan, Dónal an Chogaidh (of the strife or war), husband of Grace O'Malley, who was to become the renowned sea-queen of Clare

Island, denounced by Queen Elizabeth's officers in Ireland as 'a woman that hath impudently passed the part of womanhood and been a great spoiler, and chief commander and director of thieves and murderers at sea.'

Grace was born in about 1530; her father was Eoghan Dubhdara (black oak) O'Malley, the chieftain of what is now Murrisk on the Atlantic coast of Mayo. The O'Malleys lived as much on the sea as on the land, their motto being *Terra marique potens*; they not only raised great herds of cattle but they traded to the continent—the merchants of Galway called it smuggling—and they fished, and it was under licence from them that English, Spanish and French fishing fleets were allowed into their rich coastal waters. Grace was brought up in the castles of Belclare and Clare Island, and married Dónal—just three or four castles away down the coast from her homes—when she was sixteen or so, in about 1546. Dónal was *tánaiste* or second in command of the O'Flahertys and heir apparent to Dónal Crón of Aughnanure Castle as *taoiseach* and ruler of all Iar-Chonnacht. A few years after the marriage Dónal was implicated in a notorious murder that took place in the O'Flaherty castle at Indreabhán in south Connemara. The victim was a Walter Burke, the son of David Burke, later to become the head of the Burkes of Mayo. Walter's mother having died, David Burke had remarried, his second wife being Dónal's sister Finola. It seems that Dónal was incited to the deed by Finola, whose motive was to clear the way to power for her own son by David, Richard (later to become known as Risteard an Iarainn, Iron Dick, either from the suit of armour that seems to have been his favourite attire, or from the numerous iron mines on his territory). A future in which Dónal would rule Iar-Chonnacht and Richard the seaboard of Mayo might have been the vision behind the event. Strangely, it fell out that the belligerent Iron Dick did become the chief of the Mayo Burkes, and that Grace returned to Mayo when the equally warlike Dónal died, and married him.

Legend has it that Dónal's death occurred in the course of an attack on the Joyce Country, where he seized a castle of the Joyces, built by the O'Connors and de Burgos long ago on an island in Lough Corrib near Mám. The Joyces managed to surprise and slay him while he was hunting in the hills nearby, but when they turned to regaining their castle they found it so stoutly defended by his wife that she gained the nickname of the Hen (Dónal being the Cock), and the castle that of Caisleán na Circe, Hen's Castle. Some years afterwards the same warlike lady defended the castle against an English force, and routed them with showers of molten lead stripped from its roof. There appear to be no early sources for these tales, which the knowledgeable Sir William Wilde in his book on Lough Corrib mentions among other 'legends . . . as numerous as they are fabulous . . . some of which fables the guides and boatmen will no doubt relate to the tourist.' But whether or not they really refer to the wife of Dónal of Bunowen, they sit well with what is known more certainly of her combative nature. Her biographer Anne Chambers holds that Grace gradually superseded her husband in his authority over his followers, was active in intrigue and tribal disputes, in fishing and trading, and in leading out her swift galleys to prey upon merchant ships passing Bunowen on their way into Galway. Piracy was of great concern to the Mayor and Corporation of the little mercantile city, who appealed to the English Council about:

> . . . the continuing roads used by the O'Malleys and Flaherties with their galleys along our coasts, where they have been taken sundry ships and barks bound for this poor town, which they have not only rifled to the utter overthrow of the owners and merchants, but also have most wickedly murdered divers of young men to the great terror of such as would willingly traffic, and let and hindrance of their trade no small weakening of Her Majesty's Service.

When the English authorities, now well established in Galway and beginning to fight and scheme their way into Iar-Chonnacht, bought the loyalty of the O'Flaherty nearest and most threatening to them, Murchadh na dTua, by declaring him *taoiseach* of the clan, the result was rebellion and an outbreak of clan feuding, for under Gaelic law Dónal, as *tánaiste*, was the presumptive heir to the position. Both Dónal Crón and Dónal an Chogaidh joined the Mayo Burkes in an uprising that culminated in an indecisive battle at Shrule in Mayo and the submission of the MacWilliam, the head of the Mayo Burkes, to Queen Elizabeth. Dónal an Chogaidh must have died shortly after this—he disappears from the record, it seems—and Grace returned to her natal realms, where she assembled a band of 200 followers and made Clare Island her base for the career of maritime trade, piracy and well-judged temporization with the English powers that has made her an icon of feminism and an emblem of the national spirit. In about 1566 she married Risteard an Iarainn and moved her headquarters to his castle of Rockfleet in Clew Bay, where she later defied a siege by an English force of ships and troops and sent them packing. But one by one the chieftains of the West were submitting, and exchanging their clan rights for titles that enrolled them in the feudal system. In 1577 Grace found it politic to meet the Lord Deputy Sir Henry Sidney in Galway; his report is her first appearance in book history:

> There came to me also a most famous feminine sea captain called Grany Imallye, and offered her services unto me, wheresoever I would command her, with three galleys and 200 fighting men, either in Scot-land or Ireland; she brought with her her husband for she was as well by sea as by land well more than Mrs. Mate with him . . . This was a notorious woman in all the coasts of Ireland.

The rest of her amazing life-story—her perhaps legendary abduction of the child heir to Howth Castle; her imprisonment in Limerick and Dublin; her visit to London to face Queen Elizabeth; her many interventions in the wars and rebellions that ended in the defeat of the old Gaelic order at Kinsale; her death shortly thereafter—would take me too far from Bunowen, where she had left her two grown sons by warlike Dónal, Eoghan (Owen) and Murchadh. They had inherited Ballynahinch, as I have told in the first volume of this book, but lost the island-castle there to the English-backed upstart Murchadh na dTua, and then regained it, although their lands were ravaged by Murchadh na dTua's son

Tadhg. In the following year, 1585, the Lord Deputy Sir John Perrot brought forth the document known as the Composition of Connaught, detailing the terms on which the clan chiefs were to abjure their traditional rights and receive the clan lands as heritable personal estates held from the Queen. Both Eoghan and his brother Murchadh figure in this document, so fundamentally historic for Connemara, but neither consented to it, preferring to live and rule by the Brehon law rather than pay a faraway queen a rent and owe her knight's service for the enjoyment of what was already theirs according to the ancient ways of the clans. When the Mayo Burkes rose in revolt against this settlement, and were defeated and their leader hanged, Sir Richard Bingham sent his notorious brother Captain John Bingham into Iar-Chonnacht with 500 soldiers, to gather booty to pay the costs of the conflict. Eoghan had not joined the rebels, but he found it prudent to withdraw with his men and cattle into the island of Omey. What became of him was later recounted by his mother Grace herself, under interrogation after her own arrest:

> When they [Bingham and his men] missed both the rebels and their cattle, they came to the mainland right against the said island calling for victuals, whereupon the said Owen came forth with a number of boats and ferried all the soldiers into the island, where they were entertained with the best cheer they had. That night the said Owen was apprehended and tied with a rope with 18 of his followers; in the morning the soldiers drew out of the island four thousand cows, five hundred stud mares and horses and a thousand sheep, leaving the remainder of the poor men naked within the island, [they] came with the cattle to Bally-na-henssy aforesaid, where John Bingham aforesaid stayed for their coming; that evening he caused the said 18 persons, without trial or good cause, to be hanged, among them was hanged a gentleman of land and living, called Thebault O'Tool, being of the age of four score and ten years. The next night following a false alarm was raised in the camp in the dead of the night, the said Owen being fast

bound in the cabin of Grene O'Molloy, and at that instant the said Owen was cruelly murdered having 12 deadly wounds, and in that miserable sort he ended his years and unfortunate days.

In contrast, the second son, Murchadh, enjoyed remarkably fortunate days; he lived on at Bunowen and assembled an impressive portfolio of rights and revenues, becoming known as Murchadh na Maor, of the sergeants, from his many administrators. He led his clan to assist Red Hugh O'Donnell in his raid into the Galway region in 1599, and in the following year sailed with a fleet of galleys and 600 men to join the Earls O'Neill and O'Donnell in Kerry—but after their defeat at the Battle of Kinsale he came home again, lived a quiet life, sued successfully for a pardon and consolidated his position by obtaining English titles to Bunowen and the surrounding townlands. An enquiry or 'inquisition' of 1607 found him to be the owner of the castles of Bunowen, Ballynahinch and Renvyle, and recorded his 'fines and customs' throughout the Barony of Ballynahinch as follows:

First. That whenever anyone was robbed of a cow, the thief shall pay to the said O'Flaherty seven cows for every cow so stolen; that whenever O'Flaherty went to the General Sessions the inhabitants used to present him with a butt of sack. Moreover, that he was entitled to have yearly out of every quarter of land within the said Barony certain measures of meal called 'Sruans' in Irish [a *sruan* apparently being a 'cakelet,' an eighth part of a big cake or *bairín*], together with a sufficient quantity of butter. Further that it was customary whenever anyone took any wreck of the sea, or ambergris, without notice thereof given to O'Flaherty or his sergeants, the person so doing shall pay a fine of seven cows to O'Flaherty: And whenever O'Flaherty gave any of his daughters in marriage he was accustomed to receive one barren two year old cow out of every inhabited quarter within the aforesaid Barony.

Murchadh na Maor died in 1627 and was buried in the Abbey of St Francis in Galway. He bequeathed a large tract stretching from Cleggan Head into the heart of the Twelve Pins, 'excepting onelie the Aiery of hawkes upon Barnanoran,' to his third son, Brian (who, after the Cromwellian victory, forfeited it and had to flee to Brussels), and Renvyle to his second son, Edmund (who took part in the rebellion of 1641, leading 1,800 of what the Governor of Galway termed 'the rude kearns of Irr-Conaght' to besiege the English fort there, and was eventually hunted down at Renvyle and hanged, as I have told). The eldest son, another Murchadh, inherited Bunowen and came to own such huge herds of cattle that he was nicknamed Murchadh na Mart, of the beeves. It is said that he was visited by the Earl of Strafford, the Queen's Lord Deputy in Ireland, who risked travelling through Iar-Chonnacht to Bunowen in 1637, was entertained with a profuse but rude hospitality, and knighted his host, while spying out his lands in order to plot his dispossession. The knighthood did not buy Sir Murrough, as he now became, for long: he joined his brother Edmund in the siege of Galway fort in 1641 and after the suppression of the rebellion was denounced for his sanguinary exploits in the town. One witness stated:

At fall of night I saw in the streets of Galway one Morrogh O'Flaherty, being a tall, swarthy young man, marching down the street with about 300 Irish rebels following him, carrying torches and long swords, and they broke into the houses and stabbed five soldiers with their skenes . . .

And another:

I saw the priests of the towne and other priests, being about eight in number, going about the towne in their vestments, with tapers burning and the sacrament borne before them, and earnestly exhorting the said Sir Morrogh na Mart and his company, for Christ's sake and Our Lady's and St. Patrick's, that they would shed no more blood, if they did they would never have mercy.

Murchadh na Mart was luckier than his brother in that he got off with his life, but he was dispossessed by the victorious Cromwellians, and his castle burned. (It was an ominous presage of such changes, says Roderick O'Flaherty, that rats frequented Moycullen for one year and left overnight after devouring a carcase of mutton to the bone, and that they infested the castle of Bunowen for two years, until it was burned in January 1653.)

Bunowen, the land and the castle (whatever state it was in at that time), were forfeited and granted to a Catholic landowner whose Westmeath estates had been confiscated. The rest of Murchadh's estate was parcelled out similarly; the Earl of Westmeath got the Renvyle area, and Richard Martin of Dangan got much of the rest of Connemara, including Ballynahinch Castle. After the Restoration Murchadh tried and failed to regain his property. He probably spent his last years in the Aran Islands and had the chapel attached to the ancient church of St Enda built, for that is where he is buried, having died, in 1666, a landless man.

The new owner of Bunowen was a Geoghegan, scion of an ancient family, the MacGeoghegans, who claimed descent from Niall of the Nine Hostages, the fourth-century High King of Ireland, and whose principal seat was Castletown Geoghegan in Westmeath. The family had suffered dreadful losses in the cause of the Confederate Catholics: Art Geoghegan, who had inherited Castletown, and his brother Bryan both died in an attack on Bunratty Castle in 1649, another brother, Barnaby, was killed near Limerick, and a nephew, Thomas Óg, lost his life in the last stages of the defeat of the rebellion, at Loughrea in 1642. Another family seat, the castle of Donore, was held by a James Geoghegan, who was slaughtered there along with fifty men, women and children. Art's lands, amounting to 3,000 acres, were confiscated, but because his wife (according to a family tradition) had protected some Cromwellian officers in danger of death, his second son, Edward, was granted Bunowen in compensation; also, Art's eldest son, Hugh, somehow managed to save part of the estate out of the wreckage. Edward Geoghegan never lived in Bunowen; it was his son, another Art, who first took up residence there—but beyond that fact I can learn nothing of him.

Art was succeeded by his son Charles, and perhaps it was he who had a little mortuary chapel built, above the sandy beach just east of Doon Hill, for his tombstone lies in it. There was in his days a small church or abbey nearby, exactly at the butt of the hill, the earliest record of which (in Sir William Petty's atlas) dates from 1683, but this was in ruins by the mid nineteenth century and I could not find a stone of it when exploring the area in the 1980s. There is also an old graveyard, disused since 1820, near the chapel, an unenclosed oval area knobbly with small set boulders, all anonymous, and with one big recumbent grave-slab of Aran limestone, inscribed but illegible. So the only upstanding monument in the vicinity is the mortuary chapel itself, a roofless neglected stone chamber—some sheep ran out of it as I approached, and I had to kick a lot of sheep-droppings off the tombstone lying in a corner before I could read:

Pray for the soul of Charles Geoghegan, who dyed the 8th of Feb. 1724, aged 80; as also for his wife, Mary Geoghegan, alias Blake, who dyed 6th Feb. 1763, aged 96. Requiescat in pace. Amen.

This long-lived Mary was the third child of Walter Blake of Drum in County Galway, who under Charles II was granted Inis Ní and Inis Leacan near Roundstone and a substantial estate around what became Teach a' Bhláca or Cashel House, near An Tulaigh in south Connemara, and whose descendants were notoriously harsh landlords. Charles and Mary's son and heir, Edward, also married into the ramified Blake family, this time the Ardfry branch.

On Edward's death in 1765 his son Richard inherited, and proved to be Bunowen's most remarkable master; he was the first of the family to conform to the established Church and, as in other cases, the adoption of Protestantism went hand in hand with an interest in estate improvement. Richard went to Holland to study the science of land reclamation, and on his return had a dam built across the mouth of the *murlach*, the salt-water lagoon at

Ballyconneely, winning many acres of grazing meadow from the sea. An inscription on the dam read:

Hos terminos Deo favente posuit mari Richardus Geoghegan, qui persaepe corruentem aggerem luctando restituit, pauca ducens soler-tiae ac perseverantiae esse impossibilia. Opus perfectum fuit Anno Domini, 1758.

[These boundaries Richard Geoghegan, by the grace of God, placed on the sea. With effort he rebuilt the dam when it very frequently fell down, reckoning that with skill and perseverance few things are impos-sible. The work was completed Anno Domini, 1758.]

Richard's dam served for over a century, until it was destroyed by a great storm of 1867 and was replaced by a smaller one, which itself is now broken. I have searched its ruins in vain for the inscription.

Richard Geoghegan was an Irish patriot, resentful of the restrictions imposed by England on Irish trade, such as the Woollen Act and an embargo on the export of provisions, the purpose of which was to guarantee supplies for the British Navy and Army. When British manufacturers successfully opposed government measures to remove these injustices British goods were boycotted in Ireland, and armed Volunteers demonstrated in Dublin; as a result Lord North, the Prime Minister, announced that Ireland would be allowed to trade freely with the colonies and to export glass and wool. Richard celebrated this victory by building an octagonal pleasure-house or gazebo on top of Doon Hill, of which a scrap remains; it too had a Latin inscription, now lost:

Deo liberatori Hiberniae A.D. 1780, has aedes consecravit anno eodem, gratus et laetus, R.G.

[To God the liberator of Ireland A.D. 1780 he dedicated this building in the same year, with thanksgiving and joy.]

Shortly after his succession to the property, Richard abandoned the old castle ('it becoming unfashionable to dwell in military fortresses,' as the sardonic John O'Donovan put it) and built himself a small house on the low ridge looking down towards the beach. He married a Mary Bodkin (the Bodkins were another of the mercantile families known as the Tribes of Galway), and lived to the ripe age of eighty-three. One would like to know more of this enlightened Latinist.

Richard's son John David was a Member of the Irish Parliament until the Act of Union in 1800. In 1808, in the reign of George IV, he changed his name to O'Neill, harking back to the MacGeoghegans' illustrious ancestry. John O'Donovan thought his history was wrong and his name-change ridiculous ('the O'Neills of the north took their surname from Niall Glundubh, not from Niall of the Nine Hostages, which should have proved to Mageoghegan that he had no title to the name of O'Neill in any historical point of view'), and he indulged in some laborious sarcasms over it, in his letters back to base when researching Connemara for the first Ordnance Survey:

> . . . considering that the name Geoghegan was too barbarous for a man of his dignity and protestant feelings, [he] thought proper to change his ugly ould name to the more mellifluous but equally savage one of O'Neill, and this he did by consent of his good monarch to whom he proved that he was lineally descended from Niall of the Nine Hostages, the plunderer of Gaul and tamer of the Britons. The monarch considering this fact proved, consented, &c, that Mr. Gogh-again of Bunowen Castle in Connemara, should reject the patronymic which he and his ancestors had for eight centuries, received from their more modern ancestor Gog-again and call himself and his posterity after their more remote progenitor Niall Naoighiallach . . . and thus took the tribe name instead of the surname which had been rendered respectable by the historical reminiscences of eight centuries. This is, to my mind, august fudge . . .

John David died in 1830 and was succeeded by his son John-Augustus, who was for many years the MP for Hull and, according to O'Donovan, one of the most distinguished Orangemen of his time: 'but now he is at home at Bunowen, a very quiet and good-natured papist, and one of the best landlords in Ireland. Oh! mind of man! once a proud persecutor of his race and now a humble believer!'

By the date of O'Donovan's lightning campaign of topographical research through Connemara in 1839, John-Augustus had embarked on the project that eventually ruined him, an extensive addition to his house, using stones from the old castle, that would turn it into a rival to the Gothic castle the D'Arcys had built at Clifden. This, and the monies he expended on his election campaigns, bankrupted him, and a receiver was appointed to the estate. In 1841 John-Augustus left Bunowen to spend most of his time in London, where he died some years later in poverty. Thackeray passed by in the year after his departure from Bunowen and described the melancholy state of the place:

At length we came in sight of a half-built edifice which is approached by a rocky dismal grey road, guarded by two or three broken gates against which rocks and stones were piled, which had to be removed to give entrance to our car. The gates were closed so laboriously I presume to prevent the egress of a single black consumptive pig far gone in the family way—a teeming skeleton—that was cropping the thin dry grass that grew upon a round hill which rises behind this most dismal Castle of Bunowen. If the traveller only seeks for strange sights this place will repay his curiosity. Such a dismal house is not to be seen in all England or perhaps such a dismal situation. The sea lies before and behind; and on each side likewise are rocks and copper coloured meadows by which a few trees have made an attempt to grow. The owner of the house had, however, begun to add to it; and there unfinished is a whole apparatus of turrets and staring raw stone and fresh ruinous carpenters' work. And then the courtyard—tumble-down out-houses, staring empty pointed windows, and new smeared plaster cracking from the walls, a black heap of turf, a mouldy pump, and a wretched coal scuttle emptily sunning itself in the midst of this cheerful scene.

The Great Famine completed the humiliation of the estate; in the winter of the miserable year of 1848 a lease of the unfinished castle, its offices and a couple of acres of land was offered to and taken up by the Poor Law Commissioners in Clifden, for £80 a year; Bunowen Castle was to become an auxiliary workhouse to accommodate 500 women. Much work was required on the building, however, and it did not open until the summer of the following year. After the Famine, in 1852, the whole estate of nearly 13,000 acres was sold off, the castle, with almost 8,000 acres, going to the head of yet another branch of the Blakes, married to a daughter of yet another of those ancient Tribes of Galway who still kept so much of the county in their grasp.

Valentine O'Connor Blake of Towerhill in Mayo, and his wife Mary Ffrench of Castle Ffrench near Ballinasloe, made Bunowen into a summer residence, but three years later found it necessary to mortgage it, together with another of their estates, Lissard, to the Scottish Amicable Assurance Co. for £5,000. Valentine died in Bray in 1879, leaving Bunowen to his second son, Charles Joseph, who visited occasionally but lived near Maryborough in Queen's County (the present County Laois). In September of the contentious and distressful year of 1880 he tried to have ejectment notices served on a number of tenants who were in arrears of rent—poor fishermen who had been living on relief and could not pay, kelp-burners whose market had collapsed and some widows whose only other resource would be the workhouse—and he came up against the organized opposition of the Land League. Events of that day were reported in the *Connaught Telegraph*, unsympathetically to Mr. Blake. Seventy-eight extra policemen armed with rifles had come out from Galway to back up the unfortunate process-server, a Mr. John Browne of Clifden, 'a man dressed like an ordinary peasant, with a pale face and a hunted expression.' In command was the Resident Magistrate, Mr. Parkinson, 'a stout gentleman with white head and a benevolent expression, an aspect he very soon lost, with a luncheon bag strapped across his shoulder and an umbrella in his hand, his son by his side.' The first victim was to be a Val Clogherty, whose cabin was near the castle, and who owed two years' rent, £15 18s. 4d. His neighbours, 'great strapping fellows, dressed in yellow flannel trousers and usual vest with flannel sleeves, their faces coloured with the pure air of the Atlantic and their fists bearing big cudgels, which spoke of moral and physical force combined,' threw themselves in a mass in front of the police; but when the young curate Father Flannery assured his flock that this was only a notice, not an ejectment, Mr. Browne was allowed to affix it to the door. Then a Mr. Brennan of the Land League arrived by pony-car, to loud cheers. He had come from Dublin at the invitation of the Errismore Land League, he told the crowd, to ask them not to be guilty of any act that could disgrace Ireland; the police were only doing their duty, he said, a very disagreeable duty indeed. The people should act prudently, 'but also act as became Irishmen determined that the accursed system of landlordism must go down.'

And so the sorry work went on. The sun beat down, the sweaty police marched to and fro, the crowd of 500 or 600 people followed crying, 'God save Ireland' and 'Down with landlordism,' the children imitating the police by marching four deep. At a wretched dwelling with no window the police fixed bayonets and held a way open for Mr. Browne to walk to the door, while the occupant, an old widow woman, sat at a distance with her face in her hands crooning and wailing. Someone told Browne 'he would yet be serving processes in a warmer place and would have a police escort there too. 'Then the police marched back to the road and there ate their provisions as they waited for the pony-cars to bring them back to Clifden. Brennan addressed the people on the sands; he wished he could have called them to a more manly battle for their country's national and social regeneration, 'but it is necessary to have education of the mind as well as power of the arm . . . and we want, through public meetings, to teach you that you were not born to be the slave of any class . . . I would ask all to join in one manly struggle, in one great organization for the destruction of Irish landlordism.' If they paid rent that year, and their children died of starvation, he warned them, they would be responsible before God for their murder.

Charles Blake wrote to the newspaper to justify his proceedings, claiming that almost none of the seventy tenants had paid their rents, although he had forgiven them a half year. He had told them that the winter was likely to be a trying one and that he would not press again until the summer; in August 1880, he claimed, his brother Thomas had visited the castle and had got nothing, and he then decided to select names of persons whom he considered capable of paying, and to have ejectment notices served on them. He complained of the influence of the Land League on tenants he had known all his life and who had always exhibited towards him 'the warmest feelings of affection and regard,' and he concluded thus: 'I shall only say that, so far from driving out any of the poor tenants from their holdings, I shall retain them on my land on any terms as long as circumstances will allow me.' So, thanks to press publicity, evictions were averted, or at least delayed—for, according to Clifden's historian Kathleen Villiers-Tuthill, evictions did take place just over a year and a half later, in May 1882.

Charles never resided at Bunowen, but his younger brother Thomas did, and repaired the building in 1889–90, although by local accounts it was never quite finished. In 1909 the estate underwent the common lot of being bought out by the Congested Districts Board and divided among the tenants. The last of the Blakes of Bunowen are still remembered as occupying the front pew in the church at Ballyconneely; they were a Colonel Blake and two ladies I am told were his sisters. By their time the castle had matured enough to have its ghosts, and there was a 'fairy room' of which it was said that anyone who slept there would die within the year; a little girl of the Guinness family did so, and did not live to see her ninth birthday, or so I was told by the Bunowen blacksmith Jim O'Malley. Jim used to attend parties and dances in the castle, 'unofficially,' as he put it, and on one such occasion the hall door opened and a hand appeared over it; but when the guests rushed out, no one was there.

Now indeed there is no one there. The Blakes departed in about 1930 and the castle was abandoned. Today it is in a sad state: stripped of its roof, walls gaping, some rooms bricked up, others used as outhouses to the farm, a cattle-crush installed in the courtyard and, as I noticed last time I passed by, the whole western gable end leaning out perilously. What humiliation has been inflicted, what a petty revenge taken, here as in Clifden, for the centuries of landlordism!

One further mark of ownership has been put on this land. On the bare dome of Doon Hill, next to the stony footprint of Richard Geoghegan's 'Volunteer Tower,' is a dingy concrete structure like a small room with a fireplace and a three-windowed bay, through which the western breezes stream: a Local Defence Force lookout post from the years of 'The Emergency,' as the Second World War was euphemistically termed by the state of Éire. About a hundred such posts were built around the coast, each with a numeral of stone and concrete written large on the ground nearby to identify the coastal sector to aeroplanes. On the highest point in the Aran Islands I have come across a number 50 and the letters EIRE, perhaps intended as a reminder to lost or confused pilots that these offshore islands were part of the ground of neutral Ireland. Near the western point of Leitir Mealláin is the number 51; 52 is or was on the head-land of An Leathmhás near Carna; and here, crowning Doon Hill, I find a broken-down 53. So the earth bears the brand-marks of the state—a practical measure in time of war, this enumeration of the confines of Ireland, but now redundant, abandoned to weeds and to my adoption of it into the underpinnings of this book as a summation of all the modes of possession that have been visited on the land. Whatever clan was here before the O'Flahertys was reduced to client status or driven out. The territory may have been the common heritage of the clan as a whole according to Brehon law, but folklore associates every one of the O'Flaherty strongholds around the coast of Connemara with tyranny and oppression, and nothing in recorded history contradicts the essence of the old stories, the stored-up grudges of the centuries. The Elizabethans bought the O'Flaherty chiefs piecemeal with their own clan's territory, the Cromwellians expropriated those they did not hang and used their estates to settle out of harm's way those they had expelled from richer land elsewhere. The resilient Tribes of Galway revived their fortunes as landlords before losing them in the Famine; the best of them, like Richard Geoghegan, turned the eye of the Enlightenment on the earth to make it bring forth more wealth. The Land League crisis proved retrospectively that the Famine too, as a failure to mitigate the effects of a natural calamity, had been a question of who owned the land. The Congested Districts Board gave a revolutionary answer to that question, which Independence consolidated. Now the relics of past times, which are principally those of past owners, their powers, pieties and sorrows, are reduced to cattle-pens on the farmer's land. Property rights and possessive attitudes cut us off from even these disparaged stones, leaving us as flimsy as paper figures cut out of our backgrounds in history and nature. Where do we turn, to find a way of looking at the land, inhabiting it, loving it, other than that of ownership?

When my geologist comrade and I had parted from Sailor MacDonagh and finished investigating the basalt dyke on the beach, we followed the foreshore south-westwards and soon found ourselves scrambling between the waves and the cliffy foundations of Doon Hill. In an inlet that terminated in a vertical slit, a sea-worn cave in the rock wall, lay a line of stone blocks, the remains of a little landing stage called, I knew from earlier enquiries, Cé Aill an Bhorrtha, the quay of the cliff of the surge or swell. And at the end of our traverse we found a steep-sided inlet spanned by a natural arch of rock, Fuaigh na gColm, the creek of the rock-doves. This was a smugglers' cave, and it was here, the blacksmith had told me, that he found the small cast-iron cannon I had noticed lying in front of his house, which perhaps had been discharged by Grace O'Malley herself. And here, more importantly, my account enters another dimension of the land and the question of its ownership. For this is the doorway into Cnoc an Dúin (as I will now call the hill, it being a subject of Irish-language lore), the chief fairy stronghold of Connemara and a rival to Connacht's famous fairy hill, Cnoc Meadha, which rises mysteriously alone in the plains of east Galway just as Cnoc an Dúin does among the bogs, lakes and dunes of Errismore.

This unearthly or underearthly dimension from time to time has run parallel to the history of Bunowen as treated above. For instance one of the few humans to get the better of the fairies of Cnoc an Dúin lived 'about a hundred years ago' from the time of the first writing-down of his story in the late nineteenth century. His name was Andrew the Shoemaker, and he was employed by the Geoghegans as a herdsman. Although he took good care of their pastures he often found that more of their grass had been eaten during the night than all the cattle of Ireland would eat. This caused his masters to complain of him, so he kept watch one night. Towards midnight he heard cattle grazing and chewing the cud, but he could see nothing until he grew tired and sat down, whereupon he was able to see black cows in the meadows. Later he realized that he must have sat on the four-leaved sham-rock, a powerful charm. He grabbed the tail of the nearest cow and twisted it round his wrist, and kept his grip as the beast ran into the fairy dwelling. There were women rocking cradles there, and lots of children, and they welcomed him by his family name and forename. He was dumbfounded and nearly lost the sight of his eyes with the beauty of the place, but when his speech came back to him, 'it was no good speech':

'Why the devil are your cattle eating my master's grass?' 'Oh, Andrew, dear friend,' said the fairy women, 'you see the children; they need a drop of milk.' 'To the devil with you and your children,' said Andrew. 'Oh, Andrew! Oh! Andrew! Oh! Your mouth and your mercy, don't be saying big oaths, and we'll do whatever you demand.' 'Very well,' said Andrew, 'I want you to keep your cattle away from me and not let them eat my master's grass.' 'We're satisfied,' said the women, 'we'll do anything you want from now on for fear of the big oaths.' They made an agreement then, and since that time neither cow nor cattle came grazing the grass. Andrew was happy to be able to sleep at night, and the women kept their promise.

Fairies are extraordinarily sensitive about bad language; this is a theme in other Connemara folktales too. They are referred to as the Good People to placate them, but they still play malicious tricks on their human neighbours, as the following story, which was taken down in Irish, like the last, by Dómhnall Ó Fotharta, schoolmaster of Callow near Ballyconneely, and published in 1892. I have shortened it a bit:

Once when there was a dance on in Aill Bhreac a gentleman arrived on a fine horse, and left a lad in the saddle to mind it. No sooner had he gone into the dance but the Good People came up behind the horse and slapped it on the rump, and off it went into the lake at the foot of the hill. They kept it swimming to and fro by striking it with whips of bamboo with lashes of deerskin, until rider and horse were exhausted. Then one of them—a local man who had died recently— seized the reins and said to the rider, 'It's time for you to leave this place; go home or to my house. The little boys are awake and they'll let you in.' The Good People hit the horse, and off they all went together. They rode for three miles, and then went riding to and fro between each other like soldiers learning their drill, until cockcrow, when they were gone, as if the earth had swallowed them. The lad went to the house the dead man had told him of, and they let him in.

Another story of a familiar type from the same source is set in the timeless era of wonders, and yet has a note of rustic common sense in it:

One Hallowe'en the Good People of Cnoc an Dúin carried off the King of Leinster's daughter. About midnight, Diarmuid Súgach, Merry Diarmuid, a playful fellow who lived near the hill, and who liked walking by night as well as day, was coming home from a party when he saw a company in the road carrying, as he thought, a corpse. When they saw him coming they laid down their burden and got out of his way. He went up to the coffin and in it was a beautiful young woman. He put his hand on her forehead and felt it warm. 'Musha,' he said, 'I'm sure they were the Good People and this is a noblewoman they stole from her mother and father and were taking to their home. But I'll carry her to my own house.' So he carried her home to his mother. The woman stayed asleep for a year and a day, until Hallowe'en came round again. Diarmuid said to himself, 'I'll go back to Cnoc an Dúin tonight and perhaps I'll find out why she's in this everlasting sleep.' So he went to the fairy dwelling. The door was open before him. In he went, and hid himself behind the door. He wasn't there long before the fairies came by and began to discuss the adventure of the previous Hallowe'en. 'A year from today,' said one of them, 'Merry Diarmuid took the King of Leinster's daughter from us.' 'What good is that to him?' said another, 'She didn't give him a smile or a laugh since.' 'True for you,' said the other fairy, 'but it wouldn't be so if he pulled out the sleep-pin that's in her hair at the back of her head, and then she'd be as lively as she ever was.' 'Very well, my lad!' said Diarmuid to himself, 'I'll soon see if you're right.'

As soon as Diarmuid got home he ran to the noblewoman saying, 'I summon you and I bless you, daughter of the King of Leinster. Didn't I do the deed, taking you from the Fairy Host?' With that, he searched her hair and pulled out the sleep-pin. Her sleep and swoon left her, and her speech and hearing came back. 'Success and triumph to you, Diarmuid; the King of Leinster's daughter is yours,' said she; 'It's time for us to go home to my father's house now.' Off they went to the Province of Leinster, and told the story from beginning to end to the King. 'Musha,' said he, 'my daughter is yours.' 'My Lord and Master,' said Diarmuid, 'it's not right to mix royal blood with yokel's blood.' 'That's no objection,' said the King, 'if the girl is content.' That was what the daughter wanted, and she consented to the marriage. The wedding lasted seven days and seven nights and all the great nobles and the lesser nobles of the province were there.

After the wedding Diarmuid brought his bride back to Connemara; and there are people there today who say they are descended from that couple and that the blood of the King of Leinster runs in them. But whatever about that, there's the story for you as I heard it, and if there's a mistake or a lie in it, don't blame me.

So, once again and for the millionth time, the hero, our local Siegfried, wakes the maiden to sensual and reproductive life by his attentions—for to understand the motif of the sleep-pin withdrawn from the head we have to apply the dream-rule of 'going by opposites.' More instructive it would be to try to use the above fairy stories, and the countless other ones they remind us of, to reconfigure our outlook on the world. To imagine the consciousness of other beings is to see through their eyes, and in the case of fairies this is revelatory. The fairies dwell in the hill, not on it, nor do they look down on it from tower house or bomber. They see the land from within, as do those who briefly visit them, the village seers and shamans, and it is of dazzling splendour. So are the mist-drops threaded on a spider's web in a gorse-bush early in the morning, to glance at an item of reality that might be supposed to concern the fairies. Like the hill, even the smallest of such earth-entities are full of cradles rocking; nature is nurture to itself. In the fairy faith we can find clues to a fitting and worthy response to the generosity of the earth.

But the spider's thread is an appropriation of space, spun by fate for some flying morsel of life. A theme of Irish folklore, presumably originating in attempts by the theorists of early Christendom to accommodate the pagan deities in the new multi-story moral universe, is that the fairies are the angels thrown out of heaven for their rebellion, arrested in their fall by a late-relenting God and let inhabit the air, earth and sea, rather than plunge right down into hell. But if they are in fact the gods of old, the glorious Tuatha Dé Danaan, then their fall has been into our world of natural ecology and its gross malformed outgrowth, civilization, and they have picked up its ways. For the fairies are parasitic on honest farmers, they are sadistic practical jokers, they unfeelingly abduct children out of cottage and palace and, most importantly for the present context, they are as territorial as robins or as we humans, prone to turf wars, menacing to trespassers. That they do not exist is the greatest of their shortcomings; we should not try to re-enchant the world by peopling it with mere shadows of our twisted selves, or with any other fictive wish-fulfilling or fear-inspired entities. Hills, springs, caves, places in general, have their own modes of being, which are not those of personalities, and are to be respected. The gods are gone, and we have to live with the loss.

The interior of Cnoc an Dúin was once blindingly bright indeed. The principal interest of the hill for my geologist friend (he was Professor Paul Mohr of NUI Galway), and one of its fascinations for myself, was that it is the stump of an extinct volcano—a fact that throws a lurid light on the paltry question of who owns it.

Some sixty million years ago it would have been surmounted by a Fujiyama of congealed lava flows and consolidated ashes, piled up towards a sulphurous sky; but all that is long gone, ground down by rain, frost and wind, and carted off by streams and rivers to be dumped in the sea. Cnoc an Dúin as we see it today is a mere candle end, the column of dolerite, a coarse-grained basalt, that solidified in the throat of the dying fire-mountain.

As we picked our way around the wave-washed base of the hill, Paul pointed out various signs in the rocks of its glory days. The walls of the first cleft we came to were speckled with whitish blots he called zeolites, inclusions of aluminium silicate that had crystallized out from hot water solutions to fill little cavities in the rock, the cavities themselves being bubbles formed in the molten lava as it rose in the pipe of the volcano, fizzing like soda, as Paul put it, as the pressure on it was released. The rounded beach stones at our feet were of the same speckled rock; I brought one home to remind me of Connemara's fervid past. Then at Fuaigh na gColm, the creek with the rock arch, we saw striped pebbles, the result of a mingling and mutual drawing out of two successive pulses of molten dolerite. The inlet itself, Paul pointed out, had been formed by erosion of a two-metre-wide 'crush zone' defining the perimeter of the volcanic pipe up which the molten rock had forced its way through the ancient gneisses of Iorras Mór. The two steep sides of the creek were strikingly different in appearance, that to the west scribbled over with linear and angular grooves, the work of erosion sculpting out the layered texture of the gneiss, and that to the east composed of spheroidal blocks, gouts of lava that solidified in their flow, cracked as they cooled into hexagons, as in the Giant's Causeway, and then were rounded off by weathering.

The Doon Hill volcano was a symptom of titanic convection currents rising from thousands of miles down below, which eventually caused a new splitting apart of the Earth's crust, the separation of Greenland from Europe and the still-ongoing widening of the Atlantic Ocean. One can vaguely imagine, and science can more accurately reconstruct, what happens when the tar-slow convection currents, constantly turning over the plastic white-hot rock on which the crustal plates float, change their pattern, which they do chaotically and unpredictably, like the convection currents in a saucepan of coffee as it is heated. If upwelling begins under a continental plate the land will arch up into a vast shallow dome and gradually be torn apart by the rock-currents diverging beneath it; the furnace-hot rock begins to melt when it reaches upward to fifty or so miles below the surface, and this molten magma then works its way on up through the crust. It can prise open vertical cracks to form dykes or reefs like the one we had seen on the nearby beach, or force its way laterally between pre-existent strata to harden into horizontal sills, or burst forth in volcanic eruptions. Amid such cataclysms, the gradual foundering of basins with seas, as happened with the infant Atlantic, would have been so slow that no mortal creature could have observed them, any more than the inhabitants of Iceland, despite its active volcanos and hot springs, are routinely aware that they are riding on the mid-Atlantic ridge, the very seam from which the ocean floor is spreading out in either direction today.

Such is the story as accepted by the scientific community (who nowadays can tell it in much finer detail than suits my purposes); and in relaying it the lay person might well borrow a formula from the fireside historian I quoted above: 'There's the story for you as I heard it, and if there's a mistake or a lie in it, don't blame me. 'That the human mind can learn so much of what happened sixty or more times as long ago as the birth of the human race is wonderful;

it is as if the mite no bigger than a full stop one notices running across the page one is reading could itself read that page. Plate tectonics and mantle convection have been with us long enough as a scientific theory for us to take it into our minds as a feature of our world-picture, the backdrop of the indubitable against which other claimants to our belief parade their persuasions. And if we know in our hearts that mountains and oceans have their day then our proprietorial attitude to patches of land appears in perspective, as a littleness.

A Lake Full of Sand

One evening, back in the times when such things still happened, a lame and probably tipsy poet, staggering home along a lonely lake shore from a session of socializing, was confronted by a beautiful lady. Was she Helen of Troy herself? In any case she said she had come from Greece in search of him, having heard tell of his fine qualities, and she insisted that he go away with her. After some demurral he agreed that, if she would grant him nine days' grace to travel around consulting his former lady-friends, he would then join her in her fleet, anchored off Slyne Head.

The poem, 'Loch na Niadh,' that celebrates this unlikely affair is sung to an elaborate and delicate air which I first heard from a friend in Inis Meáin; her voice leaped lightly to and fro among notes that seemed to hang in a sparkling array like a dew-spangled spider-web.

An tráth seo aréir is mé ag siúl liom féin
Ag déanamh ar éadan Loch na Niadh,
Mo ghrua go léir do las go tréan
Le heagla ghéar, is gan fios cé faoi.

Nuair a phreab na réalta ar na spéartha
Fuair mé léargas beag ar mhnaoi,
A loit mo thaobh le saighead glan gear
Agus d'fhág an lionn dubh i lár mo chroí.

Tháinig smaoineamh eile in m'intinn
Beannú arís don mhaighre mná,
Go bhfaighinn amach cé chas in mo líon í
An tráth sin d'oíche, is uaigneas ann.

'Druid aníos liom agus dearc go grinn mé,
Is mise an fhaoileann óg ón nGréig,

Searc mo chroí thú de ló agus d'oíche,
Meabhair do chinn agus glór do bhéil.'

'Stad a chiúinbhean agus ná buail fúmsa,
Dearc mo shnua, nach bhfuil mé slán,
Tá mé stuacach, crosta, gruama
Agus páirt de mo stuaim ar easpa ball.'

'Siúil, is ná síl go gcaithfidh tú mé dhíot,
Is a liachtaí rí a chuir mé 'un báis,
Ó fuair mé scéala ar fheabhas do mhéin,
Shiúlfainn Éire le fonn thú a fháil.'

'Más fíor gach ní dá bhfuil tú a insint
Suífimid síos go n-éirí an lá,
Go bhfaighidh mé scéala an bhfuil sé in Éirinn
Ní fá'n saol a leigheasfadh grá.'

'A bhfuil in Éirinn uilig fré chéile
Nó a bhfuil sa saol den saibhreas breá,
Ní shásódh siúd mé in áit mo chlú
Gan ceangal dlúth dá bhféadfainn a fháil.'

'Tabhair dom spás go ceann naoi lá
Go siúla mé gach ceárd amach fá'n tír,
Go bhfaighidh mé fáisnéis ó na mná
A mbínn i bpáirt leo seal de mo shaol.'

'Fuigh leat is déan sin, is bí anseo arís,
Agus gheobhaidh tú mo fleet ó dheas den Cheann,
Is lóchrann oíche a gclaimhte líofa
Agus feadaíl bhinn ag an gcannonball.'

The song is a favourite among Irish-speakers in Connemara;
the above version is largely taken from a curious little book of local
folklore published by Dómhnall Ó Fotharta, the schoolmaster of
Caladh, near Ballyconneely, in 1892, *Siamsa an Gheimhridh nó cois*

an teallaigh in Iarconnachta ('Winter Entertainment, or, by the fire-side in West Connacht'), but there are many variants, each with its own obscurities, and I have transplanted a few lines from other sources to make better sense of the whole. Liam Mac Con Iomaire and myself have put together a singable English version, following the loose meter of the original and echoing as many of its internal half-rhymes as we can manage:

This time last night as I walked alone
I was fast approaching Loch na Niadh,
When all my face lit up in flame
From inexplicable sudden fear.

As the stars shone out from the firmament
I got a glimpse of a maid alone,
She pierced my side with a pointed arrow
And left deep sorrow in my heart and soul.

A sudden thought came into my mind
To speak in kindness to Her Grace,
That I might hear what brought her near
So late at night in this lonely place.

'Step up here and observe me keenly,
I'm the young queen from the land of Greece,
You're my heart's desire by day and night,
Your intellect bright and your winning voice.'

'Stop, my fair one, and don't assail me,
My face is pale and I am not well,
I'm cross and cheerless, fractious, gleeless,
My limbs are weak, as you can plainly tell.'

'Don't dare to think that you can fool me,
And the host of kings I've sent to their graves,
I would walk all Ireland to make you my own,
Once I'd been told of your splendid ways.'

'If it be true what you are saying
Let's sit down here till morning comes,
And tell me plainly, in all of Erin
Or all the world, if there's a cure for love?'

'All of the riches in the whole of Erin
Or in all the world, both near and far,
Would not repay my loss of face
If you're not mine in bonds of love.'

'Give me some space and nine days' grace
Till I visit places far and near,
And get the advice of all the ladies
With whom I've shared life in bygone years.'

'Be off and do so, and come back here again,
You'll find my fleet off the Head to the south,
Their sharpened swords like guiding lamps
And sweet whistling shots from the cannon's mouth.'

'Loch na Niadh' is the name of the song, but the sense of
the word 'niadh' in this context remains obscure. (One version is
called 'Loch na Naomh,' the lake of the saints.) Uncertainties also
surround the authorship of the song. A well-known storyteller of
Carna, the late Cóilín Ó Cualáin (he was talking on Raidió na
Gaeltachta in about 1975), said the poet was Micheál 'ac Cualáin,
familiarly known as Micheál Mharcuis after his father Marcus. Ó
Fotharta on the other hand names the poet as Miceál Ó Conghala.
  As is frequently the case with such traditional songs, the tale
of its making is also remembered and passed down. This is Ó
Cualáin's account of it, roughly translated:

He was lame, you understand, and he was able to play the
flute and the tin whistle, he was a musician as well. He used
to be going around in the áirneán time [house-visiting time,
the long nights between Hallowe'en and Christmas] as is

still the custom, though it's dying out a little now, all right. But he came home this night and maybe he was a bit late. 'You were out very late,' his wife said. 'I was,' he said, 'but I think I'm going away for good.' 'Why?' she asked. 'Ah, a young queen from Greece has come for me,' he said, 'and I think I'm going away with her.'

And the reason for this was this: when he was going home some youths who were in the visiting-house left before him, to get him to make a piece of poetry. And they placed a piece of wood that was thrown ashore, a piece of a ship, and the picture of some well-known woman was on the piece of wood—the Queen of England or some important woman— in front of him in the gap in the stone wall, wrapped in some sort of a cloth. 'There you are!' says he to the wife. 'I think I'll go away with her altogether.'

But, true to form, he set to work, and when he came to the visiting-house the next night someone asked him, 'Did you meet any ghosts on your way home the other night?' 'I didn't,' he said, 'but I met a fine-looking woman from Greece, and I'm going to elope with her.' And he lay back on the stool that was at one side of the fire and he began: 'This time last night as I walked alone . . .'

Some years ago Diarmuid Breathnach, a retired librarian whom I used to meet at the Merriman Summer School and who had become a friend, called on me looking for information on Ó Fotharta. Diarmuid, in collaboration with a former colleague, Máire Ní Mhurchú, was then compiling the fourth volume of *Beathaisnéis* ('Biographies'), a labour of love of the Irish language that has now grown to a total of nine volumes. The first five volumes comprise 700 biographical essays on people active in the Irish-language movement whose deaths fell in the period 1882– 1982, of whom perhaps sixty are fairly familiar names and the rest virtually unhonoured in the collective memory until the coming of this publication. The subsequent volumes take the roll-call back to 1560 and forward to 2006. It is a monumental, comprehensive and definitive work of reference, and if there is to be another volume every green-blooded *Gaeilgeoir* would want to be in it, but for the inconvenient entrance-condition about being dead.

All I had to offer Diarmuid towards his research on Ó Fotharta was the whereabouts of the former Calla National School in which he taught, a few miles south of Ballyconneely, so we drove round there, met the owner of the school, which is now a holiday home, were referred by him to the parish priest in Ballyconneely, and by him to the oldest resident, who could remember only that all the former pupils of 'Dan Faherty,' as he called him, 'had great Irish'; we also searched the old Ballyconneely cemetery for his grave, without success. It was an enjoyable afternoon's ramble up and down the boreens and in and out of houses, but not rich in clues to Ó Fotharta's history. However, when the fourth volume of *Beathaisnéis* appeared it contained a crisply informative essay on the almost forgotten schoolmaster.

Dómhnall Ó Fotharta was born in 1834, his father being a farmer (of Guairín in Omey Island, I have subsequently happened to learn) and his mother a Robinson, of a family who came from County Down to work on building Nimmo's quay at Cleggan. When he was fifty he married his twenty-five-year-old assistant teacher, Mary Walsh, and on his death at the age of eighty-five in 1919 left two daughters and a son, all Irish-speakers. He seems to have spent all his working life and his retirement in Caladh. As well as *Siamsa an Gheimhridh* he published a folktale in the august pages of the *Zeitschrift für Celtische Philologie*, and two other small collections of Irish-language material. The Redmondite MP Stephen Gwynn, who came holidaying by in about 1908, gives us a sketch of him in his old age:

> . . . a retired National schoolmaster, whose name—not a common one—has fine pagan associations; for, as he told me, the head of his clan fought as a chief captain under Art, son of Conn the Hundred-Fighter, at the battle of Knocklong—some seventeen hundred years ago. I found him ensconced in his study among a scholar's paraphernalia. Rare and costly Irish books were on his shelves—not a few the gift of their authors, for this old student has been

in lifelong correspondence with famous names; yet most of them were his purchases, made out of the economies of the worst paid vocation in Ireland . . . One more thing I noted as I took my leave of this old man, who is—and long may he be so—a centre of real scholarship among the Gaels of Connemara. He is a centre of culture of another sort, for dahlias and montbretias flowered in profusion about his door; and from this focus one could see them radiating outward, here a patch and there a patch outside other cottages, adding a new and most welcome feature to the Ireland of peasant ownership, which need not fear a rise in the rent . . .

Does Ó Fotharta matter nowadays? His antiquated little collection of tales, songs and riddles has solved a few puzzles for me in my work on placenames, ministering to my pedant's glee in eliciting obscure facts from even obscurer sources. I first came across him as a correspondent of the Aran Islands schoolmaster David O'Callaghan, a founding member, with Patrick Pearse, of the Aran branch of the Gaelic League. It was O'Callaghan who taught the young Irish-speaking village lad Liam O'Flaherty that there was such a thing as written Irish; thus there is a remote connection between Ó Fotharta and *Dúil*, O'Flaherty's short-story collection, through which generation after generation of schoolchildren enter into Irish-language literature. In fact without the largely unrecognized labours of Ó Fotharta and his like, the hundreds of modest, laborious enthusiasts rescued from anonymity by the compilers of *Beathaisnéis*, we would not now have access to what Ó Fotharta in the preface to his book calls '*an teanga bhinn bhríomhar, an teanga treun tuilteach, an teanga uasal árd ársa ár sinnsear féin*' ('the sweet lively tongue, the strong overflowing tongue, the noble high ancient tongue of our own ancestors'). This is the characteristic rhetoric of that passionate and idealistic band, the early Gaelic Leaguers, but there isn't a word of it I could quarrel with as a description of Irish; I don't feel excluded, as English-born, even by those 'ancestors,' for to me ancestors are the former inhabitants of whatever ground I find myself inhabiting, and learning something of their language is part of my self-investment in that ground. There were undoubtedly elements of anti-modern reaction and nationalistic introversion in the mind-mix of the old Gaeilgeoirí, which even today inhibit recognition of what was generous and creative in it. But Irish, long constricted in polemical narrows, is still a sweet, strong and overflowing tongue, and we should be able to greet it as every language should be welcomed, as a unique occasion of joy; the anxieties and ideologies of its present life-or-death situation arise inescapably, but only after, and because of, that fact of joy.

Ó Cualáin believed Loch na Niadh to be in Mannin on the north side of the peninsula of Errismore; Ó Fotharta places it a little further south-west in Errismore—but adds, 'Alas, nowadays it is filled with blown sand so that nobody would know that it ever was a lake.' Errismore was not included in the Gaeltacht when the Irish-speaking areas were officially designated as such in 1956, although there must have been many native speakers at that time; in fact the last of them died only a few years ago, and the language lies shallowly buried beneath English, so that sayings, placenames, riddles and stories come to the surface plentifully. In fact 'a lake full of sand' is such a naturally occurring image for the status of Irish here that the quest to locate the grave of Loch na Niadh suggests itself as an act of remembrance.

Ó Fotharta says that the former lake was halfway between Cnoc an Dúin and Ceann Léime or Slyne Head; that places it in or near the townland of Creggoduff. Creig an Duibh, the crag of the black stuff, is the underlying Irish of this name, referring to the mud found at the bottom of bog-holes, which was used as a dye. But it is a long time since there have been bog-holes there, or even a lake; the first edition of the Ordnance Survey, in 1839, marks the area as 'blowing sand,' and in more recent times it has been well-established machair grassland. Going back to my notes on the area made in the 1980s I was delighted to find this, taken down from a Ballyconneely man: 'Tradition that someone deposited gold (or money?) in a lake, which then filled with sand so that he couldn't refind it; on site of golf course.' And in fact most of Creggoduff was taken over by the Connemara Golf Club in 1973. Just outside the north-eastern boundary fence of the golf course

is a lake the official maps call Aillebrack Lough, from the townland it lies in; I had also forgotten that I had recorded the name
'Sand Lake' for it from the old blacksmith of that locality. Having
resurrected these indications it seemed worthwhile going to look
at Sand Lake, and so I persuaded my friend Máirtín O'Malley,
whose family came from Errismore and who knows everyone in
that district, to drive down there with me.

By the time we had passed the last of the ribbon-development
spreading westwards through Aillebrack from Bunowen the day
had turned wet and misty. We left the road and bumped along
a vague track across acres of emerald green grassland to the wire
fence of the golf course, beyond which a few hunched figures
under big umbrellas were moving like giant ambulant mushrooms.
The lake was beautiful, set in a flowery plain, with a zone of yellow sand visible in its bed all around it, but it was too large and
settled a feature of the landscape to have ever been lost to memory. We decided to call on Mr. John O'Neill, a founding member
and former president of the golf club, and, as he puts it himself,
'the oldest animal in this district,' who lives in the westernmost of
the Aillebrack houses. A stooped but vital figure, he stood in his
doorway and listened carefully as Máirtín introduced me. But he
had never heard of Loch na Niadh, or of the song about it, and I
turned away in disappointment while he had a word with Máirtín
in his role as fisherman: 'Next time you're down this way you could
bring me half a box of pollock.' But fortunately I turned back and
tried a last hint—'Maybe it was on the golf course'—and his face
suddenly focused inwardly: 'The Corrach Mór!' he said (which
means 'the big swamp'). 'I used to see water in it in the winter, and
geese gaggling on it. It's north-east of the clubhouse.' How pleas-
ingly precise—and how convincingly consistent, when I marked
it provisionally on a map, with Ó Fotharta's indication, 'half way
between Cnoc an Dúin and Ceann Léime'!

So we drove back west to the course—alien territory for me,
who tended to see it only as a regrettable intrusion into an endangered environment—and up the drive to the clubhouse, a two-and
three-storey building with terraces, much plate glass and complex
low-pitched roofs, sitting proudly on a central height of the course.

On the stairway up to the bar and lounge were hung photographs of the club's past dignitaries—presidents, vice-presidents, lady captains, etc.—among whom I noticed Mr. O'Neill in his younger days. The lounge was full of rained-off golfers and family groups of tourists; on a big TV screen rugby scrums boiled and burst. We looked out from the rain-streaked rear windows; it was impossible to make anything of the washed-out green and blonde topography of tees, fairways, bunkers and rough out there in the mist. 'There's a lake by the thirteenth,' said a man who overheard our conversation, 'the best par-three in Ireland!' But the map in the golf course brochure showed that lake as too far west to be what we were looking for. We left it for another day.

On that day I was accompanied by Cilian, the ecologist, and Sabine, the marine biologist and artist. We sneaked round behind the clubhouse, where, beyond a zone of derelict containers and piles of crates full of bottles, the ground fell away into a shallow basin of indefinite shape and extent, crossed by two or three fairways and surrounded by low grassy rises. We foraged around down there in the tousled, flower-rich sward; I had to admit that the machair was well conserved in its role as 'rough.' There was a patch of low willow scrub, which Cilian thought was possible evidence of a former lake. Hopping across a drainage channel, crossing a fairway heads down, not quite knowing the etiquette of the game or where balls might be flying at us from, we found a pond some dozen irregular yards across, full of the strange stonewort alga whose fronds are encrusted with lime and look like grey rags: Loch na Niadh, for sure, or its ghost! I was perversely delighted by the irony of identifying this residue of old, magical, poetic times subsisting in the heedless heart of contemporary banality. We looked into it; Sabine pointed out transparent newt larvae an inch long, caddis-fly grubs lurking in their sheaths of tiny pebbles and bits of plant stalk, China-mark caterpillars afloat in tiny coracles made of two ovals cut from pondweed leaves and sewn together with silk, water scorpions and other little creatures I used to know and wonder at as a child and had not set eyes on since. The pond was richly alive, it was a marvel—but in this explicit daylight with the colourfully sweatered golfers passing nearby it did not seem likely that I would find a beauty from Greece loitering around it, even in the form of a lady captain. For that, I would have to come by night, drunk perhaps, certainly alone, and maybe in thought only.

So what is she, the apparition of Loch na Niadh? In the grand old *aisling* or vision poems of the eighteenth century, of which lame Micheál Mharcuis's lame song is a belated, self-mocking echo, the forlorn but exigent lady met by the poet in a lonely place is Ireland herself, in the pride of her distress; she is not far fallen from the status of earth-goddess, an oppressed and politicized Banba, Fódla or Eriú. But now that the nation is only self-enslaved, I think she is more particularly the spirit of the Irish language, hanging around the last traces of its almost choked sources in such places as Connemara.

My own spoken Irish is badly decayed at present; that is why I am putting off writing about the Irish-speaking areas of south Connemara until I finish this present volume. My re-exploration of all those riddling peninsulas and tongue-twisting archipelagos of the south will have to wait until I have time to be born again—for to learn another language is to be reborn—as at least a competent Irish listener. Nevertheless, despite my linguistic shortcomings, my bleary face and gammy leg, the lovely language will always find me her faithful votary.

Pilgrimage and Picnic

Beyond the golf course and the rampant shanty town of mobile holiday homes that has recently colonized the machair west of it, the land suddenly becomes serious, ascetic, as if conscious that it is approaching its last end. Winds off the sea have stripped it almost bare, leaving knobbly hillocks of dark metamorphosed gabbro, between which a few sheep search the low wiry vegetation. This is private property, defended by a barbed-wire fence and 'Beware of the bull' notices, beyond which an unsurfaced track winds across barren wastes through the townland of An Caorán Mór, the big moory hill, to that of Baile na Léime, the settlement of the leap. The latter name refers to the narrow seaway between the ultimate point of the mainland, Ceann Léime, leap head, and the nearest of an archipelago of rocky islands, Oileán na Léime, leap island. (Somehow the whispering gallery of time has made first 'Slime Head' and then 'Slyne Head' out of 'Ceann Léime.') For many generations this has been the territory of a branch of the Coneys family, who used to rent it from the O'Malleys of Ceann Léime, middlemen for the Martin estate, and now own it outright. The Coneyses came to Ireland with Cromwell, according to tradition; in 1677 a Thomas Coneys obtained a 'transplanter's certificate' granting him and his heirs three townlands in the neighbourhood of what is now Clifden. His descendant Matthew lived in Ardbear (in Rushnacarra Lodge, by the bridge on the road south of the town, I believe), and 'through a long life, bore the character of an upright magistrate and an honest man,' says the Galway historian James Hardiman, in a note to his 1846 edition of O'Flaherty's *West or H-Iar Connaught*. Matthew's son was Robert, of Baile na Léime:

> On this wild point of Ballynaleame, there lived for many years, a valued friend and relative of the Editor, the late Robert Coneys, Esq., whose stormy habitation may be seen

marked on Larkin's large and small maps of the county of Galway. This gentleman held all Ballinaleame, including Duck Island, at twenty shillings yearly rent. Before the erection of the lighthouses at 'Slyne' head in A.D. 1836, he saved many lives from shipwreck, and his humanity was rewarded by 'windfalls,' as flotsam and *jetsam* are familiarly termed in Connemara; but these 'windfalls' have considerably decreased since the erection of light-houses on the coast. To sickness he and his family were strangers. He used to boast that a doctor was never known to visit Slime-head; and he considered it a bad omen, when one of the faculty settled so near as Newtown-Clifden, though several miles distant.

No one lives in Baile na Léime now, the home of the current Robert Coneys being near the little harbour of Slackport half a mile to the north. The house Hardiman mentions as marked on Larkin's maps (which date from 1819), or more likely its successor on the site, is half unroofed by gales, and the rest of it is a store for big cylindrical bales of straw to feed cattle. Mary O'Malley, the poet, remembers visiting an aged aunt who lived in this house, and having to climb over a hill of sand heaped by the wind against its west-facing door. I rambled by here recently in company with Mary's brother Máirtín and his partner Sophie. The track passes between derelict outhouses and an abandoned jeep inscribed in big white letters KEEP OUT, and fades away among blown-out dunes and knolls of rock. Flotsam and jetsam rim the low shoreline, mainly of the usual trash but including items in which Máirtín's knowledge of sea and shore ways revealed some interest: timbers riddled with the burrows of worms, prized for fencing because air can circulate in them and prevent them rotting; a plastic object like a letterbox-mouth from an American lobster pot, which allows undersized lobsters to escape and itself falls off, releasing the bigger lobsters too, if the pot goes adrift; also a striped dolphin's skull, not a cheery death's head but a long melancholy spoon-face like that of a rueful comedian, which now watches me mournfully from a shelf in my studio. Máirtín could also name the offshore rocks and shoals for me, notably Carraig na gCapall or Horse Rock, and

Carraig an Ghalúin, the rock of the bailer, so called because it has a pool on it that makes fishermen think of a bailing vessel; it is said that five mares and an 'entire,' a stallion, escaped onto the first-named rock from a wrecked ship of the Spanish Armada, and then swam across to the second, before coming ashore to contribute their distinctive genes to the breed of the Connemara pony. Once a year in the depths of winter hundreds of people make their way across the desolate moorland of An Caorán Mór to a holy well on a harsh slope that looks out southwards across a sea full of rocks the waves fight over. St Cáillín's feast day is celebrated here on 13 November, and it is an extraordinary sight, the day-long intermittent file of pilgrims huddled in their dark overcoats, picking their way along the track and then down the slope, at that bleak season of the year. At the stile in the field wall just above St Cáillín's well many take off their shoes and go on gingerly to make the rounds of the well and of the saint's 'bed' bare-footed. Tradition says that once a man came all the way from Munster on crutches, arrived at this wall, and, unable to approach nearer, cried out to the saint:

Screadaim ort, a Cháillín
A Mhic Rí Laighean,
Tá mé i mo chláiríneach
Is ní sháróchaidh mé an claí.

[I scream out for you, oh Cáillín, the King of Leinster's son,
I am a cripple, and I cannot cross the wall.]

And the cripple was instantly cured. The rhyme is still remembered in the locality; I heard it from Jim O'Malley, the blacksmith of Aill Bhreac, around 1990 (and somehow, getting a story from the local blacksmith feels like a guarantee of its soundness and rootedness in community tradition). He also had the story of the saint's most recent intervention, during the Second World War. A ship had been sunk, a lifeboat from it was at sea for days, and several of the men in it died. Of the survivors, 'one was Irish and the rest were unbelievers,' as Jim put it; the Irishman prayed all the time, and he saw a figure in dirty grey clothes in the bow who silently pointed the way. So they came to shore at last, and 'if it had taken them another quarter of an hour they wouldn't have made it.'

St Cáillín is said to have flourished about AD 560; his main foundation was the once famous abbey and monastic school at Fenagh in what is now County Leitrim, and why he is celebrated on this remote Atlantic promontory is a mystery. He was of the Conmaicne people, who reckoned themselves the seed of the mythical Fearghus Mac Róich and Queen Meadhbh and inhabited the Dunmore area in what is now north Galway. Cáillín was nursed and fostered for a hundred years by Finntan, the aged seer who alone survived the Flood in Ireland. Then he went to Rome for 200 years to learn wisdom and knowledge, and returned just twelve years after St Patrick began his mission in Ireland. It was a plea from the Conmaicne that brought him back; for they felt that their inherited lands were too confined and their blood relations too numerous, and they were projecting a horrid fratricide among themselves, until an angel counselled them to send for Cáillín. The saint then set out to find new land for them, and eventually arrived at Fenagh in the kingdom of Breifne. The local king, Fergna, sent his son Aedh with an army to drive him off, but when they saw the saint and his followers kneeling they were all converted, and Aedh gave Cáillín his fort and land on which to build a monastery. Fergna then sent his druids against him, who turned up their anuses against the air, with other obscenities that the Victorian translator of this story leaves in the decent obscurity of Middle Irish, and opened their gluttonous jaws and shouted, and were turned to stone by the saint; the many standing stones still to be seen in that vicinity are their petrified bodies. Fergna was then swallowed up by the earth, and Aedh succeeded to the kingship; but Aedh's face was as black as a beetle, which was not fitting for a king, and so Cáillín arranged for him to have the likeness of an especially handsome saint, Ríoch. Some years earlier the great king Conall had been killed in battle at Fenagh, and now Cáillín found out his grave and assembled all the saints of Ireland to fast against God until they had obtained his resurrection. Conall then was baptized out of Cáillín's great bell; thenceforth every king was so baptized, and paid tribute to Cáillín's foundation too:

Let every king of reproving valour
Into the bell of the faithful put,
As a rich visitation tribute,
Its complete fill of gold or silver.

Cáillín died at the age of 500, the most eminent of Ireland's saints after Patrick. He left a book of poems, dictated to him by an angel, which recounts the whole history of Ireland and foretells all the kings that would ever rule the land from his own time onwards till doom; it also specifies the tribute due to his monastery from all other saints and rulers in great detail, which was evidently its chief purpose. This *Book of Cáillín* is lost, but its contents survive in the *Book of Fenagh*, written in 1516 for his hereditary coarb or successor, Tadhg Ó Rodaighe, which was passed down from abbot to abbot of the O'Roddys and is now in the library of the Royal Irish Academy. In it we may read the above remarkable history.

Presumably it was the coming of the Conmaicne Mara, as part of the general dispersal of the Conmaicne mentioned in my first volume, that brought the cult of their great saint to this extremity of the territory named after them, Connemara. And under the 'Conmaicne of the Sea' he became the local patron of seafarers. The 'well' on that gaunt seashore of Caorán Mór is a *bullán*, not a spring but a hollow in a rock outcrop that rainwater lodges in, and according to Roderick O'Flaherty it 'never overflows the stone or becomes drye.' There is a low horseshoe-shaped enclosure of a few piled boulders around it, and a crude wooden cross above it. Several feet away is a shrine of boulders eked out with a few concrete blocks, holding a small statuette of the Madonna, on the edge of a grassy oval marked out with little stones and ringed about by a faint path trodden into the grass by those doing their 'rounds.' The saint's 'bed,' another such penitential station, is a slight grassy knoll fifty yards up the slope, again with a path worn about it.

The site has been somewhat refurbished of recent years, and two inscribed limestone slabs set in another low structure of cemented boulders now direct the rites:

ST CAILLINS
WELL THE WALKING IS DONE
IN BARE FEET

CAILLIN
USUAL STATION
KNEEL AT FIRST STATION
SAY A PRAYER
AND PICK UP SEVEN STONES
WALK AROUND THE MOUND
SEVEN TIMES
SAYING OUR FATHER HALE MARY
A GLORY EACH TIME AROUND
REPEAT AT WELL
LEAVE SOMETHING
THAT YOU BROUGHT WITH YOU
AT THE WELL
A COIN STONE OR MEDAL ETC
WASH YOUR FEET IN THE POOL
BESIDE THE WELL
NOT IN THE WELL

Another limestone plaque by the stile in the wall that the cripple couldn't cross tells us that these improvements were made by the Ballyconneely Community Council in 1993 and were sponsored by the staff of the Bank of Ireland, among others—a pleasing touch, in these days when one might have thought that the ATM had replaced the holy well as the station of our pilgrimages.

Cáillín is, like Macdara, a boatman's saint—the representation on the upper of the two inscribed slabs by his well of an anchor and a little currach with two occupants remind one of this—and long ago the 13 November *turas* used to be made to a ruined chapel on one of the islands of the archipelago that prolongs Ceann Léime another two and a half miles out into the Atlantic. Who were the monks that first sought out that storm-soused seagull perch is unknown; the eremitic enthusiasm of the early Irish Church drove those extremophile souls in search of penitential solitude beyond what one would have taken to be the bounds of the habitable. In legend this urge appears as the saint's compulsion to move on out of the sound of another saint's bell. I have been shown a little hollow regarded as an unfinished holy well on a furzy hillside just north-west of Ballyconneely; one local man held that it was made by St Flannan and abandoned when he heard St Cáillín's bell in the distance, while another man had the story the other way around, with St Cáillín moving on westwards out of earshot of St Flannan's devotions. No history of the chapel on the island survives, apart from a mere mention of it in O'Flaherty's *West or H-Iar Connaught*, written in 1684. There was also a holy well on the island to which pilgrimage was made on 13 November, but this seems to have been destroyed, perhaps by the elements; the OS map of 1839 shows and names it, but that of 1899 adds the words 'site of,' and at some time in that interval the *turas* was moved to the mainland well. I visited St Cáillín's chapel and that site, but found no trace of the well, with an incongruously merry party of uneremitical ladies a few years ago, on a luxurious cabin cruiser.

This boat summers in Roundstone, and Máirtín skippers it for such jaunts, courtesy of its owner, the composer Bill Whelan. Having prepared for a rock-scrambling expedition with Máirtín I was wearing my survivalist sweater, old corduroys and boots, and was surprised to be joined on the quayside by Máirtín's sophisticated and quintessentially French partner Sophie Faherty, bright-eyed Lynn of the Angler's Return and her lively daughters, two Bulgarian girls working in O'Dowd's pub, willowy Valerie Joyce of Clifden, who is an artist, and several other scantily clad and sandalled pleasure-seekers. It seems that Veronica, the Whelans' housekeeper, who was of the party, had told Bill (on the phone to the States or to China, probably) that the weather was beautiful but was forecast to break on the morrow, and Bill had said, tell Máirtín to take you out in the boat, then; that's what it's for. So we powered out of the harbour in style and within half an hour were nosing cautiously among the wave-moulded rocks and foaming shoals of Slyne Head. What a welter and plethora of place we were entering into! Every creek and each of its hidden obstacles has its name, the name of a life-threatening reality—not so much to us on this calm day, with our echo-sounder, radar and Global Positioning System receiver, but certainly to the fishermen in wooden currachs who brave it in all but the worst weathers, setting their lobster pots or salmon nets. Máirtín kept me busy scribbling on my map at every twist and turn of the way along the archipelago, noting places about which I'd been gathering lore for years but had never precisely located before.

An Clochán is the first of Béalta Chinn Léime, the 'mouths' of Ceann Léime; it is a narrow waterway between the mainland and Oileán na Léime, and is supposedly so named as being a short-cut for boats going to and from An Clochán or Clifden—though I suspect that *clochán* here merely means a stony ford, since it is crossable by foot at low water. We kept close to the mile-long, low and flat Oileán na Léime, mindful of the breakers south of it known as Na Máilleachaí, the O'Malleys, after the sea-folk who once dominated this coast and terrorized all sailors-by. Then we gingerly felt our way in close to a steeper and rockier island until we could see the drifts of stone around its summit, fallen ramparts of the ringfort that once crowned it. This island is called Dún na bhFál, the fort of the walls—at least that is how George Petrie, the first to investigate it, recorded the name in the 1820s; local people, however, pronounce and understand it as Dún Uí Mháille, asso-ciating it with the sea-going O'Malleys and in particular Grace O'Malley. Between the two islands runs a twisty and cliff-sided channel called Bealach na hUillinne or Elbow Sound; I have read of a south Connemara smuggler, Liam Ó Loideain, on his way home from Guernsey, his schooner loaded with rum, tobacco, silk and indigo dye, who escaped the Revenue cutter that was pursuing him by turning into this sound and severing his masts so that the cutter couldn't see him and went sailing by in mistaken chase of another vessel afar off.

The next channel is Joyce's Sound; a rock called Seoigheach na Cruite, Joyce of the hump, separates it from Blind Sound, which, Máirtín says, is so called because it looks as if it is wide open but is in fact full of submerged rocks. Then comes a row of three high-shouldered islets separated by narrow channels of which the first is called Pocaide, puck-goat, and the next, according to the charts, Cromwell's Sound, although the bogyman of Irish history has nothing to do with the place; I have come across similar names in Inis Meáin and it is clear that, although it isn't in the dictionaries, the word is *cromaill*, slanting cliff. Here one side of the passage leans out and the other leans back, so that it is possible to squeeze a small sailboat through between them by tilting it to keep the mast clear of the overhang. Now we were proceeding cautiously along the north side of Oileán Lachan or Duck Island, where Máirtín has seen eider duck nesting, this being the very southernmost limit of their range. It is a narrow, irregular, grassy plateau almost three miles long, very nearly cut in two, so that one can see light glimmering through a sea-cave in its cliffs where the ceaseless waves have licked out a dyke of more yielding rock. Near the far end of this island is Oileán an Teampaill or Chapel Island; the two islands almost enclose a small lagoon—and there, tucked into a sheltery hollow running down to a shelving shore, the natural landing place, we saw our goal, St Cáillín's church, lacking its roof but otherwise as spruce as when it was built, perhaps a thousand years ago.

Jim O'Malley the blacksmith once told me that there are no animals or insects that could harm you on this island, although Duck Island is teeming with rats and the two islands are separated only by a tract of seaweed-slippery rocks when the tide is out. Indeed the saint's island has an enchanted serenity about it. We anchored in the middle of the lagoon and took to the dinghy to come ashore in threes and fours. The shallows were covered with an ice-blue carpet made up of thousands—millions, I'm sure—of the little translucent jellyfish-like entities called by-the-wind sailors. I call them entities because on looking them up I learn that they are not individual organisms like true jellyfish but colonies of simpler creatures specialized for capturing food, stinging predators, reproducing their kind or keeping the composite whole afloat. Each colony is an oval raft an inch or two long, with a vertical triangular membrane that acts as a sail; hence its lovely Linnaean name *Velella velella*. In some specimens the sail crosses the raft obliquely from port stern to starboard bows, and in others it runs the other way; so that when the wind blows, the first sort sail to the left of the wind's direction and the second to the right of it, thus stirring the oceanwide gene pool from generation to generation. Why such multitudes of them had harboured here I do not know.

The chapel, especially in its unroofed state, in its relation to the rocks it sits among and the sky it opens to, is an intensification and perfecting of the island's being. Seashore plants grow on it as well as all around it: big cushions of sea-pink, shaggy beards of the white-belled sea campion and, deep down in its crevices, the ragged little sea spleenwort fern. Its orientation is not quite the conventional east-west, but east-south-east to west-north-west, the better to nestle into a natural hollow and out of the worst of the westerly gales. At the foot of the eastern gable there are narrow stones set in the ground that look like the surrounds of graves, near which a few slim bones had worked their own resurrection; Sophie, who is a doctor, looked at these and diagnosed, certainly, their humanity, and, probably, their sanctity. The doorway, in the west gable, is narrow, slightly tapered upwards, and has a flat lintel of a single long stone that makes one stoop a little to enter. The interior is one simple space, six or seven paces long by four or five wide by infinity high; there is a narrow flat-topped window opening in the east gable, with an altar that has declined into a heap of stones below it, and a projecting stone high up to the left of it, on which we found an old teapot half full of rusty pennies. We scrambled out of the hollow and looked at the chapel from roof level; there were corbels at either end of the north wall, a feature that recurs in many early churches and is said to be an imitation in stone of a constructional device of earlier wooden buildings, the prolongation of a beam on either side beyond the gable walls to provide supports for barges or end-rafters. Despite such 'primitive' features, it seems that the stone oratories of western Ireland date from the eleventh or twelfth century, that is, twenty or so generations later than the saints to whom legend attributes them. But the fervour of sanctity, the urge to praise God through the creation of beauty, shows in their masonry. We wondered at the stonework here, the boldness and tact and sense of rhythm with which large irregular blocks were juxtaposed, the perfectly judged contrast between the broad flat surfaces of these blocks and the neat bands of spalls or small slim stones tucked in between them. There is a delicate musicality to this work, for all its starkness; in fact it makes even some recent stonework I have admired locally look like exercises in bad taste.

Then we dispersed, wandered around the island, came together again in groups and unwrapped our sandwiches in sheltered, sunny spots. Near the western shore we peered into a bare-floored stone hut with a rusty tin roof, about six paces long, occasionally used by fishermen; Máirtín remembers finding fourteen men asleep in it, from Inishturk and Turbot, two islands off the Clifden peninsula. Next, he and I took the dinghy across to Duck Island, which like Chapel Island is an alternation of wind-rumpled grassland on which a few sheep eke out a life, and great shoulders of dark rock illuminated with brilliant orange patches of lichen that compose an astonishing colour-chord with the metallic blue of the sea. The eroded-out dyke we had seen from the boat earlier almost cuts the island in two parts, joined by a sagging land-bridge below which the sea heaves darkly and gurgles; the cleft is called Fuaigh na gCroisíní, from the *croisín*, a long pole with a little cross-piece at one end, used for fishing masses of seaweed out of such deep creeks—a dangerous occupation, but part of the everyday usages of offshore rocks and islets. The south-facing cliff slanting down into the cleft was white with bird droppings; men from Bunowen used to come here and throw a net down it to catch roosting cormorants, which they used to bury in the bog for three days rather than hanging them; more recently they used to stuff them with onions instead, says Máirtín.

By the time we returned to Chapel Island the girls were swimming off a cobbly beach of its western shore, observed by half a dozen seals—goggle-eyed old gentlemen voyeurs—whose heads showed above the waves at a little distance. The twin sister-and-brother blues of sky and ocean, the gold and black of the rocks, the vaporous apparition of the lighthouse island out to the west with its mysterious towers, one of them bearing the intermittent spark that marks the ultimate reach of Connemara, all astounded me yet again. The swimmers had the right of it, I briefly felt: total unreflecting immersion in the flux of the world, as opposed to my grain-by-grain hoarding of detail. If I was right, then this book might as well be thrown into the sea. But as we began to assemble below the chapel again and the dinghy came and went, the lovely generalities were enhanced and enchanted, and my ways vindicated, by the strangest of details: the iridescent, slightly undulant layer of by-the-wind sailors lay on the waters like a throng of pilgrims with faces upturned to a cathedral balcony; or perhaps they were the souls—no, better, the last breaths, caught in silver and blue bubbles—of all the fisherfolk who had ever been drowned in these waters, gathered here to confront the saint who could not save them. Another ravishing detail: long thin fronds of orange-red thong-weed lay among the by-the-wind sailors in coils and Celtic interlacings, making of the water surface an illuminated vellum, a page from that lost *Book of Cáillín*.

As soon as our boat edged out of the lagoon we felt the swell, and crashing breakers made it clear that we would not be able to land on the lighthouse island as planned; so I can reserve it for another and conclusive occasion of writing. We rounded it at a safe distance, passing outside a little half-decker from Clifden that was bucking and wallowing perilously as the two men in it wrestled with their winch and heavy net. Between machinery and wave, I thought, it is a wonder that more lives are not lost in this dreadful trade. When we had moved out into more orderly waters I suggested we visit Na Sceirdí instead, that cluster of rocks set like a doorstop to the Atlantic halfway between Connemara and the westernmost point of the Aran Islands. So the boat was put on an automatic compass course and thrummed away like a laborious arrow for most of an hour, except for when a girl's hat blew off and we gallantly but vainly looped back to try to rescue it. Gannets followed us, their Concorde noses down as they eyed our wake from a great height and then plummeted into it. A little rainbow formed in the spray from our bows, so close it seemed fixed like a paddle-wheel to the side of the boat. We came into a stillness again among Na Sceirdí—surly, unvegetated, wave-blackened, round-shouldered plateaus of scoured granite, not a loose pebble to be seen—and exchanged uncomprehending stares with dozens of lugubrious grey Atlantic seals. An utterly alien world; we did not delay in it. Máirtín with great care manoeuvred us out of a complex of shoals and headed for Roundstone Bay. Soon we were passing Roundstone Rock, and the village, borne on its hillside, came swivelling into view, reassembled in a defamiliarizing upward perspective from water level. M in a long dress ran out onto the flat roof of the Folding Landscapes studio by the old pier and greeted us with the extravagant and ancient gesture—arms flung wide—that says, 'Welcome safely home from the sea, sailors, whether ye come guided by a saint, follow a compass course, or sail by the wind.'

To the Dark Tower

The lighthouse, because of its steadfast endurance in an extreme situation where the mineral world gives way to the liquid, its dramatic but routine role in welcome and warning to mariners approaching this interzone fraught with more dangers than either land or sea, its loneliness, the kernel of hermetic domesticity it holds or used to hold, is so richly fogbound in symbolism that it can almost be left to do its own work as emblematic endstop to a book. So, in writing up Slyne Head Light, I will begin with bare facts.

Oileán Imill ('or Bordering Island, as being the outmost border of the west,' as Roderick O'Flaherty puts it) is the last and largest of the Slyne Head archipelago, and lies about two miles offshore from Baile na Léime; it is a largely naked outcrop of dark and twisted gneiss, a third of a mile long and 200 or 300 yards across, rising to a height of 119 feet. There are two lighthouse towers on it, both built during the 1830s. One of them is disused and lacks its turret, the other, 150 yards nearer the north-western shoulder of the island, is still in use but no longer manned. The idea of the two towers was to warn of dangerous rocks north and south of the island, which approaching vessels could clear by keeping the further tower visible to the west of the nearer one.

From 1810 onwards the officials, dignitaries and merchants of the growing port town of Galway had been requesting the establishment of lighthouses at Slyne Head and on the Aran Islands, to mark the mouth of Galway Bay, and on Mutton Island in the approaches to the port itself. The Mutton Island light came into operation in 1817 and the Aran light, on the highest point of Árainn, the westernmost of the three Aran Islands, in 1818, but it was only after many representations from the captain of the coast-guard vessel covering this sector of the coast, and from inhabitants of the new settlements of Clifden and Roundstone, as well as from the Galway authorities, that Trinity House sanctioned the two lights of Slyne Head. The island was bought in 1831 for £210, of which £199. 14s. went to J. A. O'Neill of Bunowen and £10 to the tenants who would lose a bit of grazing, and some curious little amounts to three gentlemen who had claims on it through marriage relationships: Lord Plunkett (4s.), the Marquis of Clanrickard (1s.) and a William le Grand (1s.). The towers, dwellings and outhouses were built of the island's own gneiss except for the window and door surrounds, coign stones and stairs, which were of imported granite, and the sandstone flagging of the courtyards. During the work a man was drowned while bringing in provisions; his widow and four children were awarded 20 guineas. Then a boat over-turned with the loss of eight men; two widows, one of whom also lost a son in the accident, received pensions of £6 per annum, some children were awarded £3 per annum, and donations of £3 were made to three sisters who had been supported by one of the men. A coppersmith covered the domes of the two towers for a price of £60 each, and a J. Dove of Edinburgh constructed the apparatus for the north tower, which was to have a revolving light. Both towers were painted white, and both were seventy-nine feet high. They came into operation in October 1836, although not quite finished; the total cost to completion was a closely calculated £40,314. 19s. 3d., plus the few lives mentioned above.

In the early years keepers' wives shared the rigours of life 'on the rock,' and this claustral situation sometimes produced a potent brew of malice or despair. In 1859 Mrs Gregory, the principal keeper's wife, was committed for trial on a charge of poisoning an assistant keeper, and was in prison for months, separated from her large family of young children, before it became clear that the accusation was groundless and that the man had drowned, per-haps in suicide. When in 1894 two keepers, Harris and Harrison, were dismissed for insobriety and leaving the station without per-mission, their wives claimed that those who had lodged the com-plaint (one of them a King) were themselves frequently had up for drunkenness and fighting. A few years later Slyne became a reliev-ing station, the keepers spending six weeks 'on' and two weeks 'off.' Cottages were built for keepers and their families by the quay at Clifden, and were occupied from 1906.

Supply of the lighthouse, until the helicopter came into use in recent times, was traditionally in the hands of the King family of Slackport, a hamlet on a little bay about a mile up the coast from the tip of Baile na Léime, where there is a slip and a boathouse. When a keeper and a crew of six were drowned on their way to the island in 1852, three of the boatmen were Kings. (I have been unable to find out the origin of the placename 'Slackport,' which does not occur on Ordnance Survey maps or Admiralty charts but is well established orally. The Kings are familiarly known as the Slacks, but I think the nickname derives from the place rather than the other way around. The local origin myth is that some sailors came ashore here once and enquired for the pub; when they learned that it was five miles away in Ballyconneely they said, 'Well, this is a very slack port!')

The routine of supplying the lighthouse was primitive and complicated. When the boatman at Slackport decided that the weather was suitable he would hoist a 'bat' against a wall near his cottage as a signal to the keepers on the rock. He would then go to Bunowen, two and a half miles away, by horse or, later, bicycle, or send a message by a child going to school there. Thence a contractor with a cart would go to the cottages at Clifden, pick up the relief keeper and supplies, and return to the contractor's cottage near Bunowen, from whence the goods would be taken on donkey-back over the hills to Slackport and rowed out the three miles to the lighthouse.

Various technical changes were made to the lights over the years. The south lighthouse was decommissioned in 1898 and its lantern was removed so as not to obstruct the north light, which now became a fixed light showing white to seaward and red to the sector that watched over the rocks and islands to landward. In 1907 both towers were painted black, and two years later the six-wicked oil lamps of the north light were replaced by incandescent paraffin vapour burners. A new optical apparatus was installed in 1939, giving the double white flash every fifteen seconds that is still a familiar rhythm of nights in westernmost Connemara, and the red landward sector was discontinued. Electricity replaced paraffin vapour in 1977. The helicopter from Clifden replaced the boat from Slackport, and then humans were replaced by automatic mechanism in April 1990, when the last resident keeper, Seán Faherty of Clifden, locked the door for the last time.

Since I have no car Máirtín came to collect me for the long-awaited trip out to the lighthouse. He keeps his own little boat in Mannin, and on the way there we passed what had been Erriseask House, a pleasant small hotel esteemed for its cuisine and its 'unspoiled' site overlooking a long arm of sand and grassy dunes that shelters little salt-marshes and tranquil lagoons from the waves of Mannin Bay, and gives the area its name, Iorras Iasc, promontory of fish. Here I got a nasty shock, a reminder that even here we are subjects of a new, postmodern Ireland, the Old Woman of the Four Green-field Sites. The hotel had suddenly acquired long barracks-like extensions and two outlying blocks of holiday apartments, which looked as if they had been rammed down on the yielding machair in lumpish indifference to its soft contours and delicate horizons. Each of these new two-storey constructions is of three parts stuck end to end, the outer sections with eaves-lines in the gibbering-gables style that now infests the Irish countryside, and the central one workhouse-plain. The buildings were not quite finished, and some perceptive fly-by-night critic had scrawled 'EYESORE' in huge letters on one of the unplastered gable ends. On my way as I was to some hoped-for conclusive identification of the quintessence of Connemara, I had to pause and consider the significance of this addition to the scene. Is it actually part of Connemara? Or does it belong to some Anticonnemara that threatens to neutralize the place, to drag it down into globalized nullity? Connemara is both a certain tract of the Earth's surface and an accumula-tion of connotations: wild shores and tiny fields, famine and folk-song, mountains, lakes, heathers and lichens, the O'Flahertys and the O'Malleys, deserted cottages and russet-sailed turf boats, Patrick Pearse's vision of Connemara as 'a little Gaelic kingdom,' the Sublime and lots more, some of which I have been patiently weaving into this book. I should mention too the qualities of Wittgenstein's 'pool of darkness,' or of what dregs remain to us from it: tremendous silences, shadowy retreats from the competi-tive lights of the city, untimetabled hours and non-calendrical days.

(There are of course countless entities, good and necessary in their ways, within the geographical extent of Connemara that I have not mentioned because they are elements of the world at large rather than particular to the place.) Everyone who knows and attends to Connemara will have such a mental list of associations, which will overlap largely with mine. Thus Connemara has acquired a name rich in suggestions, which name—harmonious and persuasive resumé of all one means by Connemara—itself belongs among these riches. That is the nature of certain places—not of those that are mere locations with an arbitrary label attached, or of places too small or simple to resonate, or of cities that are already too heterogeneous to refuse any addition to their components, but of what I might call deep places, places that demand fidelity to their truth, like the three I have lived with for years: Aran, the Burren, Connemara. To see (or feel) if some attribute or object belongs to Connemara, one consults its assembled elements, among which is the accepted (and perhaps contested) idea of Connemara. But if this idea is a multiplicity that includes itself, Russell's paradox threatens, making Connemara a 'suspect terrane,' suspected, that is, of not existing, of being, as people mindlessly say it is, 'a state of mind rather than a place.' And, rather than venture into logicophilosophical acrobatics on the shaky trapeze of paradox, I will stay down-to-earth and say that a deep place is a historical and ongoing process, a slow event, in which, at every stage of its development or degradation, its current name is the touchstone of eligibility for the proposed new element. Thus a place ripens or rots; thus, in this instance, if Connemara is to conserve its truth to its name it must decisively reject certain so-called 'developments.' And such a conceptual rejection can have long-term objective consequences—in the present case, I hope, the eventual demolition of these two senseless blocks built to profit from that which they degrade, a shore blessed by Manannán.

Well, at least I have to thank the originator of these buildings for suggesting a train of thought; but I must not allow the gross intrusion too much attention, for the real Connemara awaits me in all its plenitude. Máirtín's sea-beaten old boat was moored off a beach further along the southern shore of Mannin Bay. An eighteen-foot wooden currach painted white and blue, it was full of marine clutter: buoys, ropes, an anchor, a plastic bottle of holy water attached in the prow, a fishing rod mounted vertically, a pair of narrow-bladed oars and quite a bit of water sloshing to and fro, some of which Máirtín scooped overboard now and again with a sawn-off plastic container. Soon the outboard engine was rumbling satisfactorily and the boat was champing at little waves. We had waited through a summer of rain and wind for an interval of calm long enough for the seas to settle down before we made this trip. Today promised little wind, and the tide time-tables indicated that its tidal fluxes would suit the course Máirtín had planned. The sea was a grand deep blue although the skies were argumentative: the sun high and bright but attenuated by thin cloud, and great grey piles of cumulus over the distant rim of mountains. Máirtín stood at the tiller, a narrow Nile-green wake of churned-up water behind him, the silver-flashing bow waves diverging to either side of it.

A mile to the north-west we rounded the cliffy hillock of An Cnoc and the rocks lying off it, then headed south-westwards along a low coast of alternating beaches of yellow sand and low dune-capped promontories with rocky foreshores. Off Dún Locháin a chain of islands and rocks begins that parallels the coast; we edged between the first of them, Inis Duga, dock island, and the little fishing quay it shelters and from which it gets its name. Here the sea surface, sheltered from the westerly wind, was sleek and black, muscular with the powerful flow of the tide. After that, the water being still too low for us to continue 'inside the islands,' we headed out towards what looked like an empty horizon—on which, however, Máirtín pointed out far-off rumpuses of foam where billows rolling in from the west were breaking over Carraigín Bhuí, small yellow rock, and Carraig na nGiúróg, barnacle rock, and others he knew from a lifetime spent knocking about these waters. Out here we had to take account of the rollers, heading into the bigger ones and running along the lesser ones. The boat was kicking up spray; I felt a touch of the romance of seafaring, of the swift black Homeric ships I had been reading about the night before, which needed no steering oars as they knew where their masters wanted to go, and of the bold Captain O'Malley heading off for Guernsey in his *Slúipín Vaughan*. The unfamiliar dimension of depth beneath the little boat was exhilaratingly scary; I had not been so far out in such a small boat before. I think no wave was as tall as a standing man and they posed no threat—not with An Caiptín Máilleach himself at the helm—but it was awe-inspiring to see how each one in turn lifted the horizon on its back and bore it towards us, then relinquished it to the next as it divided smoothly around our prow and shouldered past the boat. The possibility of their being aware of us, these blank-eyed horses of Manannán, seemed as remote as that of our warning them of the iron coast behind us, on which they would soon be broken.

Sailing between an isolated pair of wave-pounded islets a mile or so offshore known as Carraig an Róin, the seal's rock, we saw several bobbing seal-heads withdraw into the water on our approach, and a coven of shags taking off in weird black silhouette against the dazzling west. The round of the horizon was punctuated now by the two slim towers of Slyne Head a couple of miles to the south-west. If all this was high adventure to me it was a workplace to the local fishermen; again and again we had to alter course a shade to slide past a brightly coloured balloon-like buoy marking a lobster pot down below, and as we approached Oileán Imill we passed a boat hardly larger than ours, piled high with pots, lurching up and down as a solitary figure hauled yet more pots aboard.

Then we slid into the shelter of an inlet on the eastern shore of the island and docked against a small quay of massive stones all white and rough with close-packed barnacles, from which a flagstone-paved way mounted bare rocks ahead of us; the two towers, a quarter of a mile away at the other end of the island, showed dark against the western sky. On the opposite side of the inlet, where the landing place must have been before the quay was built, there were flights of steps chiselled out of the blackish, contorted strata of sea-washed rock. After the first 200 yards or so the way was flanked by shoulder-high stone walls, clearly intended to give the lighthouse personnel some shelter against gales and spray. Dips in the central plateau of the island held shapeless brackish lakes; on a rock in the middle of one of these someone had built a foot-high model of a lighthouse, not the black tower of Slyne, but white with a black band—do lighthouse men feel nostalgia for other lights? Dozens of buoys lay in grassy hollows on either side of the way, blown ashore and rolled inland until stopped by its walls. A branch of the walled way, to the left, led us into the ruinous yards around the disused and truncated tower, which had been weather-proofed with slates but was largely stripped of them by the wind now and stood ankle-deep, as it were, in smashed slates. The walls of the living quarters, with their wide brick-built fireplace recesses and chimney flues, looked as ragged-topped as if gales had torn the roofs off bodily. Here poor John Doyle sank into melancholy, Mrs. Gregory was torn from her children, Mrs. Harris and Mrs. Harrison wrangled with the drunken assistant keepers. Now all was wreck and desolation.

We turned to the functioning tower, which loomed black and ominous. The slow-turning apparatus of lenses half visible in the glass turret above seemed to move like a restless prisoner in a cell. A bell rang constantly all the time we were there, like an unanswered telephone trying to tell me something—as it might be, some fact I have misunderstood or misrepresented about Connemara. The yard gates were padlocked; we peered through the bars, explored all around but found no other entrance; the bell followed us with its increasingly desperate appeal. To the north of the lighthouse enclosure the land fell away seaward. A thick copper cable, no doubt the earth connection of the tower's lightning conductor, went snaking down this slope and disappeared into a slimy green rock pool. Flights of concrete steps with a handrail rope led us down to a narrow bridge across a smooth-sided fissure cutting right across a shoulder of the island, about four feet wide and fifty feet deep, through which white surges were rushing to and fro. Beyond that the steps went steeply down to a quay, usable when the main landing place is beset by easterly winds, in a wide cliff-sided inlet called Fó na gCacannaí, the creek of the droppings, the white guano left by cormorants. Looking back from there up to the black, locked tower with its urgent bell, rising out of rocks like the ruins of precipices overthrown and chaotically flung together, I thought I'd never felt a place so far from home.

The southern aspect of the island, which falls in terraces and easy slants, was more welcoming. Every sheltered nook was carpeted with the inch-wide daisy-flowers of scentless mayweed and softened by thick springy mounds of sea-pink. Rabbits burst forth from under our feet and scampered over the near skylines. By the inlet where our boat was waiting we ate chocolate and watched a little flock of turnstones shuffling about on the foreshore, unworried by our presence.

Then we took to the sea again, and, as it was now high water of an opulent spring tide answering to the full moon that would rise in the evening to come, we were able to work our way in and out of usually impassable channels of the archipelago between the lighthouse island and the tip of the mainland peninsula. At Chapel Island a huge bull seal humped and floundered himself off a rock as gracelessly as a cow might have done, and then turned sleek and swift and evanescent underwater. Just north of the point of Baile na Léime we sheltered for a few minutes below the water-echoing cliffs of Fó na nGlasóg, the cove of the rockfish, until a thundershower that curtained off a large sector of the horizon passed by to the south of us and the clouds above tore open to reveal a sunlit sky, with a fading contrail like a ribbon from the unwrapping of some huge gift. The declining afternoon was transformed, the inland dunes became heaped gold dust, the boat was animated by a thought of home. Máirtín steered in long carefree exploratory arcs among the rocks and islands. When he saw a pink buoy that was evidently adrift he went in pursuit of it, nuzzled the side of the boat against a shelving rock, saying, 'That will hold it for a moment,' leaped out onto slithery seaweed, made another leap, scooped up the buoy and flung it aboard with a laugh on noticing that—unbelievable!—a name was painted on it: ROBINSON. The bell, and now this, when already the world seemed supersaturated with self-reference and the moment of writing was coming so dangerously close to the moment of experience! Engaged as I was in consciously enacting the last paragraph of my last chapter, I fancied myself, first, answerable

to an unanswerable demand, and now, the recipient of personally addressed flotsam—two hints that it is time to throw my
book away, a paper boat adrift on the unknown waters of other
people's minds, unballasted with summation or conclusion.

Bibliography

Anon., *Hand-Book to Galway, Connemara, and the Irish Highlands* (London and Dublin, 1854).

Anon., *The Saxon in Ireland* (London, 1851).

Artaud, Antonin, *Oeuvres Complètes*, vol. 7 (Paris, 1967). Badiou, Alain, *Being and Event* (London, 2005).

Barrett, John, and Yonge, C. M., *Collins Pocket Guide to the Seashore* (London, 1958).

Bede, The Venerable, *The Ecclesiastical History of the English Nation*, 1st edn (1475).

Blake Family, *Letters from the Irish Highlands* (published anonymously, London, 1825; republished Clifden, 1995).

Blake, Martin J., 'An Account of the Castle and Manor of Bunowen,' *Journal of the Galway Historical and Archaeological Society*, vol. 2 (Galway, 1902).

Bowen, Desmond, *The Protestant Crusade in Ireland, 1800–70* (Dublin, 1978).

Breathnach, Diarmuid, and Ní Mhurchú, Máire, *Beathaisnéis*, vols. 1–9 (Dublin, 1986– 2007).

Bright, John, *The Diaries of John Bright*, ed. R. A. J. Walling (London, 1930).

Browne, Charles R., 'The Ethnography of Inishbofin and Inishshark, County Galway,' *Proceedings of the Royal Irish Academy*, series 3, vol. 2 (Dublin, 1893).

Burke, Edmund, *A Philosophical Enquiry into the Origin of our Ideas of the Sublime and Beautiful* (1st edn 1757; Oxford, 1990).

Butler, Hubert, *Ten Thousand Saints: A Study in Irish & European Origins* (Kilkenny, 1972).

Cannon, Moya, *Carrying the Song* (Manchester, 2007).

Chambers, Anne, *Granuaile: The Life and Times of Grace O'Malley* (Dublin 1979; revised edn 1998).

Clarke, Paddy, *The Marconi Wireless Station at Derrigimla–Clifden and Letterfrack* (Dublin, n.d.).

Clesham, Brigid, *A Descriptive List of Part of the Salruck Papers* (unpublished typescript, 1979).

Cody, Eamon, and Walsh, Paul, 'Seán Ó Nualláin 1926–2006,' *Archaeology Ireland*, vol. 20, no. 3 (Autumn 2006).

Colgan, John, *Acta Sanctorum Hiberniae* (Louvain, 1645). Collins, Timothy (ed.), *Decoding the Landscape* (Galway, 1993).

Commission to Inquire into Child Abuse, *Third Interim Report* (Dublin, 2003). Commissioners of Inquiry into the State of the Irish Fisheries, *First Report* (Dublin, 1836).

Concannon, Kieran (ed.), *Inishbofin Through Time and Tide* (Inishbofin, 1993).

Costeloe, M. P. L., 'The History of Slyne Head Lighthouse 1836–1990,' Irish Lights Office, republished in Gibbons, 1991.

Dallas, Mrs., *Incidents in the Life and Ministry of the Reverend Alexander R. C. Dallas* (London, 1873).

De Latocnaye, Le Chevalier, trans. John Stevenson, *A Frenchman's Walk Through Ireland 1796–7* (Belfast, 1917).

Diderot, Denis, 'Paradoxe sur le comédien,' *Oeuvres Esthétique* (Paris, n.d.).

Edgeworth, Maria, *Tour in Connemara (1833)*, first appeared in an unpublished memoir (1867), reprinted with additional material, ed. H. E. Butler (London, 1950).

Feeney, Marie, *The Cleggan Bay Disaster* (Penumbra Press, 2001).

Feynman, Richard P., *QED: The Strange Theory of Light and Matter* (Princeton, NJ, 1985; Harmondsworth, 1990).

Flowers, F. A. (ed.), *Portraits of Wittgenstein*, vol. 4 (Bristol, 1999). Flynn, Mannix, *Nothing to Say* (Dublin, 1983; revised edn 2003). Fouéré, Olwen, website: www. olwenfouere.com.

Fouéré, Yann, *Towards a Federal Europe: Nations or States?* (Swansea, 1980).

————, *La Maison du Connemara: Histoire d'un Breton* (Rennes, 1995).

————, Fondation Yann Fouéré website: www.fondationyannfouere.org.

Frege, Gottlob, *Translations from the Philosophical Writings of Gottlob Frege*, ed. Peter Geech and Max Black (Oxford, 1966).

Fry, Right Hon. Sir Edward, *James Hack Tuke: A Memoir* (London, 1899). Gannon, Paul (ed.), *The Way It Was* (Renvyle, 1999).

Gibbons, Erin (ed.), *Hidden Conamara*, (Letterfrack, 1991).

Gibbons, Michael, and Gibbons, Myles, 'Hiberno-Norse Ringed Pin from Omey Feichín, Connemara,' *Journal of the Galway Archaeological and Historical Society*, vol. 57 (Galway, 2005).

Gibbons, Michael, and Higgins, Jim, 'Connemara's Emerging Prehistory,' *Archaeology Ireland*, vol. 2, no. 2 (Summer 1988), reprinted in Gibbons, 1991.

Gogarty, Oliver St John, *As I Was Going Down Sackville Street* (London, 1937).

————, *Rolling Down the Lea* (London, 1950).

Gosling, Paul (ed.), *Archaeological Inventory of County Galway, vol. 1, West Galway* (Dublin, 1993).

Gregory, Lady Augusta, *Gods and Fighting Men* (London, 1904).

Griffith, Richard, *Valuation of the Several Tenements in the County of Galway* (Dublin, 1855).

Gwynn, Stephen, MP, *A Holiday in Connemara* (London, 1909). Hall, S. C., and Mrs. Hall, *The West and Connemara* (London, 1853). Harbison, Peter, *Pilgrimage in Ireland* (London, 1991).

Hardiman, James, *The History of the Town and County of the Town of Galway* (Dublin, 1820).

Harmon, Maurice (ed.), *Richard Murphy: Poet of Two Traditions* (Portmarnock, 1978).

Hayes, Richard, *The Last Invasion of Ireland* (Dublin, 1939).

Heather, Alannah, *Errislannan: Scenes from a Painter's Life* (Dublin, 1993).

Hennessy,W. M. (ed.), and Kelly, D. H. (trans.), *Book of Fenagh in English and Irish, originally compiled by St. Caillin* (facsimile of 1875 edition, Dublin, 1939).

Hutchinson, John, and Malone, Sheena (eds.), *Leaves and Papers 1–6*, Douglas Hyde Gallery (Dublin, 2008).

Inglis, H. D., *A Journey Throughout Ireland, 1834* (London, 1835).

Irish Church Mission Society, *A Mission Tour-Book in Ireland* (London, n.d.).

————, *The Story of the Connemara Orphans' Nursery* (Glasgow, 1877).

————, *The Banner of the Truth in Ireland* (1851–90).

Johnson, Joan, *James and Mary Ellis: Background and Quaker Family Relief in Letterfrack* (Dublin, 2000).

Kaule, Prof. Giselher, *The Future of the Cultural Landscape and Rough Grazing in Western Connemara* (unpublished LACOPE discussion document, 2006).

Kenney, James F., *Sources for the Early History of Ireland* (New York, 1929). Kilroy, Patricia, *The Story of Connemara* (Dublin, 1989).

Kinahan, G. Henry, 'The Ruins on Ardillaun, Co. Galway,' *Proceedings of the Royal Irish Academy*, vol. 10 (1869).

Larkin, William, *Map of County Galway, 1819* (Dublin, 1989).

Lavelle, Rory, 'The Mayo Rebels of '98 in Connemara,' *Connemara: Journal of the Clifden and Connemara Heritage Group*, vol. 1, no. 1 (Clifden, 1993).

————, 'John Reilly and the San Patricios,' *Connemara: Journal of the Clifden and Connemara Heritage Group*, vol. 2, no. 1 (Clifden, 1995).

Ligniti, Emily (ed.), *Dorothy Cross*, exhibition catalogue, Irish Museum of Modern Art (Dublin, 2005).

Lydenberg, Robin, *Gone: Site-Specific Works by Dorothy Cross* (Boston, 2005).

Lynam, Shevawn, *Humanity Dick Martin 'King of Connemara' 1754–1834* (Dublin, 1989). Mac Giolla Choille, Breandán (ed.), *Books of Survey and Distribution, vol. III, County of Galway* (Dublin, 1962).

Mac Giollarnáth, Seán, *Annála Beaga ó Iorrais Aithneach* (Dublin, 1941).

————, *Conamara* (Cork, 1954).

MacAlister, R.A. S., 'The Antiquities of Ardoiléan, Co. Galway,' *Journal of the Royal Society of Antiquaries*, Part III (Dublin, 1896).

McGrath, Walter, *Some Industrial Railways of Ireland* (Cork, 1959).

MacLoughlin, Dr C. P., 'From Sellerna to Harley Street,' *Connemara: Journal of the Clifden and Connemara Heritage Group*, vol. 1, no. 1 (Clifden, 1993).

Magee, Revd Hamilton, *Fifty Years of 'The Irish Mission'* (Belfast, n.d.).

Marshall, Jenny White, and Rourke, Grellan D., *High Island: An Irish Monastery in the Atlantic* (Dublin, 2001).

Meyer, Kuno (trans.), *Selections from Ancient Irish Poetry* (London, 1911). Monk, Ray, *Ludwig Wittgenstein: The Duty of Genius* (New York, 1990).

————, *Bertrand Russell: The Spirit of Solitude* (London, 1996).

Mulloy, Sheila, 'Inishbofin—The Ultimate Stronghold,' *The Irish Sword*, vol. 17, no. 67 (Winter 1987–Summer 1988).

———— (ed.), *Ó Máille: The O'Malley Clan Annual* (Westport, 1989). Murphy, Gerard (trans. and ed.), *Early Irish Lyrics* (Oxford, 1970). Murphy, Richard, *Collected Poems* (Oldcastle, Co. Meath, 2000).

————, *The Kick* (London, 2002).

Napoléon Bonapart, *Correspondence de Napoléon 1er, publiée par ordre de l'Empereur Napoléon III* (Paris, 1858–6).

Neary, Revd John, 'History of Innishbofin and Innishark,' *Irish Ecclesiastical Record*, vol.15 (Jan.–June 1920).

Newman, John Henry, *Apologia Pro Vita Sua* (London, 1994).

Newsome, D., *The Parting of Friends: The Wilberforces and Henry Manning* (Cambridge, MA, 1966).

Ní Fhlathartaigh, Ríonach, *Clár Amhrán Bhaile na hInse* (Dublin, 1976). Nicholson, Asenath, *Ireland's Welcome to the Stranger* (London, 1847).

Ó Coigligh, Ciarán (ed.), *Raiftearaí. Amhráin agus Dánta* (Dublin, 1987). O'Connor, Ulick, *Oliver St. John Gogarty* (London, 1964).

O'Donnell + Tuomey Architects, *Transformation of an Institution: The Furniture College, Letterfrack* (Cork, 2004).

O'Donovan, John, *Ordnance Survey Letters, Co. Galway, 1839* (typescript copy in National Library of Ireland).

O'Flaherty, Roderick, *West or H-Iar Connaught* (written 1684), ed. James Hardiman (Dublin, 1846, reprinted Galway, 1978).

Ó Fotharta, Dómhnall, *Siamsa an Gheimhridh nó cois an teallaigh in Iarconnachta*, (Dublin, 1892).

Ó hÓgáin, Dr Daithí, *Myth, Legend and Romance* (London, 1990).

O'Keefe, Tadhg, 'Omey and the Sands of Time,' *Archaeology Ireland*, vol. 8, no. 2 (1994). Ó Máille, Mícheál agus Tomás, *Amhráin Chlainne Gael*, ed. William Mahon (Indreabhán, 1991).

Ó Máille, Tomás, *Micheál Mhac Suibhne agus Filidh an tSléibhe* (Dublin, 1934).

O'Malley, George, unpublished autobiography (typescript in National Library of Ireland).

Ordnance Survey Name Books (field notes on placenames, with occasional comments by John O'Donovan; 1839, unpublished manuscript).

Orme, Antony R., 'Drumlins and the Weichsal Glaciation of Connemara,' *Irish Geography*, vol. 5 (1967).

O'Rourke, Brian, *Blas Meala: A Sip from the Honey-Pot: Gaelic Folksongs with English Translations* (book and cassettes, Blackrock, 1985).

Osborne, Hon. and Revd S. Godolphin, *Gleanings in the West of Ireland* (London, 1850). Otway, Caesar, *A Tour in Connaught* (Dublin, 1839).

Petrie, George, *The Ecclesiastical Architecture of Ireland*, vol. 1 (Dublin, 1845).

——, 'An Essay on Military Architecture in Ireland Previous to the English Invasion,' *Proceedings of the Royal Irish Academy*, vol. 72C (Dublin, 1972).

Plunkett, Revd W. C., *Short Visit to the Connemara Mission* (London, 1863).

Redington, M., 'An Island's Story,' *Galway Historical and Archaeological Society Journal*, vol. 10 (Galway, 1917–18).

Rhees, Rush (ed.), *Ludwig Wittgenstein: Personal Recollections* (Oxford, 1981).

Robinson, Sir Henry, *Further Memories of Irish Life* (London, 1924).

Robinson, Tim, *Setting Foot on the Shores of Connemara* (Dublin, 1996).

——, *Stones of Aran: Labyrinth* (London, 1997).

——, *My Time in Space* (Dublin, 2001).

——, *Olwen Fouéré in The Bull's Wall* (Ballybeg, 2001; reprinted in Tim Robinson, *Tales and Imaginings* (Dublin, 2002)).

Russell, Bertrand, *Autobiography* (London, 2000).

Ryan, K. M., 'Geochemical Fingerprinting of Sedimentary Basins Using a Revised South Mayo Lower Palaeozoic Stratigraphy' (National University of Ireland, Galway, unpublished dissertation, 2005).

Ryan, K. M., and Williams, D. M., 'Testing the Reliability of Discrimination Diagrams for Determining the Tectonic Depositional Environment of Ancient Sedimentary Basins,' *Chemical Geology*, no. 242 (2007), pp. 103–25.

Ryan, P. D., and Dewey, J. F., 'The South Connemara Complex Reinterpreted: A Subduction-accretion Complex in the Caledonides of Galway Bay, Western Ireland,' *Journal of Geodynamics*, vol. 37 (2004).

Salruck Papers, largely unpublished; see Clesham, 1979.

Scott, Thomas Colville, 'Journal of a Survey of the Martin Estate, 1853,' in *Connemara After the Famine*, ed. with introduction by Tim Robinson (Dublin, 1995).

Smith, the Revd Joseph Denham, *Connemara: Past and Present* (Dublin, 1853).

Somerville, E. Oe., and Ross, Martin, *Through Connemara in a Governess Cart* (London, 1893).

Speed, John, *A Prospect of the Most Famous Parts of the World* (1627).

Spencer Brown, George, *Laws of Form* (London, 1969).

Stenson, Nancy (ed.), *An Haicléara Mánas: A Nineteenth-century Text from Clifden, Co. Galway* (Dublin, 2003).

Stokes, Whitley (trans.), *Martyrology of Oengus the Culdee* (Dublin, 1984). Thackeray, W. M., *The Irish Sketch Book of 1842* (London, 1843).

Tully Cross Guild I.C.A., *Portrait of a Parish: Ballynakill, Connemara* (Renvyle, 1985). Villiers

Tuthill, Kathleen, *History of Clifden, 1810–1860* (Clifden, 1981).

——, *Beyond the Twelve Bens: A History of Clifden and District 1860–1923* (Clifden, 1986).

——, *Patient Endurance: The Great Famine in Connemara* (Dublin, 1997).

——, *History of Kylemore Castle and Abbey* (Kylemore, 2002). Wakeman, William, *A Week in the West of Ireland* (Dublin, n.d., *c*.1850). Walsh, Mary, *A Piece of Yellow Chalk* (unpublished typescript).

Walsh, Paul, 'Cromwell's Barracks: A Commonwealth Garrison Fort on Inishbofin, Co. Galway,' *Journal of the Galway Historical and Archaeological Society*, vol. 42 (Galway, 1989–1990).

Webb, D. A., and Scannell, Mary J. P., *Flora of Connemara and the Burren* (Cambridge, 1983).

Westropp, Thomas J., 'Inishbofin, History and Archaeology,' *Clare Island Survey*, Proceedings of the Royal Irish Academy, vol. 31, section 1, part 2 (Dublin, 1911–15).

Whelan, Irene, *The Bible War in Ireland* (Dublin, 2005). Wilde, Sir William, *Irish Popular Superstitions* (Dublin, 1852).

Williams, Guy St John (ed.), *Renvyle Letters: Gogarty Family Correspondence* (Monasteries, 2000).

Winter, A., and Siesser, W. G. (eds.), *Coccolithophores* (Cambridge, 1994).

Wittgenstein, Ludwig, *Tractatus Logico-Philosophicus*, 1st English edn, trans. C. K. Ogden (1922); 2nd English edn, trans. D. F. Pears and B. F. McGuinness (London, 1961).

——, *Philosophical Investigations*, trans. G. E. M. Anscombe, 2nd edn (Oxford, 1958).

Sources

PREFACE: THE DARK NIGHT OF THE INTELLECT

xi   (last pool of darkness) Wittgenstein's remark was made to Father Fechin O'Doherty, who attended his lectures in Cambridge; it is recorded in two slightly different forms by George Hetherington in Flowers, 1999.

xi   (drawing in mud) Murphy, 2002.

xi   (duck-rabbit, landscape) Wittgenstein, 1958.

x   (logic or sins) Russell, 2000; Monk, 1990.

A SUSPECT TERRANE

1   (St Roc and the Devil) Hall and Hall, 1853.

2   (Bina McLoughlin) Máirtín Ó Catháin, *Connacht Tribune*, 23 February 2001.

3   (maps) Speed, 1627; Larkin, 1819.

5–10   (geology) Ryan, 2007. I am also grateful to Paul Mohr for corrections to my account, and to Simon Wellings for a useful hint.

8–9   (Iapetus suture) Ryan and Dewy, 2004.

FAULTS

I am grateful to the late Mrs. Willoughby for giving me access to the Salruck Papers, and to Brigid Clesham for a copy of her descriptive list of them.

13–20   (The Thomsons) Hall and Hall, 1853; Clesham, 1979; Villiers-Tuthill, 1997; Kilroy, 1989;Tully Cross, 1985.

14   (graveyard) Photo in Tully Cross, 1985; Somerville and Ross, 1893.

19   ('Feeding Time') Tully Cross, 1985.

21   (Festy Mortimer) Gannon, 1999.

THINKING ON THE OCEAN'S EDGE

24   (Richard Murphy) Murphy, 2002.

24–34   (Drury) Rhees, 1981; Monk, 1990; Flowers, 1999. Hetherington, 'A Sage in Search of a Pool of Darkness,' in Flowers, 1999.

25–27   (Russell's paradox and Frege) Frege, 1966; Russell, 2000; Monk, 1996.

27–29   (*Tractatus*) Wittgenstein, 1922.

31–32   (*Philosophical Investigations*) Wittgenstein, 1958.

THE MERMAID

35   (mermen) Gannon, 1999; Gibbons, 1991.

35–40   (Cross) Lydenberg, 2005; Ligniti, 2005; Hutchinson and Malone, 2008.

41   (village lore) Information from Peter Ward, Tuaina Beola.

MOANING ABOUT THE CHIMNEYS

43–44   (séance) Gogarty, 1937.

45–47   (O'Flahertys) Hardiman's appendices to O'Flaherty, 1846; O'Malley; De Latocnaye, 1917.

47–55   (Henry Blake) Blake Family, 1825; Edgeworth, 1867 (Pierce Marvel is the chief character in her story 'The Will');Thomson's letter was printed in Kilroy, 1989.

55–56   (Caroline Blake) Tully Cross, 1985.
56–57   (evidence to Special Commission) *The Times*, 10 November 1888;
          Somerville and Ross, 1893.
59–62   (Gogarty) Gogarty, 1937; O'Connor, 1964;Williams, 2000.
63   (conglomerate) Information from Paul Mohr, who also supplied the
          quote from a letter to the *Galway Vindicator*, 7 September 1864, by
          John Birmingham, an amateur geologist of Tuam.
64   (pondweeds) Webb and Scannell, 1983; information from Cilian
          Roden.
64–65   (tower house and chapel) Gosling, 1993.
65–66   (Caití and Mairéad) Information from Paddy Fitzpatrick recorded
          by Dave Hogan, in Gibbons, 1991.
66   (Caroline Blake's story) *Today's Woman*, 6 April 1895; copy kindly
          supplied by Jenny Conboy among material collected by Tully Cross
          Guild I.C.A.
68   (song) Sung by Treasa Bn. Uí Chongaile in O'Rourke, 1985, who
          gives the Irish words, prose translation and a singable English
          version.

THE SUBLIME AND THE RELIGIOUS
70–71   (the Picturesque, the Beautiful and the Sublime) Inglis,
          1835;Anon., *Hand-Book to Galway*, 1854 (I thank Neville Figgis for
          the sight of this book); Thackeray, 1843.
72–74   (Wilberforces) *Oxford Dictionary of National Biography*; Newsome,
          1966; Newman, 1994.
74–75   (Eastwoods) Osborne, 1850; Particulars of Sale, Landed Estates
          Court, Dublin, 1862.
75–83   (Kylemore) Mitchell Henry, the Manchesters and the Benedictine
          nuns are treated in detail in Villiers-Tuthill, 2002.
76–77   (description of the castle) Documentation of the 1902 sale, on the
          Mitchell-Henry Family Website, www.mitchell-henry.co.uk.
85   (Irish diamonds) Hall and Hall, 1853.
86   (the Sublime) Burke, 1757.

UNFINISHED HISTORY
87   (*frag*) A suggestion from Dónall Mac Giolla Easpaig,
          Placenames Branch, Dept. of Arts, Heritage, Gaeltacht and the
          Islands.
88   (Lynches) Ordnance Survey Name Books, 1839.
88–89   (Grahams) Griffith, 1855;Tully Cross, 1985; Bright, 1930;Wilde,
          1852.
89–93   (Ellises) Wakeman, n.d.; Johnson, 2000.
93–97   (Tuke) Fry, 1899.
95–96   (Letterfrack murders) Villiers-Tuthill, 1986.
97–101   (Christian Brothers); Flynn, 1983; *Sunday Tribune*, 4 July 2004;
          Irish Times, 29
          November 2003, 23 May 2006; Commission to Inquire into Child
          Abuse, 2003. I am grateful to Patrick Gageby for his advice on this
          topic.
101–105   (new buildings) O'Donnell + Tuomey, 2004.

SMUGGLER AND FABULIST
107   (song) 'Caiptín Ó Máille,' in Ó Máille, 1991, and other collections; translation by Liam Mac Con Iomaire.
108–109 I am grateful to Eileen O'Malley for first showing me a typescript of George O'Malley's memoirs, to Sheila Mulloy for her notes on them, and to Ann O'Malley Kelly for lending me another typescript of Part 1.
110   (Givet bridge) Napoleon Bonaparte, 1858–69, letter of 12 November 1811. 121–2
119–120 (workhouse) John O'Dowd, 'Some Tales from Fallduff,' 1964, in Mulloy, 1989.
121   (fairy kings) 'Rí Cathair a' Dúin agus a' Dúinín Mhóir,' Roinn Bhéaloideas Éirinn, Iml.229; printed in Gibbons, 1991.

TWILIGHT ON OLD STONES
122   (Éamonn Láidir) Hardiman's appendices to O'Flaherty, 1846.
123   (Na Síáin placenames) Information from Patrick Conroy, Na Síáin.
124   (Garraunbawn) Information from the late Cecil Hodson, formerly of Garraunbawn House. This account originated as part of 'A Connemara Fractal,' a talk given to the First Conference of the Centre for Landscape Studies, UCG, 1950, and published in Collins, 1993.
125–132 (megaliths) Gibbons and Higgins, 1991; Gosling, 1993.
127   (Gleninagh stone row) See 'Through Prehistoric Eyes' in Robinson, 1996.
129   (Seán Ó Nualláin) Cody and Walsh, 2006.

AN EAR TO THE EARTH
133   (St Gregory) O'Flaherty, 1846; Butler, 1972; Robinson, 1997.
133   (jasper) Information from Paul Mohr.
135–136 (Twining) Scott, 1995;Villiers-Tuthill, 1986. I am grateful to Hugh and Nicola Musgrave for access to their family papers.
138–143 (ecology) information from Prof. Giselher Kaule; Kaule, 2006.

FATE
144   (drumlins) Orme, 1967.
145–146 (Cleggan village) Blake Family, 1825; Nimmo's report, in Commissioners of Inquiry into the State of the Irish Fisheries, 1836.
147   (Lighton) Osborne, 1850.
149   (white stones in ballast) Concannon, 1993.
149   (Freyer) Oxford Dictionary of National Biography; MacLoughlin, 1993.
150–154 (Cleggan Disaster) Feeney, 2001; Murphy, 2000; Murphy, 2002.
151   (Laffey, and the restless sea) Gannon, 1999.

REFLOATING INISHBOFIN
155–156 (legend) O'Donovan, 1839; Otway, 1839.
156–157 (Royal Oak) Ordnance Survey Name Books, 1839; information from Paddy O'Halloran, North Beach.
157–158 (1780 wreck) Redington, 1917–18.
159–167 (Carraig na dTairní) Information from Paddy O'Halloran, North Beach. (Kitty Brigg) Concannon, 1993.
158   (drownings) Concannon, 1993.

159–167   (history) Neary, 1920; Mulloy, 1987–8.
161–162   (Guairim, Bosco) Browne, 1893;Westropp, 1911–15.
163–165   (fort) Westropp, 1911–15;Walsh, 1989–90.
165–166   (Hildebrand) Concannon, 1993; Scott, 1995.
166–167   (ICMS) Neary, 1920.
167–169   (Wilberforce, Allies) Concannon, 1993; Newsome, 1966.
168   (gunboats) Robinson, 1924.
170   (St Scaithín) Stokes, 1984 (notes to Jan. 1–6).

IN THE MIST
I am grateful to the late Mary Walsh for allowing me to copy part of her draft
autobiography, and to Olwen Fouéré for her company and material relating
to her family.

183   (Olwen Fouéré) www.olwenfouere.com.
183–185   (Artaud) Artaud, 1967; Robinson, 1995.
185   (crayfish) Information from Noel King, Roundstone.
186   (Coneys family) Griffith, 1855.
187–188   (Tony White) Murphy, 2002.
189–191   (Yann Fouéré) www.fondationyannfouere.org (includes the 1961
           Times interview tape);Yann Fouéré, 1980, 1995 (unpublished trans-
           lation by Rozenn Barrett).
192   (paradox) Diderot, n.d.

PLAGUE AND PURITY
193   (High Kings) Life of St Gerald of Mayo, in Kenney, 1929.
194   (mine) Blake Family, 1825.
196–202   (archaeology) Marshall and Rourke, 2001; Michael Herity, 'The
           High Island Hermitage,' in Harmon, 1978; Kinahan, 1869;
           O'Donovan, 1839; MacAlister, 1896; Petrie, 1845.
197   (marine pilgrimage) Harbison, 1991.
202–204   (Richard Murphy) Harmon, 1978; Murphy, 2000; Murphy, 2002.
           I am grateful to Richard Murphy for permission to print his poem
           'Moonshine,' and for supplying copies of many documents relating
           to High Island.
204   (storm petrels) Information from Richard Nairn, Irish Wildbird
           Conservancy, 1985.

SOMETIME ISLAND
208   (Kearney) Murphy, 2002. 211–13
209–210   (grazing, ecology) Kaule, 2006.
211   (St Féichín) Colgan, 1645; O'Flaherty, 1846.
212–213   (archaeology) Gosling, 1993; O'Keefe, 1994; Gibbons and Gibbons,
           2005; Connacht Tribune, 31 August 1990, 1 January 1993.
213   (hexagon) Murphy, 2002.

CONTROVERSIAL PITCH
216   (John Reilly) Lavelle, 1995.
217   (Gleann Eoghain) Ordnance Survey Name Books, 1839. 219–20
217–218   (Honor) Irish Church Mission Society, 1877.
219   (The Times) Osborne, 1850.
220–221   (castle) Inglis, 1835; Anon., The Saxon, 1851.

221–222   (D'Arcy family) Hardiman, 1820;Villiers-Tuthill, 1981.
223   (grotto) Nicholson, 1847.
223–224   (town development) 10th Fishery Report, 1829; Fishery
           Commissioners, 1836; Wakeman (n.d., c.1850); Ordnance Survey
           Name Books, 1839;Villiers-Tuthill, 1981.
224   (D'Arcy letter) State of the Country Papers, National
           Archives,SOC.1831/126 (I am grateful to Dr Kevin Whelan for
           drawing my attention to this document.)
225   (assaults; Daniel O'Connell) Villiers-Tuthill, 1981.
227   (Baile Mac Conraoi) Hardiman's notes to O'Flaherty, 1846;
           O'Donovan, 1839.
227–228   (rectory) Blake Family, 1825.
228   (Seymour) Whelan, 2005.
229–237   (ICMS) Bowen, 1978; ICMS 1851–1890, 1877, *Mission Tour Book*,
           n.d.; Magee, n.d.; Plunkett, 1863; Smith, 1853. I thank Patrick
           Gageby for copies of documents and books relating to this topic.
234   (D'Arcy on priests) Villiers-Tuthill,1986.
235   (death of Dallas) Dallas, 1873.
237–238   (burning of orphanage; the mother) Heather, 1993.
238–239   (priest's wife's shift) Information from Rory Lavelle, Clifden. ('Slán
           leat, a Dhia') information from Michael Gibbons, Clifden.

FROM BALLINABOY
240   ('*Tá mo mhac le cur*') Rory Lavelle, Clifden.
240   (Ballinaboy Fair) Hardiman's notes to O'Flaherty, 1846.
240–246   (Father Prendergast) Hayes, 1939; Lavelle, 1993.
241   (proposed airport) 'The Echosphere' in Robinson, 2001.
243–244   (Raftery) 'Na Buachaillí Bána' in Ó Coigligh, 1987.
244   (his escape from Castlebar) Mac Giollarnáth, 1941 (my translation).
246   (grave of the man he shot) Information from Rory Lavelle.
247   (his appeal to Martin) Lynam, 1989.
248   (Affy Gibbons' lament) Ó Máille, 1934.
250–251   (St Flannan) O'Flaherty, 1846; 'Clare People' website, www.clareli-
           brary.ie/ index.htm.
252   (O'Leys) Mac Giolla Choille, 1962.
252–253   (four heirs) Ordnance Survey Name Books, 1839;Villiers-Tuthill,
           1986; Morris family papers (I am grateful to the late Colonel
           Anthony Morris for access to these).
253–254   (Revd Wall) Heather, 1993.
257–258   (Mac Suibhne) Ó Máille, 1934.
259–262   (Mánas) I thank the Dublin Institute for Advanced Studies (School
           of Celtic Studies) for permission to quote from *An Haicléara Mánas*,
           Stenson, 2003.

PHOTONS IN THE BOG
263–267   (Marconi) www.marconicalling.com; Clarke, n.d.; Villiers-Tuthill, 1986.
266   (railway) McGrath, 1959.
267–268   (Alcock and Brown) Villiers-Tuthill, 1986. *Connacht Tribune*, 10
           June 1994.
271–272   (photons) Feynmann, 1985.

THE KINGDOM OF MANANNÁN

275 (seashore life) Barrett and Yonge, 1958.
276 (coccolithophores) Winter and Siesser, 1994; *Emiliana huxleyi*, Science Net Watch website, www.soes.soton.ac.uk/staff/tt.
277–278 (Bodach) 'Echtra Bhodaigh an Chóta Lachtna' on An Chartlann website, www. craobhcrua.org/fc0009.html.
278 (Ceithearnach) Ó hÓgáin, 1990; Gregory, 1904.
279–280 (Bran) Meyer, 1911; Murphy, 1970.
280 (Oirbsiu, Oileán Mana) Ó hÓgáin, 1990.
281–282 ('Shells') I thank Carcanet Press and Moya Cannon for permission to quote this poem from Cannon, 2007.
282–283 (maerl) 'Ecological role of Maerl,' www.ukmarinesac.org.uk/ communities/ maerl/m3_2.htm.

WHO OWNS THE LAND?

290 (Doon Hill) O'Flaherty, 1846.
290–294 (O'Flahertys and Grace O'Malley) Chambers, 1998; Hardiman's notes to O'Flaherty, 1846.
297–299 (Geoghegans) Blake, 1902; O'Donovan, 1839; Geoghegan clan website, www. geoghegan.org/clan.
298–299 (dam, folly) I thank Ann Mohr for translations of the Latin inscriptions.
301 (Thackeray) Thackeray, 1843
302 (evictions) Villiers-Tuthill, 1986. 307–10
306–311 (folktales) Ó Fotharta, 1892.

A LAKE FULL OF SAND

314–315 (song) Ó Fotharta, 1892; sung by Máire Áine Ní Dhonnchadha on *Deora Aille* (CD).
317 ('Loch na Naomh') Ní Fhlathartaigh, 1976.
317–318 (Ó Cualáin) I thank Liam Mac Con Iomaire for his translation of this Raidió na Gaeltachta talk.
318–319 (*Beathaisnéis*) Breathnach and Ní Mhurchú, 1986–2007.
319–320 (Ó Fotharta) Breathnach and Ní Mhurchú, vol. 4, 1994; Gwynn, 1909; Ó Fotharta family lore, for which I thank Clare Dixon.

PILGRIMAGE AND PICNIC

325–326 (Coneys family) Hardiman's notes to O'Flaherty, 1846.
327 (Armada horses) Local lore from the late Jim O'Malley, Aill Bhreac.
327 (the cripple's rhyme) Jim O'Malley; Mac Giollarnáth, 1941.
328–329 (St Caillín) Hennessy and Kelly, 1875.
332 (smuggler) Mac Giollarnáth, 1941.
332 (Dún na bhFál) Petrie, 1972; Ordnance Survey Name Books, 1839.

TO THE DARK TOWER

338–341 (lighthouse history) Costeloe, 1991.
241 (automation) *Connacht Tribune*, 23 March 1990.
341–343 (deep places) Perhaps this 'train of thought' could be developed along the lines of the theory of the event in Badiou, 2005, with respect to another domain, that of the Earth.

A cartographer and writer, **TIM ROBINSON** (1935–2020), studied mathematics at Cambridge and worked for many years as a teacher and visual artist in Istanbul, Vienna, and London, among other places. In 1972 he moved to the Aran Islands. In 1986 his first book, *Stones of Aran: Pilgrimage*, was published to great acclaim. The second volume of *Stones of Aran*, subtitled *Labyrinth*, appeared in 1995. He also published collections of essays and maps of the Aran Islands, the Burren, and Connemara. *Connemara: Listening to the Wind*, first published in 2006, won the Irish Book Award for Nonfiction.

ABOUT SEEDBANK

Just as repositories around the world gather seeds in an effort
to ensure biodiversity in the future, Seedbank gathers works of
literature from around the world that foster reflection on the
relationship of human beings with place and
the natural world.

SEEDBANK FOUNDERS

The generous support of the following visionary investors
makes this series possible:

Meg Anderson and David Washburn

Anonymous

The Hlavka Family

milkweed
EDITIONS

Founded as a nonprofit organization in 1980, Milkweed Editions is an independent publisher. Our mission is to identify, nurture, and publish transformative literature, and build an engaged community around it.

Milkweed Editions is based in Bdé Óta Othúŋwe (Minneapolis) within Mní Sotą Makhóčhe, the traditional homeland of the Dakhóta people. Residing here since time immemorial, Dakhóta people still call Mní Sota Makhóčhe home, with four federally recognized Dakhóta nations and many more Dakhóta people residing in what is now the state of Minnesota. Due to continued legacies of colonization, genocide, and forced removal, generations of Dakhóta people remain disenfranchised from their traditional homeland. Presently, Mní Sota Makhóčhe has become a refuge and home for many Indigenous nations and peoples, including seven federally recognized Ojibwe nations. We humbly encourage our readers to reflect upon the historical legacies held in the lands they occupy.

milkweed.org

Milkweed Editions, an independent nonprofit publisher, gratefully acknowledges sustaining support from our Board of Directors; the Alan B. Slifka Foundation and its president, Riva Ariella Ritvo-Slifka; the Amazon Literary Partnership; the Ballard Spahr Foundation; Copper Nickel; the McKnight Foundation; the National Endowment for the Arts; the National Poetry Series; and other generous contributions from foundations, corporations, and individuals. Also, this activity is made possible by the voters of Minnesota through a Minnesota State Arts Board Operating Support grant, thanks to a legislative appropriation from the arts and cultural heritage fund. For a full listing of Milkweed Editions supporters, please visit milkweed.org.

Interior Design by Mary Austin Speaker
Typeset in Adobe Caslon

Adobe Caslon Pro was created by Carol Twombly
for Adobe Systems in 1990. Her design was inspired by
the family of typefaces cut by the celebrated engraver
William Caslon I, whose family foundry served
England with clean, elegant type from the early
Enlightenment through the turn of the
twentieth century.